NATURE, SEX, AND GOODNESS
IN A MEDIEVAL LITERARY TRADITION

Nature, Sex, and Goodness in a Medieval Literary Tradition

HUGH WHITE

OXFORD
UNIVERSITY PRESS

OXFORD
UNIVERSITY PRESS

Great Clarendon Street, Oxford OX2 6DP
Oxford University Press is a department of the University of Oxford.
It furthers the University's objective of excellence in research, scholarship,
and education by publishing worldwide in

Oxford New York

Athens Auckland Bangkok Bogotá Buenos Aires Calcutta
Cape Town Chennai Dar es Salaam Delhi Florence Hong Kong Istanbul
Karachi Kuala Lumpur Madrid Melbourne Mexico City Mumbai
Nairobi Paris São Paulo Shanghai Singapore Taipei Tokyo Toronto Warsaw
with associated companies in Berlin Ibadan

Oxford is a registered trade mark of Oxford University Press
in the UK and in certain other countries

Published in the United States
by Oxford University Press Inc., New York

British Library Cataloguing in Publication Data

Data available

Library of Congress Cataloging in Publication Data

White, Hugh.
Nature, sex, and goodness in a Medieval literary tradition / Hugh White.
p. cm.
Includes bibliographical references and index.
1. English literature—Middle English, 1100–1500—History and criticism. 2. Nature in
literature. 3. Guillaume, de Lorris, fl. 1230. Roman de la Rose. 4. French literature—To
1500—History and criticism. 5. Alanus, de Insulis, d. 1202—Ethics. 6. Chaucer, Geoffrey,
d. 1400—Ethics. 7. Jean, de Meun, d. 1305—Ethics. 8. Gower, John, 1325?–1408—Ethics.
9. Ethics, Medieval, in literature. 10. Good and evil in literature. 11. Sex in literature. I.
Title.

PR275.N3 W47 200
820.9'36—dc21   00-057120
ISBN 0-19-818730-0
1 3 5 7 9 10 8 6 4 2

Typeset in Swift
by Kolam Information Services Pvt. Ltd, Pondicherry, India
Printed and bound in Great Britain
on acid-free paper by
T. J. International Ltd,
Padstow Cornwall

To my mother in memory of my father

Acknowledgements

The debts I have incurred in writing this book are manifold. I am very conscious of how much I owe to the scholarly tradition and the editions, translations, and critical writings it has produced, on which this book so thoroughly depends. I am conscious too of how much I have gained from discussions of nature and other matters with many people in various academic fora formal and informal. I have enjoyed much support from my former and present colleagues in the Department of English at University College London and at St Catherine's College, Oxford. I should like to thank the latter institution and the University of Oxford for granting me leave from teaching which greatly assisted the completion of this book. Several individuals have generously taken time to offer advice on all or part of the book (I have particularly profited from the superior knowledge of others of some of the languages with which I have had to deal). My gratitude, then, to Helen Barr, Marilyn Corrie, Peter Ganz, Malcolm Godden, Richard Hamer, Anne Hudson, Richard Parish, Roger Pensom, J. C. Smith, Simon Tabbush, Jane Taylor, Carolinne White, and to those who read this book for the Oxford University Press for information and insights of various kinds; I regret not always having made the best use of what they offered. Aby Bidwell and Lizzie Andrews, the Fellows' Secretaries at St Catherine's, have been unfailingly patient and helpful in the face of many demands. Several generations of students have had my musings on nature inflicted on them, their suffering being to my benefit, and my family has endured patiently over the years my absences and abstractions in pursuit of the natural. The dedication acknowledges my least repayable debts.

H.W.

Contents

Abbreviations

AHDLMA	Archives d'histoire doctrinale et littéraire du moyen âge
An. M.	*Annuale medievale*
Ant.	*Anticlaudianus*
Arch.	*Architrenius*
Ayenbite	*The Ayenbite of Inwit*
BD	*The Book of the Duchess*
BVV	*The Book of Vices and Virtues*
CA	*Confessio Amantis*
CB	*Cinkante Balades*
CHLMP	*Cambridge History of Later Medieval Philosophy*
CM	*Cursor mundi*
Cosm.	*Cosmographia*
CP	*De consolatione Philosophiae*
CT	*Canterbury Tales*
DPN	*De planctu Naturae*
EA	*Les Echecs amoureux*
EETS	Early English Text Society
ELXIII	*English Lyrics of the Thirteenth Century*
EWS	*English Wycliffite Sermons*
EWWHU	*The English Works of Wyclif Hitherto Unprinted*
FNM	*La filosofia della natura nel medioevo*
JEGP	*Journal of English and Germanic Philology*
JMRS	*Journal of Medieval and Renaissance Studies*
Lam.	*Lamentations*
MED	*Middle English Dictionary*
MES	*Middle English Sermons*
MLQ	*Modern Language Quarterly*
MO	*Mirour de l'omme*
MP	*Modern Philology*
NHC	*Northern Homily Cycle*
OED	*Oxford English Dictionary*
OLD	*Oxford Latin Dictionary*
PC	*The Pricke of Conscience*
PF	*The Parlement of Foules*
PG	*Patrologia Graeca*

PL	*Patrologia Latina*
PMLA	*Publications of the Modern Language Association of America*
PP	*Piers Plowman*
PQ	*Philological Quarterly*
RC	*Renart le Contrefait*
RD	*Le Roman des deduis*
RES	*Review of English Studies*
RLXV	*Religious Lyrics of the Fifteenth Century*
RR	*Le Roman de la Rose*
SCG	*Summa contra Gentiles*
SEL	*The South English Legendary*
SE Lit.	*Studies in English Literature (Japan)*
Sent.	*Sententiae*
SEWJW	*Select English Works of John Wyclif*
SEWW	*Selections from English Wycliffite Writings*
SP	*Studies in Philology*
ST	*Summa theologiae*
TC	*Troilus and Criseyde*
VC	*Vox clamantis*

Introduction

Nature is constantly associated not with blind passion or instinct but with Reason.[1]

[T]he law of *nature* is conceived as an absolute moral standard against which the laws of all nations must be judged and to which they ought to conform.[2]

The orthodox [medieval] idea [is] that Nature is the symbol of order, beauty and perfection, while everything vicious and wicked is against Nature.[3]

Kynde (Nature) in medieval thought is always an aspect of God ... the law of nature is the moral order as known to man through his indwelling powers of conscience and reason. ... the rule of nature is the rule of reason and order.[4]

Since natural law is the exclusive property of rational beings, an acceptable synonym for 'natural law' would be 'rational law'.[5]

---

[1] J. A. W. Bennett, *The Parlement of Foules* (Oxford, 1957), 132.

[2] C. S. Lewis, *Studies in Words* (Cambridge, 1960), 61. Lewis's influence over the modern understanding of medieval Nature would seem to have been considerable. For another trenchant but, in my view, misguided statement of his on Nature, see below at the end of Ch. 2. Gareth W. Dunleavy entitles an article 'Natural Law as Chaucer's Ethical Absolute'. This appears in Willi Erzgräber (ed.), *Geoffrey Chaucer* (Darmstadt, 1983), 196–206. Erzgräber's own piece ' "Kynde" und "Nature" bei Chaucer', in G. W. Weber (ed.), *Idee, Gestalt, Geschichte: Festschrift Klaus von See* (Odense, 1988), 117–35, paints a largely positive picture of Nature (with much reference to Aquinas); Erzgräber, however, thinks that Chaucer wishes to draw attention not only to the value but also to the limitations of the natural as it impinges on human beings (134 f.).

[3] Shinsuke Ando, 'Chaucer's Conception of Nature' in Yoshio Terasawa (ed.), *Key-Word Studies in Chaucer*, i (Tokyo, 1984), 1–14 (7). It should be said that Ando thinks that there is in Chaucer 'a certain tincture running counter to the strictly orthodox pattern of medieval nature' (3), though this is not, according to Ando, really apparent in an analysis of Chaucer's Nature and Kynde terminology (10, 12).

[4] Helen Phillips (ed.), *The Book of the Duchess* (Durham, rev. repr. 1984), 143, note on l. 56.

[5] Linda Barney Burke, 'Genial Gower: Laughter in the *Confessio Amantis*', in R. F. Yeager (ed.), *John Gower: Recent Readings* (Kalamazoo, Mich., 1989), 39–63. (47).

These remarks articulate a view often, I think, taken for granted by modern students of medieval Nature—Nature as God's agent, deputy, 'vicar',[6] presides over a benign cosmic and moral order, an order to which human action ought to be conformed; the law of nature, 'rational law', lays out one's moral duty. This view, widespread, even dominant, though it appears to be, will not do—and this matters a great deal; because how people conceive Nature is intimately and ineluctably bound up with their opinions on all sorts of important matters—on the existential predicament of human beings, on the possibilities for moral behaviour, on God. If we are wrong about what people think about Nature, we will be hopelessly wrong about what they think—and feel—full stop.

That Nature need not be on the side of the angels in the Middle Ages and may be quite explicitly opposed to Reason is apparent if we consider her treatment in *The Assembly of Gods*.[7] In this allegory the triumph of Virtue in the contest for control of the field Microcosm[8]—i.e. the human being—involves the submission of Sensuality to Sadness, a submission which, we are told, is 'somewhat ageyn [Sensuality's] hert'.[9] Nature objects to the restraining of Sensuality and in this shows herself ill disposed to what is right. Virtue's rejoinder to her complaint indicates how the unconditioned operations of Nature through Sensuality are morally flawed:

> ... Sensualyte shall nat performe your lust
> Lyke as he hath do before thys, yef I may.
> Therfro hym restrayn Sadnesse shall assay.[10]

For all the accommodation of Nature made by Virtue and by the poem—Virtue allows Nature liberty within the field Microcosm[11] —it is clear that she has a tendency to work contrary to Reason and

---

[6] The term becomes standard for the personification Nature in the medieval literary tradition.

[7] *The Assembly of Gods* is a 15th-century poem formerly attributed to Lydgate. Quotations are from the edition by O. L. Triggs, EETS es 69 (London, 1896).

[8] The text reads 'Macrocosm' throughout, but it is clearly 'Microcosm' that is meant.

[9] 1266. Sensuality is the side of human beings concerned with the physical senses; it need not be seen as bad in itself, but is often understood to have a tendency towards sin. Sadness should be understood as Seriousness, Gravity, or Discretion.

[10] 1277–9.

[11] 1280 f.

Virtue. So we find Virtue warning Reason to be careful not to allow Sensuality, now under the control of Sadness, to be 'shent' by Nature's efforts.[12] When Resydyuacion,[13] bent on mischief, is thwarted in his approach to Sensuality he turns (indicatively) to Nature for advice. She replies:

> ... Euer syth Vertew of Vyce wan the pryse,
> Reson with Sadnes hath rewlyd the fylde so,
> That I and Sensualyte may lytyll for the do.
> For I may no more but oonly kepe my cours.[14]

And the opposition of Nature and the bodily to reason and what is right is plainly apparent when we are told

> that fylde [Microcosm] thus rewled Reson with Sadnes
> Mawgre Dame Nature for all her carnall myght.[15]

The dubious Nature of *The Assembly of Gods* shows us clearly that Nature in the Middle Ages is not always a benign and reasonable figure, standing for proper moral order and in harmony with Reason.[16]

D. W. Robertson, Jr. has a formulation which allows for the badness of nature: 'the medieval mind distinguished two "natures" with reference to man, one "nature" which made virtue natural before the Fall, and one which made vice natural thereafter';[17] yet this too is unsatisfactory.[18] The Natures and the natural human

---

[12] 1305 f.   [13] Relapse (into sin).   [14] 1354–7.   [15] 1380 f.

[16] The rule of Reason, whatever exactly that term may mean (see John A. Alford, 'The Idea of Reason in *Piers Plowman*', in Edward Donald Kennedy, Ronald Waldron, and Joseph S. Wittig (eds.), *Medieval English Studies Presented to George Kane* (Cambridge, 1988), 199–215), is the rule of right.

[17] *A Preface to Chaucer* (Princeton, 1962), 398.

[18] Robertson's perspective is highly Augustinian. There is certainly a strand in medieval thought according to which only the primal state of innocence is truly natural and it was possible to understand the natural law as that which pertained before the Fall (see below, p.11, p.17 n. 33), but it is also true that much of the discourse of Nature in medieval times emerges from classical conceptions of the constitution of human beings where, of course, there is no question of a radical alteration in the constitution of human nature at a Fall. See Brian Tierney, '*Natura, id est Deus*: A Case of Juristic Pantheism?', *Journal of the History of Ideas*, 24 (1963), 307–22 (321–2.). Jeremy Cohen, 'Original Sin as the Evil Inclination: A Polemicist's Appreciation of Human Nature', *Harvard Theological Review*, 73 (1980), 495–520 (especially 504–10, where Aquinas' views are usefully contrasted with those of Augustine) Jeremy Cohen, '*Be Fertile and Increase, Fill the Earth and Master It*' (Ithaca, NY, 1989), 290 ff., and Pierre J. Payer, *The Bridling of Desire* (Toronto 1993), 49–50.

behaviour with which we shall be concerned exist within the post-
lapsarian world, but are by no means dismissable as evidently and
simply bad; while it is true that sin can be regarded after the Fall as in
a sense natural to the human condition,[19] what we tend to find are
acknowledgements that Nature operates for the good, or perhaps
does so, coupled with reservations as to whether the natural is
totally, or genuinely, good. One may well suppose that the fascination Nature holds for medieval writers is very much bound up with
her ambivalent moral status, the issue being whether and how her
claims to be an agent of the purposes of God[20] can be harmonized
with her involvement in carnality and in particular sexuality.[21] The
fascination issues in hesitations, uncertainties, and reluctances over
what is to be said about Nature more often than it produces the cut-
and-dried. And because Nature is so central a concept in a world-
view, not being able to affirm with conviction the goodness of the
natural is connected to scepticism about the satisfactoriness of the
human condition and perhaps ultimately of God.

The smart response to receipt of the information that someone is
working on nature is to ask which nature, which of the *x* senses
discernible.[22] Nature is indeed one of the more polysemous terms
one could wish for and this book is nothing like a review of all the
semantic and conceptual territory which can be marked out by the
use of nature terminology.[23] I am not, for instance, writing about
scientific enquiry into the natural world or about how the natural
world is presented and reviewed in literary texts, exept in so far as

[19] See Ch. 1 below for some discussion of this in relation to Augustine.

[20] The formulation 'natura, id est Deus', considered by Tierney, '*Nature*', shows
agency becoming identity on the grounds that it is God (*natura naturans*) who creates the
order of nature.

[21] See Cohen, *Be Fertile*, 271–305. Note how in *The Assembly of Gods* a Nature plainly
inclined to give trouble on the moral front is nevertheless allowed her liberty within the
human being—she has to be, for this is, after all, the arrangement in creation.

[22] In *Primitivism and Related Ideas in Antiquity* (Baltimore, 1935) Arthur O. Lovejoy
and George Boas remark that the word 'nature' is 'probably the most equivocal in the
vocabulary of the European peoples' (12); they adduce sixty-six meanings (447–56).
There is much of interest in this book on ideas of the natural.

[23] The Middle Ages recognized the polysemy of Nature. For instance in the *Didascalicon* (ed. C. H. Buttimer, Washington, 1939) Hugh of St Victor comments on the
problematic quality of the term and analyses ancient usage into three major meanings (1.
10), whilst in his *Distinctiones* (a kind of theological dictionary) Alan of Lille gives eleven
(PL 210, 871).

that bears on my central concern. That concern is with such over-lapping questions as whether that provision with which human beings are endowed by nature tends towards their good, whether the natural circumstances of human beings conduce to their happiness, whether by nature human beings are inclined to the good, whether the law of nature directs human beings to the good; in short is Nature benign and moral? This concern means what follows is not an exhaustive study of Nature in the literature of the Middle Ages— I am not sure how many volumes and how many years that would take.[24] But even within the limitations imposed by this concern, there is nothing like exhaustiveness. My focus lies on certain literary works in Latin, French, and English in which the idea of nature figures prominently and which may be said to constitute a tradition, in that later works are significantly shaped by the earlier ones;[25] and even here, though focus on the end-point is not absolutely conditioning, there is a certain teleological shaping of my treatment of the tradition, which I read with a view to the light it sheds on the works of Chaucer and Gower. In a sense, though I hope this function does not exhaust their interest, the first five chapters of this book are prolegomena to the readings of Chaucer and Gower contained in Chapters 6 and 7.

Sometimes, especially with Chaucer, it is possible to see a direct response to antecedent works in the nature tradition, but I am also interested in the evidence the tradition provides for what might be thinkable about nature by an educated author in England in the later fourteenth century. So having reviewed in Chapters 3 and 4 material

[24] George D. Economou covered considerable ground in *The Goddess Natura in Medieval Literature* (Cambridge, Mass., 1972). Like Economou, I discuss the 'Chartrian' tradition and the *Roman de la Rose*. I am less concerned than Economou is with Nature in Classical literary material but I discuss medieval theological writing in much greater detail than he does. My Chs. 2, 5, and 6 consider material outside Economou's chosen scope and my discussion of Chaucer in Ch. 7 is not confined, as is Economou's, to *The Parlement of Foules*. Besides Economou, other important studies of Nature in the Middle Ages include E. C. Knowlton's articles 'The Goddess Nature in Early Periods', *JEGP* 19 (1920), 224–53, 'Nature in Middle English', *JEGP* 20 (1921), 186–207, 'Nature in Old French', *MP* 20 (1922), 309–29, and the appendix, 'Natura, Nature, and Kind', to Bennett's *Parlement*, 194–212.

[25] In *Nature and Salvation in Piers Plowman* (Cambridge, 1988) I discuss Langland's view of Nature, a view which seems to me very distinct from that of Gower or Chaucer and comparable to that of Julian of Norwich in its ultimately positive assessment of the natural.

much of which Chaucer and Gower would probably or certainly have read, in Chapter 5 I consider some French works most of which they probably or certainly would not have read. I do not, though, think it self-evident that it is only the literary tradition which informs the thinking of Chaucer and Gower on Nature, and so in my first chapter I offer a broad (though again by no means exhaustive) review of theological and legal material. Here I do not seek to construct what one might call a stemma of influences in order to be able to assert that Chaucer or Gower found such and such a view on Nature in such and such an authority; I doubt this is a feasible enterprise. Rather, I present a range of quotations from theological and legal discourse to demonstrate the kinds of idea about nature which I take it would have been available to or excogitatable by Chaucer and Gower. In the second chapter, I review English vernacular writings, mainly homiletic and didactic, more or less contemporary with Gower and Chaucer. This survey, like that conducted in the first chapter, attempts to be representative rather than completely comprehensive; as such it is able to demonstrate, I think, that a spectrum of views as to the moral status of nature broadly similar to that discernible in the material considered in the first chapter is also evident in English writings pitched at a lower academic level. This both confirms the availability to Gower and Chaucer of understandings of nature according to which nature is not unequivocally good, and, by suggesting that such understandings would have been easily acceptable to that section of their audience not familiar with the more elevated academic discourse, increases the plausibility of the claim I shall be making that these relatively negative understandings of the natural indeed have a presence in their works.

The teleological thrust of this study towards Gower and Chaucer in part explains why it does not engage as much as it might have done with the historical positionedness of some of the writings it considers, with the agendas the writers may have been pursuing within their own social and political contexts. There are indeed interesting directions to be pursued here. Such matters, however, will not receive much attention in what follows, for it seems to me that an attempt to chart the way in which ideas about nature might be implicated in the political stances of various writers would require considerable space and might not, given the complexity of such ideas and the ambivalence of the natural for many writers, yield anything other than speculative uncertainty. To demonstrate the complexity of the tradition of thought of which Gower and Chaucer were heirs is in itself a legitimate aim. With Gower and Chaucer themselves I shall be more concerned to suggest how their views dealing with Nature are implicated in their wider understanding of the way things are, though here my explicit perspective will be more metaphysical than socio-political.

One further limitation. In what follows I consider what the medieval (and Classical) writers themselves nominate natural. My consideration is thus very much bound to certain lexical items; mainly to *natura* and terms related to it in Latin, French, and English and to *kynde* and related terms in English.[26] It would have been possible to pursue the natural where nature terms did not actually appear, but this would have been likely to produce a false impression of a particular writer's perspective and emphasis.[27] It is not as if the limitation to particular items of lexis—even in combination with the other kinds of limitation—leaves an over-confined field of study.

[26] As far as I can see, there is no attempt among Middle English writers to make a semantic distinction between nature- and *kynde*-terms. See, however, R. F. Yeager, 'Learning to Speak in Tongues: Writing Poetry for a Trilingual Culture', in R. F. Yeager (ed.), *Chaucer and Gower: Difference, Mutuality, Exchange*, English Literary Studies Monograph Series 51 (Victoria, 1991), 115–29.

[27] Dunleavy, 'Ethical Absolute', seems to me to fall foul of this difficulty when he assesses various Canterbury pilgrims for adherence or otherwise to the *lawe of kynde*. It is of course possible to measure a medieval writer for signs of something which from a modern perspective can be related to nature and to track this in passages where nature-terms do not appear, as Ando, 'Chaucer's Conception', does in the case of Chaucer and 'modern Naturalism'. I have preferred to concentrate on what the medieval concepts of nature are rather than on what they might have been but are not. (In fact, a case for seeing the seed of 'modern Naturalism' in Chaucer's own nature terminology is made by Shunichi Noguchi in 'Chaucer's Concept of Nature', in Toshiyuki Takamiya and Richard Beadle (eds.), *Chaucer to Shakespeare: Essays in Honour of Shinsuke Ando* (Cambridge, 1992), 25–31.)

CHAPTER ONE

Academic Natures

This chapter considers how the natural was treated in a broad range of academic writings (philosophical, theological, legal, medical) from antiquity to the fifteenth century. It is particularly concerned to show that though much academic writing understood the natural to be good, this was by no means unequivocally the case for all writers in all circumstances. The chapter is organized into several sections. 'The Goodness of the Natural' reviews ways in which the natural is understood to be good and to promote virtue in human beings. This leads into a section on the Natural Law, which was held to provide moral guidance available in virtue of their rationality to all human beings, and what the content of that law was taken to be. However, one very important definition of Natural Law, a definition attributed to the Roman jurist Ulpian, associates it with animal behaviour rather than with human reason. This raises questions as to what behaviour is properly regarded as natural in human beings and whether certain kinds of behaviour which may be considered natural are also to be considered right. Ulpian's definition and the way it and its ramifications were dealt with by scholastic commentators are discussed in 'Human Nature, Animal Nature, and Ulpian' and 'Nature, Sex, and the Discriminating of Natures'. It is in the area of sexuality that Ulpian's definition is most challenging for moral orthodoxy, and scholastic commentary is much exercised over questions as to the naturalness of fornication, concubinage, and polygamy; these scholastic reflections are considered at some length. The scholastics discriminate between an animal nature and a rational nature in human beings which raises the question of whether one of these might be *more* natural. The section 'The Primacy of Nature-as-Instinct' shows that it was possible to take humanity's non-rational, animal side as more fundamentally natural than the rational, so that 'nature' and 'reason' within the human being can be at odds.

A final section, '"Natural" as Moral Middle Term', points out how sinning 'naturally' in the sexual sphere was better than sinning against nature and suggests that this adds to the instability of the natural as a term in moral discourse, an instability inevitable when the natural is understood, as this chapter shows it regularly to have been, to refer to an order (the animal) ultimately God-sanctioned but which nevertheless incorporates energies which urge towards that which is not right.

THE GOODNESS OF THE NATURAL

A sense of the close relationship between what is and what is right is, it has been claimed, central to the religious view of life. In the West, the idea of Nature has played a highly significant role in articulating this sense.[1] Within the Christian moral tradition from very early on it was possible to see the natural as pointing to the right and to think of what was unnatural as wrong. In Romans St Paul writes:

> Their women exchanged natural relations for unnatural, and the men likewise gave up natural relations with women and were consumed with passion for one another, men committing shameless acts with men and receiving in their own persons the due penalty for their error.[2]

And in another passage from the same Epistle, a passage which was to be of the greatest importance for medieval writers on natural law, Paul states: 'When Gentiles who have not the law do by nature what the law requires, they are a law to themselves, even though they do not have the law. They show that what the law requires is written on their hearts.'[3] Remarks such as these do not attempt sophisticated philosophical analysis of the goodness of the natural, but they do

---

[1] In *Islam Observed* (New Haven, 1968), 97, Clifford Geertz writes: 'The heart of . . . the religious perspective . . . is the conviction that the values one holds are grounded in the inherent structure of reality, that between the way one ought to live and the way things really are there is an unbreakable inner connection.' As with 'nature' in the West, in some Eastern systems a key term brings together what can be distinguished as the realms of fact and of value. On *jen* in Confucianism see Raymond Dawson, *Confucius* (Oxford, 1981), 37–40. In Hinduism one's *dharma* is both what one is and what one should be.

[2] Romans 1: 26 (Revised Standard Version).

[3] Romans 2: 14 f.

provide secure biblical justification for seeing the natural as something good, and in this way they ground the more academic reflections of later theologians on nature's goodness.

Outside the Bible, perhaps no authority was more revered in the Middle Ages, or more influential, than St Augustine.[4] If St Paul's remarks on nature bear some relation to Stoic ideas,[5] the thinking of Augustine in this area owes much to the Platonic equation between being and goodness.[6] This equation, of course, is easily assimilable to the Christian view that creation is the work of a benevolent deity: what there is must be in essence good, if it proceeds from a good God.

In Platonic vein, then, Augustine asserts that to be, to be a nature, is to be good, and to be bad is to fail to be a nature, to be against nature. For him, 'omnis natura, in quantum natura est, bona est.'[7] [Every nature, inasmuch as it is a nature, is good.] In so far as the devil is a *natura*, he is good.[8] On the other hand, if you take away what is good from a thing, it ceases to exist, to have or be a nature:

Si ergo malo illo adempto manet natura purgatior, bono autem detracto non manet ulla natura: hoc ibi facit naturam quod bonum habet; quod autem malum, non natura, sed contra naturam est.[9]

[If therefore, when that evil has been removed, nature remains in a purer condition, on the other hand, when good is taken away, no nature remains. That which possesses good constitutes a nature; what possesses evil, however, is not a nature, but is against nature.]

Evil in this understanding is parasitic on what is good, unable to exist without it:

---

[4] For instance, a very large number of the citations from past authorities in Peter Lombard's *Sentences*, probably composed between 1148 and 1150 and regularly commented on thereafter by theologians, are from Augustine. See also Henry Chadwick, *Augustine* (Oxford, 1986), 3.

[5] On this see, e.g., Rudolf Bultmann, *Theology of the New Testament* (British edn., London, 1952), i. 71.

[6] On this equation in Platonic thought see, e.g., G. M. A. Grube, *Plato's Thought* (London, 1935; repr. 1980), 23 f.

[7] *De libero arbitrio* 3. 13 (*PL* 32, 1289). See also, for example, *Contra epistolam Manichaei* 34 (*PL* 42, 199); *De natura boni* 1 and 17 (*PL* 42, 551 and 556).

[8] See *Opus imperfectum contra Julianum* 6. 16 (*PL* 45, 1537) and *De civitate Dei* 19. 13. 2 (*PL* 41, 641).

[9] *Contra epistolam Manichaei* 33 (*PL* 42, 199).

Nulla enim natura, in quantum natura est, malum est; sed prorsus bonum, sine quo bono ullum esse non potest malum: quia nisi in aliqua natura ullum esse non potest vitium; quamvis sine vitio possit esse, vel nunquam vitiata, vel sanata natura.[10]

[For no nature, in so far as it is a nature, is bad, but rather good, without which good no evil is able to exist—for no flaw is able to exist except in some nature, whereas there can exist without flaw a nature never flawed or one healed.]

For Augustine, what there is—natures—is fundamentally good, though natures are subject to vitiation; nothing evil is truly natural and the natural condition of a thing is identical with the way it ought to be. This, of course, applies for human beings even though the Fall in Augustine's view has radically affected the nature of human beings for the bad so that human nature is now *vulnerata, sauciata, vexata, perdita* (wounded, damaged, tormented, lost).[11] The effects on human nature of the Fall mean that there is a sense in which it is possible to speak of sin as natural,[12] but it is a secondary sense. St Paul speaks of how human beings are 'natura filii irae'.[13] Commenting on this Augustine distinguishes two definitions of *natura*:

Sic etiam ipsam naturam aliter dicimus, cum proprie loquimur, naturam hominis, in qua primum in suo genere inculpabilis factus est: aliter istam, in qua ex illius damnati poena, et mortale et ignari et carni subditi nascimur; juxta quem modum dicit Apostolus, *Fuimus enim et nos naturaliter filii irae, sicut et caeteri.*[14]

[Thus also we define the nature of man in one way, when we are speaking correctly, as that nature in which he was created blameless in his kind and in another way as that in which as a result of the penalty for that condemnation we are born mortal, ignorant and in submission to the flesh. In accordance with this way the Apostle says, *For even we also were naturally sons of wrath just like the others too.*]

Furthermore, a natural power for good still remains, because the image of God which defined original, prelapsarian human nature

---

[10] *Opus imperfectum contra Julianum* 3. 206 (*PL* 45, 1334).

[11] *De natura et gratia* 53. 62 (*PL* 44, 277).

[12] See the chapter on Augustine in J. Mehlmann's *Natura filii irae*, Analecta Biblica 6 (Rome, 1957).

[13] Ephesians 2: 3. Discussions of this text by patristic writers and later theologians are reviewed in Mehlmann, *Natura filii irae*.

[14] *De libero arbitrio* 3. 19 (*PL* 32, 1297).

still remains and exerts influence: the tendency even of man's fallen nature is not altogether evil. As Augustine puts it:

Verumtamen quia non usque adeo in anima humana imago Dei terrenorum affectuum labe detrita est, ut nulla in ea velut lineamenta extrema remanserint, unde merito dici possit etiam in ipsa impietate vitae suae facere aliqua legis vel sapere; si hoc est quod dictum est, quia *Gentes quae legem non habent*, hoc est, legem Dei, *naturaliter quae legis sunt faciunt*, et quia hujusmodi homines *ipsi sibi sunt lex*, et *scriptum opus legis habent in cordibus suis,* id est, non omni modo deletum est, quod ibi per imaginem Dei cum crearentur impressum est.[15]

[However, the image of God in the human soul is not so destroyed by the pollution of earthly affections that there do not remain in it, as it were, the last traces, on account of which it is possible to say of it deservedly that even in the impiety of its life it fulfils or has knowledge of certain requirements of the law-if this is what is meant by *the Gentiles who do not have the law*, that is, the law of God, *do naturally the things of the law*, and because men of this kind *are a law to themselves* and *have the work of the law written in their hearts*, that is, what has been imprinted there by the image of God when they were created has not been completely destroyed.]

If Augustine invokes St Paul, later writers might look to Aristotle on matters of nature and morality. Alan of Lille writes:

Natura convenit omnis potentia, quae sit virtus, homini a creatione, ut naturaliter aptus sit secundum hanc, vel illam potentiam ad hoc vel illud faciendum, ut sicut est natus ad ratiocinandum, vel ad intelligendum; ita aptus natus ad reddendum unicuique quod suum est, ad diligendum Deum, et proximum: quod satis insinuat Aristoteles, quod homo est mansuetus natura. Sub hoc nomine *mansuetus* intellexit illas naturales virtutes.[16]

[By nature every potentiality which may be a virtue is present to man from his creation so that he is naturally fitted in respect of various potentialities to do various things; so that just as he is naturally fitted to reasoning and to understanding, so he is born fitted for rendering to each person what is theirs, for loving God and neighbour. This Aristotle implies with sufficient

---

[15] *De spiritu et litera* 28 (*PL* 44, 230).

[16] *Theologicae regulae* 88 (*PL* 210, 667). Alan of Lille was born *c.*1116 and died in 1202 or 1203. His allegories of Nature are considered at length in Ch. 3. The remark of Aristotle cited is from *De interpretatione* 20[b] (in *The Organon*, ed. H. P. Cooke, Loeb Classical Library (London, 1949), vol. i). Aristotle's word is ἥμερον: it is rendered 'mansuetum' by the translators of the Latin Aristotle. See *Aristoteles Latinus*, ed. L. Minio-Paluello, ii. 1–2 (Bruges, 1965), 23, 53.

clarity in saying man is 'mansuetus' [domesticated, civilized] by nature. Under this term, *mansuetus*, he understood those natural virtues.]

The natural foundations for virtue are present, then, though for both Aristotle and Alan these natural dispositions to the good are not in themselves true virtue.[17]

Aristotle was, of course, a major formative influence on the thinking of the great thirteenth-century Dominican theologian Thomas Aquinas, and Aristotelian notions are evident in Aquinas' opinions on the nature of things in general and human beings in particular. Aquinas held that God had created things in such a way that 'all beings by their nature have within themselves inclinations which direct them to the end that is proper to them'.[18] So human beings were naturally equipped with the germs of the natural virtues, which it was their natural end to develop.

These three theologians, Augustine, Alan of Lille, and Aquinas, speak in other ways too about a natural inclination within human beings towards the good. In a sense, according to Aquinas, humans naturally desire God, since they naturally desire the *beatitudo* which is, whether an individual realizes it or not, found in the possession of God.[19] Augustine likewise thinks human beings have an innate desire for happiness which can only be satisfied in union with God.[20] Alan of Lille writes of the natural love by which any rational creature loves God.[21]

---

[17] See Aristotle, *Nicomachean Ethics*, ed. H. Rackham, Loeb Classical Library (Cambridge, Mass., 1926), 6. 13. 1144[b]. According to the Stoics, man was naturally guided in the right direction by his reason, though the full achievement of virtue called for strenuous effort. See A. A. Long, *Hellenistic Philosophy* (London, 1974), 182, where *Stoicorum veterum fragmenta*, ed. J. ab Arnim (Leipzig, 1903–24), i. 566 and Seneca's *Epistle* 120, 4 are cited.

[18] The formulation of Aquinas' position is D. E. Luscombe's in the chapter entitled 'Natural Morality and Natural Law' in Norman Kretzmann, Anthony Kenny, and Jan Pinborg (eds.), *The Cambridge History of Later Medieval Philosophy* (*CHLMP*) (Cambridge, 1982), 705–19 (709). Aquinas (*c.*1225–74) exercised considerable influence in the later Middle Ages, though the adoption of his teaching as official Roman Catholic doctrine is a post-medieval development.

[19] On this see E. Gilson, *The Philosophy of St Thomas Aquinas*, trans. E. Bullough, ed. G. A. Elrington (2nd edn., rev., Cambridge, 1929), 58 f.

[20] As in the famous quotation from the *Confessions*, ed. James J. O'Donnell, 3 vols. (Oxford, 1992), i. 3: 'fecisti nos ad te et inquietum est cor nostrum donec requiescat in te' [you have made us for yourselves and our hearts are restless until they rest in you].

[21] *Summa de arte predicatoria* 20 (*PL* 210, 153).

Notwithstanding the innate desire for a happiness which is to be found in possessing God, medieval thinkers held (unsurprisingly) that human beings can pursue wrong ends in the mistaken belief that in these lies happiness.[22] However, a direct, immediate, and irremovable attachment to what is in fact good is also commonly attributed to human beings. Peter Lombard remarks:

Recte ... dicitur homo naturaliter velle bonum, quia in bona et recta voluntate conditus est. Superior enim scintilla rationis, quae etiam, ut ait Hieronymus, in Cain non potuit exstingui, bonum semper vult et malum odit.[23]

[Man is rightly said naturally to desire the good, because he is established in a good and upright will. For the higher spark of reason, which even, as Jerome says, 'in Cain cannot be extinguished', always desires good and hates evil.]

This 'superior scintilla rationis' is what later writers, drawing the term from the passage of Jerome to which Peter Lombard refers,[24] call *synderesis*. *Synderesis* is what guarantees the attachment of human beings to the sovereign good, sinners though they be. Aquinas, associating it with the practical reason, understood it as an innate *habitus* by which a person knows the precepts of the natural law.[25] It is not always, however, taken as an aspect of the reason: Bonaventure understood it as an aspect of the will, a *naturale quoddam pondus* [a certain natural weight] in persons taking them towards the good (the good being perceived partly through the help of a *naturale lumen* which acquaints human beings with moral first principles).[26]

---

[22] See, for instance, Boethius, *De consolatione Philosophiae* 3 p. 3 (ed. S. J. Tester, Loeb Classical Library (Cambridge, Mass., 1973)).

[23] *Sententiae* 2. 39. 3 (*Sententiae in IV libris distinctae (Grottaferrata, 1971)*).

[24] See Jerome, *Commentaria in Ezechielem* 1. 1 (verse 7) (PL 25. 22).

[25] See *Summa theologiae* (Aquinas, *Opera omnia*, ed. R. Busa, 7 vols. (Rome, 1980), vol. ii), 1. 2 q. 94 a. 1 and a. 2. For Aquinas's view of the relationship betweeen *synderesis* and natural law see P. M. Farrell, 'Sources of St. Thomas' Concept of Natural Law', *Thomist*, 20 (1957), 237–94 (283) and M. B. Crowe, 'Synderesis and the Notion of Law in St Thomas', in *L'Homme et son destin d'après les penseurs du moyen âge*, Actes du Premier Congrès International de Philosophie Médiévale (Louvain, 1960), 601–9. See also O. Lottin, *Le Droit naturel chez Saint Thomas d'Aquin et ses prédécesseurs* (2nd edn., Bruges, 1931), 79–81. and T. C. Potts, *Conscience in Medieval Philosophy* (Cambridge, 1980), 45–6. On *synderesis* generally see O. Lottin, *Psychologie et morale au XIIe et XIIIe siècles*, 6 vols. (Louvain, 1942–60), Potts, *Conscience*, and the entry in A. Vacant and E. Mangenot (eds.), *Dictionnaire de théologie catholique* (Paris, 1903–72).

[26] Or, alternatively, according to some textual witnesses, as *voluntas cum illo pondere* [the will with that weight]. See Bonaventure (*c.*1217–74), *Commentarium in IV libros*

THE NATURAL LAW

Synderesis can be identified with *naturale ius* and is frequently treated in connection with it.[27] The idea of natural law was extensively discussed by theologians and both civil and canon lawyers in the Middle Ages and what they say about it sheds much light on the literary tradition of a personified Nature.[28] The development of medieval natural law theory owed much to Stoic thought. The Stoics held that the prime moral obligation was to follow the law of nature, which in the case of humans meant to follow reason, since humans are by nature rational.[29] Cicero, one of the main transmitters of Stoic thought to the Christian Middle Ages,[30] states that

---

sententiarum, 4 vols. (Quaracchi, 1882–9) (vols. i–iv of the *Opera omnia*), 2 d. 39 a. 2 q. 1 and comments on this by Lottin, *Psychologie*, ii. 206 ff. and T. C. Potts, 'Conscience', in *CHLMP* 687–704 (695–70).

[27] See Lottin, *Psychologie*, ii. 108 and 74 n. 3, where a passage from Simon of Bisiniano making the identification is quoted. See also 83 with n. 2. Rufinus, *Summa decretorum* (ed. H. Singer, Paderborn, 1902), 6 (mentioned in this context by Lottin, *Psychologie*, ii. 108), defines natural law as 'vis quedam humane creature a natura insita ad faciendum bonum cauendumque contrarium' [a certain capacity of the human creature put in it by nature for doing good and avoiding its opposite].

[28] For discussion of medieval treatments of natural law see, besides Lottin, *Droit naturel*, R. W. Carlyle and A. J. Carlyle, *A History of Medieval Political Theory in the West*, 6 vols. (Edinburgh, 1903–36); P. Delhaye, *Permanence du droit naturel*, Analecta Mediaevalia Namurcensia 10 (Louvain, 1960); Tierney, '*Natura*'; Rudolf Weigand, *Die Naturrechtslehre der Legisten und Dekretisten von Irnerius bis Accursius und von Gratian bis Johannes Teutonicus* (Munich, 1967); A. P. d'Entrèves, *Natural Law* (2nd edn. London, 1970); Michael B. Crowe, *The Changing Profile of the Natural Law* (The Hague, 1977); Luscombe, 'Natural Morality'.

[29] The *nomos/physis* [law/nature] distinction in Greek thought gave rise to the initially paradoxical notion of a *nomos physeos* [law of nature], which became central in Stoicism (see C. Morris, *Western Political Thought*, i: *Plato to Augustine* (London, 1967), 129). At the highest level, for the Stoics, to follow the law of nature was to follow reason, but there was also an accommodation of instinct (see Long, *Hellenistic Philosophy* 189–92). For nature as reason in Stoic thought see G. Watson, 'The Natural Law and Stoicism', in A. A. Long (ed.), *Problems in Stoicism* (London, 1971), 223, 228 and the citations under 'God' in A.L. Motto, *Guide to the Thought of Lucius Annaeus Seneca* (Amsterdam, 1970).

[30] For Stoic influence in general on the Middle Ages and its channels of transmission see G. Verbecke, 'L'Influence du Stoïcisme sur la pensée médiévale en Occident', in *Actas del 5° Congreso Internacional de Filosofía Medieval* (Madrid, 1979), 95–109 and M. L. Colish, *The Stoic Tradition from Antiquity to the Early Middle Ages*, 2 vols. (Leiden, 1985). Verbecke considers the notion of *synderesis* indebted to Stoic thought. The respect in which a Stoic writer might be held in the Middle Ages is made clear when in his *Fons philosophiae* (written *c*.1175) Godfrey of St Victor claims an authority for Seneca in moral

humanity's possession of law is a function of its endowment by nature with reason:

Quibus enim ratio <a> natura data est, isdem etiam recta ratio data est; ergo et lex, quae est recta ratio in iubendo et vetando.[31]

[For to those to whom reason has been given by nature, right reason has also been given; and therefore law as well, which is right reason as it gives commands to action or forbids it.]

Elsewhere Cicero identifies *recta ratio* as *vera lex*, the true law, to rebel against which is to rebel against one's nature as a human being:

est quidem vera lex recta ratio, naturae congruens, diffusa in omnis, constans, sempiterna, quae vocet ad officium iubendo, vetando a fraude deterreat, quae tamen neque probos frustra iubet aut vetat, nec improbos iubendo aut vetando movet. huic legi nec obrogari fas est, neque derogari aliquid ex hac licet, neque tota abrogari potest . . . sed et omnes gentes et omni tempore una lex et sempiterna et immutabilis continebit, unusque erit communis quasi magister et imperator omnium deus: ille legis huius inventor, disceptator, lator; cui non parebit, ipse se fugiet, ac naturam hominis aspernatus hoc ipso luet maximas poenas, etiamsi cetera supplicia quae putantur effugerit.[32]

[True law is right reason, in harmony with nature, diffused in everyone, constant, eternal, which calls to duty when it commands, deters from deceit when it forbids, and which neither commands nor forbids the virtuous in vain, nor moves the wicked when it commands or forbids. It is not right to counter-legislate against this law, nor is it permissible to repeal any of it and possible for it to be abrogated entirely, . . . but one eternal and immutable law will rule all nations and in every age, and God will be, as it were, the one common teacher and ruler. He is the author, promulgator and decreer of this law, and he who fails to obey it will be in flight from himself, and, rejecting his nature as a human being, will in virtue of that fact incur the most grievous punishments, even if he should escape other torments which are thought of.]

---

matters scarcely less than that of the Gospels (*Fons philosophiae*, ed. P. Michaud-Quantin, Analecta Mediaevalia Namurcensia 8 (Namur, 1956), ll. 409–12).

[31] *De legibus*, ed. K. Ziegler and W. Görler (Freiburg, 1979), 1. 12. 33. See also *De legibus* 1. 6. 18: 'Lex est ratio summa, insita in natura, quae iubet ea quae facienda sunt, prohibetque contraria.' [Law is the highest reason, implanted in nature, which commands those things which ought to be done and forbids the opposite.]

[32] *De re publica*, ed. K. Ziegler (Leipzig, 1969), 3. 22. 33.

This passage adumbrates certain characteristics generally attributed to the natural law in the Middle Ages-its universality, its availability to and binding power over all human beings, its immutability,[33] and its derivation from God.

Cicero's conception of the natural law as a law 'non scripta, sed nata' [not written, but spontaneously arising][34] accords well with the passage from the second chapter of Romans, given above, in which Paul speaks of how 'Gentiles who have not the law do by nature what the law requires', thereby showing that 'what the law requires is written on their hearts'. Paul's formulation of the inscription on the heart is recurrent in medieval theological writing,[35] but the interiority and spontaneous availability of the natural law is also sometimes explicitly related to man's rational capacity. In his *Distinctiones*, Alan of Lille exemplifies the meaning of *natura* 'naturalis ratio' with the Romans passage:

Dicitur [natura] naturalis ratio, unde Apostolus ait quod *gentes, quae legem non habent, naturaliter quae legis sunt faciunt*, id est naturali instinctu rationis.[36]

[[Nature] is defined as natural reason, on account of which the Apostle says 'the gentiles, who have not the law, do by nature what the law requires', that is, by the natural instinct of reason.]

Aquinas regards the first principles of the natural law as 'scripta in ratione naturali' [written in the natural reason] and as 'per se nota

---

[33] See, e.g., Gratian, *Decretum* (in *Corpus iuris canonici*, vol. i, ed. A. Friedberg (Leipzig, 1879)), P. I 6, 18. (The *Decretum*, compiled *c*.1150, was the central document of medieval canon law. It is a codification of patristic texts, conciliar decrees, and papal pronouncements.) However, it came to be argued that the natural law was not completely immutable. Aquinas held that the first principles of natural law were immutable, but that the natural law contained also precepts deduced from these first principles which were subject to change (see *ST* I. 2 q. 94 a. 25 (also a. 4) and Lottin, *Droit naturel*, 32). The Fall might be understood to have brought about changes in the natural law: whereas before the Fall community of possession and universal liberty were part of the natural law, private property and servitude are 'per legem naturalem' after the Fall. See, e.g., Alexander of Hales (attrib.), *Summa theologica*, ed. B. Klumper, 4 vols. (Quaracchi, 1924–48), 3. 247 ad 1 (this work is not, in fact, all by Alexander). By the end of the 12th century the view of the Augustinian tradition that the law of nature was the law of man's innocent, unfallen nature was rather old fashioned: see Tierney, 'Natura', 322 and n. 47.

[34] *Pro Milone*, ed. A. B. Poynton (2nd edn. Oxford, 1902), 4. 10.

[35] See, e.g., Augustine, *Ennarationes in Psalmos* 57. 1 (*PL* 36, 673) and Hugh of St Victor, *De sacramentis* 1.2 (*PL* 176, 347).

[36] *Distinctiones* (*PL* 210, 871).

rationi humanae' [self-evident to human reason].[37] In the *Decretum*, a work of the first half of the twelfth century profoundly influential on later writers, Gratian ties the law of nature to rationality when he says that the natural law began with the coming into being of the rational creature.[38] And Aquinas, again, calls the natural law 'nihil aliud . . . quam participatio legis aeternae in rationali creatura' [nothing other than the participation of the rational creature in the eternal law].[39]

As for the content of the natural law, Alan of Lille continues his remark just cited as follows:

et secundum hoc solet dici quod natura dictat homini ut non faciat aliis quod sibi non vult fieri, id est naturalis ratio.[40]

[and accordingly it is customary to say that nature commands a man not to do to others what he does not wish done to himself—that is, natural reason.]

That prohibition and the corresponding positive commandment are indeed frequently taken to constitute the essence of the natural law.[41] This permits the natural law to be identified with the morality of the Old and New Testaments. Thus Gratian writes:

Ius naturae est, quod in lege et evangelio continetur, quo quisque iubetur alii facere, quod sibi uult fieri et prohibetur alii inferre quod sibi nolit fieri.[42]

[The law of nature is what is contained in the Law and the Gospel, according to which everyone is commanded to do to another that which they desire to be done to themselves and are forbidden to do to another what they do not wish to be done to themselves.]

Several authors held that the promulgation of the Old Law involved a reiteration of the natural law.[43] Peter Abelard speaks of the moral precepts of the Gospel as a *reformatio*, a reshaping, of the natural law:

[37] *ST* 1. 2 q. 100 a. 3 and a. 3 ad 1. See Lottin, *Psychologie*, ii. 97. I would not wish to give the impression that Aquinas' views on the natural law are adequately encapsulated in the remarks cited here. For the complex and developing nature of Aquinas' thinking see Crowe, *Changing Profile* and Oscar Brown, *Natural Rectitude and the Divine Law in Aquinas* (Toronto, 1981).

[38] *Decretum* 1 d. 5. 1. 1.

[39] *ST* 1. 2 q. 91 a. 2.

[40] *Distinctiones* (PL 210, 871).

[41] See Lottin, *Psychologie*, ii. 71–3.

[42] *Decretum* 1 d. 1 dictum ante c. 1.

[43] See Carlyle, and Carlyle, *History*, i. 104 f.

Si enim diligenter moralia Evangelii praecepta consideremus, nihil ea aliud quam reformationem legis naturalis inveniemus, quam secutos esse philosophos constat.[44]

[Should we consider carefully the moral precepts of the Gospel, we will find them to be nothing other than a reshaping of the natural law, which it is agreed that the philosophers followed.]

However, not all the precepts to be found in the Old and New Testaments were regarded as part of the natural law. The ceremonial stipulations of the Old Testament, for instance, were not included.[45] Abelard illuminates the relationship between natural law and biblical precept in the following passage from his *Dialogus* (a Philosopher is speaking to a Christian):

Ipsae quoque leges quas divinas dicitis, Vetus scilicet ac Novum Testamentum, quaedam naturalia tradunt praecepta, quae moralia dicitis, ut diligere Deum vel proximum, non adulterari, non furari, non homicidam fieri, quaedam vero quasi positivae justitiae sint, quae quibusdam ex tempore sunt accommodata, ut circumcisio Judaeis et baptismus vobis et pleraque alia quorum figuralia vocatis praecepta.[46]

[Those laws which you call divine, that is the Old and the New Testament, convey certain natural precepts, which you call moral precepts, such as to love God or neighbour, not to commit adultery, not to steal, not to become a murderer; and certain precepts, on the other hand, which are features of what one might call a posited justice, and which are appropriate to particular people at various times, as, for example, circumcision to the Jews and baptism to you and many other things the precepts in relation to which you call figural.]

Aquinas writes that the *prima et communia precepta* [primary and general precepts] of the natural law are love of God and of one's neighbour, making the law of nature in its fundamental essence Christ's summary of the law.[47] In a widely shared understanding,

[44] *Theologia Christiana* (written c.1123–4) 2 (PL 178, 1179), cited in Luscombe, 'Natural Morality', 706.

[45] See Carlyle, and Carlyle, *History*, ii. 108–10.

[46] *Dialogus* (PL 178, 1656). The 13th-century canonist Azo speaks of the *ius naturale decalogi*. On the relation of the natural law to the Old Law see also Aquinas, ST I. 2 q. 100 a.1 and a. 3 ad 1. Tierney, '*Natura*', 310 f., comments on the matter.

[47] ST I. 2 q. 100 a. 3 ad 1. On the notion of *prima et communia praecepta* see n. 33. In his *Summa de arte praedicatoria* (PL 210, 109–72) Alan of Lille writes, 154, 'Consule naturam, illa te docebit diligere proximum tuum sicut te ipsum' [Consult nature; she will teach you to love your neighbour as yourself] .

in fact, the central moral precepts of Christianity are dictates of the natural law. A quotation from the Alexandran *Summa* encapsulates the broad scope and high moral authority which the law of nature might be taken to possess: 'omne malum secundum se est contra dictamen legis naturalis' [all intrinsic evil is against the dictate of the natural law].[48]

HUMAN NATURE, ANIMAL NATURE, AND ULPIAN

So far the picture of what is truly natural to human beings has been ethically positive, for all that their true nature has, in the Augustinian view, been damaged by the Fall.[49] But natural law theory in the Middle Ages is profoundly conditioned by a definition of what natural law is which we have not so far considered, and which introduces some ethically challenging possibilities as to what kind of behaviour might be regarded as natural in human beings. Further, the disparity between this definition of natural law and other definitions invites consideration of what is the primary meaning of 'natural', and this semantic issue brings with it ontological questions as to what human nature is.

This charged definition of natural law occurs in the *Corpus iuris civilis*, compiled under the Emperor Justinian in the first half of the sixth century, which codified the opinions of Roman legal writers on the whole range of law and which was much commented upon in the Middle Ages.[50] Various views on what natural law is are discernible in this compilation, but the most prominent and explicit definition in both the *Digest* and the *Institutes*, two different components of the *Corpus*, is one ascribed to Ulpian:[51]

Jus naturale est, quod natura omnia animalia docuit: nam jus istud non humani generis proprium, sed omnium animalium, quae in terra, quae in

---

[48] *ST* 3. 365 ad 8.

[49] Tierney, '*Natura*', 322, finds the Augustinian tradition according to which only the state of primal innocence was truly natural very much in eclipse by the end of the 12th century.

[50] The *Corpus* was the particular province of civil lawyers, but the ideas on natural law contained in it received commentary far beyond the civil law tradition in the works of canon lawyers and theologians.

[51] There has been some discussion as to whether this definition is not a later interpolation. See Crowe, *Changing Profile*, 47 f.

mari nascuntur, avium quoque commune est. Hinc descendit maris et feminae coniunctio, quam nos matrimonium appellamus, hinc liberorum procreatio, hinc educatio . . . . Jus gentium est, quo gentes humanae utuntur. Quod a naturali recedere facile intellegere licet, quia illud omnibus animalibus, hoc solis hominibus inter se commune sit.[52]

[Natural law is what nature has taught all animals: for this law is not peculiar to the human race, but common to all animals that are born on land or in the sea and to the birds as well. From it comes the union of male and female, which we call marriage, from it comes the procreation of children and their bringing up. The law of nations is what human nations use. This law may easily be understood to be distinct from natural law, because the one is common to all animals, the other common only to human beings.]

Considerable difficulties arise with regard to this definition, a definition which nevertheless carries considerable authority; though some writers regard it as improper, many feel they have to come to terms with it.[53] The theologians may have felt that their negotiations with the definition demonstrate how its problematic aspects can be neutralized, but the very energy with which they undertake this task means that the problems they are dealing with are given wide currency, and whether all who confronted the difficulties via the master theologians (directly or indirectly) felt those difficulties had been satisfactorily resolved would seem by no means certain, as later chapters will suggest.

NATURE, SEX, AND THE DISCRIMINATING OF NATURES

The difficulties centre on this: the natural law is something given by God[54] and so must tend to the good; yet the natural law as Ulpian defines it seems to promote behaviour not allowable in the ortho-

---

[52] Vol. i of the edition of the *Corpus iuris civilis* by P. Krueger and T. Mommsen (16th edn., Berlin, 1954) contains the *Digest* and the *Institutes*. The extract given is from *Digest* 1. 1. i. The *Institutes* substitute Gaius' definition of the *ius gentium* for Ulpian's; see Crowe, *Changing Profile*, 45.

[53] On this see Michael B. Crowe, 'St. Thomas and Ulpian's Natural Law', in *St. Thomas Aquinas 1274–1974: Commemorative Studies* (Toronto, 1974), i. 261–82 (267 ff.). In *The Changing Profile of Natural Law*, Crowe claims that for canonists the Ulpianic definition of natural law is the primary one.

[54] In the phrase 'Natura, id est Deus' (on which see Tierney, '*Natura*') the *natura* understood to teach all animals is actually identified with God.

dox Christian moral scheme. The Ulpianic definition instances *coniunctio maris et feminae* [union of male and female] as one of the things to which natural law prompts, and it is in the field of sexual behaviour that most of the problems associated with Ulpianic nature arise. What, for instance, about polygamy; it cannot be held that nature has taught monogamy to all animals, so why should human beings be monogamous? What follows shows medieval theologians negotiating this and other difficulties arising out of the plausibility which the Ulpianic definition gives to the notion that alarmingly unrestricted sexual behaviour is natural and therefore permissible.

But it is not just the witness of Ulpian in the *Corpus*. The high authority of St Augustine supported the view that polygamy could in certain circumstances be acceptable: he had expressed the opinion that the plural sexual relations of the patriarchs had been legitimate, since these did not run counter to the law of nature. Such relations were not contrary to the natural law because the patriarchs were not polygamous out of lust, but in the interests of procreation, this being the proper end of sexual activity, that towards which it is ordered.[55] In the *Sentences* Peter Lombard cites Augustine's opinion:

Antiquis iustis non fuit peccatum, quod pluribus feminis utebantur: neque contra naturam hoc faciebat, cum non lasciviendi causa, sed gignendi hoc facerent.[56]

[Having sexual relations with several women was not a sin for the just men of ancient times and they were not acting against nature, because they did this not out of lust but for the sake of having children.]

The implication of Augustine's remark seems to be that having sexual relations with more than one woman is not against nature, given procreative intent. Augustine may be speaking to a particular situation now past, but his views here might still be regarded as dangerous, given that if an action is in accordance with nature, it will tend to be seen as permissible.

---

[55] For discussion of patristic and medieval opinion on the purpose of marriage see Jean-Louis Flandrin, *L'Église et le contrôle des naissances* (Paris, 1970), 19–65, James A. Brundage, *Law, Sex, and Christian Society in Medieval Europe* (Chicago, 1987), and Payer, *Bridling*, 60–72.

[56] *Sententiae* 4. 33. 1. The Augustine passage cited by Peter Lombard comes from *De bono coniugali* 25. 33 (*PL* 40, 395). See also Augustine's *Contra Faustum*, 22. 47 (*PL* 42, 428).

At any rate, later theologians are at pains to deny that the natural-ness in the Ulpianic sense of sexual activity legitimizes polygamy or other dubious forms of sexual activity. Vincent of Beauvais, for example, moves swiftly to prevent the Ulpianic notion that the natural law includes the conjoining of male and female being taken as justification for non-monogamous behaviour:

Quia vero dictum est supra, iuris naturalis esse coniunctionem maris, & feminae, quam natura omnia animalia docuit, ne per hoc videatur quod liceat alicui carnem suam in plures diuidere.[57]

[But because it is said above that the joining of man and woman is a matter of natural law, it should not on that account appear that it is permissible for people to share out their bodies among several.]

But why not? After all, *nullus actus naturalis est peccatum*, surely?[58] Medieval lawyers and theologians have a variety of answers. One response is to insist on the sinfulness of the action in question and take this as proving that the act cannot be in accordance with natural law. So on the statement in the *Decretum* that the *coniunctio* of a man and a woman is *de iure naturali* the twelfth-century canonist Simon of Bisiniano writes:

Hic queritur de qua coniunctione hoc possit intelligi. De fornicaria non, quia ipsa est peccatum et ideo de iure naturali esse non potest.[59]

[Here the question is of what union this may be understood. Not of a union through fornication, because that union is a sin and therefore cannot be of the natural law.]

The union of marriage is what is in question. Similarly Huguccio (twelfth century) thinks the union should be understood 'de con-iunctione carnali matrimoniali, non fornicaria, cum ex iure naturali

---

[57] *Speculum maius* 2. 7. 41 (Venice, 1591).

[58] Such a contention that 'no natural act is a sin' occurs in the discussion of 'Utrum inseparabilitas matrimonii sit de lege naturali' [whether inseparability in marriage is a matter of natural law] in the Alexandran *Summa*, *ST* 3. 256. The resolution is achieved by means of the distinction between genus and species and the different ideas of the natural deriving from these categories. See further below.

[59] On d. 1 c. 7, quoted by Weigand, *Naturrechtslehre*, 286. The union between man and woman that *is* of the natural law is marriage. See also *Ecce vicit leo* which understands the *coniunctio* referred to to be a union of souls rather than bodies, 'coniunctio enim corporum sepius est fornicatio et sic peccatum et sic esse non potest de iure naturali' [for the union of bodies is often enough fornication and so a sin and so cannot be of the natural law] (quoted by Weigand, *Naturrechtslehre*, 287).

peccatum non possit esse' [as referring to the union of the flesh in marriage, not to union through fornication, since sin cannot proceed from the natural law].[60]

Other responses allow that in some sense the questionable act is in accordance with natural law, but set the Ulpianic definition against other understandings of the law of nature so as to show that at least one other non-Ulpianic law of nature demands orthodox moral behaviour. Thus, under the article 'Utrum habere plures uxores sit contra legem naturare' [Whether to have several wives is against the law of nature] in Aquinas' *Commentary on the Sentences*, we find Ulpian's definition invoked in support of the contention that polygamy is allowable under natural law:

Praeterea, jus naturale est quod natura omnia animalia docuit, ut in principio digestorum dicitur. sed natura non docuit hoc omnia animalia, quod sit una unius; cum unum mas in multis animalibus, pluribus feminis conjungatur. ergo non est contra legem naturae habere plures uxores.[61]

[Besides, the law of nature is what nature has taught all the animals, as is said at the beginning of the *Digest*. But Nature has not taught all the animals that one female should belong to one male: in fact in many species of animal one male has sexual relations with several females. So it is not against the law of nature to have several wives.]

Aquinas responds to this by saying that there are several ways in which the law of nature may be understood. He says that a law may be called natural 'ex principio, quia a natura est inditum' [in relation to first principle, because [it] is implanted by nature].[62] He then moves on to the equation of natural law with the contents of the Old Testament Law and the Gospel. There follows a third possibility:

tertio dicitur ius naturale non solum a principio, sed a natura, quia de naturalibus est. et quia natura contra rationem dividitur, a qua homo est homo; ideo strictissimo modo accipiendo jus naturale, illa quae ad homines tantum pertinent, etsi sint de dictamine rationis naturalis, non dicuntur esse

---

[60] On d. 1 c. 7 quoted by Weigand, *Naturrechtslehre*, 291. Huguccio sees marriage as in accordance with the natural law as 'instinctus naturae' and with the natural law as 'ratio' because immediately supervening on the urges of the natural appetite of the sensuality to bodily union between man and woman is the command of reason that such union shall only be between man and wife and in a legitimate manner (ibid.).

[61] Aquinas, *In quattuor libros sententiarum*, in vol. i of *Opera omnia*, ed. R. Busa, 7 vols. (Rome, 1980), 4 d. 33 q. 1 a. 1 ag. 4.

[62] *Sent.* 4 d. 33 q. 1 a. 1 ad. 4.

de jure naturali: sed illa tantum quae naturalis ratio dictat de his quae sunt homini aliisque communia; et sic datur dicta definitio, scilicet: jus naturale est quod natura omnia animalia docuit. pluralitas ergo uxorum quamvis non sit contra jus naturale tertio modo acceptum, est tamen contra jus naturale secundo modo acceptum, quia jure divino prohibetur; et etiam contra ius naturale primo modo acceptum, ut ex dictis patet, quod natura dictat animali cuilibet secundum modum convenientem suae speciei; unde etiam quaedam animalia, in quibus ad educationem prolis requiritur solicitudo utriusque, scilicet maris et feminae, naturali instinctu servant conjunctionem unius ad unum, sicut patet in turture et columba, et hujusmodi.[63]

[Thirdly, natural law is so called not only from first principle but from nature, because it has to do with natural things. And because nature is distinguished from reason, by which the human being is a human being, in the strictest way of taking natural law, things which pertain only to the human being, although they may be dictated by natural reason, are not said to be of the natural law, but only those things which natural reason dictates with reference to what is common to human beings and other creatures. And so the stated definition is given: that is, 'natural law is what nature has taught all animals'. So although having several wives is not contrary to the natural law understood in the third way,[64] it is contrary to the natural law understood in the second way, because it is forbidden by divine law and also to natural law understood in the first way, as is clear from what has been said, that nature dictates to each animal according to the mode that suits its species, and accordingly, even certain animals, among whom care from each—that is, male and female—is required for bringing up their offspring, preserve a monogamous relationship by natural instinct, as is clear with the turtle dove and the dove and similar things.]

In his *Commentary on the Sentences* Bonaventure also finds the example of the turtle dove useful. In dealing with the question (closely related to that of Aquinas just considered) 'utrum contra legem naturae sit habere concubinam' [whether it is against the law of nature to have a concubine], Bonaventure resolves the opposing arguments by discriminating between three senses of the law of nature. In one sense 'Ius naturale est quod in Lege et Evangelio continetur' [Natural law is what is contained in the Law and the Gospel], in another it is 'quod est commune omnium nationum'

---

[63] Ibid.

[64] Crowe finds this concession odd, a symptom of Aquinas' 'diffidence' in handling the formidable legacy of Ulpian (*Changing Profile*, 145–6).

[what is common to all nations],[65] and in the third it is 'quod natura docuit omnia animalia' [what nature has taught all animals]:

et hoc modo non est contra naturam, nec tamen omnino secundum naturam; et hoc, quia quaedam animalia bruta sunt, licet non omnia, quae coniunguntur in individuam copulam, ut sunt turtures; et quoniam, sicut vult Philosophus, omnes virtutes quae sunt in animalibus dispersae, in homine colliguntur, sicut arma omnium animalium in manu hominis, quamvis non omnia alia animalia habeant instinctum, tamen natura homi- nis habet: unde ad hoc inclinatur recta natura hominis, ut, si adhaeret mulieri, sic adhaereat ut pro ipsa patrem et matrem deserat, et sic accipiat in copulam individuam.[66]

[And in this way of understanding, it [i.e. having a concubine] is not against nature, but it is not, however, altogether in accordance with nature. This is so because there are some brute animals, though not all, who are linked in an indivisible bond, as for instance turtle doves; and since, as the Philo- sopher [i.e. Aristotle] has it, all the virtues dispersed in animals are gathered together in man, as the weapons of animals in the hand of a man, although not all other animals have the instinct [to indivisible monogamy], man's nature does: and so the right nature of man is inclined to this, so that, if he adheres to a woman, he should do so in such a way as to leave for her his father and mother, and thus he should receive her in an indivisible bond.]

Whereas the turtle dove in Aquinas is not brought to bear on the implications of the Ulpianic definition, Bonaventure uses the dove to block the possible claim that the Ulpianic definition allows one to see concubinage as in a sense natural to man; the example of the turtle dove shows, in the light of the Aristotelian observation, that the nature of human beings must in fact incline them to mono- gamy.[67]

Despite Aquinas' remark that nature is distinguished from reason, neither of these passages makes a clear distinction between an

---

[65] A *ius gentium* [law of nations], however, was often distinguished from the *ius naturae*.

[66] *Sent.* 4 d. 33 a. 1. q. 1, resp.

[67] Aquinas seems to be thinking in terms of characteristics shared by all animals, and polygamy (or concubinage) would for him, I think, be both *non contra* and also *omnino secundum* the teaching of nature that male and female should be joined. Bonaventure, on the other hand seems to be treating 'all animals' as a variegated set of different entities such that it is not the case that concubinage accords entirely with what nature has taught these different animals. Bonaventure's next *quaestio* again refers to the differing natures of animals, and proves that man's nature being what it is, having two wives is against the law of nature.

instinctual side and a rational side in the human being. For Aquinas
here, even in the Ulpianic understanding the law of nature as it
pertains to human beings seems to be a matter of what natural reason
dictates, as if what is taught by nature is not so much the instinctual
goals as the appropriateness of those goals for the human being—
natural reason sees that these goals are to be pursued.[68] In Bonaventure too, it is at least possible that the natural inclinations of human
beings are not experienced as expressions of a sub-rational, animal
nature. Other commentators argue that the union of man and
woman to which the Ulpianic definition refers is not, or not
necessarily, to be understood as union of the body. So in the *Glossa
ordinaria* on Gratian's *Decretum* Johannes Teutonicus writes:

Si intelligas de coniunctione corporum, secundum hoc est ius naturale ex
sensualitate proveniens. Si intelligis de coniunctione animorum, est ius
naturale ex ratione proveniens.[69]

[If you understand it to refer to the joining of bodies, it is accordingly
natural law proceeding from the sensuality. If you understand it to refer to
the joining of souls, it is natural law proceeding from the reason.]

For Laurentius the connection of physical union with the sensuality
is a reason for not seeing physical union as of the natural law:

motus coniunctionis quo mas mouetur ad feminam est de iure naturali. Vel
coniunctio animorum, non corporum, quam matrimonium appellamus . . . non corporum, quia illa est ex sensualitate.[70]

[the impulse for union, by which the male is moved towards the female is
of the natural law. Or rather the union of souls, not of bodies, which we
call marriage . . . not of bodies, because that [union] proceeds from the
sensuality.]

Huguccio sees the *coniunctio* as *animorum*. He asks 'ad quod ius
naturale spectat hec coniunctio' [to what natural law does this union
have reference] and answers 'ad rationem'.[71]

Nevertheless, it was certainly possible to understand the Ulpianic
definition as not having anything to do with human reason. Commenting on the *Institutes* the thirteenth-century canonist Azo
writes:

---

[68] See Crowe, *Changing Profile*, 144.
[69] Quoted by Weigand, *Naturrechtslehre*, 298.
[70] Quoted ibid. 299.   [71] Quoted ibid. 290.

Ius autem naturale pluribus modis dicitur. Primus est ut dicatur a natura animati motus quidam instinctu naturae proveniens, quo singula animalia ad aliquid faciendum inducuntur. unde dicitur, ius naturale est quod natura, id est, ipse deus, docuit omnia animalia.[72]

[The law of nature is defined in several ways. The first way defines it with reference to the nature of an animate being as a certain motion proceeding from the instinct of nature, by which each animal is led to do something, and accordingly it is defined as follows: Natural law is what nature, i.e. God himself, has taught all animals.]

Azo then explains how this understanding takes *natura* in Ulpian's definition as nominative, but that it is also possible to take *quod* as the nominative and the subject of *docuit*, so that *natura*, now an ablative, means *per instinctum naturae*.[73] Azo continues:

et hoc est quod dicitur, primi motus[74] non sunt in nostra potestate, secundi vero sunt. et ideo si res procedat in oblectamentum, id est, delectationem, veniale tantum contrahitur peccatum, nisi progrediatur ad aliquid componendum, ut exerceat quod turpiter cogitavit. et tunc dicetur tertius motus mortale contrahere peccatum. Et est illud notandum, quod qua ratione iustitia est voluntas etc., habito respectu ad rationalia tantum, eadem dicitur ius naturale motus, ut dixi, habito respectu ad omnem creaturam rationalem vel irrationalem.[75]

[And this is what is meant when it is said that the first impulses are not in our power, but the second are. And so if things go as far as pleasure, i.e. delight, venial sin only is contracted, unless things should proceed further

---

[72] *Summa institutionum* (Spirae, 1482) 1. 2, cited in F.W. Maitland, *Select Passages from Bracton and Azo*, Selden Society 8 (London, 1985), 32. The adaptation of Azo by the influential English lawyer Bracton (d.1268) tends to make Ulpian's definition *the* definition of the law of nature. Azo's scrupulous recognition of a variety of other senses is not found in Bracton; Bracton, for instance, makes no acknowledgement of the fact that in one understanding of the law of nature it can be identified with the *ius gentium*. See Maitland, *Select Passages*, 34–41. On Bracton and natural law see also Charles M. Whelan, 'The "Higher Law" Doctrine in Bracton and St. Thomas', *Catholic Lawyer*, 8 (1962), 218–32, 245. Full appreciation of Bracton's views on natural law is hampered by the state of the text of his work, on which see Thorne's introduction to the standard edition of it, *De legibus et consuetudinibus Angliae*, ed. George Woodville, trans. with revisions and notes by Samuel E. Thorne, 4 vols. (Cambridge, Mass., 1968).

[73] *Summa institutionum* 1. 2, in Maitland, *Select Passages*, 32.

[74] On the 'primi motus' see O. Lottin, *La Doctrine des mouvements premiers de l'appetit sensitif aux 12e et 13e siècles*, AHDLMA 6 (Paris, 1932); Lottin, *Psychologie*, ii. 493–589; also Payer, *Bridling*, 50–3. With the passage from Azo quoted compare, e.g., Aquinas, *Sent.* 2 d. 24 q. 3 a. 4, co.

[75] *Summa institutionum* 1. 2, in Maitland, *Select Passages*, 32, 34.

to planning something, so that a person can do what he has basely thought about, then it will be called the third motion and mortal sin will be contracted. And this is to be noted, that for the reason that justice is will, etc. in respect of rational creatures only, so by that reason natural law is impulse, as I said, in respect of all creatures, whether rational or irrational.]

Here natural law is the order of instinctual, pre-rational, pre-voluntary *motus* to which human beings and animals are both subject. In this understanding natural law for human beings is the order of impulses which lie beyond the control of the free rational will. A little later Azo points out that

Prima autem definitio [Ulpian's] est secundum motum sensualitatis, aliae autem assignatae sunt secundum motum rationis.[76]

[The first definition is given in accordance with the operation of sensuality, the others are assigned in accordance with the operation of reason.]

The distinction between an Ulpianic natural law which relates to the sense side of the human being, a side shared with the animals,[77] and one which relates to the reason, which is peculiar to human beings, can be expressed through the Aristotelian terminology of genus and species. We find this terminology used in treatments of the question of the consonance of certain kinds of sexual behaviour with the natural law. So, for example, the Alexandran *Summa* invokes the distinction between genus and species with reference to concubinage:

distinguendum quod est lex naturalis a natura generis, sicut dicit Isidorus, 'Naturale ius est quod natura docuit omnia animalia, ut masculus cum femina', et hoc modo verum est [that concubinage is not against the natural law]. Item, est lex naturalis a natura speciei, scilicet rationalis, ut 'non facies

---

[76] *Summa institutionum* 1. 2. Payer, *Bridling*, 50 f. cites Peter Lombard's definition of *sensualitas* as 'quaedam vis animae inferior, ex qua est motus qui intenditur in corporis sensus, atque appetitus rerum ad corpus pertinentium' (*Sententiae* 2. 24.4) ['Sensuality is a lower power of the soul giving rise to motion that focuses on the senses of the body; it is the appetite for things pertaining to the body' (trans. Payer)]. Sensuality need not carry negative connotations, but as Payer points out (50 ff.) it could be understood as a morally negative force.

[77] As we have seen, not all commentators see natural law in Ulpian's sense as relating exclusively to the animal and non-rational.

alii quod tibi non vis fieri et fac alii' etc. Et hoc modo est contra legem naturalem.[78]

[A distinction is to be made recognizing a law of nature defined with reference to the nature of the genus, as in Isidore's remark 'Natural law is what nature has taught all the animals, such as [the union of] male with female' and according to this understanding it is true [that concubinage is not against the natural law]. On the other hand, the natural law may be defined with reference to the species, that is the rational nature, such that 'you should not do to others what you do not wish done to yourself', etc. And according to this understanding concubinage is against the law of nature.]

The *Summa* deals with the claims of *fornicatio simplex* to be in accord with the natural law in similar fashion:

Ad illud ergo quod obicitur quod 'naturalis usus est viri cum muliere', patet responsio ex praedictis, quia a natura generis verum est, 'secundum quam est ius, quod natura docuit omnia animalia, ut masculus cum femina'; a natura speciei, quae est rationalis, non erit naturalis usus nisi sit viri cum muliere sua. Unde fornicatio non est naturalis actus hoc modo.[79]

[Then to the objection that sexual activity between man and woman is a natural practice the response is clear, that this is true with reference to the nature of the genus, according to which it is a law, which nature has taught all animals, that the male [should mate] with the female: with reference to the nature of the species, which is rational, the practice will not be natural, unless between a man and his wife. So fornication is not in this latter understanding a natural act.]

Clearly here there is a determination to show that the orthodox moral positions on non-marital, non-monogamous sexual behaviour do not run counter to what is natural for human beings. Yet

---

[78] *ST* 3. 365 ad 8. Ulpian rather than Isidore is the source of the quotation at the beginning of the passage. Isidore actually writes: 'Ius naturale [est] commune omnium nationum, et quod ubique instinctu naturae, non constitutione aliqua habetur; ut viri feminae coniunctio, liberorum successio et educatio, communis omnium possessio, et omnium una libertas'. (*Etymologiae*, ed. W. M. Lindsay (Oxford, 1911), 5. 4.) [Natural law [is] the common possession of all nations, and what is observed everywhere by an instinct of nature, not through any decree, such as the union of man and woman, the succession and education of children, common possession of everything and a single liberty for all.] The invocation of the 'do (not) unto others' principle rests on the consideration that 'Nullus vult quod uxor dividat se cum pluribus' [No one wants his wife to divide herself among several men] (see *ST* 3. 256 sol.).

[79] Alexander of Hales, *ST* 3. 366 ad 1.

there is implicit in the passage an understanding of the natural for human beings as something which need not necessarily involve the reason. This understanding perhaps becomes more explicit in the following remarks by an anonymous author:

Natura in homine consideratur dupliciter, scilicet ut est natura generis, uel ut est natura speciei rationalis ... homo enim est animal et est animal rationale. Primo modo habere duas uel plures non est contra naturam ...; quia enim femine appetunt saluare speciem, plures aliquando sequuntur unum masculum et prouocant ipsum, cum tamen quelibet mallet habere unum et suum ut verbi gratia est in ceruis et in apris. Secundo modo est contra naturam: natura enim rationalis dictat uiri ad mulierem equalitatem federis et obligationis et amicitie conjugalis, et etiam uitam indiuiduam ut dicit Commentator super 8 Ethicorum, que omnia uir cum pluribus seruare non potest.[80]

[Nature in the human being is regarded in two ways, that is as the nature of the genus or as the nature of the species and rational ... for the human being is an animal and also a rational animal. According to the first way of regarding nature, to have two or several females is not against nature ..., for because females desire to preserve the species, many sometimes follow one male and stimulate him, whilst, however, another may prefer to have one male as her own, as is the case for example among deer and boars. According to the second way it is against nature: for the rational nature requires of the man towards the woman equality of compact, obligation, and conjugal friendship, and also an undivided life, as the Commentator on Ethics 8 says, all of which a man cannot fulfil with many wives.]

A passage such as this, which explicitly speaks of two kinds of human nature and sets before us the notion that man is an animal as well as a rational animal, allows the question 'is polygamy natural to human beings' to be answered 'in a sense, yes', rather easily; certainly more easily than do the passages of Aquinas and Bonaventure quoted above, which do not force us to countenance a two-sided human nature. And in the sense in which it is true that polygamy is natural to man, the natural will not include man's rational capacity.

The perspectives more or less evident in the last three passages quoted are confirmed by Peter of Tarentasia:

---

[80] This passage appears as a marginal note in an Avignon manuscript containing the *Commentary on the Sentences* by Peter of Tarentasia (*c.*1224–76), who became Pope Innocent V in the year of his death. The passage is given by Lottin, *Psychologie*, ii. 92 n. 1.

Contra ius naturale illud dicitur esse quod est contra instinctum et dicta-men nature. Instinctus uero nature duplex est: unus nature generalis qui est communis nobis et brutis; et hic est preter rationem et discretionem; alter uero specialis qui est proprius nobis, et hic est cum ratione et discretione. Primus instinctus generalis, quia sine ratione est, non distinguit sufficienter inter suam et non suam. Unde cognoscere non suam <non>[81] est contra ius naturale generale. Secundus instinctus, quia cum ratione est distinguit sufficienter inter suam et non suam; unde cognoscere non suam est contra ius naturale speciale. Huiusmodi enim ius, scilicet ratio naturalis, dictat sic utendum actu generationis ut inde proueniat debitus finis et intentio generatiue in natura rationali; hoc prouenire non potest nisi per com-munem curam parentum longo tempore adhibitam in filiorum educatione tam corporali quam spirituali.[82]

[That which is against the instinct and dictate of nature is said to be against the natural law. But the instinct of nature is two-fold: one is of nature-as-genus, which is common to us and the beasts, and this operates without reference to reason and discretion; the other is of nature as species, which is peculiar to us and which operates with reason and discretion. The first genus-instinct, being without reason, does not distinguish sufficiently between what is a person's own and what is not. So to have sexual relations with a female not one's own is <not> against the law of nature-as-genus. The second instinct, being possessed of reason, does make sufficient dis-tinction between what is one's own and what is not, so to have sexual relations with a female not one's own is against the law of nature-as-species. For law of this kind, that is natural reason, dictates that the act of generation should be so performed as to bring about the proper end and intention of the generative force in the rational nature; this is not able to come about except through the parents living together for a long time so as to see to the bringing up, both bodily and spiritual, of the children.]

THE PRIMACY OF NATURE–AS–INSTINCT

It could be said that the theologians examined in the last section of this chapter all seek in one way or another to make the concept of

[81] Lottin's insertion of a negative particle is essential for the run of the argument. One wonders, however, whether its omission in the manuscript points to an automatic assumption on the part of an inattentive scribe of consonance between orthodox sexual morality and the law of nature.

[82] Peter of Tarentasia, *Commentary on the Sentences*, given by Lottin, *Psychologie*, ii. 93 n. 1.

the law of nature safe for use in moral discourse. The potentially subversive implications of the Ulpianic definition are defused so as to make it clear that polygamy, concubinage, and fornication are indeed in some sense or senses against the natural law for human beings. Nevertheless, the careful discriminations we have seen the theologians making also legitimize, and give currency to, an understanding of the law of nature and of the natural which separates these from the law of nature as reason and from the rational and aligns them with an animal endowment in human beings. Questions now arise as to how the different understandings are to be aligned. Is one kind of natural law more natural than another? The *instinctus naturae* is *duplex*, but is one kind of instinct more truly natural in the human being than the other? Both semantic and ontological issues present themselves and intertwine; what is the proper meaning of 'natural' and what is fundamentally natural in the constitution of the human being?

It is possible to balance the claims of each instinct, of *sensualitas* and *ratio*, *genus* and *species*, to determine what is truly natural for human beings. Albert the Great disposes of the notion that monogamy is not natural by adverting to the 'perfecta natura rei':

perfecta natura rei non est tantum in natura generis nec tantum in natura differentiae, sed in natura utriusque simul, et ideo, quod convenit homini secundum naturam generis et differentiae simul, scilicet secundum quod rationalis est, perfecte et proprie naturale est. Unde coniunctio maris et feminae, quae naturalis est ex natura generis, non dicitur simpliciter naturalis homini, sed talis coniunctio, quae completur secundum bonum rationis.[83]

[the full nature of a thing is not only in its nature as member of the genus nor only in its nature as defined by its differentiating characteristics, but in its nature as both of these at the same time; and so, what man has in virtue of genus-nature and differentia-nature as well—that is what he has in virtue of being rational—is fully and properly natural. So the conjoining of male and female, which is natural with reference to genus-nature, is not said to be natural to man unqualifiedly, but rather that kind of conjoining which is accomplished in accordance with the good defined by reason.]

Here neither genus nor species has priority in what is deemed most natural for man; neither does either have priority for the meaning of

[83] Albert the Great (*c.*1200–1280), *Super ethica*, ed. Wilhelm Kübel (*Opera omnia*, xiv/ 2 (Aschendorf, 1987)), bk. 8, lectio xii, 759 (642).

'natural'. But such equilibrium is by no means always proclaimed. William of Auxerre seems to deny it when he distinguishes between ways of defining the natural law as follows:

Sciendum ergo quod ius naturale quandoque large, quandoque stricte dicitur. Large, secundum quod ius naturale dicitur quod natura docuit omnia animalia, ut est coniunctio maris et femine, et similia; et secundum hoc ius, non est virtus vel vicium, quoniam secundum communia omnibus animalibus non est virtus vel vicium, sic enim bruta susceptibilia essent virtutis et vicii. Stricte sumitur ius naturale secundum quod ius naturale dicitur quod naturalis ratio sine omni deliberatione aut sine magna dictat esse faciendum, ut Deum esse diligendum et similia.[84]

[One must be aware that natural law is sometimes strictly defined and sometimes broadly. Broadly as when natural law is defined as what nature has taught all animals, such as the conjoining of male and female and the like; and there is no virtue and vice with reference to this law, for if there were it would follow that the beasts were capable of virtue and vice. Natural law is taken strictly when defined as what natural reason says without any deliberation, or without much, should be done, such as that God is to be loved and the like.]

Here 'stricte' seems likely to imply a precision which would make the natural reason definition the preferable one.[85] If this is so, primacy would be given to reason and species in the ranking of meanings of nature, and perhaps, by implication, in understanding the nature of the human being. A similar preference for reason and species as definers with respect to human beings of what is most truly natural, both semantically and ontologically, may perhaps be perceived when the Alexandran *Summa* has 'specialiter and proprie dicitur ius naturale, quod dictat naturaliter ratio faciendum' [what reason naturally pronounces should be done is called the natural law *specialiter et proprie*],[86] where 'specialiter et proprie' is the third adverbial in a sequence containing also 'communissime' and 'communiter'. The question is whether 'proprie' is simply being used, like 'specialiter', in contrast with 'communissime' and 'communi-

[84] *Magistri Guillelmi Altissiodorensis summa aurea*, ed. Jean Ribaillier, 4 vols. and introduction (Paris, 1981–7), Tractatus 18, *init.* (iii/1. 369). William was born *c.*1150 and died in 1231.
[85] Possibly 'stricte' is a non-evaluative antithesis to 'large', which is itself value-neutral.
[86] *ST* 3. 368 sol. 2.

ter' to connote particularity, or whether it also has connotations of accuracy and propriety.[87]

If this evidence from William of Auxerre and the Alexandran *Summa* points in one direction, that from Bonaventure and Aquinas points the other way. Bonaventure says that the Ulpianic sense of the law of nature is that in which 'dicitur ius naturale propriissime',[88] where 'with most particular reference' does not seem a possible meaning for 'propriissime', since the other definitions given are no less particular in reference. 'Propriissime' accordingly must refer to the accuracy and appropriateness of this particular definition over against others. When Aquinas writes of natural law being so called 'from nature' and continues:

et quia natura contra rationem dividitur, a qua homo est homo; ideo strictissimo modo accipiendo ius naturale, illa quae ad homines tantum pertinent, etsi sint de dictamine naturalis rationis, non dicuntur esse de jure naturali[89]

[and because nature is distinguished from reason, by which the human being is the human being, therefore in the strictest way of taking natural law, those things which pertain only to human beings, although they may be dictated by natural reason, are not said to be of the natural law]

it seems, as with William of Auxerre, that 'strictissimo' connotes accuracy rather than narrowness.[90] Furthermore, there is the remark 'natura contra rationem dividitur'. This shows that the natural may be defined in contradistinction to the rational. But if the natural can *mean* the non-rational as opposed to the rational, then the non-rational may well seem to have a truer claim to be called natural than the rational, and, within man, the non-rational side to have a right to be regarded as more fundamentally natural than the rational.

[87] See *OLD* s.v. 'proprie' 2 and 3.

[88] *Sent.* 4 d. 33 a. 1 q. 1, resp. (Bonaventure, like the Alexandran *Summa*, contrasts *communiter* with *proprie*, but in Bonaventure's case *communiter* seems to mean 'in the ordinary manner of speaking' rather than 'in a general sense', as in the Alexandran *Summa*. See *OLD* s.v. 'communiter' 2 and 3b.) On the strength of this passage Crowe, 'St. Thomas', 270, speaks of Bonaventure's 'preferring Ulpian's definition' of the law of nature.

[89] *Sent.* d. 33 q. 1 a. 1 ad 4.

[90] After all, the contents of the Law and the Gospel, which define the law of nature in the second sense, might reasonably be held to cover a narrower range than the instruction of Nature to the animal kingdom at large.

Bonaventure and Aquinas are not alone in testifying to a felt primacy of non-rational nature. Notwithstanding its remark just quoted, when the Alexandran *Summa* has 'Ius enim naturale in homine debet regulari ratione' [For the law of nature in the human being ought to be regulated by reason],[91] the implication is that for the writer an unqualified reference to natural law in man is to the non-rational, Ulpianic understanding of that law, and this is evidence for the primacy of that sense over the *naturalis ratio* sense.

In Giles of Rome's *De regimine principum*, Ulpianic natural law, which embraces both humans and animals, is considered more natural than the kind of natural law specific to human beings alone.[92] Giles states that natural law as opposed to positive law is 'quid commune, quid notum et quid immutabile' [something common, something known and something unchangeable],[93] and this definition provides terms in which one variety of natural law can be accounted more natural than another. The *ius gentium* is said to be the foundation of contracts and is designated *ius naturale contractum*.[94] This natural law is specific to human beings. Giles continues:

Ius itaque illud quod natura omnia animalia docuit, et quod sequitur inclinationem nostram naturalem vt communicamus cum animalibus aliis, respectu iuris gentium dicitur esse naturale. Nam si considerentur dicta in praecedenti capitulo, ius naturale est quid commune, quid notum, et quid immutabile. Quanto ergo ius aliquod est communius, quam ius gentium: tanto magis meretur nomen iuris naturalis. Ius ergo, quod omnia animalia docuit et in quo omnia animalia communicant, est communius quam ius gentium, et per consequens est notius: quia sunt nobis nota confusa magis. Quanto enim aliquid est vniuersalius, tanto est intellectui nostro notius, et prius cadit in apprehensione nostra. Est etiam huiusmodi ius immutabilius, quia regulae iuris quanto magis applicantur ad materiam specialem, tanto plures defectus contrahunt, et in pluribus casibus non sunt obseruandae, et maiorem mutationem suscipiunt: merito igitur huiusmodi ius naturale dicitur respectu iuris gentium.[95]

---

[91]   *ST* 3. 255 ad 2.

[92]   Giles of Rome (*c*.1247–1316) wrote the *De regimine principum* around 1285. It was very popular and was translated into several vernacular languages. The 14th-century English version is probably by John Trevisa.

[93]   *De regimine principum* (Rome, 1556), 3. 2. 25 (308).

[94]   Ibid.

[95]   Ibid. Giles considers *most* natural the law embracing humans, animals and also beings lower than animal, by which all seek survival and what for them is good.

The fourteenth-century English translation renders this passage as follows:

Also þat riȝt and lawe þat kynde techeþ alle beestes and folweþ oure inclinacioun in þat we accorden wiþ oþere beestes is icleped kynde riȝt in comparisoun to þe riȝt þat hatte ius gencium. For ȝif thinges þat ben iseid in þe nexte chapitre ben iknowe, kynde riȝt is som what comyne and som what yknowe. And þe more riȝt is iknowe and þe more comyne it is and þe more vnchangeable, þe more it is worþi to be cleped kynde riȝt. And þat riȝt þat kynde techeþ alle bestes and by þe whiche alle beestes acordeþ is more comyn þan þe riȝt þat hatte ius gencium; and so it is more yknowe, for þyng þat is most comyne is most iknowe to vs. For þe more general a þyng is, þe better we knowen it. Also suche riȝt is more vnchangeable; for þe more þe rewles of lawe ben applied to a special matere, þe mo defautes þei drawen and failleþ in þe moo caas and ben þe more chaungeable. Þanne suche a riȝt is worthi to be clepede kynde riȝt in comparisoun to þe riȝt þat hatte ius gencium.[96]

Primacy of the Ulpianic sense of natural law and of a corresponding understanding of the natural in man is evident rather late in the medieval period in the *De natura legis naturae* of Sir John Fortescue.[97] In part I, chapter 31 he writes:

si de lege naturae diffinitionem ejus interrogemus, diffinitio illa genus legis, sed non speciem nobis revelabit; quia descriptio juris naturae generalis legem naturae qua disciduntur lites quam nos querimus non segregat a lege naturae qua procreatur proles, lege etiam qua foetus et partus suos omnia sentientia faciunt, nec a lege qua nidificant aves pullos que educant et similibus, cum ipsa descriptio omnes has leges sub uno contextu amplectatur, dicens, 'Jus naturale est quod natura omnia animalia docuit.' Quid obscurius indistinctiusve dici poterit ut non una legum species discernatur ab alia, quum omnes eas sic passim in uno quasi fasciculo complectitur? Species est quam querimus et non genus: genus namque causas hominum judicare non poterit, sed species, immo verius aliquid individuum speciei.[98]

[if we inquire after a definition of the law of nature, that definition will reveal to us the genus of the law, but not the species, because the generic

[96] John Trevisa, *The Governance of Kings and Princes* 3. 2. 25.

[97] Sir John Fortescue (?1394–?1476) composed his *De natura legis naturae* c.1462. Quotations are given from *The Works of Sir John Fortescue*, ed. Thomas (Fortescue), Lord Clermont (London, 1869).

[98] *De natura legis naturae* part I, ch. 31 (93).

description of the natural law makes no distinction between the law of nature by which disputes are settled, which is the law we are in search of, and that law of nature by which offspring are procreated, the law also by which all sentient things make their foetuses and give birth, nor from the law by which birds make their nests and bring up young and so on, since that definition includes all these laws in one embrace, stating that 'the law of nature is what nature has taught all animals'. What definition could be more indistinct or more obscure, when no species of law is discriminated from another, but all are in this way entirely embraced in one bundle as it were? The species is what we are looking for and not the genus, for the genus is not able to deliver judgements in men's lawsuits, but the species, or rather, in fact, something individual to the species.]

But though he registers its limitations forcefully, Fortescue takes the Ulpianic definition as where he has to start from, as the primary generic meaning of the law of nature. This is apparently because he thinks of what nature has taught all animals as the totality of nature's endowment of all animals, rather than what they have in common, a totality which includes the ability of the human being to recognize a natural moral law. This means that though Fortescue acknowledges a primacy for the Ulpianic definition, he would not see himself as thereby attaching naturalness primarily to the order of animal instinct rather than to the natural moral law. However, when he goes on to discuss the various species of meaning embraced under the generic definition as this pertains to human beings, his remarks do demonstrate a way of thinking about human nature that makes the animal side primary. Fortescue offers a rather whimsical allegory in which the different species of the law of nature are figured as the sons of Jesse.

Et nunquid difficultas Samueli prophetae non minima fuit, placidissimum Deo qui regeret populum Israel de filiis Jesse eligere, cum septem de filiis ejus in domo una invenisset? Major vero difficultas est multo, unam de tot speciebus quas continet jus naturae eligere ad regendum orbem. Quid si Sensualitas, quae sub hac diffinitione complectitur et primogenitus humanae naturae esse videtur, ut Eliab primogenitus Jesse, adducitur coram Propheta ut ungatur ad regendum populum? Credo quod diceretur de ea quod de Eliab dictum est a Domino, 'ne respicias vultum ejus quoniam abjeci eam.' Et si secunda, ut Abinadab filius secundus Jesse, adducatur coram Propheta Ratio, videlicet naturalis, quam post sensualitatem secundam gignit humana natura, nunquid diceretur de ea ut de Abinadab dixerat Spiritus, 'nec hunc elegit Dominus?'[99]

[And surely the prophet Samuel's problem was not of the smallest in having to choose the most pleasing to God of the sons of Jesse to rule the people of Israel, when he found he had seven sons in one house. But it is a much greater problem to choose one species from the many the law of nature contains to rule the world. Supposing Sensuality, which is embraced under this definition and appears to be the first-born of human nature, is put forward, as Eliab, Jesse's first-born, was led out before the Prophet to be anointed for the rule of his people. I think that there would be said about it what the Lord said of Eliab, 'do not look upon his face, since I have rejected him'. And if the second, Reason, that is natural reason, which human nature brings forth second after sensuality, like Abinadab, the second son of Jesse, were led out before the prophet, surely of it it would be said as the Spirit spoke of Abinadab, 'neither has the Lord chosen this one'.]

Fortescue shows clearly that there was a potentially confusing mass of conflicting definitions of natural law, but he recognizes, as do other writers, the propriety of understanding the law of nature as the law of *sensualitas*, the human being's non-rational, animal side. Further, for Fortescue this side of the human being is prior to reason in the constitution of human nature.

A body of evidence can be produced, then, to show that it was possible to take the Ulpianic understanding of the law of nature not only as *a* legitimate, but as a *more* legitimate understanding than its rivals. This means that the way is very much open for thinking of the animal in human beings, and the not wholly regulated sexual behaviour in which the human being's animal side may be expressed, as more natural than the rational side and the behaviour which reason counsels. But if the animal as opposed to the rational is to be taken as having priority in the natural constitution of the human being, then what is most truly natural in the human becomes morally ambiguous, not necessarily on the side of the right, since the natural-as-animal can prompt to immoral action.

It is worth noting that in the discourse of medicine 'natura' and related terms are used to refer to the sub-rational physiological

---

[99] *De natura legis naturae* part 1, ch. 31 (93 f.). The requisite sense of natural law is in fact very much bound up with reason, being 'justitiae ueritas quae recta ratione poterit reuelari' [the truth of justice which is able to be revealed by right reason] (ibid. 94).

dimension of the human being. This is likely to have been a usage influential on how people in general thought of nature. The following passage from Gerard of Berry's Glosses on the *Viaticum*[100] implicitly opposes naturalness to conscious rational operations:

Galenus inquit uirtus anime. id est, operatio uirtutis. *complexionem sequitur* etc. quia secundum complexionem corporis mouetur anima ad operandum. Naturaliter dico, quia aliter secundum mores acquisitos a philosophia uel a conuictu, quia secundum complexionem colericam mouetur ad iram et sic de aliis.[101]

[*Galen says: the faculty of the soul*: that is, the function of the faculty, *follows the complexion, etc.*: for the soul is moved to acting according to the complexion of the body. [It acts in this way] according to nature, I mean, for otherwise [it acts] according to habits acquired from philosophy or conviction, since a choleric complexion moves it to wrath and similarly for the others.]

In his *Quaestiones super Viaticum* Peter of Spain makes a revealing distinction between two aspects of stimulation to sexual intercourse, the latter itself being subdivided:

Quedam est animalis proper fortem impressionem rei dilecte factam in virtute estimativa, et hec est cerebro. Quedam est naturalis, et hec est duplex: aut fluens, et sic est ab epate. Ponit enim Constantinus quod desiderium in coitu venit ab epate. Quedam autem est naturalis fixa in uno membro et hec est in testiculis.[102]

[one aspect is mental, on account of the strong impression of the beloved object made in the estimative faculty, and this is from the brain. One aspect is natural, and this is double: either flowing, and this is from the liver. For Constantine asserts that sexual desire comes from the liver. The other however is located stably in one member, and this is in the testicles.]

A medical sense for 'natura' is recognized in Alan of Lille's *Distinctiones* when we are told that it can mean 'naturalis calor, unde

---

[100]   The *Viaticum* of Constantine the African (d. *c*.1087), a translation into Latin from Arabic sources, became an authoritative medical textbook in medieval universities.

[101]   This, like the passage following, is taken from Mary Frances Wack, *Lovesickness in the Middle Ages* (Philadelphia, 1990), 204, 206, ll. 79–81.

[102]   *Quaestiones*, Version B, Wack, *Lovesickness*, 236, ll. 92–8.

physicus dicit esse pugnam inter morbum et naturam' ['natural heat, according to which meaning the doctor says there is a battle between disease and nature']. Alan also glosses natura as 'complexio', a usage he links to the field of medicine.[103]

The possibility of conceiving nature in respect of the human being as something quite distinct from reason, and the various indications that non-rational nature was frequently considered to be most truly nature, make it unsurprising that we should find occasions on which nature and the natural cover the human being's instinctual side and stand in opposition to the human being's rational endowment. This happens, for example, in a passage from John Damascene's *De fide orthodoxa*:

Ὅθεν καὶ τὰ ἄλογα οὐκ εἰσὶν αὐτεξούσια · ἄγονται γὰρ μᾶλλον ὑπὸ τῆς φύσεως, ἤπερ ἄγουσι· διὸ οὐδὲ ἀντιλέγουσι τῇ φυσικῇ ὀρέξει, ἀλλ ἅμα ὀρεχθῶσί τινος, ὁρμῶσι πρὸς τὴν πρᾶξιν. Ὁ δὲ ἄνθρωπος, λογικὸς ὢν, ἄγει μᾶλλον τὴν φύσιν ἤπερ ἄγεται· διὸ καὶ ὀρεγόμενος, εἴπερ ἐθέλοι, ἐξουσίαν ἔχει ἀναχαιτίσαι τὴν ὄρεξιν, ἢ ἀκουλουθῆσαι αὐτῇ.

[Irrational things are not in possession of free will, for they are controlled by their nature rather than controlling it. For this reason they do not reject natural desires, but as soon as they desire anything, move towards practical fulfilment. But man, being rational, controls his nature, rather than being controlled by it. For this reason when he desires, if he wishes, he has the power to restrain the desire or to follow it.[104]]

Here the φύσις of the human being is the set of impulsive desires, of a kind with those found in animals, which he experiences. These sometimes need to be held in check by reason. These ideas were influential on later Latin authors. In the thirteenth century, for instance, there is this passage in the Alexandran *Summa*:

Praeterea, irrationabilia non habent vim per quam possint diiudicare naturales actus et probare probandos et reprobare reprobandos, immo appetitiva in eis est subiecta instinctui naturae; unde non est in eis potestas contradicendi naturali appetitui; homo vero habet potestatem diiudicandi

---

[103] *Distinctiones* (PL 210, 871). *Kynde* appears in a sense similar to Alan's 'natural heat' in Chaucer's *The Book of the Duchess* and there are passages in Gower's *Confessio Amantis* where 'natural heat' would be an appropriate meaning (see below).

[104] *De fide orthodoxa* 2 c. 27 (PG 94, 960 f). The work was translated into Latin in the 12th century.

naturales motus et probandi et reprobandi et etiam contradicendi naturali appetitui, et ideo est liber arbitrio.[105]

[Besides, irrational creatures do not have a faculty by which they are able to judge between natural acts and approve those that are to be approved and dismiss those that are to be dismissed, the appetitive faculty in them being subject rather to the instinct of nature, and therefore they have no power of contradicting natural appetite; but the human being has the power of judging between natural motions, approving and dismissing them, and even of contradicting natural appetite, for which reason his will is free.]

Here, where a contrast between appetite and reason, both of them natural, might have been offered, what we in fact find is a contrast between nature's motions, acts, and appetites and the rational power which assesses those motions, acts, and appetites from a moral point of view. In this perspective, what is truly natural in human beings would seem to be not reason, but instinctive appetites.[106]

Elsewhere the *Summa* understands motions of nature in such a way as to allow of natural rational motions, but the discriminations made suggest that, even so, non-rational motions are regarded as more fundamentally natural than rational ones. Sexual morality in relation to natural law is again the issue, the passage coming from the *solutio* of the question '*Utrum de dictamine legis naturalis sit quod una sit unius*':

Dicendum quod triplex est dictamen naturae, secundum quod natura tribus modis movetur. In natura enim rationali aliquando movetur natura ut natura, aliquando natura ut ratio, aliquando ratio ut ratio. Et secundum hoc diversificatur dictamen naturae, quia secundum quod natura movetur ut natura, dictat masculum coniungi feminae ad multiplicationem speciei. Secundum autem quod natura movet ut ratio, dictat quod unus cum una coniungi debet, vel secundum congruentiam status et temporis opportunitatem unus cum pluribus, eo dispensante qui est supra naturam, quia natura ut ratio confert [e]t legit quod non est faciendum alteri quod sibi non vult fieri: unde natura ut ratio dictat unum debere coniungi cum una simpliciter vel cum pluribus, exigente statu et tempore, eo dispensante qui est supra naturam. Secundum autem quod ratio movet ut ratio, ulterius confert et dictat natura quod unus debet coniungi cum una inseparabiliter coniuncta. Et sic patet quo modo habere plures est contra dictamen naturae

---

[105]   *ST* 1–2. 403 r.
[106]   Compare the *Summa*'s remark on natural law in human beings needing to be restrained by reason (see above at n. 91).

et quo modo non, quia, secundum quod natura movet ut natura, non est contra dictamen naturae habere plures; nec secundum quod natura movet ut ratio, eo modo quo dictum est, alio modo sic.[107]

[It should be said that the dictate of nature is threefold, according as nature is moved in three ways. For in a rational nature sometimes nature is moved as nature, sometimes nature is moved as reason and sometimes reason is moved as reason. And according to this scheme the dictate of nature varies, in that according as nature is moved as nature, it dictates that the male should be joined with the female for the multiplying of the species; but according as nature moves as reason, it dictates that one male ought to be joined with one female, or in accordance with what is appropriate to the circumstances and opportune for the time, one male with many females— with the one who is above nature giving dispensation—because nature as reason decrees and demands that one must not do to another what one does not wish done to oneself; on account of which nature as reason dictates that one man ought to be joined to one woman simply, or to many, if the circumstances and time demands and he who is above nature gives dispensation. But according as reason moves as reason, nature further decrees and dictates that one man ought to be joined to one woman linked to him inseparably. And thus it is clear in what way to have several wives is against the dictate of nature and in what way it is not, because according as nature moves as nature, it is not against the dictate of nature to have several, nor according as nature moves as reason—in the way stated above, though in the other way it is against it.]

The process of discrimination here results not merely in a recognition that the natural in man can be the non-rational, but in a refinement of terminology such that the term 'nature' is used to specify that in man which is natural and non-rational ('natura ut *natura*') as opposed to that in him which is natural and rational ('natura ut *ratio*'). Such a linguistic procedure would seem to reflect a feeling that the most fundamental meaning of nature excludes the rational, and that the animal side of human beings is what is most fundamentally natural to them.[108]

It is abundantly clear that, as Sir John Fortescue rather querulously recognized, medieval academic writing presents a complexly

[107] *ST* 3. 255 sol. See also Philip the Chancellor as quoted by Lottin, *Psychologie*, ii. 77 n. 2. According to Lottin, Philip, writing around 1233 or 1234, introduced the *natura ut natura, natura ut ratio, ratio ut ratio* schema for categorizing kinds of *ius naturae*.

[108] An opposition between *ratio* and *natura* is also to be found when Latin theologians seek to render the distinction between *thelesis* and *boulesis* which they find in John

variegated picture of the moral status of the natural. Whilst it is true that an association between nature and reason is widespread and that nature is frequently seen as good—the natural defining a proper state of being for all things, and human beings possessing natural desires towards God and the good—it is also the case that a far from negligible strain in medieval thought associates the natural with the animal and the irrational and recognizes that there is a sense of nature in which nature can move to the bad. Part of the human being which may need to be kept in check can be called natural in contradistinction to that which does the checking. Nature and reason in the human being can in fact be understood to be at odds.

'NATURAL' AS MORAL MIDDLE TERM

There is a further complexity in regard to the moral status of the natural. The natural, even when bad, is better than the unnatural. So to follow natural animal instinct may lead one into sin, but such a sin will be less heinous than one which nature cannot be held to have taught.[109] We might say that whilst the patterns of nature-as-genus

Damascene (see Lottin, *Psychologie*, i. 393 ff.). To speak of the will as it spontaneously seeks the human being's proper end Aquinas uses *voluntas ut natura*, of the will as it deliberates and chooses regarding the means to that end, *voluntas ut ratio* (see Lottin, *Psychologie*, i. 415 and i. 169 for Odo Rigaldus' distinction between *uoluntas ut natura* and *uoluntas vel deliberata sive consiliata*). A similar distinction between *ratio* and *natura* in terms of spontaneity against deliberation is to be found in Odo's consideration of synderesis: *ratio ut natura* refers to the reason as it tends automatically to its true end and *ratio ut ratio* is contradistinguished from it (see Lottin, *Psychologie*, ii. 197). The natural in these cases is not the non-rational, but shares with non-rational impulse a spontaneous and unbidden character, being something that the human being does not choose to have operate. Such usages would seem to reinforce any tendency the language has to propose the animal as more truly natural than the deliberations of reason. We might also consider in this connection the distinction between *appetitus naturalis* and *appetitus uoluntarius* (see Lottin, *Psychologie*, i. 301 f. n. 4). Cf. Boethius, *De consolatione* 3. p.11 89–102.

[109]   Its not having to do with reason, the possession of which enables moral choice, might seem to disqualify Ulpianic nature from having any moral resonances, but in fact a long-standing tradition of thought in the Middle Ages found moral guidance in the behaviour of animals. Animals may be held to behave according to patterns designed by God and so to provide in certain areas examples to be followed. This is what happens in *Piers Plowman* B 11; here Langland in a striking because apparently paradoxical formulation has Reason following the beasts but not humans (though Reason means primarily right reasonableness, not the faculty of Reason, see Alford, 'Idea'). Flandrin, *L'Église*, 33

do not provide a sufficient guide to the moral life, they do set certain moral limits on behaviour. So, for instance, the Alexandran *Summa* sees 'fornicatio simplex' as natural in the Ulpianic, nature-as-genus sense, but impermissible because not in accordance with nature as species; it goes on, however, to remark: 'peccatum vero sodomiticum contra naturam est utroque modo, et ideo nefandissimum'[110] [but the sin of sodomy is against nature according to either understanding, and hence of extreme evil]. Here sin against nature in the Ulpianic sense is worse than sin which is in accord with nature so understood.

That natural sin is preferable to unnatural had been explicitly affirmed by Augustine:

Usus feminae naturalis est, cum ejus masculus illo membro utitur, quo natura ejusdem generis animantium propagatur.... Usus itaque naturalis et licitus est, sicut in conjugio; et illicitus, sicut in adulterio: contra naturam vero semper illicitus, et procul dubio flagitiosior atque turpior; quem sanctus Apostolus et in feminis et in masculis arguebat, damnabiliores volens intelligi, quam si in usu naturali, vel adulterando, vel fornicando peccarent.[111]

[The natural use of a woman is when the man uses the organ of hers by which a nature of the same kind of living things is propagated.... And so the natural use is both licit, as in marriage, and illicit, as in adultery: but the use against nature is always illicit and without doubt more criminal and disgraceful; this the holy Apostle condemned in both men and women,

---

writes: 'Clément, Ambroise, Jérôme, prennent, comme le leur suggérait Sénèque, la conduite animale comme modèle de ce qui est naturel puisque, ajoutent-ils, non souillé par le péché originel' [Clement, Ambrose and Jerome took animal conduct, on the strength of what Seneca suggested to them, as the model of what is natural, since (this they added) it was not sullied by original sin]. On the selectiveness of the use by medieval writers of the animal realm in establishing moral behaviour, see John T. Noonan, *Contraception: A History of its Treatment by the Catholic Theologians and Canonists* (Cambridge, Mass., 1966) 241 and Brundage, *Law,* 7. Certain kinds of behaviour could be stigmatized precisely as animal.

[110] Alexander of Hales, *ST* 3. 366 ad 1. On the 'sin against nature' and 'sodomy' and what exactly these terms meant see Noonan, *Contraception*, 224 ff. and Vern L. Bullough, 'The Sin against Nature and Homosexuality', in Vern L. Bullough and James Brundage (eds.), *Sexual Practices and the Medieval Church* (Amherst, NY, 1994), 55–71. It was standard to stigmatize non-inseminative sexual practice and unorthodox sexual position as *peccatum contra naturam*.

[111] Augustine, *Opus imperfectum contra Julianum* 5. 17 (PL 45, 1450 f.). The reference to St Paul is to Romans 1: 26.

wishing them to be considered more culpable than if they sinned, either in fornication or adultery, according to the natural use.]

In the *Summa theologica* Aquinas confirms this opinion. He demonstrates the proposition that the vice against nature is the worst of all species of lechery. He counters the argument that this cannot be so since the sin against nature need involve no harm to another, whilst in other kinds of sexual sin such as adultery and rape injury is done to a person, with the argument that the heinousness of unnatural sexual vice lies in its being an offence directly against God:

sicut ordo rationis rectae est ab homine, ita ordo naturae est ab ipso deo. et ideo in peccatis contra naturam, in quibus ipse ordo naturae violatur, fit iniuria ipsi deo, ordinatori naturae.[112]

[as the order of right reason is from man, so the order of nature is from God Himself. And so in sins against nature in which the order of nature is violated, injury is done to God Himself, the ordainer of nature.]

Not merely the propriety but the sanctity of the natural is here affirmed.

These passages suggest behaviour may be analysed according to a three-tier system: there is the natural and the right, the natural but wrong, and the unnatural, which is, just in virtue of being unnatural, wrong. This establishment of the unnatural as wrong, indeed as the extremity of wrong, indicates and reinforces a presumption in favour of the goodness of whatever may be styled natural. But that presumption, together with the existence of the unnatural as the negative pole of the moral spectrum, makes for a certain lack of absoluteness in respect of the 'natural but wrong' category. The natural may sometimes not be right, but it cannot be *so* wrong—at least the wrong behaviour is not unnatural: as compared with being unnatural, being natural is relatively good—even when bad; after all, the order of nature is from God himself, so being natural must basically be all right. The three-tier system may well be thought to encourage this kind of (admittedly rather loose) thinking. The system tends, in fact, to enhance the instability of the idea of the

---

[112] Aquinas, *ST* 2. 2 q. 154 a. 12 ad 1. The sense of the natural here may not exactly be the Ulpianic one, but—and this is so also for nature in the Augustine passage just quoted—it is very congruent with it. We should note how Aquinas here, as elsewhere (see above at n. 89), uses 'natura' as a term to cover something distinguishable from the rational.

natural in moral discourse. I say 'enhance' because the instability is inevitable once the idea is used to cover an ultimately God-sanctioned order which nevertheless includes forces which urge towards actions not necessarily right. We have seen how the theologians try to stabilize the various senses of nature and to clear up the ambivalence attaching to nature's moral status which those different senses generate. With the poets we shall often find, contrariwise, that the idea of the natural is allowed its instability and ambivalence, and precisely because of that acquires enormous poetic power as the focus of contesting energies within individual poems.[113]

---

[113] For some similar remarks see Cohen, *Be Fertile*, 295.

CHAPTER TWO

The Moral Status of the Natural in Middle English Vernacular Writings

The previous chapter outlined the moral profile of the natural in certain medieval academic discourses conducted in Latin. The natural, however, was also a highly important concept for those who wrote less academically elevated devotional works, sermons, and moral treatises in the Middle English vernacular.[1] This chapter reviews such writings,[2] which may well have helped shape Chaucer's and Gower's thinking about the natural, and which will certainly have played a part in forming views on the natural held among their first readership. What follows shows that the moral profile of the natural in these works looks very similar to that apparent in the academic writings considered in Chapter 1—not surprisingly, since the vernacular writings of devotional and moral instruction are drawing on an inheritance of academic clerical discourse. The overlap between the sub-section headings in this chapter, 'The Goodness of the Natural', 'Problematic Nature: *Kynde* and Lechery', ' "Natural" as Moral Middle Term', and those of the previous one points to this basic consonance between Middle English vernacular homiletics and Latin theology and law in the matter of the natural.

THE GOODNESS OF THE NATURAL

There is a widely diffused sense in Middle English of the moral goodness of what is natural. In the following passage from *The South*

---

[1] In Middle English the concepts of Nature and naturalness are often covered by *kynde* (noun and adjective) and related words.

[2] There is also some consideration of writings which, though they could not strictly be called sermons or moral treatises, may be felt to have a measure of moral and homiletic purpose and which deploy the idea of the natural in moral contexts.

English Legendary the easy movement from the idea of *riȝte* to that of *cunde* demonstrates the proximity in the writer's mind of the right and the natural.

> Mid riȝte þi soule maister is. & þi bodi hire hyne shal beo
> If þanne þi bodi maister is. & þi soule his hyne
> Aȝe cunde þanne hit is & þu worst. þerfore in helle pyne.[3]

The normative force possessed by the idea of the natural is evident—'aȝe cunde' is a moral judgement—whilst the explicit message of the passage is that subversion of a natural hierarchy is culpable. A similar passage occurs in a Wycliffite sermon:

> And heerfore seiþ Poul heere þat *we ben not dettid to þe fleshe þat we lyve aftir þe flesche*, for þanne we maden þe seruaunt maystir; and, aȝenus þe lawe of God, we loueden more þat he loueþ lesse. And whoeuere þus reuersiþ God, and chaungiþ in loue þe ordre of kynde, God mot nedis reuerse hym, and resoun turneþ his loue to hate.[4]

Again, the appeal to *kynde* is a potent one, because the *kynde* is taken to be self-evidently proper, and subversion of the natural order is understood to be not merely wrong, but wholly perverse.

Because of the goodness of the *kynde* many things are subject to moral condemnation as *unkynde* or against *kynde*. It is indeed possible to regard all sin as *unkyndely*: 'whanne men synneþ aȝenys God, and mut nede be punysched of hym, þis ys one vnkyndely dreede, as it is unkyndely to synne.'[5] The following passage implies that nature

---

[3] *The South English Legendary*, ed. C. d'Evelyn and A. J. Mill, EETS 235, 236, 244 (London, 1956–9), 535, ll. 60–2.

[4] *English Wycliffite Sermons* (*EWS*), ed. Anne Hudson and Pamela Gradon, 5 vols. (Oxford, 1983–96), i. 637, no. E38. See also the similar reference to a natural hierarchy of soul and body in a passage in *Middle English Sermons* (*MES*), ed. W. O. Ross, EETS os 209 (London, 1940), 267, ll. 8–16: 'Now ȝitt foure thynges may mak vs vondre of suche lewdenes of ȝounge men: first, nature; þe secound, reson; þe thirde, policie; þe fourte, þe callyng of God.

Mans nature, I sey, moveþ man to wondir why ȝonge men beth vnthryfty. For man seyth he is made of soule so wurthy a creature, and of body so sympull and so lowe a creature. Þan it is wondre þat he leueþ all þe vertevous desires of þe soule and ȝeueþ hym to þe foule lustus of þe foule and vnclene parte, the body.' It would be appropriate to recognize that the large number of references to the natural in Wycliffite writings may have something to do with its particular anticlerical agenda. Nevertheless, I think the evidence of the citations in this chapter suggests that remarks about the natural emerging from a Wycliffite context are not unusual and eccentric in comparison to those found in more orthodox texts.

[5] *EWS* ii. 274 (no. 108).

objects to sin in general because sin is ingratitude (*unkyndenesse*) to God:

Poule moeueþ in þis epistele for former kyndenesse of Crist to be kynde to hym aȝeen. For clerkis seien, and sooþ it is, þat boþe God and kynde haten þat a man dwelle vnkynde aftir greet kyndenesse þat he haþ takun; for sooþ it is þat alle synne turneþ to vnkyndenesse to God.[6]

If sinning in general can be held to be unnatural, doing God's will and obeying his commandments in general can be seen as a function of the nature of the human being, a nature given by God and therefore good. So in *The Pricke of Conscience* we find:

> Alle thing he ordaynd aftir is wille
> In sere kyndes, for certayn skylle;
> Whar-for þe creatours þat er dom,
> And na witt ne skille has, er bughsom
> To lof hym, als þe boke beres wytnesse,
> On þair maner als þair kynd esse.
> For ilk a thyng þat God has wroght,
> Þat folowes þe kynd and passes it noght,
> Loves his maker and hym worshepes,
> In þat at he þe kynd right kepes;[7] . . .
> Mans kynd es to folow Goddes wille
> And alle hys comandements to fulfille.[8]

There are some lines of similar import in a Vernon lyric:

> To god an mon weore holden meste
>   To loue and his wraþþe eschuwe.
> Now is non so vnkuynde a beeste
>   Þat lasse doþ þat weore him duwe;

---

[6] *EWS* i. 643 (no. E40).

[7] We shall see that Boethius makes very much this kind of claim, whilst Chaucer for one seems to be sceptical about such optimistic naturalism. In fact, *The Pricke of Conscience*, citations of which are from the edition by R. Morris (Berlin, 1863), is soon talking about the 'wrechednes of mans kynde' (351), to which, we are told, the first part of the book is devoted (see also 9536), and how 'foul' it is (587) in such a way as to make one wonder how committed it is to its opening perspective on the *kynde*.

[8] *PC* 47–56, 63 f. In the lines omitted play is made of the distinction between animals and human beings arising out of the possession of reason by human beings. Possession of reason, which permits moral perception, makes it particularly incumbent on man to worship God in his *kynde*. For man to fail to live by the faculty of reason and so 'knaw | The werkes of God and gode law' and what he himself is is to live like 'an unskylwys best' and 'agayn his kynde' (159 ff.).

For Beestes and foules, more & leeste,
Þe cours of kynde alle þei suwe;
And whonne we breken Godes heste,
Aȝeynes kuynde we ben vn-trewe.
For kuynde wolde þat we him knewe,
And dradde him most in vre doing.[9]

In *Cursor mundi* the obligation to fulfil God's commandments is presented as the *lawe of kynde* (in contradistinction with the *lawe possitiue*, here understood as establishing what must *not* be done):

Lawes two wer set on sise
To Adam in paradise
As in holy writt we fynde
Þe firste was þe lawe of kynde
Þat is to seye kyndely to do
Al þat hym was beden to
Þe toþer haþ possitiue to nam
Þat was fully forbeden Adam.[10]

The same high and wide-ranging authority is accorded in rather different terms to *kynde* in the fifteenth-century *Dives and Pauper*. This sees 'on precept of kende' as encapsulating both the Ten Commandments of the Old Law and Christ's command to love God and one's neighbour:

alle þe ten comandementis ben conteynyd in þe two preceptis of charite and þe two preceptis of charite ben conteynyd & knyt in þis on precept of kende: Quod tibi non vis fieri alteri ne facias, . . . And so, . . . al þe lawe is conteynyd in þis on precept of kende: þat þu wil nout ben don to þe, do þu it to non oþ-ir.[11]

A Wycliffite writer refers the positive counterpart to this 'on precept' as commanded by Christ to the *lawe of kynde*: 'And of þe lawe of kynde criste spekiþ in þe gospelle, seyinge þus: "Alle þingis þat ȝe

[9] *Religious Lyrics of the XIVth Century*, ed. Carleton Brown, 2nd edn. rev. G. V. Smithers (Oxford, 1957), no. 95, ll. 121-30. See below for passages in which nature is said to be responsible for the acknowledgement of God as their Creator made by all creatures.

[10] *CM* 9427-34. Citations are from *The Southern Version of Cursor mundi*, ed. Sarah M. Horrall et al., 5 vols. (Ottawa, 1978–2000).

[11] *Dives and Pauper*, ed. P. H. Barnum, EETS 275, 280 (Oxford, 1976, 1980), vol. i, pt ii, 28.

wollen þat oþer men done to ȝou, do ȝe to hem."[12] The high
authority and broad scope of the *lawe of kynde* are again evident in
a passage from a demonstration of the unnaturalness of beggary:

and so þis is lawe of kynde þe which mai not be dissolued. For as Crist
myȝte not, so he dissoluede no such lawe, but perfourmede hem and
declaride þe ful perfeccioun of þe moraltees of þe oold lawe.[13]

The fourteenth-century *Book of Vices and Virtues* also relates a far-
reaching moral injunction to nature when it cites Cicero to the
effect that the pursuit of common profit is something we are taught
by *kynde*:

Tullius þe philosophre seiþ, 'We schulde þenke wel þat al þat is made in
þis world is made for to serue man, and þe man is made eueriche to helpe
oþere, and þerto be þei bigete.' Þan seiþ he, 'Do we þan þat þat we be bore
in þis world fore and þat kynde techeþ vs, and seche we al comune profiȝt,'
for, as seynt Poule seiþ, we beþ alle membres of o body.[14]

This passage understands natural morality to be derivable from a
consideration of the purpose of human beings—*kynde* perhaps *techeþ*
us as we reflect on what our natural end is, rather than through a
natural impulse to mutual support. How exactly *kynde* is understood
to teach creatures in the following is not specified, but again, what is

---

[12] *The English Works of Wyclif Hitherto Unprinted* (*EWWHU*), ed. F. D. Matthew,
EETS os 74 (London, 1880), 387. It was, as we have seen in Ch. 1, standard to regard
these negative and positive injunctions as the content of the natural law. See also '*Þe
secounde maundement . . . byddiþ þe loue þin neiȝ-ebore as þow louest þiself*, and þat artow tawt
by kynde', *EWS* i. 293 (no. 18); 'And to þis entent spekiþ Ione þat man shulde kyndeli
loue his broþir', *EWS* i. 610–11 (no. E31) (i.e. humanity in general); 'And if þei [the
friars] did þus, þei did as þei wolden þat men did to hom; and þis is þo lawe of gospel and
kynde' (*Select English Works of John Wyclif* (*SEWJW*), ed. Thomas Arnold, 3 vols.
(Oxford, 1869–71), iii. 421).
[13] *Selections from English Wycliffite Writings*, ed. Anne Hudson (Cambridge, 1978), 95,
ll. 65–7. In this passage, as in the previous one, the Bible text to which reference is made
speaks of the Law (meaning the Jewish law) not the *lawe of kynde*. Another kind of
bestowal of biblical status on the *law of kynde* occurs when it becomes one division of
holy writ: 'Þe firste wynge [of the four beasts of the Apocalypse] was lawe of kynde, þe
toþir was lawe of Moyses, þe þridde was lore of prophetis, þe feerþe was lawe of þe
gospel, þe fyueþe was lore of oþere apostelis, and þe sixeþe was prophecye of Ion and
story of Luke. By þes sixe partis of holy writt fleen alle þes foure beestes' (*EWS* i. 606
(no. E30)).
[14] *The Book of Vices and Virtues* (*BVV*), ed. W. N. Francis, EETS os 217 (London,
1942), 146, ll. 6–13. *Ayenbite of Inwit*, ed. R. Morris, EETS os 23 (London, 1866; corr.
Pamela Gradon, 1965) has a very similar passage at 147 (not surprisingly, since both
Middle English works translate the *Somme le roi* of Lorens d'Orléans).

taught has wide-ranging and spiritually benign implications: 'And alle creaturis seyn to God þat he made hem, for þis is kyndeli seiing, þat kynde techiþ Goddis creaturis.'[15]

However exactly *kynde* may be thought to teach in various passages,[16] human beings do seem to be in possession of natural impulses drawing them towards their own spiritual good and right behaviour towards others. So we are told (we may be reminded of Augustine and Aquinas)[17] that 'Yche man coueytuþ kyndely to haue blisse þat God haþ ordeyned to mankynde to reston inne'[18] and that 'by vey of keende' man desires to come to heaven.[19] We hear of a universal desire for Christ[20] and that the heathen exhibit 'a kyndly wille to wyte þe trewþe and stonde þerinne'.[21] Besides these God-centred positive desires there is also 'drede': 'men han kyndely drede of God and of his lawe.'[22] The natural shame of sin spoken of in the following passage is a natural impulse tending to promote righteousness:

but fro þey [Adam and Eve] hadden synnede, þei wisten þat þei weron nakyd, and þei foundon in lemes of gendrure rebellion to resoun; and þei shamedon herof, and hulyden þes lemes, for man shameþ kyndely of werkis of synne.[23]

---

[15] *SEWJW* iii. 52 f. See also 'Siþ ech creature seiþ kyndely þat God made it of nouȝt, ech creature schulde by kinde blesse God' (*SEWJW* iii. 62). See also n. 12 above and p.55 and nn. 16, 23, 38 below for other instances of *kynde* teaching.

[16] At *SEWJW* iii. 220 where 'kynde techiþ synful men to ȝeve goodis to here children', the natural impulse of parental love is presumably in question.

[17] See Ch. 1.

[18] *EWS* i. 476 (no. E1). The passage goes on to say that 'monye men contraryen hemself' in that their 'lust and fleschly wyt letton hem to wynne þis blis'. Compare the following, which implies rather than declares a natural longing to reach one's natural fulfilment: 'monnis soule is ordeyned þus to be filde wiþ hir God, and vanyte of þis worlde makes hir to long aftir hym, ffor ho haves not kyndely ende to whiche monnis soule is made' (*SEWJW* iii. 150). Here avarice is seen as unnatural because it diverts from man's true end: 'þo avarous mon coveytis unkyndely to fille his soule wiþ þing þat on no wyse may fille hit.'

[19] *MES* 95, ll. 11 ff.

[20] *EWS* ii. 170 (no. 84) (Christ as 'a blessyd worm, þat alle men coueyte kyndely').

[21] *EWS* i. 306 (no. 21). See also the following, from a discussion of the parable of the Prodigal Son in which the Prodigal is understood to figure the heathen: 'And so þis fer cuntre is þe lijf of man in synne . . . Þis hungir þat fel in þis cuntre is wanting of knowing of truþe wiþ kyndely desijr to knowe truþe' (*SEWW* 53, ll. 47–8, 53–5).

[22] *EWS* ii. 296 (no. 115).

[23] *EWS* ii. 230 (no.95). See also 'It is knowon to experte men þat man shameþ kyndely to do monye synnys in lyȝt, þat he wolde do in derknesse, as ben lecherye and

Elsewhere we learn, more positively, that 'ilche man loueþ kynde-liche holynesse of his broþer'[24] and that human beings, in common with other creatures of God, are said to have a natural appetite pressing them to charity towards other things: 'God mot loue kyndeli, and eche creature of God haþ kyndeli an appetyt to sauyng of hymself, and to helping of oþir þyngis.'[25] *Kyndeli* self-interest is appealed to in arguments designed to show that the avoidance of sin and the practice of virtue are dictated by individuals' natural inclina-tion to look to their own welfare. Why, one sermon writer asks, does a man flee from an adder or other venemous beast?

For he knoweth well þat it is þinge contrarius to is own liff, and þerfore naturally of keend he hateþ itt.

Now goostely to speke, by þis skill þou may see þat meche pepull in þis world ben ful vnkeend, for þei neþur luf hem-selfe ne here own sowles, for þei lede all here liff in lechery, in pride, and glotenye, and in all þinge þat is likynge vn-to þe bodie. Þat þenkeþ hem beste to do. But certen, more contrarious þinge is not in þis werld þan synne and mans sowle.[26]

In another sermon we are told that God desires our good and so requires us to love him and do deeds of charity, because by so doing we will reach heaven. The appeal to nature follows:

And þer-fore, sirs, ryght as a man is beholden by þe veye of keende to vayte is owne profette, ryght so he is beholden be keend to loue is Lord God. And þer-fore, fore owre profett, 'Diligamus Deum', Iohanis xv°—'loue we God'.[27]

Certain invocations of the natural in these vernacular writings show the animal world looked to as an indication of what is natural. So animal behaviour, by exemplifying what is truly natural, can demonstrate what is right for human beings:

Þe first þing þat schulde moue man or womman to mercy is kynde. For as þe boke þat spekeþ of kynde of beestes seiþ, non foule wole ete of a-noþer

þefte and money oþre syche synnys þat man doþ in derknesse of nyȝt, and schameþ of hem in lyȝt of day' (*EWS* i. 478 (no. E1)), where a shame of sin apparently more confined in scope is spoken of, and 'Bot se þo filthe of lecchorie, hou mon schulde kyndely hate hit. Iche mon by lore of kynde schames to do hit opunly' (*SEWJW* iii. 165), where only lechery is in question as an object of *kyndely* shame.

[24] *EWWHU* 315. Though this proposition is presented as part of an argument of the devil, there seems no reason to doubt it.

[25] *EWS* i. 609 (no. E31).   [26] *MES* 198, ll. 22–31.   [27] *MES* 96, ll. 22–6.

foule þat is of his kynde. After, þat self boke seiþ þat on meere wole
norische þe colt of þat oþer whan sche is ded. After, men haue ofte y-
seie and proued þat wolues norisscheden caste children & defendede hem
from oþer wolues and oþer bestes.[28]

As for mercy, so for the honouring of father and mother:

and ouer alle oþere, men ben holde to straungers and principalliche to
fadre and modre, whan men seen hem nedeful, for þat techeþ kynde and
God hoteþ it. Þe storke norischeþ his fadre & modre whan þei ben holde
and mowe not purchasen hem, wher-bi kynde techeþ wel þat men schul
doo to here fadres and modres, and who-so doþ nou3t, he is vnkynde and
synneþ a3ens kynde and a3ens God, þat comaundeþ to honoure fadre and
modre.[29]

One of the seven acts of mercy, burying the dead, is in the following
passage shown to be incumbent upon humans through reference to
the behaviour of dolphins:

and to þis dedee schulde kynde moue a man, wherfore men seyn in the
boke of kyndes of bestes þat þe dolfyn, whan þei seen a dolfen ded, þei
gader hem to-gidre and beren hym in-to þe depeste of þe see and þere þei
birien hym. And 3if kynde and pitee moueþ þes sarazenes and Iues and
mysbileuyng folke to birie þe deede, moche more scholde moeue vs rewþe
and pitee and cristene bileue.[30]

The association of *kynde* with the animal realm here is clear: what is
not so clear is whether man is understood actually to share certain
natural impulses which direct him to good moral action with the
animals, or whether the behaviour of the animal world simply
defines the natural and sets before man a programme of action
which he ought to adopt, without any presumption as to the state
of his impulses.

Whether or not these passages think in terms of animal impulse
within man, the action that *kynde* teaches man is good, and this
shows that even when the natural order is understood to be defined

[28] *BVV* 190 f. See the analogous passage at *Ayenbite*, 185 f. The doctrine that every
animal loves its like is used to prove the naturalness to humanity of the love of God at
MES, 303, ll. 33–9, and is invoked to support the contention that every man 'kuyndely
and skilfully schulde fleo and eschuwe' manslaughter at *BVV* 325 f. (a passage from a
variant treatise on the Ten Commandments found in some manuscripts of the work).
[29] *BVV* 213, ll. 13–21. See also *Ayenbite* 193, where the heron is the filial bird.
[30] *BVV* 211, ll. 18–25.

by the being and behaviour of non-rational creatures, it can still demonstrate what is right; the order of natural non-rational impulse is, after all, ordained by God.[31]

PROBLEMATIC NATURE: *KYNDE* AND LECHERY

An understanding that the natural is good is, then, very frequent in these vernacular writings. However, it is also sometimes recognized that the natural is not always unequivocally good and that therefore it may be necessary to hold natural impulses within the human being in check.[32] For example, in the afterlife a natural desire to help their friends will be evoked in those in heaven by the spectacle of those friends suffering in hell. The natural desire, though, will not hold sway: 'ʒif somme seyntes coueyton kyndely to counforten her frendis, þei han strengure wille to conformen hem to Godys wille.'[33] The possibility of the natural love of relations needing to be held in check in favour of the love of God is recognized in the following passage also, where Christ's saying 'þat *he cam to parte a man aʒenus his fadur*' is being discussed:

for he [Christ] techeþ how a sowle schulde more loue God þan owt ellys; and so loue þat man schulde haue to God schulde passe loue and lawe of kynde. For al such kyndely bond schulde serue to þe loue of God.[34]

---

[31] See above Ch. 1 n. 109. We should also note how *kynde* or *nature* can be invoked in various ways as guides to consumption. So, for instance: 'þe multitude of craftis nout nedful, usid in oure chirche, norsschith michil synne in wast, curiosite and disgysing. Þis schewith experience and resun prouith, for nature with a fewe craftis sufficith to nede of man' (*SEWW* 28, ll. 163–6). One Wycliffite sermon tells us that man harms his soul by having 'godis of siche ordris [friars]' over and above 'ʒiftis of kynde þat ben susteyned to his nede' and goes on to say: 'And so it semeþ þat Crist wolde seye þat eche man schulde go nye þe staat of kynde and serue God, and leeue superflu þat man haþ foundid by errour of his wille' (*EWS* iii. 265 (no. 214)). In another we read: 'þey [friars] shulden not haue in comune þat were not nedeful to þer staat, for þis hauyng more aʒenus kynde is more hatid of Crist and seyntis' (*EWS* iii. 260 (no. 212)).

[32] That something is natural may render it, if not good, at least excusable. So we are advised of the grieving of the Virgin Mary for her son Christ: 'Blame her nat, hit was but kynde' (*RLXV* 97. 75). There seems to be a sense here, however, that what is natural is not quite ideal. See below on the intermediate moral status of the ideal (and above in Ch. 1).

[33] *EWS* i. 225 (no. 1).

[34] *EWS* ii. 95 (no. 72).

In this last passage what *kynde* directs to and what the law of God demands come into conflict, but the impulse which needs to be checked would in other circumstances be a positively good one. Elsewhere, however, this is not the case, the natural motion being morally neutral, or worse. The natural fear of death can be appropriately suspended by charity: 'And where deþ is þe moste þing þat man dreeduþ heere, þis loue [charity] passeþ kynde, and makeþ men to coueyte such deþ.'[35] The *Northern Homily Cycle* has natural promptings working against the proper obedience of one man to another:

> By þis ensample may we se
> þat gude it es bowsum to be,
>
> Bot mans hert, kind to fulfill,
> Wald wirk efter his awin will,
>
> And right rewle of obedience
> Sall do oþer mens cumandmentes.[36]

This shows us *kynde* clearly in the wrong. The following passage, which contrasts the teaching of *kynde* to God's law, suggests that the *lawe of kynde* might not always prompt to what is right:

Also freris ben adversaries of Crist and disciplis of Sathanas, not ʒeldinge gode for yvel, as Gods lawe techis, ne gode for gode, as kynde and monnis lawe techen; bot ʒelding yvel for gode, as þo fendis lawe techis.[37]

whilst another invocation of this tripartite division of law is explicit on the moral unsatisfactoriness of the 'myddul lawe':

---

[35] *EWS* i. 464 (no. 53). That dread of death here is not in itself bad is suggested by the fact that Christ himself is said to have experienced it at *EWS* ii. 273 (no. 108): 'Kyndely drede was in Crist whanne he dredde to suffre deþ.' (Contrast a passage in Chaucer's *Tale of Melibee* (*CT* 7. 1585 f.) which suggests that fear of death is unnatural.)

[36] *The Northern Homily Cycle*, ed. S. Nevanlinna, *Mémoires de la Société Néophilologique de Helsinki*, 38, 41 (1972, 1973), ll. 13339–44. In the continuation of this passage it is 'Oure flesly willes' (13360) that stand in the way of obedience to God, suggesting that in this instance *kind* is involved with the propensity to evil of the flesh. At *Piers Plowman* B 17. 332 (see below at n. 66) *kynde* is said to 'contrarie' the soul, as if it is equivalent to the soul's usual opposite, the body (the flesh is mentioned in the previous line in relation to sin). However, frequently in English vernacular writings the flesh, and not nature, is made responsible for motions to evil experienced by human beings which appear automatic and inevitable.

[37] *SEWJW* iii. 393.

Lawe of God, þat Poul techeþ, is moste resonable and liʒt: to ʒelde men good for yuel, for so doþ God þat may not fayle. Þe secounde lawe of þe world is to ʒelde good for good, and yuel for yuel; for, as men seyon, þus kynde techeþ men to do. Þe þridde lawe of þe feend is to do yuel for good, ... Poul forfenduþ here þe myddul lawe þat men schulden ʒelden yuel for yuel. . . . And þis lawe of þe world brynguþ in lawe of þe feend. For it is takon for a rewle among worldly werryouris þat þei schulden anoye þer enemyes on what maner þat þei may, and it is holdon a riʒtwisnesse to do a wrong for anoþur. And ʒeet Godis lawe bidduþ to ʒelde not an yuel for an yuel. . . . And þis, holdon comun lawe of men, is turned into fendis lawe, for no lawe reuersuþ Godis lawe, but ʒif it be þe feendis lawe.[38]

It seems likely that *kynde* in these passages is understood as the impulsive and covers the automatic, unthinking reaction of human beings to what is done to them. At any rate, we are dealing with a different idea of the natural from that which sees it as urging people to do as they would be done by, as teaching what is taught by the Law and the Gospel. The natural here occupies an intermediate moral status—*fendis lawe* is worse—but there is at least partial opposition between the *lawe of kynde* and *Godis lawe*; indeed, in the second of these passages, the teaching of *kynde*, 'myddul lawe' though it is, seems closer to the law of the devil than to that of God.

In the *South English Legendary* we find a devil advocating the attempt to do one's enemy down with a reference to nature— 'And echmon may be riʒte cunde . fonde is fon to schende'[39]— and a Wycliffite Antichrist invokes the animal realm to substantiate the same kind of claim:

---

[38] *EWS* i. 517 f. (no. E10). One wonders whether the 'as men seyon' might register a certain unease about the notion of *kynde* teaching men to act according to the law of the world. But the following passage from Sermon 5 (*EWS* i. 242) in which God's law is likened to a net seems to make a close association between 'lif of kynde' and 'wordly lif': 'And so þese nettys þat fyscherus fysche wiþ bytoken Godys lawe in whyche vertuwes and trewþus ben knytted; and oþer propretes of nettis tellen propretes of Godes lawe, as voide places bytwene knottys bytoknen lif of kynde þat men han bysyde uertues; and fowre cardynal vertuwes ben fygured by knyttyng of þe net. Þe net ys brood in þe bygynnyng and aftur streyt in þe ende to teche þat men, whan þei ben turnyd furst, lyuen a brod worldly lif but afturward, whan þei ben depyd in Godis lawe, þei kepen hem streiʒtlier fro synnes.' The life of virtue is apparently specifically dissociated from the 'lif of kynde', which seems to be conceived as a mode of living which of itself has no interest in the cultivation of virtue.

[39] *SEL* 298, l. 199.

Bot ȝitte argues Anticrist, to mayntene mennis feghtyng, þat kynde techis þat men schulden by strenght agenstonde hor enmyes. Sith a nedder by hir kynde stynges a mon þat tredes on her, why schulde we not feght ageynes oure enmyes?[40]

One might suppose that the invocation of *kynde* in these passages was illegitimate, but this is not explicitly claimed in what follows either of the quotations—and then another passage denounces lords who 'go to straunge londes to werre wiþ þere enmyes' rather than combating error close at hand and claims that if the Church 'stode clenly bi þe ordynaunce of Crist, wiþowten fendes novelries', 'þan schulde men begynne to werre on enmyes nexst hem, as mede and nede and kynde teches Cristen men'.[41] Here there is no suggestion that what is said about the teaching of *kynde* is false.[42] This and the previous passages which have *kynde* teaching people to return evil for evil suggest that there might indeed be a legitimate understanding of the natural in terms of which what the devil and Antichrist say about *cunde* is right.

There is certainly an awareness among moralists of arguments which enlist the support of *kynde* for immoral activities:

to þis riching of persouns kyn moueþ þe fend þes ipocritis bi feyned mersy & bi kynde; & boþe he seiþ comen of god. What man shulde not haue mersy on his pore kyn to helpe hem, for heere is more cause of mersy þan to helpe oþere straunge men; as a man loueþ bi kynde more his lemes þan oþere mennus, so bi kynde he shulde loue more his kyn þan oþere strange men.[43]

But to act in this way is to pervert the natural feelings of affection that exist between relations, as lechery perverts natural sexual desire. The passage continues:'& þus þes prelatis þat turnen þis loue synnen boþe in god & man, & disusen kyndely wille as don synneris in leccherye.'[44] The comparison with lechery here perhaps arises out of an awareness that that sin is on occasion defended through an appeal to the natural. The following passages see such a defence as a damaging attempt to excuse the inexcusable:

[40] *SEWJW* iii. 137.
[41] *SEWJW* iii. 181 f.
[42] Had the writer drawn back from his immediate polemical purpose, he might have been prepared to concede that what *kynde* taught was not unequivocally good, and that the natural had an intermediate moral status.
[43] *EWWHU* 439
[44] *EWWHU* 440.

Poul bidduþ here to trewe men þat *no mon bygyle hem* in byleue *by veyne wordis* whiche þei spekon, þat þes be none synnes or lyȝte—as lecherye is kyndely as þei seyn, and man schulde kyndely haue loue of his owne excellense, siþ þat God haþ ȝouen it hym, and God haþ ȝouen þis world to man to serue hym by help þerof. Syche veyn wordis þat excuson synne don myche harme among men.[45]

Prestis weiward of lif...colouren...lecherie bi helpynge forþ of þe world & kyndely dede; & þis þei don to excuse here owene synne, & norischen oþere men þer-inne for þank and worldly wynnynge.[46]

Lo! how þe deuel baptisiþ synnes vndir þe names of honestee þat þei be þe lasse orrible to men. Þus is now pride callid honestee, veniaunce manhood, glotenye good felouship, leccherie kyndely solace,...[47]

The idea that sinners conveniently rename sins is an ancient one,[48] by no means confined to Wycliffite writing. A passage in the *Ludus Coventriae* has a devil renaming lechery 'naterall kend':

> I haue browth ȝow newe namys, and wyl ȝe se why
> Ffor synne is so plesaunt, to ech Mannys intent
> Ðe xal kalle pride· oneste· and naterall kend lechory
> And covetyse wysdam· there tresure is present.[49]

And a poem in MS Bodley 416 on the corruption of the present age notes the same problematic designation as one of a series:

---

[45]   *EWS* i. 554 f. (no. E18).

[46]   *EWWHU* 174.

[47]   The Sermon of William Taylor, in *Two Wycliffite Sermons*, ed. Anne Hudson, EETS 301 (Oxford, 1993), 14, ll. 418–21. See also *SEWW* 81, ll. 255–62 and *Jack Upland*, 46–53 (*Jack Upland, Friar Daw's Reply and Upland's Rejoinder*, ed. P. L. Heyworth (London, 1968)). Interestingly, Roger Dymmok, *Rogeri Dymmok liber contra XII errores et hereses lollardorum*, ed. H. S. Cronin (London, 1921), refuting the Lollard Conclusions of 1395, claims (275) that the 11th Conclusion (condemning clerical celibacy) affirms the necessity of lasciviousness through reference to 'naturalis inclinacio' [natural inclination] and 'delectatio naturalis' [natural pleasure] (xi. 2). See also iii. 6 (80). It may be that the Lollard position on clerical celibacy privileges what is taken to be natural to the extent that it affirms the danger of ignoring natural drives; this is not quite the same as affirming that because sexuality is natural it is good, as implicitly occurs in these renaming examples. So it is not clear that Dymmok is justified in suggesting that his Lollard opponents are making illegitimate use of the benign connotations of the natural, though such a suggestion is polemically advantageous to him.

[48]   There is an example in Gregory the Great, *Moralia in Job* 32. 45 (PL 76, 662): see Hudson's note on the Taylor passage cited in the previous note.

[49]   *Ludus Coventriae*, ed. K. Block, EETS ES 120 (London, 1922), Passion Play 1, 228, ll. 109–12. The meaning of *kend* here may be '(natural) sexual impulse', such as seems to be in play when Myrc writes in his *Instructions for Parish Priests*, ed. Edward Peacock,

> richesse is clepud worþynes,
> and lecherie kyndely þing.[50]

The poem goes on to speak of the legitimization of sloth through reference to *kynde*:

> slouþe men clepen nedfulnes
> to norshe mennes kynde.[51]

It is not clear whether these writers are simply indicating disapproval of the attempt to excuse sin involved in the use of the concept of nature, or whether they would also have disallowed the claim that these sins were natural. Would they have thought what was said entirely incorrect, as well as mischievously making the abhorrent seem excusable? Perhaps only the latter: Latin academic writing, after all, shows that there were ways of regarding illicit sexual behaviour as natural. When in those writings sex is said to be *contra naturam* without further explanation,[52] it is specific kinds of sexual behaviour (non-inseminative practices and unorthodox position) which are so designated rather than any kind of lechery at all. Such seems likely to be the case when *The Book of Vices and Virtues* tells us that the last bough of the sin of lechery

> is so foule and hidous þat [it] scholde not be nempned, þat is synne aȝens kynde, þat þe deuel techeþ to a man or to a womman in many wises þat mowe not be spoken, for þe matere is so foul þat it is abhomynacioun to speke it.[53]

Non-inseminative practice (not to mention unorthodox position) is part of what is involved in the unnatural sexual behaviour of those who perished in the Flood in this passage from *Cursor mundi*:

EETS OS 31 (London, 1868): 'to gret synne forsoþe hyt ys, | For any mon þat bereþ lyf | To forsake hys wedded wyf | And do hys kynde other way, | Þat ys gret synne wyþowte nay' (227–31). At any rate, the existence of such a meaning, and others relating directly to sexual matters, no doubt increases the plausibility of presenting lechery as something natural. On this and other meanings of *kynde* in the sexual sphere see *MED*, s.v. 'kinde', 14a.

[50]   *Historical Poems of the Fourteenth and Fifteenth Centuries*, ed. Rossell Hope Robbins (Columbia, NY, 1959), no. 57, ll. 7 f.

[51]   Ibid. 12 f. *Kynde* here may mean something like natural vigour (compare certain usages in Gower and Chaucer, discussed below).

[52]   See above, Ch. 1 n. 110

[53]   *BVV* 46, ll. 3–8. See also *Ayenbite*, 49. On the complications in respect of sexual sin against *kynde* in *BVV* and *Ayenbite* see n. 70 below.

Euer þei ȝaf her lyf to lust
Þat shende her soulis al to dust
Wymmen as we hit fynde
Wente togider aȝeyne kynde
And men also þe same wyse
As þe deuele wolde devyse
Of soþfastenes as seiþ þe sawe
Þei left euer þe good lawe
Þe lawe of sooþnes ny of kynde
Wolden þei no tyme fynde
Al wexe wicked & in stryf
Þe broþer took þe oþeres wyf
Her kursednes was not vnkid
Þe lawe of kynde þei so fordid
Þe shame & synne þat þere was oute
To telle were sumdel doute.[54]

What also seems to be against *kynde* here is the incestuous practice of a man sleeping with his brother's wife.[55] Nevertheless, there is no suggestion that sexual irregularity of any kind at all is unnatural.

On the other hand, Augustine, as we have seen, could write in such a way as to make procreative intention the criterion for sexual behaviour being in accordance with the law of nature and so as to imply a distinction between natural sexual behaviour and lust.[56] In this passage from Trevisa's translation of Bartholemaeus Anglicus' *De proprietatibus rerum* it is not entirely clear whether 'aȝenst þe . . . lawe of kynde' refers to non-procreative practice, or non-procreative intent:

But many mysusen þis membres, þat vsyn ham nouȝt to þe frute but more aȝenst þe ordre of resoun and lawe of kynde, and nouȝt to gete children but to foule lust and likynge of lecherye.[57]

If what is thought unnatural is non-procreative intent (possible even where the sexual act is open to procreation), this passage, with its contrast of procreative intent and lechery, would seem to imply that all lechery is unnatural. Again, the comment that '[þ]o fifft maner of

---

[54] *CM* 1567 ff.
[55] This kind of incest is designated *vnkyndenes* in the story of Herod and John the Baptist at *CM* 13015 ff.
[56] See above, Ch. 1 at n. 56.
[57] *On the Properties of Things*, ed. M. C. Seymour et al. (Oxford, 1975), 5. 48 (263).

lecchorye is þo synne of Sodome, and is more unkyndely þen any oþer lecchorye'[58] implicitly affirms the unnaturalness of lechery in general, albeit there are differences of degree in this unnaturalness. However, the following Wycliffite passage apparently admits a kind of naturalness in all sorts of sinful sexual practice, though they are also partly unnatural:

> As God hafs ordeyned instrumentis and powere to do þis dede, so he ordeynes mariage and feyth of wedded folk. And þus in iche lechorye is sum þing by kynde, and sum þing ageyns kynde; and þerinne stondes synne. Ffor synne is so feble and noȝt worth of hym, þat hit myght not be bot if gode of kynde groundid hit. And he þat excusis synne, or preysis hit herfore, excusis þo fende and dispreyses God.[59]

In the light of this we might recall the passage above[60] which spoke of the 'disuse' of *kyndely wille* in lechery, implying that there is something *by kynde* in it. It may be, in fact, that claims that sexual sin is natural would not necessarily be seen to involve a positive misuse of language: to rename lechery 'naterall kende' may not be very discriminating, perhaps, and may therefore be misleading, but it is not simply deceitful. The plausibility of the renaming, without which, after all, it would be pointless, is not entirely specious.

Indeed, it seems that some, even though not they are not trying to 'colouren lechorie', would have been happy with the renaming, albeit that would imply that the vice was in a straightforward way natural. Whilst the passages given above suggest that their authors would have wanted some very careful hedging of any claim that lechery was natural in the interests of proper explanation of exactly how this might be so and how it might not, *The Ayenbite of Inwit* seems to grant the designation 'kendlich' to lechery without a qualm when the author writes: 'And hue is hit [Lechery] uoul dede zeþþe hit is kendlich? uor þet god hit uorbyet ine his spelle.'[61] There is certainly no disputation over lechery's naturalness. *Cursor mundi*, which, as we have seen, speaks of 'þe kyndely synne wiþ wommen', seems to think that a tendency to fall into sins of the flesh is endemic to human *kynde*. It is the 'caytif kynde' which brings Solomon low:

---

[58] *SEWJW* iii. 162. There is a passage of similar import at *EWWHU* 68. No doubt the sin of Sodom is more unnatural because traditionally designated 'against *kynde*'.

[59] *SEWJW* iii. 161–2.   [60] See at n. 44.   [61] *Ayenbite*, 47.

[Solomon's] dedis couþe no mon amende
Suche grace god hym sende
But harde hit was þe dede of synne
Þat ordeyned was to adames kynne
Þat sorweful werk hemself hit souȝte
Þat al her sede in sorwe brouȝt
Man to falle in fulþe of flesshe
Þourȝe fourme of kynde þat is nesshe
Ouer þast hym haþ þat caytif kynde
And made kyng salamon al blynde.[62]

'NATURAL' AS MORAL MIDDLE TERM

In these two last passages the claim that sexual sin is natural does not seem to be offered up to ironic scrutiny. We do need to recognize such a possibility, however, when in *The Owl and the Nightingale* sexual sin is linked by the Owl to *kinde* in a way which mitigates the offence.

ȝef maide luueþ dernliche
 Heo stumpeþ & falþ icundeliche;
For þah heo sum hwile pleie
Heo nis nout feor ut of þe weie.[63]

It might be argued that the Owl, intent on putting one over on the Nightingale, is not to be trusted, and that we are meant to see what she says as a culpable colouring of lechery, into which she is led by the illegitimate spirit of a self-serving contentiousness. We might also harbour reservations about the attempted mitigation of the seriousness of lechery which Langland puts in the mouth of Mede in *Piers Plowman* when she claims that it is 'a cours of kynde, wherof we comen alle'.[64] But the alternative possibility—that what the Owl and Mede say about the naturalness of lechery is to be taken at face value—gains ground if we consider other moments in *Piers Plowman*. It is much more difficult to accuse Reason of conceptual impropriety than it is to accuse Mede, and Reason says that man must suffer *wo*

[62] *CM* 8979–89.
[63] *The Owl and the Nightingale*, ed. Eric Stanley (London, 1963), 1423–6.
[64] *Piers Plowman* B 3. 56. References are to A. V. C. Schmidt's edition of the B-Text (London, 1987).

In fondynge of the flessh and of the fend bothe.
For man was maad of swich a matere he may noght wel asterte
That som tyme hym bitit to folwen his kynde.
Caton acordeth therwith—*Nemo sine crimine vivit!*[65]

The implication is that the sins of the flesh, lechery among them, of course, proceed from the nature of the human being and could therefore legitimately be designated 'naterall kende'. Again, the Samaritan, a figure of Christ and therefore as trustworthy as anyone in *Piers Plowman*, speaks of

> oure wikked flessh that wol noght be chastised,
> For kynde clyveth on hym evere to contrarie the soule.[66]

Now the Samaritan's remark comes in a vehement protestation against *unkyndenesse*, which is presented as something which quenches God's mercy: *kynde* sins are by contrast excusable and 'lightly' forgivable.[67] We seem here to be faced with a three-tier system in which the natural can occupy a place between the absolutely good and the absolutely bad, a conception which matches that found in certain writings examined in the first chapter.

A passage from *Cursor mundi* which comments on the fate of Sodom shows very clearly the natural in this intermediate position:

> Ensaumple bi þis wooful wrake
> Þat al for lecchery done was
> Þe foulest þat euer coom on plas
> Þat hit was wicked was wel sene
> Bi þat wreche þat was so kene
> Hoot & stynkynge is þat lake
> Fuyr & brymstone was þe wrake
> Out of kynde her synne was done
> Þerfore her kynde lost was soone
> Fleeþ þat synne al þis werde
> For þis wreche þat 3e haue herde
> God forbede 3e do þat synne
> Þat 3ee in helle þerfore brynne
> But if 3e nede synne shal do

---

[65] *PP* B 11. 399–402.
[66] *PP* B 17. 331–2. One wonders whether present in these Langlandian usages of *kynde* (or gestured at by them) is the meaning 'natural sexual impulse'. See n. 49 above.
[67] See *PP* B 17. 330–51.

Þe synne of kynde holde ȝou to
Þe kyndely synne wiþ wommon
But sib ne spoused take ȝe noon
So fer ȝoure synne folweþ nouȝt
To forgete him þat ȝow wrouȝt.[68]

The natural is also found in an intermediate position in *The Book of Vices and Virtues*.[69] A passage in this work's discussion of Confession implies that sin is more or less bad according as it is against nature or in accordance with it.

After, men schul seye þe condicion of þe synne, for it is wel more synne in a womman maried or in a maide or in a man or a womman of religion or in a persone þat haþ ordre of holi chirche, as prest or dekne or subdekne, and as þe ordre is hiȝ or lowe. And after, ȝif þe synne be bi weye of kynde or aȝens kynde.[70]

These vernacular writings, then, very often understand the natural as the good, as something which urges human beings along the path of virtue; this can be so even when *kynde* is closely associated with the animal realm. But there is a recognition that certain natural motions fall short of the highest virtue and that to follow nature can be to fail in one's obligations to God. There seems to be some reluctance among moralists and homiletic writers to allow that sin can be the result of natural pressures, but the explicit rejection of this idea suggests that it was in fact current, a suggestion confirmed by the practice of Langland and others. That a plea of naturalness could be entered in mitigation of a sin shows the power of nature as a normative concept: there is a sense that if something is natural it is in some degree acceptable, or at least undepraved.

---

[68]   *CM* 2882–900.

[69]   See also *Ayenbite*, 175 f., for the analogous passage.

[70]   *BVV* 178, ll. 11–17. Though the context is a discussion of confession in general, it seems possible, indeed likely, given the reference to marriage and virginity, that uppermost in the writer's mind here is sexual sin and perhaps the intermediate moral status of the natural in *BVV* (and *Ayenbite*) is effectively confined to this area.
       The treatment of the sin of lechery in *BVV* and *Ayenbite* does not quite deliver the clear-cut evaluation of what is against *kynde* being worse than what is in accordance with *kynde* which one might expect, since though the enumeration of the branches of lechery culminates with sin *aȝens kynde* as the fourteenth, sin *aȝens kynde* is also involved in the relatively unheinous sixth branch (sin between husband and wife). Quite what the difference is between the practices constituting the sin against *kynde* in the sixth branch and in the fourteenth branch is unclear.

The last two chapters have prepared for the consideration of the more strictly literary inheritance of Chaucer and Gower by attempting to sketch out some of the ideas about the natural that might have helped to form the thinking about nature of a later Middle English writer and which seem likely to have been part of the shared conceptual background of such writers and their audiences. C. S. Lewis held that:

A medieval poet would have been surprised to find Great Mother Nature inspiring sins, for he would have supposed that her 'inspiration', so far as concerned man, lay in the *nature* (*animal rationale*) appointed by her for man.[71]

Having considered Latin academic theology and English moral writings, we are in a position to see that this is something of an oversimplification. Very frequently, to be sure, the natural is good and right. A standard conception is that the natural law enshrines the moral dictates of natural reason, another, consonant with this, that the natural law is to be identified with the moral commands of the Old Law and the Gospel. One may do naturally the things of the law, in the Pauline phrase, because Nature has endowed one with reason. But it is also perfectly standard to see the natural as what the human being shares with the animal and this animal side of the human being does not necessarily (though it may) press towards goals reason would endorse and is therefore not guaranteed to direct to what is good. The medieval understanding of Nature as it bears upon human beings (if we are to think of a single understanding) is unstable at just this point. What is it truly natural for the human being to do—what indeed is a human being's true nature? Should one regard the human being as fundamentally rational, as *rationale* first and *animal* second, or should it be the other way round? If the other way round, can the natural order still be seen as morally benign? These kinds of question lie at the heart of the medieval literary tradition of Nature, and we shall find much less certainty about Nature and much less confidence in her as an agent of good than did Lewis and his medieval poet.

[71] *Studies in Words*, 71 f.

CHAPTER THREE

Natura Vicaria Dei

Our scrutiny of the moral status of the natural in medieval writing turns now to a literary tradition in which Nature is personified as a power operative in the constitution and organization of the universe. This personification becomes very visible in the twelfth century, but is not, of course, a creation *ex nihilo* of that era. For the formation of medieval Nature Plato's *Timaeus* and commentaries on it are extremely important, the critical concept being the world-soul, intermediary between the material and the immaterial world.[1] In several places Aristotle offers a personified, or quasi-personified, Nature who represents the tendency within things to achieve their best possible states and who can be presented as presiding over the orderedness and purposiveness of the universe in close connection with God. So we are told that God and Nature create nothing that does not fulfil a purpose.[2] There are also presentations in Latin poets known to medieval authors, such as Statius and Claudian, of Nature figures of considerable dignity and power whose activity is benign.[3] These things—benignity, power, and proximity to the divine—are attributes which various different parts of the Classical heritage through various different routes all propose for the medieval Nature figure.

---

[1] See Economou, *Goddess*, 10–13 on this, and Economou's first two chapters generally for the Classical inheritance of the medieval Nature figure. On the Platonic influences in 12th-century thought see Tullio Gregory, 'The Platonic Inheritance', in Peter Dronke (ed.), *A History of Twelfth-Century Western Philosophy* (Cambridge, 1988), 54–80.

[2] Aristotle, *De caelo* 1. 4. 271^a and the citations given by David Ross, *Aristotle* (5th edn. rev., London, 1949), 78 f.: *De generatione animalium* 744^{b}16^{a}36; *De caelo* 291^{b}13^{a}24; *De partibus animalium* 686^{a}22. See also *Metaphysics* 5. 4. 1015^a and *Physics* 2. 1. 193^b.

[3] Economou, *Goddess*, 42–52.

BOETHIUS

The classical background to the medieval Nature figure has been extensively discussed by several writers, and I shall not consider in full detail the indebtedness to past writers of Bernardus Silvestris, Alan of Lille, and Johannes de Hauvilla, whose contributions to the Nature tradition are the main concern of this chapter.[4] However, I do want to discuss one particular late Classical work, Boethius' *De consolatione Philosophiae*, and that for several reasons. First, it has been said that the *De consolatione* 'reaffirms and clarifies several of the major classical concepts of nature'.[5] Second, it is a work whose importance for the Middle Ages in general and the Nature tradition in particular cannot be overemphasized: it was, in fact translated by two later contributors to that tradition, Jean de Meun and Chaucer.[6] Third, in it there becomes apparent a certain continuity between the personification Nature and some of the ideas considered in the first chapter.[7]

In the *De consolatione Philosophiae* arguments about the natural make up a significant strand in Philosophy's attempts to demonstrate the benignity of the providential order. Boethius was profoundly influenced by Plato and by Neoplatonist writers such as Proclus,[8] and his debt to the Platonic tradition is evident in the way he has Philosophy align closely being, goodness, and nature, so that to lapse into evil is to fail to preserve one's nature and to lose being:

[4] Besides Economou, see, e.g., Knowlton, 'Early Periods', Winthrop Wetherbee, *Platonism and Poetry in the Twelfth Century* (Princeton, 1972), Marc M. Pelen, *Latin Poetic Irony in the Roman de la Rose*, Vinaver Studies in French 4 (Liverpool, 1987).

[5] Economou, *Goddess*, 50.

[6] On the general influence of Boethius on the Middle Ages, see Margaret Gibson (ed.), *Boethius* (Oxford, 1981); Wetherbee, *Platonism*, 74 ff., presents Boethius as a major seminal figure for writers in the Nature tradition. See also M. D. Cherniss, *Boethian Apocalypse* (Norman, Okla., 1987). Paul Piehler, *The Visionary Landscape: A Study in Medieval Allegory* (London, 1971), 46, writes that Alan of Lille's *De planctu Naturae* 'seems to be not merely influenced by [Boethius' *De consolatione Philosophiae*] but even a conscious attempt to produce something in the same genre'.

[7] It might also be said that *CP* bridges the gap between the kinds of writing reviewed in Ch. 1 and this chapter. In so far as it is a piece of philosophy it might have been dealt with in Ch. 1, but since it has certain mythopoeic elements which link it generically to the later writing considered in this chapter and in view of the evident indebtedness to *CP* of later writers in the Nature tradition, it is considered here.

[8] See, e.g., Henry Chadwick, *Boethius: The Consolations of Music, Logic, Theology and Philosophy* (Oxford, 1981), pp. xi–xv.

Nam qui mali sunt eos malos esse non abnuo; sed eosdem esse pure atque simpliciter nego.

Nam uti cadaver hominem mortuum dixeris, simpliciter vero hominem appellare non possis, ita vitiosos malos quidem esse concesserim, sed esse absolute nequeam confiteri. Est enim quod ordinem retinet servatque naturam; quod vero ab hac deficit, esse etiam, quod in sua natura situm est, derelinquit.[9]

[For those who are evil, I do not deny to be evil; but that they are, purely and simply, I do deny. For as you would say that a corpse was a dead man, but you could not call it simply a man, so I concede of the vicious that they are indeed evil, but I cannot admit that they are, absolutely. For that *is* which keeps its order and preserves its nature; and whatever falls from this also abandons being, which is dependent on its nature.]

Conversely, to abide by one's nature is to be and therefore also to be good. The keeping of one's nature guarantees that one will be in harmony with the will of God, as Philosophy and the character Boethius agree:

'Nihil est igitur quod naturam servans deo contraire conetur.' 'Nihil,' inquam.[10]

['There is therefore nothing,' she said, 'which while remaining true to its nature would try to go against God?'
'Nothing,' I said.]

And Philosophy has just stated that there is a natural tendency in all things to the good:

eademque omnia sicuti docui ad bonum naturali intentione festinent.[11]

[and all these same things, as I have taught you, hasten towards the good by a natural inclination.]

In human beings the *naturalis intentio* towards the good is bound up with a vestigial perception of their true *principium* and *finis*:

Vos quoque, o terrena animalia, tenui licet imagine vestrum tamen principium somniatis verumque illum beatitudinis finem licet minime perspicaci qualicumque tamen cogitatione prospicitis eoque vos et ad verum bonum naturalis ducit intentio et ab eodem multiplex error abducit.[12]

---

[9] *CP* 4. p. 2 104–12. References to the *De consolatione Philosophiae* are to the Loeb edition (Cambridge, Mass., 1973) from which the text and S. J. Tester's translation (sometimes adapted) are taken.
[10] *CP* 3. p. 12 56–7.   [11] *CP* 3. p. 12 49–50.   [12] *CP* 3. p. 3 1–6.

[And you also, earthly creatures that you are, have some image, though hazy, in your dreams of your beginning; you see, though with a far from clear imagination yet with some idea, that true end of your happiness. A natural inclination draws you towards that end, to the true good, though mistaken notions of many kinds lead you away from it.]

This *naturalis intentio* operates even in evil men:[13]

Vide enim quanta vitiosorum hominum pateat infirmitas qui ne ad hoc quidem pervenire queunt ad quod [i.e. the *summum bonum*] eos naturalis ducit ac paene compellit intentio. Et quid si hoc tam magno ac paene invicto praeeuntis naturae desererentur auxilio?[14]

[For see how plainly great is the weakness of corrupt men, who cannot attain even to that towards which a natural inclination draws and almost compels them. And what would it be like if they were deprived of this great and almost invincible aid, of nature leading the way.]

Even when they pursue false goods, men are motivated by a 'mentibus... veri boni naturaliter inserta cupiditas' [a desire of the true good naturally put into their minds].[15] Behind the agreement of all human beings in the pursuit of good can be detected *naturae vis*:

Bonum est igitur quod tam diversis studiis homines petunt; in quo quanta sit naturae vis facile monstratur, cum licet variae dissidentesque sententiae tamen in diligendo boni fine consentiunt.[16]

[The good is therefore that which human beings pursue in so many different endeavours; and we can easily see how great is nature's power in this, since although opinions vary and differ so much, yet they agree in loving the same end, the good.]

Boethius then goes on to celebrate Nature, now clearly personified,[17] as the regulative force of the universe, the power which endows particular creatures with their specific natures:

> Quantas rerum flectat habenas
> Natura potens, quibus immensum
> Legibus orbem provida servet
> Stringatque ligans inresoluto

---

[13] One is reminded of the scholastic notion of *synderesis* discussed in the first chapter.
[14] *CP* 4. p. 2 75–9.   [15] *CP* 3. p. 2 13 f.   [16] *CP* 3. p. 2 76–9.
[17] It is not always possible to know whether a particular reference to nature relates immediately to this personified power, or to the nature of a particular thing (see, e.g., the *naturae vis* of the passage just quoted); but because general Nature endows particular natures, this difficulty is not in the end a very troubling one.

Singula nexu, placet arguto
Fidibus lentis promere cantu.[18]

[I have decided now
In clear song, with my pliant strings to show
What great control Nature in her power
Wields over all things, with what laws
She in her foresight keeps the vast universe
Tied fast, each single thing, in indissoluble bonds.]

Examples follow to demonstrate Nature's power: the tamed lion, the caged bird, and the bent sapling all have a natural tendency to return to the original condition which they enjoyed prior to the intervention of human beings.

Repetunt proprios quaeque recursus
Redituque suo singula gaudent.[19]

[Each thing seeks its own way back
And coming back is glad.]

One might be tempted to entertain doubts about the lion, which turns violently on its trainer, but that the return to the original mode of behaviour is positively conceived seems clear from the fact that this *metrum* follows on from and is immediately succeeded by statements of the natural tendency of human beings to the good.[20] Here, then, Nature is both potent and benign.

Evident in Nature's binding things to regular courses of behaviour is a concern for order, and a concern for order and harmony lies behind her refusal to allow the joining of unlike things: 'respuit ut contraria quaeque iungantur.'[21] Here, too, Nature is to be understood as a force for good, benign in her operations.

In book 3 *prosa* 11 Boethius demonstrates a natural desire for the good in all things by making an equation between unity and goodness;[22] he goes on to present death and destruction as involving a breakdown of unity and finds that all creatures naturally seek to

---

[18] *CP* 3. m. 2 1–6.

[19] *CP* 3. m. 2 34 f.

[20] The *metrum* is preceded by the passage 'Bonum est igitur . . .' (*CP* 3. p. 2 76–9) and followed by the 'Vos quoque, o terrena animalia . . .' passage (*CP* 3. p. 3 1–6), which are both quoted above. Jean de Meun and Chaucer (see below) may both have had doubts as to how positive the returns to nature instanced by Boethius here in fact are.

[21] *CP* 2. p. 6 43.

[22] *CP* 3. p. 11 18 ff.

avoid death and destruction and hence may be said to desire unity (and so goodness).[23] In the demonstration of the natural desire of plants and trees for continuing existence Boethius speaks of the provision made by Nature for different species in different habitats:

Sed dat cuique natura quod convenit et ne, dum manere possunt, intereant, elaborat.[24]

[But nature gives to each what is fitting for it, and labours to prevent their dying for as long as they can endure.]

Nature is also said to be concerned for the propagation of plants and trees: 'Iam vero quanta est naturae diligentia, ut cuncta semine multiplicato propagentur' [Again, how great indeed is nature's care, that all things should be propagated by the multiplication of seeds].[25] She is involved too in the processes of human reproduction: it is she who brought Boethius forth from his mother's womb.[26] In this interest in reproduction and concern for the continuation of the species despite the death of individuals, Boethius' Nature clearly foreshadows the Nature figure of later writers in the tradition.

Nature's concern for life is explicitly registered as good, being in effect a concern for unity and therefore goodness. However, the discussion of the natural instinct for self-preservation which all creatures have reveals the possibility that natural impulse might incline to action questionable on moral grounds:

nam ne in animalibus quidem manendi amor ex animae voluntatibus, verum ex naturae principiis venit. Nam saepe mortem cogentibus causis quam natura reformidat voluntas amplectitur, contraque illud quo solo mortalium rerum durat diuturnitas gignendi opus, quod natura semper appetit, interdum coercet voluntas. Adeo haec sui caritas non ex animali motione sed ex naturali intentione procedit. Dedit enim providentia creatis a se rebus hanc vel maximam manendi causam ut quoad possunt naturaliter manere desiderent; quare nihil est quod ullo modo queas dubitare cuncta quae sunt appetere naturaliter constantiam permanendi, devitare perniciem.[27]

[For not even in living things does the love of survival proceed from acts of will of the soul, but from principles of nature. For often for compelling reasons the will embraces death, which nature fears and avoids, and on the

---

[23] *CP* 3. p. 11 27 ff.   [24] *CP* 3. p. 11 60–2.   [25] *CP* 3. p. 11 69 f.
[26] *CP* 2. p. 2 9.   [27] *CP* 3. p. 11 89–102.

other hand, though nature always desires it, the will sometimes restrains that act of generation by which alone the perpetuation of mortal things is assured. So this love of self proceeds not from a motion of the soul but from a natural inclination; for providence has given to her creatures this most important cause of enduring, that by their nature they desire to endure so far as they can. Therefore there is nothing that in any way could make you doubt that all things that are seek naturally the continuance of their own survival, and avoid destruction.]

We can think of the kind of circumstances which might make it morally incumbent not to allow expression to natural instincts: one might be right to choose death rather than to flee it at the cost of virtue, and the urge to reproduce will certainly have to be held in check if orthodox moral demands are to be met. In this area of sex we have already found the natural presenting difficulties, and we shall do so again—rather more obviously, in fact. But it is worth noting that even here, where the concern is to celebrate the goodness of the natural, certain problems associated with nature as instinct demand at least a degree of attention.

THE TWELFTH CENTURY

The *De consolatione Philosophiae* is a major influence on writers on nature in the twelfth century,[28] but the fact that even so great an authority as Boethius has things to say about nature and deploys a personified Nature is clearly not sufficient to explain the importance which the Nature figure assumes in the literature of the period; we need to pay attention to the general cultural climate.[29] As part of what has been styled the Twelfth-Century Renaissance there emerged what might be called a more scientific attitude to the natural world. M.-D. Chenu writes as follows of the vision of the natural world in the Middle Ages prior to the twelfth century:

[28] See n. 6.
[29] On this see, e.g., C. H. Haskins, *The Renaissance of the Twelfth Century* (Cambridge, Mass., 1927); M. Clagett, G. Post, and R. Reynolds, *Twelfth Century Europe and the Foundations of Modern Society* (Madison, 1961); R. W. Southern, *Medieval Humanism and Other Studies* (Oxford, 1970); M.-D. Chenu, *Nature, Man, and Society in the Twelfth Century*, ed. and trans. Jerome Taylor and Lester K. Little (Chicago, 1966).

The diffuse Christian spirituality hitherto dominated by the Augustinian view of the universe had seen the omnipotence of God revealed as plainly by the buds of spring as by the flowering of Aaron's rod, as much by the squeezing of wine from grapes as by the miracle of Cana, as much by the daily birth of infants as by the raising of a dead man to life. This constricting religiosity, undervaluing secondary causes, had operated within a symbolic vision of the world which tended to let slip the explanation of phenomena by reference to immediate causes and to stress the meaning such phenomena might acquire *sub specie aeternitatis*.[30]

Tullio Gregory takes a similar view of the pre-twelfth-century attitude towards the natural world, which he characterizes as 'allegorico-symbolique':

chaque phénomène physique est étudié surtout pour sa signification d'ordre spirituel ou moral; alors on renvoie directement du phénomène non pas à la *causarum series* physique mais directement à des enseignements que les phénomènes peuvent donner.[31]

Physical phenomena were of interest for the symbolic or moral teachings they might offer rather than as a nexus of physical cause and effect, and it is these teachings and the interpretation of the allegory of creation, rather than the system of secondary causation, with which treatises *De natura rerum* before the twelfth century are primarily concerned.[32]

What happens in the twelfth century might be characterized as the emancipation of nature from the realm of the sacred: the study of

---

[30] Chenu, *Nature*, 41 f. See also Tullio Gregory, 'L'idea di natura nella filosofia medievale prima dell'ingresso della fisica di Aristotele: ll secolo XII', in *La filosofia della natura nel medioevo*, Atti del Terzo Congresso Internazionale di Filosofia Medievale (Milan, 1966), 27–65 (36 f.) and Tullio Gregory, 'La Nouvelle Idée de Nature et de savoir scientifique au XIIe siècle', in J. E. Murdoch and E. D. Sylla (eds.), *The Cultural Context of Medieval Learning*, Boston Studies in the Philosophy of Science 26 (Dordrecht, 1975), 212 f. In *Nature, Miracle and Sin: A Study of St. Augustine's Conception of the Natural Order* (London, 1916), 27, T. A. Lacey remarks that Augustine 'tended not to personify nature as a worker, since he saw in nature nothing but the direct work of God'.

[31] Gregory, 'Nouvelle Idée', 213. [Each physical phenomenon is studied above all for its spiritual or moral significance; thus direct reference is made back from the phenomenon not to the physical *sequence of causes* but directly to whatever teachings the phenomena are able to give.] Contrast, however, Lynn Thorndike's view in *A History of Magic and Experimental Science*, 8 vols. (New York, 1923–58), i. 501–3 that 'medieval men... studied nature from scientific curiosity and not in a search for spiritual allegories'.

[32] See Gregory, 'L'idea', 31, and Gregory, 'Nouvelle Idée', 193.

the natural realm shakes itself free, in some measure at least, from theology.[33] A demarcation is established between the direct creativity of God and that which operates through secondary causes.[34] Accordingly, William of Conches held that God's direct creative action was limited to the creation of the elements and the human soul.[35] The marking off of God's creative activity from that residing in secondary causes permits the exploration of how the system of those causes operates and allows Nature to be seen in certain ways. Gregory puts it as follows:

n'étant plus conçue comme une simple *voluntas Dei* ou comme *sacramentum salutaris allegoriae*, mais comme *vis genitiva*, *ignis artifex*, *causarum series*, *qualitas planetarum*, *regula mundi*, elle devenait l'objet d'une *ratio naturalis* que la culture du haut moyen âge avait ignorée, et qui était destinée à conditionner tout discours philosophique ou théologique.[36]

---

[33] This is not to say that the world could no longer be regarded symbolically. Chenu, *Nature*, 114–15, 117 and Gregory, 'L'Idea', 27–9, both cite Hugh of St Victor and Alan of Lille to demonstrate a 12th-century symbolist mentality existing alongside the new 'naturalism'. The works to which they refer are Hugh's *De tribus diebus*, in which the idea that the world is a book written by God is to be found (see *PL* 176, 814b), and the *Rhythmus alter* of Alan, which begins as follows: 'Omnis mundi creatura, | Quasi liber, et pictura | Nobis est, et speculum. | Nostrae vitae, nostrae mortis, | Nostri status, nostrae sortis | Fidele signaculum' (*PL* 210, 579; 1–6). [The whole wordly creation is as it were a book, a picture, a mirror for us; a trustworthy sign regarding our life, our death, our condition, our fate.] See also Wetherbee's distinction (*Platonism*, e.g. 4–5, 16–18, 57–65) between 12th-century 'symbolism' and 'rationalism', two emphases in intellectual discourse which he finds converging in writers such as Bernardus Silvestris and Alan of Lille.

[34] This is worked out in terms of a distinction between God's operations *in constitutione mundi* and Nature's ensuing creativity in Peter Abelard's *Expositio in hexameron* (*PL* 178, 746).

[35] Gregory cites William's *De philosophia mundi*, 1. 23 (*PL* 172, 55 f.). See Gregory, 'Nouvelle Idée', 195 (also 213). These creative activities of God apart, the organization of the world was, for William, in the charge of secondary causes and in particular the stars. Their movement created life and even the bodies of Adam and Eve.

[36] Gregory, 'Nouvelle Idée', 195 [being no longer conceived as a simple *will of God* or as *a sacrament of saving allegory* but as *a birth-giving power, artificing fire, sequence of causes, character of the planets, rule of the world,* [nature] became the object of a *natural reason* of which the culture of the High Middle Ages had been unaware, and which was destined to condition all philosophical and theological discourse]. For the terms see Peter Damian, *De bono religiosi status* (*PL* 145, 771), *sacramentum salutaris allegoriae*; John of Salisbury, *Metalogicus* 1. 8 (*PL* 199, 835C), *vis genitiva*; Hugh of St. Victor, *Didascalicon* 1. 10, *ignis artifex*; John of Salisbury, *Entheticus* 607 (*PL* 199, 978), *causarum series*; the anonymous *Liber Hermetis Mercurii Triplicis de VI rerum principiis*, ed. T. Silverstein, AHDLMA 22 (Paris, 1955), 282, *qualitas planetarum*; Alan of Lille, *De planctu Naturae*, 7. 8, *regula mundi* (for edition see n. 72). See also Gregory, 'L'idea', 42.

The object of an examination of the natural world was not the recovery of significations of sacred import, but achieving an understanding of the 'legitima causa et ratio'[37] of the natural event:

dans la mentalité qui se forme au XIIe siècle, on cherche à dégager cette *causarum series* du contexte symbolique... et... à pouvoir constituer une physique pour expliquer la connexion des causes. C'est la première fois qu'on va reconnaître aux causes physiques une consistance vraiment autonome, toujours à l'intérieur, évidemment, d'une idée de la nature comme créature.[38]

So, for example, Thierry of Chartres writes a *Hexemeron*, dealing with the process of creation at the beginning of the world, which specifically excludes allegorical and moral readings and seeks to interpret Genesis 'secundum physicam et ad litteram'.

De septem diebus et sex operum distinctionibus primam Geneseos partem secundum physicam et ad litteram ego expositurus,... ad sensum litterae historialem exponendum veniam, ut et allegoricam et moralem lectionem, quae sancti expositores aperte executi sunt, ex toto praetermittam.[39]

[I am going to expound the first part of Genesis, about the seven days and the divisions between the six works, in relation to physics and the literal sense.... I shall proceed to the exposition of the historical literal sense, so I shall completely leave aside both the allegorical and moral readings, which holy expositors have lucidly accomplished.]

In the *Hexemeron* Thierry sees fire with its *virtus*, *calor*, as the active agent in the creation of the world subsequent upon God's creation of the elements.[40] Twelfth-century writers took up the Stoic idea of

[37] R. Klibansky, 'The School of Chartres', in Clagett, Post and Reynolds, *Twelfth Century Europe*, 6, cites John of Salisbury, *Entheticus* 607–14 (*PL* 199, 978) for the search for the *ratio* of all things.

[38] Gregory, 'Nouvelle Idée', 213 [the attitude of mind which comes into being in the 12th century seeks to disengage this *sequence of causes* from the symbolic context... and... to be able to arrive at a physics to explain the causal connections. It is the first time that a truly autonomous consistency in physical causes will be recognized, always, of course, within the concept of nature as creature].

[39] Thierry of Chartres, *De sex dierum operibus*, ed. N. Häring, AHDLMA 22 (Paris, 1955), 184–200 (184), cited by Tullio Gregory, *Anima mundi* (Florence, 1955), 182 n. 2 and Gregory, 'L'idea', 42).

[40] *De sex dierum operibus*, 186–90. See Gregory, *Anima mundi*, 182–3 and 'L'idea', 44.

Nature as *ignis artifex*, the principle of movement and life both in the heavens and on the earth.[41] In the *Didascalicon* of Hugh of St Victor we find Nature in a procreative role—a role of great significance in writings of the period—defined as *ignis artifex*:

Natura est ignis artifex ex quadam vi procedens in res sensibiles procreandas. physici namque dicunt, omnia ex calore et humore procreari.[42]

[nature is an artificing fire proceeding from a certain force to the procreation of sensible things. For physicists say that everything is procreated out of heat and moisture.]

The influence of heavenly motions is for some writers the foundation of the system of secondary causation and sometimes Nature herself is identified with planetary influence.[43] Thus she is the *qualitas planetarum* through which the divine *dispositio* is realized in the *Liber Hermetis Mercurii Triplicis de VI rerum principiis*,[44] whilst for Bernardus Silvestris the heavens constitute *natura elementans*:

Est igitur elementans Natura celum stelleque signifero pervagantes, quod elementa conveniant ad ingenitas actiones.[45]

[This elementing nature, then, is in fact the firmament, and those stars which traverse the circle of the Zodiac, for it is these that summon together the elements to their natural activity.]

Or again, Herman of Carinthia identifies the *anima mundi* of the Platonic tradition with the Nature of the Stoics.[46] In all these transformations Nature remains the force by which things come to be and by which the physical universe is governed.

---

[41] See Gregory, 'Nouvelle Idée', 200 and 'L'idea', 44. For the Stoics see Cicero, *De natura deorum*, ed. A. S. Pease (Cambridge, Mass., 1955–8), 2. 57 and the editor's citations at this point.

[42] *Didascalicon* 1. 10. The translation given here is that of Jerome Taylor (New York, 1961).

[43] See Gregory, 'L'idea', 48–50, Gregory, 'Nouvelle Idée', 203. See also John of Salisbury, *Entheticus*, 1059–61 (*PL* 199, 988).

[44] *Liber Hermetis*, 282, cited by Gregory, 'L'idea', 49–50.

[45] *Cosmographia* 1. 4. 7. See Wetherbee, *Platonism*, 154 n. 131 and Peter Dronke's edition of the *Cosmographia* (Leiden, 1978), 8.

[46] Hermann of Carinthia, *De essentiis*, ed. M. Alonso (Comillas, 1946), 48, 51–2, 89–92 (cited by Gregory, 'Nouvelle Idée', 201). Tullio Gregory, *Platonismo medievale* (Rome, 1958), 122–50, describes a process of assimilation of the concept of the *anima mundi* to that of Nature.

The new respect for Nature also makes itself apparent outside the sphere of cosmology. A naturalistic exegesis of Scripture develops. Hugh of St Victor reacted against over-hasty allegorization of Scripture, insisting that a full understanding of the letter, the literal sense, of Scripture, an understanding opened up by study of the liberal arts, was essential before the *sensus allegoricus* could be unfolded.[47] Andrew of St Victor was clear that one should only have recourse to miracle in the exposition of Scripture when all the possibilities of natural explanation have been exhausted.[48] Andrew played a central role in naturalistic exegesis, which in Chenu's words 'demands that history too and not merely nature, be taken at face value and read literally'.[49] Chenu also speaks of 'the elaboration, side by side with supernatural morality, of a secular moral science based on the natural'.[50] Allied developments include a secularizing tendency in regard to history and to the moral education of rulers: in both cases the biblical is no longer entirely constraining and pagan Classical sources come to be used. The apostolic movement out of which the orders of the Friars emerged can be seen as intimately bound up with a new and positive attitude to the world in which humanity finds itself: the monastic model of the spiritual life in which the world is shut out and a spiritual oasis cultivated behind the walls of the monastery is challenged by the idea that an engagement with the world should be made so that the world in all its parts can be made perfect. The whole world is capable of being formed to the service of God—there is no irreducible element of the profane.[51] The natural is a proper object of loving attention.

---

[47] See Beryl Smalley, *The Study of the Bible in the Middle Ages* (Oxford, 1952), 99–102, 106 and Wetherbee, *Platonism*, 49.

[48] See Smalley, *Bible*, ch. 4, esp. 144 and 388 f.; also Chenu, *Nature*, 17.

[49] Chenu, *Nature*, 17.

[50] Ibid. 27. See also ibid. 233 for the high valuation of pagan ethics. For Godfrey of St Victor's esteem of Seneca in moral matters see above, Ch. 1 n. 30. On the debt of 12th-century thinkers to the Stoics see Michael Lapidge, 'The Stoic Inheritance', in Dronke (ed.), *History*, 81–112.

[51] The preceding paragraph draws extensively on Chenu, *Nature*. The optimism about the natural which Chenu detects in the culture of the period may not always be expressed unequivocally in the texts considered in this chapter; see Winthrop Wetherbee, 'Philosophy, Cosmology, and the Twelfth-Century Renaissance', in Dronke (ed.), *History*, 21–53, especially 46 ff.

BERNARDUS SILVESTRIS AND THE *COSMOGRAPHIA*

Returning to the narrower perspective of the literary tradition and to cosmology, we find a personified Nature[52] a central figure in Bernardus Silvestris' *Cosmographia*.[53] This work, an allegorical cosmogony in two parts much indebted to Neoplatonic categories, describes creation.[54] The first part, the *Megacosmos*, describes how the world is made by the imposition of form on formless matter. The second, the *Microcosmos*, tells of the creation of human beings. Nature's goodness is apparent from the outset. At the beginning of the first book Nature laments the formlessness of matter[55] and begs Noys, the providence and reason of God, and in Bernardus' allegory Nature's own mother,[56] to make the world more beautiful by imposing order upon it. Nature here appears as an intermediary between earth and heaven, between the material and the immaterial, in a fashion reminiscent of other platonizing schemes.[57] She desires order, but unlike Boethius' Nature is not represented as herself responsible for the order of the cosmos. This order proceeds from the fashioning of primordial matter according to the pattern of the divine ideas (which are beyond Nature's control) and this is the work of Noys.[58] Noys also generates the world-soul, Endelichia.[59] Her role and that of Nature are summarized in the account of the creative operations of the various powers at the end of book I:

Sicut enim divine voluntatis semper est pregnans, sic exemplis eternarum quas gestat imaginum Noys Endelichiam, Endelichia Naturam, Natura Imarmenen quid mundo debeat informavit. Substantiam animis

---

[52] On the development of the figure of Nature and her moral role see Gregory, *Platonismo*, 122–50.

[53] Quotations from the *Cosmographia* are taken from the edition by Dronke and translations (with some adaptation) from Winthrop Wetherbee, *The Cosmographia of Bernardus Silvestris* (New York, 1973). Little is known for certain about Bernardus' life and work; it seems likely that he studied and taught at Tours and Chartres. The *Cosmographia* seems to have been in existence by 1147. See further Wetherbee, *Cosmographia*, 20 ff.

[54] On the macrocosm/microcosm idea see the references given by Wetherbee, *Cosmographia*, 130 n.10.

[55] *Cosm.* I. I.   [56] *Cosm.* I.2. I.   [57] See above, n. I.

[58] *Cosm.* I.2. 7 f.

[59] *Cosm.* I.2. 13. On Endelichia see Peter Dronke, *Fabula: Explorations into the Uses of Myth in Medieval Platonism* (Leiden, 1974), 109–18.

Endelichia subministrat; habitaculum anime, corpus, artifex Natura de initiorum materiis et qualitate conponit. Imarmene,[60] que continuatio temporis est, et ad ordinem constituta, disponit, texit et retexit que conplectitur universa.[61]

[For as Noys is forever pregnant of the divine will, she in turn informs Endelichia with the images she conceives of the eternal patterns, Endelichia impresses them upon Nature, and Nature imparts to Imarmene what the well-being of the universe demands. Endelichia supplies the substance of souls, and Nature is the artisan who compounds bodies, the dwelling places of souls, out of the qualities and materials of the elements. Imarmene, who stands for temporal continuity, in its aspect as a principle of order, disposes, joins together, and rejoins the universe of things thus comprised.]

In the second book Nature is enlisted by Noys in the task of creating human beings.[62] Noys recognizes that to accomplish this is beyond the unaided capacities of Nature:

Humane quidem sementem anime, et in anima iubar vivacitatis eterne vel facere vel fundare, utrumque subtilitati mee singulare perspitio, quia id operis et tuam, Natura, prudentiam et cuius velis numinis facultatem sicut estimatione ponderis, sic auctoritate maiestatis excedit.[63]

[Yet I recognize that the generation of the human soul, and the creation or instillation in this soul of the radiance of eternal vitality, are both tasks particularly demanding of my keenness. For it is a task beyond your own understanding, Nature, and the faculties of any power you might muster, either to assess the soul's value or to express its majesty.]

Again the theme of the limitation of Nature's capacities appears: it is to be a significant one in the tradition. She has a specific and limited role in the creation of the human being as we learn when Noys speaks of the task of creation:

Trina igitur tribus superincunbit opera, cuique sua. Compositio anime: ex Endelichia, et virtutum edificatione; corporis, ex materie preparatione; utrorumque corporis et anime formativa concrecio, de celestis ordinis

---

[60] On Imarmene see R. B. Woolsey, 'Bernard Silvester and the Hermetic Asclepius', *Traditio*, 7 (1949), 340–4 and Wetherbee, *Platonism*, 39, 156 n. 149. Dronke, *Cosmographia*, understands Imarmene as Destiny (see his note on *Megacosmos* 4. 14).

[61] *Cosm.* 1. 4. 14. On these lines see Dronke, *Cosmographia*, 167.

[62] *Cosm.* 2. 3. 2.

[63] *Cosm.* 2. 3. 3.

emulatione. Prior igitur ad Uraniam, secunda ad Physim, tertia ad te, o Natura, dinoscitur pertinere.[64]

[This task imposes obligations on the three of you, each their own: the composition of a soul from Endelichia and the edifying power of the virtues; the composition of a body by the conditioning of matter; and the formative uniting of the two, soul and body, through emulation of the order of the heavens. The first task plainly belongs to Urania, the second to Physis, the third, O Nature, to you.]

Distinction of function is not absolute, however. The *liber recorda- tionis* [Book of Memory] with which Noys equips Physis shows, among other things, the *ratio* by which Nature gives varying physical attributes and other characteristics to different kinds of animal.[65] When we recall in addition that in the first book Nature is said to create bodies, the similarity between this kind of creativity on Nature's part and that attributed to Physis will be apparent. In fact, there seems to be some overlap, for in the course of detailing how Physis disposes the parts of the body and the senses and balances the humours within man, Bernardus approves *Nature's* carefulness (*dili- gentia*),[66] and the specific arrangements for procreation are attributed to Nature—fittingly enough, since she is the *mater generationis* [mother of generation]:

> Defluit ad renes, cerebri regione remissus,
>   Sanguis, et albentis spermatis instar habet.
> Format et effingit sollers Natura liquorem,
>   Ut simili genesis ore reducat avos.[67]

[Blood sent forth from the seat of the brain flows down to the loins bearing the image of the shining sperm. Artful Nature moulds and

---

[64] *Cosm.* 2.11.1. Nature has been dispatched by Noys to find Urania and Physis. On Urania, see Wetherbee, *Platonism*, 173 n. 30 and Wetherbee, *Cosmographia*, 42 and for her responsibility for the human soul, which she endows with knowledge of such things as the law of Fate, the mutability of Fortune, the limitations of free will, and the possibility of the recollection of this knowledge while on earth, see *Cosm.* 2. 4. Physis is characterized as a student of *naturalia* and a medical practitioner who is concerned to avert the damage inflicted by mutability through an application of the curative proper- ties of things into which she has the most penetrating insight (see *Cosm.* 2. 9. 6 f.) Physis is found by Nature in the paradisal garden Gramision, a place of generation, which burgeons at Nature's approach, Nature being *mater generationis* (2. 9. 4 ff.). In Alan of Lille's *De planctu Naturae* the motif of the earth flowering at nature's approach is repeated (4. 45 ff.). The tradition stresses Nature's associations with spring and fecundity, though it can also grant her responsibility for all the seasons (see, e.g., *DPN* 8. 47–52).

[65] *Cosm.* 2. 11. 11.   [66] *Cosm.* 2. 13. 8.   [67] *Cosm.* 2. 14. 167–70.

shapes the fluid, that in conceiving it may reproduce the form of ancestors.]

Their names show Nature and Physis to be closely related, and one might feel that in certain respects Physis is an aspect of Nature,[68] Bernardus using both figures to build up a composite picture of Nature's activities. But this connection with Physis, as well as other features, indicates that in Bernardus' conception Nature is profoundly implicated in the material.[69] In the Neoplatonic frame of reference of Bernardus' allegory this involvement with the material might have been morally compromising,[70] and we shall find instances later in the tradition where such involvement does seem to be bound up with a moral dubiousness in Nature. Bernardus, however, makes Nature a principle, though a subordinate principle, of right order in the cosmos, who has connections and important dealings with the realm of the spirit and whose aspirations and performance are entirely in tune with the divine.[71]

---

[68] Wetherbee views Physis as representing the *artifex* aspect of Nature (*Cosmographia*, 156 n. 148). On the relationship between Physis and Natura see Brian Stock, *Myth and Science in the Twelfth Century* (Princeton, 1972), 193–7. See also n. 64 above.

[69] The emphasis of Physis' *liber recordationis* is on the material (see *Cosm.* 2. 11. 11). Nature's implication in temporality and mutability is evident in the *tabula fati* [Table of Fate] which Noys gives her. The *tabula* is said to be 'non ... aliud ... quam eorum que geruntur series, decretis fatalibus circumscripta' ['nothing else but the sequence of those things which come to pass by the decrees of fate'] and in which 'naturalia et que temporis sunt porrectiore spacio tenebantur' ['natural events and those taking place in time were contained ... in extensive array'] and the 'longa longis hystoriis fatorum series' ['long chain of fate and history'] following on from the first human being is shown (see *Cosm.* 2. 11. 8 f.). Urania is given the *speculum providencie* [Mirror of Providence] in which to view the divine ideas (2. 11. 4 ff.: the *speculum* is identified as the *mens eterna* [eternal mind]). From this the *tabula* of Nature differs by the mutability in time of what it chiefly displays.

[70] Bernardus is clear about a tendency to evil in Silva (primordial matter) which even Noys's efforts do not seem entirely to remove. See *Cosm.* 1. 2. 2; 1. 2. 8.

[71] Wetherbee draws attention to Bernardus' projection of the problems that beset Nature's ambitions. Generation involves human beings with 'the mindless forces of earthly nature' (*Platonism*, 184 and see 182 ff.). Elsewhere ('Philosophy', 48), Wetherbee writes of the 'murkiness of life as viewed from the existential vantage-point of Bernardus' Nature and Physis'. Responsibility for what is less than ideal does not, however, seem to be laid at Nature's door.

ALAN OF LILLE: *DE PLANCTU NATURAE*

The *Cosmographia* influenced two works by Alan of Lille, the *De planctu Naturae* and the *Anticlaudianus*.[72] The *Anticlaudianus*, the later work,[73] is perhaps the closer of the two in its conception of Nature to the *Cosmographia*. In the *De planctu*, as generally in the post-Bernardan Nature tradition, Nature remains subordinate to God,[74] but she nevertheless has power in areas outside the jurisdiction of Nature in the *Cosmographia* and the *Anticlaudianus*. In particular, the Nature of the *De planctu* is responsible for endowing man with reason.[75]

In the *De planctu* Nature appears to the poet in a vision to lament how human beings have perversely fallen away from the behaviour proper and natural to them. Nature explains her God-given agency in the functioning of the universe and how it is that humanity has come to flout her rule. At the end of the work she summons Genius,[76] her priest, a power of generation, to anathematize all who fail to obey her laws.

---

[72] References to the *De planctu Naturae* are to the edition by N. Häring in *Studi medievali*, 19 (1978), 797–879, those to the *Anticlaudianus* to the edition by R. Bossuat, Textes Philosophiques du Moyen Âge 1 (Paris, 1955). The translations given (with occasional alterations) are from those by James J. Sheridan, *Anticlaudianus* (Toronto, 1973) and *The Plaint of Nature* (Toronto, 1980). Alan was born between 1114 and 1120 and died at Cîteaux in 1202. He taught at Paris and in the Midi (at Montpellier and perhaps Le Puy). Alan was an original theologian who wrote extensively in a variety of fields. For discussion of Alan, besides the works by Gregory and Wetherbee cited above, see G. Raynaud de Lage, *Alain de Lille: poète du XIIe siècle* (Montreal, 1951), G. R. Evans, *Alan of Lille: The Frontiers of Theology in the Later Twelfth Century* (Cambridge, 1983).

[73] Sheridan dates the *Anticlaudianus* to between 1181 and 1184 (25 of his translation) and the *De planctu* to between 1160 and 1165 (*Plaint*, 29).

[74] Here we might note a distinction between Bernardus and his successors and Boethius, for in Boethius there is no real separation between God and Nature. Boethius' position in this respect is alignable with that evident in certain remarks of Aristotle (see n. 2 above).

[75] See *DPN* 6. 36 f. Like the *Cosmographia* (and Boethius' *Consolation of Philosophy*) the *De planctu* alternates sections of prose and poetry. The *Anticlaudianus* is all in verse.

[76] On the figure Genius see E. C. Knowlton, 'Genius as an Allegorical Figure', *Modern Language Notes*, 39 (1924), 89–95; C. S. Lewis, *Studies in Medieval and Renaissance Literature* (Cambridge, 1966), 169–74; Jane Chance Nitzsche, *The Genius Figure in Antiquity and the Middle Ages* (New York, 1975); Denise N. Baker, 'The Priesthood of Genius: A Study of the Medieval Tradition', *Speculum*, 51 (1976), 277–91.

The dignity and authority possessed by Nature in the *De planctu Naturae* is apparent in the following passage which presents some of the most important characteristics of the figure:

> O dei proles genetrixque rerum,
> Vinculum mundi stabilisque nexus,
> Gemma terrenis, speculum caducis,
>   Lucifer orbis.
> Pax amor uirtus regimen potestas
> Ordo lex finis uia dux origo
> Vita lux splendor species figura
>   Regula mundi.
> Que, tuis mundum moderans habenis,
> Cuncta concordi stabilita nodo
> Nectis et pacis glutino maritas
>   Celica terris.
> Que, Noys puras recolens ideas,
> Singulas rerum species monetas,
> Rem togans forma clamidemque forme
>   Pollice formans.[77]

[O child of God, mother of creation, bond of the universe and its stable link, bright gem for those on earth, mirror for mortals, light-bearer of the world: peace, love, virtue, guide, power, order, law, end, way, leader, source, life, light, splendour, beauty, form, rule of the world: you, who by your reins guide the universe, unite all things in a stable and harmonious bond and wed heaven to earth in a union of peace; who, working on the pure ideas of Noys, mould the species of all created things, clothing matter with form and fashioning a mantle of form with your thumb.]

---

[77] *DPN* 7. 1–16. This passage has a Boethian pedigree; see *CP* 3. m. 2. In *Latin Poetic Irony* Marc Pelen argues that Boethius is invoked in *DPN* for ironic ends. Alan's Dreamer 'looks for substitutes in Nature and Genius for the sublime religious teaching of Lady Philosophy' (96) and is foolish in so doing since all that Nature can offer is naturalistic teaching, when what is required for the healing of moral disorder in the world is, as Boethius' *Consolation* has shown, religious faith beyond human reason (90). Whilst there are questions to be asked about Alan's Nature—questions which Alan himself may be raising—I think Pelen's irony thesis leads him severely to underestimate the seriousness of Nature's concern with morality in general and the value of what she has to say on moral matters. Although she is certainly much concerned about illegitimate sex, Nature is surely also genuinely concerned about the whole range of sin; and whilst it seems to be true that she is ineffectual in the face of human sinning, this does not mean that her views on what ought to be are mistaken, or that her intentions are invalid. If human beings were to follow the law of Nature, which is the law of reason in *DPN*, they would be in harmony with God's purposes.

In her creativity, Nature is, in a characterization that will recur in the tradition, *vicaria Dei*, God's deputy.[78] This shows that she carries forward God's purposes, though, as she herself recognizes, her creativity is inferior in various respects to that of God. The passage culminates in a contrast between Nature's activity and the re-creation, the rebirth of human beings accomplished by God according to Christian soteriology.[79] However, Nature has her appointed, and highly important, creative function, which is to secure the continuation of species following their initial creation by God:[80]

> Sed postquam uniuersalis artifex uniuersa suarum naturarum uultibus inuestiuit omniaque sibi inuicem legitimis proportionum connubiis maritauit, uolens ut nascendi occidendique mutue relationis circuitu per instabilitatem stabilitas, per finem infinitas, per temporalitatem eternitas, rebus occiduis donaretur rerumque series seriata reciprocatione nascendi iugiter texeretur, statuit ut expresse conformationis monetata sigillo sub deriuate propagationis calle legitimo ex similibus similia ducerentur.
>
> Me igitur tanquam pro-deam, tanquam sui uicariam, rerum generibus sigillandis monetariam destinauit ut ego, in propriis incudibus rerum effigies conmonetans, ab incudis forma formatum deuiare non sinerem sed mei operante sollertia ab exemplaris uultu, nullarum naturarum dotibus defraudata exemplati facies diriuaret.[81]

[When the artisan of the universe had clothed all things in the outward aspect befitting their natures and had wed them to one another in the relationship of lawful marriage, it was His will that by a mutually related circle of birth and death, transitory things should be given stability by instability, endlessness by endings, eternity by temporariness and that the series of things should ever be knit by successive renewals of birth. He decreed that by the lawful path of derivation by propagation, like things, sealed with the stamp of manifest resemblance, should be produced from like.

Accordingly he appointed me as his substitute, his vice-regent, the mistress of his mint, to put the stamp on the different classes of things so that I should mould the images of things, each on its own anvil, not allow the product to deviate from the form proper to its anvil but that, by my

---

[78] DPN 8. 224.

[79] DPN 6. 128–48.

[80] Nature is concerned that the species should continue in the *De consolatione Philosophiae*. See above, at n. 25.

[81] DPN 8. 217–28.

diligence in work, the face of the copy should spring from the countenance of the exemplar and not be defrauded of any of its natural gifts.]

But Nature is not simply an agent of reproduction. As the abstract nouns defining her in the first passage from the *De planctu* quoted above suggest, she also has moral force: Alan combines in the one figure both physical and moral scope and thus endows Nature with enormous power and authority.[82] There is a moral dimension to Nature's creation of human beings. She has, on the advice of Reason, constituted humans both sensual and rational, an arrangement which involves them in moral struggle:

Rationis enim motus, ab ortu celestium oriens, occasum pertransiens terrenorum, considerando regiratur in celum. Econtrario uero, sensualitatis motus planetici contra rationis firmamentum in terrestrium occidens oblicando labuntur. Hec mentem humanam in uiciorum occasum deducit ut occidat. Hec in orientem uirtutum ut oriatur inuitat. Ista hominem in bestiam degenerando transmutat. Illa hominem in deum potentialiter transfigurat. Hec contemplationis lumine mentis noctem illuminat. Hec concupiscentie nocte mentis lumen eliminat. Ista hominem facit disputare cum angelis. Illa eundem cogit debachari cum brutis. Ista in exilio docet hominem patriam inuenire. Illa in patria cogit hominem exulare. Nec in hac re hominis natura mee dispensationis potest ordinem accusare.

De rationis enim consilio tale contradictionis duellum inter hos pugiles ordinaui, ut, si in hac disputatione ad redargutionem sensualitatem ratio poterit inclinare, antecedens uictoria premii consequente non careat. Premia enim uictoriis comparata ceteris muneribus pulcrius elucescunt.[83]

[For the movement of reason, springing from a heavenly origin, escaping the destruction of things on earth, in its process of thought turns back again to the heavens. On the other hand, the movements of sensuality, going planet-like in opposition to the fixed sky of reason, with twisted course slip down to the destruction of earthly things. The latter, then, draws man's mind down to the destruction arising from vice so that he may fall, the former invites him to come to the source of virtue so that he may rise; the one, corrupting man, changes him into a beast, the other has the power to transform man into a god; one illuminates the dark light of the mind with the light of contemplation, the other removes the light of the mind by the dark night of concupiscence; one enables man to hold converse with angels, the other drives him to wanton with brute beasts; one shows the

---

[82] On this see Gregory, *Platonismo*, 122–50 and Wetherbee, 'Philosophy', 50
[83] *DPN* 6. 55–69.

man in exile how to get back to his fatherland, the other forces the one in his fatherland to go into exile. Nor in this matter can the blame for man's nature be laid on my order and arrangement. It was on reason's advice that I arranged such antagonism and war between these contestants, so that if reason could in this debate turn sensuality into an object of ridicule, the first reward of victory would not be without subsequent ones.[84] For rewards obtained from victories shine more fair than all other gifts.]

We saw in Chapter 1 that it was possible to consider the *sensualitas*, the generic, animal side of the human being, as what determined the law of Nature. Here such a way of thinking is not in question; though Nature endows man with the *sensualitas*, she repudiates its operations in man and intends that so shall man himself. Her law is here implicitly defined as the operation of what is contrary to the motions of the *sensualitas*.[85] Nature in the *De planctu* very clearly takes her stand on the side of Reason; she is a Nature tailored to C. S. Lewis's cut, her blueprint for man, the *animal rationale*, involving the dominance within him of the *ratio*.[86]

Nature's alignment with reason is further emphasized by the fact that she designs man in the way she does precisely on the advice of Reason. This indicates that the arrangements she has made are proper ones, as she claims; yet in spite of this self-vindication—indeed, because of it—we perhaps here catch sight of an apprehension recurrent in the Nature tradition that what is imposed on man by Nature, given him in his very nature, may be morally prejudicial. The tradition frequently raises questions as to whether Nature's immense power over human beings is benignly exercised. Even with the *De planctu*, though one may take Nature's remarks just cited as evidence of her benign intentions, one might feel that what she says raises, and is not sufficient entirely to allay, doubts about the natural dispensation. We shall return to this point.

However, what we might call the official line of the *De planctu* points the moral finger elsewhere than at Nature. The frustration of her purposes for man is figured by a tear in Nature's tunic at the point where the proper activity of mankind is imaged:

[84] Sheridan's translation here may be incorrect. Perhaps better, 'so that if . . . victory going before as antecedent should not be without reward as the consequent'.

[85] On the negative moral inflexion of the term in some medieval theological writing see Payer, *Bridling*, 51.

[86] See above, Ch. 2 at n. 71.

In huius uestis parte primaria homo, sensualitatis deponens segniciem, directa ratiocinationis aurigatione, celi penetrabat archana. In qua parte tunica, suarum partium passa dissidium, suarum iniuriarum contumelias demonstrabat.[87]

[On the first section of this garment, man, divesting himself of the indolence of sensuality, tried to run a straight course through the secrets of the heavens with reason as a charioteer. In this section the tunic had suffered a rending of its parts and showed the effects of injuries and insults.]

This is the only part of the garment damaged, since all creatures other than humans behave as Nature would have them.[88] This general indictment of humanity is given more specific detail in the course of the work. Man, Nature tells us, 'nature naturalia denaturare pertemptans, in me soloecistice Veneris armat iniuriam'[89] [tries to denature the natural things of nature and arms a lawless and solecistic Venus to fight against me], for sexual unnaturalness is the first object of Nature's complaint against human beings (as, indeed, it had been the author's first theme and the ostensible motivation of the whole work[90]). The charge continues:

Solus homo, mee modulationis citharam aspernatus, sub delirantis Orphei lira delirat. Humanum namque genus, a sua generositate degenerans, in constructione generum barbarizans, Venereas regulas inuertendo nimis irregulari utitur metaplasmo.[91]

[Man alone turns with scorn from the modulated strains of my cithern and runs deranged to the note of mad Orpheus' lyre. For the human race, fallen from its high estate, adopts a highly irregular (grammatical) change when it inverts the rules of Venus by introducing barbarisms in its arrangement of genders.]

In the myth of the *De planctu* this decadent state of affairs is ultimately laid at Venus' door, being the result of Venus' rebellion from Nature. Nature has appointed Venus as *subvicaria* to assist her in her reproductive task:

Venerem in fabrili scientia conpertam meeque operationis subuicariam in mundiali suburbio collocaui, ut ipsa sub mee preceptionis arbitrio, Ymenei

---

[87] DPN 2. 232–5.   [88] See DPN 2. 235–8.   [89] DPN 8. 20 f.
[90] DPN 1. 1 ff.
[91] DPN 8. 54–7. Orpheus' turn to pederasty is mentioned by Ovid in *Metamorphoses* 10.

coniugis filiique Cupidinis industria suffragante, in terrestrium animalium
uaria effigiatione desudans, fabriles malleos suis regulariter adaptans incudibus, humani generis seriem indefessa continuatione contexeret, ne Par-
carum manibus intercisa discidii iniurias sustineret.[92]

[I stationed Venus, learned in the artisan's skill, on the outskirts of the
Universe to be the subdelegate in charge of my work that she, under my
will and command, with the active aid of Hymenaeus, her spouse, and
Desire, her son, might exert herself in the reproduction of the varied
animal-life of earth and, fitting her artisan's hammer to its anvil according
to rule, might tirelessly maintain an unbroken linkage in the chain of the
human race lest it be severed by the hands of the Fates and suffer damage by
being broken apart.]

Nature instructs Venus in the correct grammar of sexual relations, a
grammar determined, at least in part, by the requirement that sex
should aim at procreation.[93] For a while Venus diligently performs
her reproductive function, battling against the inroads made into
the human species by death. But then she becomes bored, and,
wanting an easy life, turns to idleness and over-indulgence, and
commits adultery with Antigenius.[94] The adultery with Antigenius
signifies Venus' turning away from her task of procreation, Genius,
Nature's priest and 'her other self', being a power presiding
over reproduction.[95] We are told that Venus 'malleos ab incu-
dum exheredans consortio adulterinis dampnauit incudibus'[96]
['dispossessed the hammers of fellowship with their anvils and
sentenced them to counterfeit anvils'], what is at issue being that
non-inseminative sexual activity standardly understood as *contra
naturam*.[97.]

---

[92] DPN 8. 240–6.
[93] See DPN 10. 35 ff.
[94] DPN 10. 118–36. Some manuscripts have 'Antigamus' rather than 'Antigenius'.
The adulterous Venus might well be understood as anti-marriage, but to have her
connected with Antigenius would figure her turning sex away from its proper end of
reproduction (Genius being a power of reproduction). This sin, which can of course
occur within marriage, would seem to be more fundamental than opposition to
marriage in the moral universe of *DPN* and so 'Antigenius' is the more satisfactory
reading in terms of the inner logic of *DPN*.
[95] DPN 16. 175 (Genius Nature's priest), 16. 187 f. (Genius Nature's other self).
Genius is also, apparently, Nature's son (18. 94 f.). Genius' reproductive efforts are
detailed at *DPN* 18. 64 ff.
[96] DPN 10. 135–6.
[97] See above, Ch. 1 n. 110.

Nature stands for moderation and restraint in sexual behaviour[98] as well as inseminative orthodoxy. It is temperance that prevents the influence of Cupido[99] over human beings from being disastrous. Nature indicates how disasters can occur[100] but it seems that their occurrence is not an inevitable consequence of the nature of Cupido. Having detected the narrator's interest in Cupido, Nature first develops an extravagantly extended series of paradoxes in description of him,[101] but then returns to less elevated prose to vindicate his basic nature:

Non enim originalem Cupidinis naturam inhonestatis redarguo, si circumscribatur frenis modestie, si habenis temperantie castigetur, si non genuine excursionis limites deputatos euadat uel in nimium tumorem ipsius calor ebulliat, sed si eius scintilla in flammam euaserit uel ipsius fonticulus in torrentem excreuerit, excrementi luxuries amputationis falcem expostulat, exuberationis tumor solatium medicamenti desiderat, quoniam omnis excessus temperate mediocritatis incessum disturbat et habundantie morbidantis inflatio quasi in quedam apostemata uiciorum exuberat.[102]

[I bring no charge of dishonourable conduct against the basic nature of Desire, if it restrains itself within the bridle of moderation,[103] checks itself with the reins of temperance, avoids over-stepping the assigned bounds of its natural ambit or allowing its ardour to boil forth in excessive passion, but only if its tiny flame turns into a conflagration, if its little fountain grows into a torrent, if its luxurious growth calls for the pruning-hook to shorten it, if its excessive swelling needs treatment to heal it. For every excess interferes with the progress that comes from the temperateness of the mean and distention from unhealthy surfeit swells and causes what we may call ulcers of vice.]

---

[98] The Stoic idea that life according to nature was a life of moderation in respect of bodily appetite fed the Nature tradition here. See Lapidge, 'Stoic Inheritance', 96 f.

[99] DPN 9 begins by describing *amor* and moves on to detail the effects of Cupido. Alan does not seem to wish to keep the two distinct, as representing distinguishable things. Sexual desire is what is in question. (By the end of this *metrum* Alan is speaking of Venus in reference to sexual desire.)

[100] In DPN 9 after unfolding the paradoxical nature and effects of love, Nature (37 ff.) mentions a number of mythical women whom love caused to commit crimes.

[101] DPN 9. 1–18.

[102] DPN 10. 8–16. We might note here the traditional teaching that the excessively ardent lover of his own wife was an adulterer. See e.g. Brundage, *Law*, 90 f., where Jerome, *Adversus Jovinianum* 1. 49 (*PL* 23, 281) is cited.

[103] Perhaps better 'modesty'.

Here the use of the idea of moderation makes room within an orthodox moral scheme for a natural impulse—Nature acknowledges that Cupido is related to her[104]—which is recognized as potentially troublesome to the ambition to lead the moral life. Her setting of limits through the appeal to moderation also tends to prevent Nature from being compromised by association with the moral problematicness of the sexual urge. That Nature makes these remarks on Cupido implies, in fact, that what is truly natural is for the natural sexual impulse to express itself in a restrained manner.[105] We may then conclude that fully natural sexual behaviour is not over-passionate, occurs within marriage (Alan tells us that Cupido is the legitimate son of Venus and Hymenaeus, the god of marriage[106]), and aims at, or is at least open to, procreation (as we have seen, Venus' revolt from Nature involves the desertion of Hymenaeus for Antigenius, which implies a contempt for the procreative purpose of marriage).[107]

Her lament of sexual depravity and her espousal of reasonableness in sexual behaviour demonstrate Nature's high moral standing, but

[104] *DPN* 10. 4 f.

[105] We are, I think, dealing with post-lapsarian sexuality even with the *originalis natura* of Cupido. The primary function of Nature, the continuation of the species, and with that the role of sexuality in general, in *DPN* is predicated on the (post-lapsarian) reality of death. So the *originalis natura* of Cupido cannot, it would seem, be prelapsarian sexuality. In fact, Cupido is likely to be in close relation with concupiscence, which comes into being, at least according to standard Augustinian accounts, with the Fall. *Concupiscentia* is seen as bad at *DPN* 6. 61 f.; on the complexity of Augustine's views see Payer, *Bridling*, 54–6. I am not sure that Wetherbee is right (*Platonism*, 196) to suppose that *DPN* 9 is about what Cupido has become rather than his *originalis natura*; I suspect that Alan sees the kind of irrationality *DPN* 9 documents as intrinsic to the nature of Cupido as sexual desire, but that this is acceptable when circumscribed by temperance.

[106] *DPN* 10. 149–56.

[107] Piehler, *Visionary Landscape*, 68, thinks that Nature urges a flight from Venus, which would seem to suggest that sexual activity in general is in a sense unnatural; and since Venus now behaves in ways contrary to what Nature wishes, the sexuality over which she presides could indeed be understood as at least in some degree unnatural. However, what Nature actually says is that if one wishes to avoid the chaos which submission to love involves, one must flee it (*DPN* 9. 67–72). This suggests that celibacy might be a sensible option, but does not constitute an instruction from Nature to avoid sexual love, on which love, morally problematic though it may be, the procreation with which Nature has been charged by God after all depends. But it may be that Alan has not fully reconciled a feeling that Venusian sexuality must be condemned with a desire to approve sexual reproduction as natural and part of God's current dispensation.

this is further enforced by the fact that sexual depravity is not all that Nature laments.[108] She moves on to condemn sin of all kinds. As earlier she complained that man abandons reason and follows *sensualitas*, now, lamenting the domination of virtue by vice,[109] she accuses man of abandoning his proper condition for that of an animal:

> Esse pudicum
> Iam cunctis pudor est absque pudore
> Humanos hominis exuit usus
> Non humanus homo. Degener ergo
> Bruti degeneres induit actus
> Se sic exhominans exhominandus.[110]

[To have a sense of shame is now a shame in every eye. Without shame, a man, no longer manlike, puts aside the practices of man. Degenerate, then, he adopts the degenerate way of an irrational animal. Thus he unmans himself and deserves to be unmanned.]

The unnaturalness of sin in general is strongly suggested in this talk of man abandoning his humanity (which is after all his nature) and being man no more. The following passage makes explicit reference to nature:

> Vides enim qualiter homines originalis nature honestatem bestialibus illecebris inhonestant, humanitatis priuilegialem exeuntes naturam, in bestias morum degeneratione transmigrant.[111]

[For you see how men dishonour the dignity of their original nature by succumbing to bestial allurements, and abandoning a nature with the privilege of humanity, cross over to join the beasts by degeneration in their morals.]

This passage comes from a letter Nature writes to Genius when she summons him to excommunicate the vicious.[112] In this she acts as representative of the Virtues, Chastity, Temperance, Generosity, and Humility, who, oppressed by vice, have gathered around

---

[108] It has been argued that the sexual sin against which Nature rails is a synecdoche for sin in general. See Marc-René Jung, 'Jean de Meun et l'allégorie', *Cahiers de l'Association Internationale des Études Françaises*, 28 (1976), 21–36 (32).

[109] *DPN* 11. 1–4.

[110] *DPN* 11. 43–8.

[111] *DPN* 16. 197–9.

[112] *DPN* 16. 187–213.

Nature.[113] This allegorical tableau demonstrates how in the *De planctu Naturae* Alan ranges the natural on the side of the right. Nature has her limitations: we have seen how she defers to the superior creativity of God and acknowledges how the rebirth effected by Grace is beyond her capacities, whilst in her address to the Virtues before she writes to Genius Nature confesses that she has only limited ability to restrain vice.[114] But that her efforts are directed towards the good and that her intentions are in harmony with reason is clear.

The limitations of Nature, however, are not the only difficulty. The Nature tradition will make much of the relationship between the divinities of love, Venus and Cupido, and Nature. In the *De planctu* Nature sets a distance between herself and the Venus who has rebelled against her and she draws a line between legitimate and unacceptable behaviour by Cupido, condemning the latter. She thus places the responsibility for human sexual misbehaviour on shoulders other than her own. Later writers will suggest that this clean separation between a morally correct Nature and a morally problematic Venus and Cupid perhaps ought not to be made, and will thus intimate that Nature herself is implicated in the moral unsatisfactoriness of human sexuality. Even in the *De planctu* there may be some implicit criticism of Nature; Nature, after all, arranges the system that goes wrong. We are perhaps invited to find questionable Nature's appointment of Venus as her subvicar because this appointment is made with a view to Nature's own comfort, her desire to escape the disquietudes of the the realm she is supposed to superintend.[115] The initiation of the system in a kind of selfishness may, in fact, despite Alan's mythic presentation of an originally satisfactory sexual system, be a metaphorical way of pointing to a radical moral unsatisfactoriness in human sexuality, to the impossibility of conceptualizing sex as we know it as wholly good.[116] That

---

[113] *DPN* 16. 43–154.   [114] *DPN* 16. 171 f.

[115] See *DPN* 8. 235 ff. Perhaps a contrast is implied here with the activity of Christ in the Incarnation: Christ is prepared to be immersed in the unsatisfactorinesses of the earthly and so (unlike Nature) is able to save humanity. One should note that Nature says that she will put the finishing touches to what Venus produces (*DPN* 10. 21–4).

[116] This would, of course, be in line with an understanding widely diffused in the Middle Ages that all sexual expression, even when legitimate, was in some degree morally compromised (see, e.g., Payer, *Bridling*, 18 f., 50–60). Note too how the product of the legitimate union between Venus and Hymenaeus is Cupido, whose nature at least tends towards—but I suspect inevitably involves—a disruption of human reason.

Nature in any case remains engaged in a now corrupt system is indicated when Genius, who stands in the closest possible relation to her, is depicted as drawing (an image for generation) figures not only representing the proper channels of human activity (these with his right hand), but also (these with his left) those representing the deformed and the debased: Thersites, Paris, Sinon, Ennius, and Pacuvius.[117] Here we see that the activity of generation which is at the centre of Nature's purpose gives rise to what is bad as well as what is good. And then the Cupido whose *originalis natura* causes Nature no problems (though it appears not to be utterly satisfactory) now tends to operate beyond the boundaries of temperance—and yet this malfunctioning cannot annul the consanguinity between Cupido and Nature.[118] Again, the rebellion of Venus suggests her deep corruption, and though Genius makes reference to legitimate sexual behaviour over which Venus presides,[119] behaviour which we may understand will carry forward Nature's reproductive purposes, we are entitled to ask questions about the complicity of Nature with this corrupt figure whose commitment to procreation is much less than absolute. In fact, though Nature may seek to place blame elsewhere, she is bound in to the moral unsatisfactoriness of process and result in which human generation is now involved, and, as we have seen, there are reasons for doubting that the sexual system which she initiated could ever be wholly satisfactory and so for doubting that Nature could ever be the blameless, if limited, figure she apparently takes herself to be.

ALAN OF LILLE: *ANTICLAUDIANUS*

The *Anticlaudianus*, so called because where the Latin poet Claudian's *Against Rufinus* depicts the wholly evil man, Alan's work

---

[117] DPN 18. 81–91.

[118] DPN 10. 4 f. Cupido is paralled by Iocus, the illegitimate offspring of Venus and Antigenius, but it is not clear that this debased Iocus embraces all kinds of problematic sexual behaviour. There would seem to be difficulties even with the marital and procreative sex which the legitimate Cupido seems to represent. See n. 105 above.

[119] He condemns the person who 'legitimum Veneris obliquat incessum' [blocks the lawful path of Venus (perhaps better: deflects the lawful advance of Venus)] at *DPN* 18. 146 and goes on to say 'Qui a regula Veneris exceptionem facit anomalam, Veneris priuetur sigillo' [Let him who makes an irregular exception to the rule of Venus be deprived of the seal of Venus] (18. 151 f.).

presents the completely good man, is an epic poem in nine books. Nature decides to remedy the defects in her creation by making a perfect man. Because Nature is unable to create souls, she sends Prudentia to ask God to create the soul for this new creature. Much of the poem is made up of a description of Prudentia's journey to heaven, which constitutes an allegory of the mind's ascent to God. God grants Prudentia's petition, she returns to the earth, and the so-called New Man is brought into being. He leads the forces of good in a battle between the Virtues and the Vices, the defeat of the latter in which brings in a new Golden Age.

In the *Anticlaudianus* Alan presents a Nature figure with many similarities to Nature in the *De planctu*. Nature is again *regula mundi*:

> Singula decernens sensu Natura profundo,
> Sedibus hiis sua iura tenet legesque figurat
> Prouida, quas toto sparsim promulgat in orbe.[120]

[Nature, who decrees every single thing with profound wisdom, has her own ordinances for these abodes and with far-seeing eye shapes the laws which she promulgates throughout the wide world.]

And she also again operates in subordination to God:

> Diuinum creat ex nichilo, Natura caduca
> Procreat ex aliquo; Deus imperat, illa ministrat;
> Hic regit, illa facit; hic instruit, illa docetur.[121]

[The Divine creates from nothing. Nature makes mortal things from some material; God commands, she serves; He directs, she acts; He instructs, she accepts instruction.]

In fact, the work is concerned to emphasize Nature's limitations. Nature is, as in the *De planctu*, by intention very much on the side of the good—this is evident, for instance, in her being sister to the virtues.[122] Nevertheless, and despite her power over creation, Nature finds that her work is flawed and determines that she and her sisters should set about making the perfect man:

> nichil invenio quod in omni parte beate
> Viuat, quin multas nobis deferre querelas
> Possit, si hanc nostram uelit accusare Mineruam. . . .
> Hoc in mente diu scriptum mihi sedit, ut omnes

---

[120] *Ant.* 1. 187–9.   [121] *Ant.* 2. 72–4.   [122] See, e.g., *Ant.* 1. 18 ff.

Et simul instanter, caute, solerter ad unum
Desudemus opus, in quo tot munera fundat
Quelibet, ut post has dotes uideatur egere,
Nostrorum crimen operum redimatur in uno,
Vnius probitas multorum crimina penset.[123]

[I find no living thing that is perfect in every way and could not bring many complaints against us, should it choose to attack our art. . . . Long has this idea lain impressed upon my mind that all of us together, with zeal, care and skill, should exert ourselves on one work: that each should pour on it so many gifts that, when these gifts are given, she may seem herself to be in need: that the faults of our work be redeemed in one work: that the perfection of that one work make up for the faults of many.]

But the imperfection of Nature's work seems to figure the necessity of supernatural, divine action if creation is to be set to rights. For it becomes apparent that the remedy cannot be provided by Nature's efforts. Prudentia,[124] while supporting her sister's initiative, points out the difficulty:

Incudem nostram corpus mortale fatetur,
Artifices nostros et nostram postulat artem.
Artifices alios anime natale requirit,
Artificis melioris opem celestis origo
Postulat et nostram fugit eius forma monetam,
Diuinique loquens operis miracula, nostrum
Spernit opus, ridens artis uulgaria nostre.[125]

[The mortal body recognizes our anvil, calls for our artisans and our art; the birth of a soul demands other artisans: a heavenly origin demands the aid of a higher artisan and its form is beyond our mint. Showing the wonders of a divine product, it spurns our work and it smiles at the ordinariness of our art.]

Ratio, another of Nature's sisters, endorses this view:

Corpus ad esse suum uocat artis regule nostre;
Excipit hanc hominis animam, que semper ab istis
Legibus excipitur, meliori pollice ducta.[126]

[123] *Ant.* 1. 216–18, 228–33.
[124] On Prudentia (otherwise Phronesis) see Sheridan, *Anticlaudianus,* 35 f. and Wetherbee, *Platonism,* 211–18.
[125] *Ant.* 1. 372–8.
[126] *Ant.* 2. 62–4.

[Our customary art brings man's body into being: it does not extend to the soul of man which is ever exempted from these laws of yours and is fashioned by a higher hand.]

So a human soul has to be sought from heaven. Prudentia is deputed to present prayers to God in heaven that he should favour the sisters' plan with the soul they need.[127] Prudentia is brought on her way heavenwards by Ratio,[128] and when Ratio, confronted by divine mysteries impenetrable to human reason, fails, by Theologia, and then later by Fides [Faith].[129] In heaven Prudentia is given the soul of the New Man[130] which is brought back to earth[131] and united by Concordia to a body made for it by Nature:

> Postquam materiem Nature dextra beauit
> Vultibus humanis, animam Concordia carni
> Federat et stabili connectit dissona nexu.[132]

[After Nature's right hand enriched the material with human features, Concord joins soul to flesh and unites discordants by a stable bond.]

As compared with her role in the creation of man in the *Cosmographia* this represents something of a demotion for Nature, a stricter binding to the material. And whilst in the *De planctu* Nature claims responsibility for the arrangement of man's whole nature, for the relationship between reason and sensuality, in the *Anticlaudianus* this would seem to be beyond her range. Nevertheless, Nature's restriction to the material in the making of the New Man does not mean she lacks moral scope. It is she, after all, who initiates the project of creating the New Man (rather as Natura in the *Cosmographia* initiates the formation of the cosmos), and she who sends the New Man to fight against Allecto and the Vices.[133] The eventual victory of the New Man and the Virtues is registered as a triumph for Nature:

> Pugna cadit, cedit iuueni Victoria, surgit
> Virtus, succumbit Vicium, Natura triumphat,
> Regnat Amor, nusquam Discordia, Fedus ubique.[134]

---

[127] See the speeches of Ratio and Concordia in the first part of book 2 and Prudentia's speech at *Ant.* 5. 178–242.

[128] *Ant.* 4. 213 ff.   [129] *Ant.* 5. 243–64; 6. 185 ff.   [130] *Ant.* 6. 428–65.

[131] *Ant.* 6. 466–88.   [132] *Ant.* 7. 56–8.   [133] *Ant.* 8. 198–201, 336 f.

[134] *Ant.* 9. 384–6.

[The battle ceases, Victory falls to the New man. Virtue rises, Vice sinks, Nature triumphs, Love rules, nowhere is there Disagreement, but Agreement everywhere.]

Honestas has, in fact, commended to the New Man the following of Nature in a way which closely approximates the natural and the virtuous. She counsels him:

> Vt uicium fugiat, Naturam diligat, illud
> Quod facinus perperit damnans, quod praua uoluntas
> Edidit, amplectens quicquid Natura creauit;
> Non homines sed monstra[135] cauens et crimina uitans.[136]

[To flee vice, love Nature, condemning what villainy has spawned or an evil will has brought forth and embracing whatever Nature has created, guarding not against men but against monsters and shunning reproach.]

Man's moral capacity may be laid up in his rational soul, but Nature's inability to create the soul does not here distance her from Ratio, the *mensura boni* [measure of good].[137] Prudentia and Ratio implicate themselves and all the other sisters of Nature in Nature's limitation, and Ratio's own limitation in the face of the divine mysteries clearly marks her as in a sense natural, as one not privy to what is penetrable only with the aid of supernatural revelation and faith. In fact, it seems that we should regard her sisters as in some sense aspects of Nature, their endowment of the New Man as a natural endowment.[138] Nature may not make human souls, but certain virtues developed in the soul can be regarded as natural.[139] Alan's insistence on Nature's inability to make the soul is not an attempt to align her with *sensualitas* against Ratio, but a declaration of the transcendence of the divine.[140]

---

[135] It is interesting to note that the *Architrenius* attributes the creation of *monstra* to Nature. See below, n. 145.

[136] *Ant.* 7. 208–11.

[137] *Ant.* 1. 28. Later in the tradition it seems that this limitation to the material does pull Nature away from Reason.

[138] See Raynaud de Lage, *Alain*, 88. The *Summarium* to the *Anticlaudianus* (found in some manuscripts, but not written by Alan) separates the Virtues and Nature. See Bossuat, *Anticlaudianus*, 199.

[139] In his treatise on the Virtues and Vices, ed. O. Lottin, *Medieval Studies*, 12 (1950), 20–56 Alan says all virtues have their beginning [*initium*] in nature.

[140] In the *Roman de la Rose*, as we shall see, Nature's inability to create the rational soul is bound in with her moral dubiety.

The *Anticlaudianus*, then, differs somewhat in its conception of Nature's scope from the *De planctu Naturae*, but Nature is clearly on the side of the right, however limited her power in comparison to the divine. However, the *Anticlaudianus'* view of human sexuality seems more negative than does that of the *De planctu Naturae*. The earlier work presents Venus as originally part of a system which operated satisfactorily—that, at any rate is Nature's view—but in the *Anticlaudianus* there is no hint that she has ever been anything but malign in her influence on human beings.[141] She fights on the side of the Vices and is eventually defeated by the New Man, who achieves his victory, in accordance with the traditional prescription, by fleeing from her.[142] The *De planctu* suggests that, if it can be kept within proper bounds, sexual passion is acceptable, but no such accommodation is made in the *Anticlaudianus*. This may not constitute a repudiation of human sexual behaviour in general—Nature begins the work at her anvil, which presumably, as in the *De planctu*, images sexual activity.[143] Perhaps it may only be to say, traditionally enough, that the highest virtue, as embodied in the New Man, involves sexual abstinence. Yet the question arises, given the viciousness of Venus in the work, as to whether it is possible for human beings to be sexual and sinless. To put it another way, can the work at Nature's anvil be carried out without Venus? The doubts sexuality casts over Nature in the *De planctu* are not far in the background of the *Anticlaudianus*.

Before we leave Alan of Lille it is worth pointing out that his presentations of moral struggle envisage human beings as essentially free agents, working out their own destinies through the exercise of deliberate choice. In the *De planctu* Nature structures humans in such a way as to require of them a decision in favour of their rational side over their sensual side, so that when they act naturally, this will be the result of their choosing the reasonable course of action rather than following the promptings of a spontaneous impulse, a Boethian

---

[141] A distinction between two Venuses was sometimes made in medieval writing (see, e.g., G. D. Economou, 'The Two Venuses and Courtly Love', in Joan M. Ferrante and G. D. Economou (eds.), *In Pursuit of Perfection: Courtly Love in Medieval Literature* (Port Washington, 1975), 17–50). The Venus of the *Anticlaudianus* would seem to be wholly the *Venus scelestis* as opposed to the *Venus caelestis* of this duality.

[142] In *DPN* Nature urges that overcoming Venus requires fleeing from her (9. 67–72).

[143] *Ant.* 1. 8–11.

naturalis intentio. Likewise the perversity of human behaviour is something deliberate. Responsibility for evil is thus made to lie with human beings. Other writers in the Nature tradition, however, will find it possible to present human beings as in the grip of a Nature understood to preside over spontaneous impulsive activity which can sometimes produce evil, and this makes it easy to lay moral blame on a Nature which can be thought of as victimizing human beings.

JOHANNES DE HAUVILLA: *ARCHITRENIUS*

The *Architrenius* of Johannes de Hauvilla describes the journey of its eponymous hero to find Nature, to whose treatment of him he objects, a journey which takes him through such places as the court of Venus, the house of Gluttony and the Schools of Paris (this permitting a satirical review of the later twelfth-century scene). On his journey Architrenius also receives moral instruction from an array of philosophers. The poem ends with his finding Nature, who arranges his marriage with Moderancia, a marriage which will produce the remedy for the unsatisfactoriness Architrenius had detected in his condition.

Architrenius, the Arch-Lamenter, reckons himself a victim of Nature, not because she positively urges him to forbidden activity but because she fails to protect him against vice.[144] It may be that reflection on how the systems over which Alan's Nature figures preside give permission to vice prompted Jean to invert the direction of complaint in the *De planctu* and have his hero complain about Nature, rather than Nature complain about humankind.[145] Nature's

---

[144] *Arch.* 1. 225–33. See below. The edition of the *Architrenius* used here is that of P. G. Schmidt (Munich, 1974). Winthrop Wetherbee, *Architrenius* (Cambridge, 1994), reprints Schmidt's text with his own parallel translation, which (occasionally adjusted) I cite here. Jean was born in 1150 and died betweeen 1208 and 1216. He is associated with Rouen. The *Architrenius* seems to have been completed by 1184. See further the introduction to Wetherbee's translation.

[145] In the *Anticlaudianus*, Nature comments that there is nothing alive which would not be justified in complaining against her (1. 216–18). In the *De planctu* we are assured, as part of the praising of Nature, that she does not create *monstra*; in the *Architrenius*, we are told that Nature *does* create *formas monstrorum* (see below). Here too, perhaps, we can see a reworking of an Alanian detail in which scepticism about the benignity of Nature is allowed some rein. On Johannes' relation to earlier 12th-century works see Wetherbee, *Architrenius*, p. xxv.

creativity and power extend far and wide: she rules over earth and
heaven:

> Illud enim supraque potest nullaque magistras
> Non habet arte manus, nec summa potencia certo
> Fine coartatur: astrorum flammeat orbes,
> Igne rotat celos, discursibus aera rumpit,
> Mollit aque speram, telluris pondera durat,
> Flore coronat humum, gemmas inviscerat undis,
> Phebificans auras, stellis intexit Olimpo.
> Natura est quodcumque vides, incudibus illa
> Fabricat omniparis, quidvis operaria nutu
> Construit, eventusque novi miracula spargit.[146]

[Nature can do all of this and more. There is no art that her hand has not
mastered, and her supreme power knows no limit. She kindles the starry
orbs, makes the heavens revolve by her vital heat, stirs the air with conflicting movements, makes the watery region fluid and hardens the bulk of
the earth. She decks the land with flowers, plants precious gems in the deep,
imbues the air with Phoebus' light and adorns the firmament with stars.

Whatever you behold is Nature; she labours at her all-creating forge,
creates at will whatever she pleases, and spreads abroad a miraculous array of
new products.]

But this power has its disquieting aspects:

> Ipsa potest rerum solitos avertere cursus,
> Enormesque serit monstrorum prodiga formas,
> Gignendique stilum variat, partuque timendo
> Lineat anomalos larvosa puerpera vultus.[147]

[She has power to alter the normal course of events, and prodigally litters
the world with huge and monstrous forms. The style of her conceptions is
ever changing, and the fearful labor of her fantastic fertility gives shape to
abnormal creatures.]

A passage de monstruosis [on strange creatures] follows. This kind of
creativity contrasts with that of the Nature of the De planctu, who is
appointed by God to oversee the production of like from like and to
make sure that individual creatures do indeed represent their proper
species, that the shape of the exemplar is properly stamped upon the
individuals of a given class in a process characterized by regularity
and non-deviance.[148] The Nature of the Architrenius would appear

---

[146] Arch. 1. 234–43.   [147] Arch. 1. 244–7.   [148] DPN 8. 224–8.

to have a capricious streak and in view of this seeming capriciousness
it is not entirely surprising that Architrenius has complained of what
Nature has done for humankind. Architrenius, finding his life without virtue, accuses Nature of having brought him into the world
only to abandon him to vice:

> 'Mene istos' inquit 'in usus
> Enixa est Natura parens, me misit ut arma
> In superos dampnata feram, divumque reatus
> Irritent odium? legesque et iura meique
> Preteream decreta Iovis? viciine potestas
> Mortales eterna premit? facinusne redundat
> Diis invisa palus? mater quid pignora tante
> Destituit labi nec, quem produxit, alumpno
> Excubat, ut nullis maculam scelus inspuat actis?'[149]

['For such purposes as these did mother Nature give me birth?' he asks.
'Has she sent me forth to wage impious war against the gods, that my guilty
acts may arouse their hatred? Am I to ignore laws and statutes decreed by
Jove? Does sin have power to oppress human life eternally? Is our guilt like
some boundless swamp, hateful to the gods? Why has my mother abandoned her charge to such peril? Why does she not keep watch over the
child she has borne, so that his actions may remain untainted by guilt?']

Architrenius details instances of Nature's remarkable and unusual
provision for certain races and individuals[150] and contrasts this with
what he sees as her neglect of him.

> me pestiferis aliis exponit inhermen
> Anguibus et tortis viciorum deteror idris.
> Non michi pacifico nudum latus asperat ense,
> Non Calibum plumis lorice recia nodat,
> Non surgente caput animosum casside cristat,
> Non clipei telis obtendit menia: nec, quos
> Det Natura, timent scelerum Stimphalides arcus,
> Nec furtim lesura nefas deterret harundo.[151]

[Nature has left me unarmed amid poisonous vipers of another kind,[152] for
I am ensnared by the twisting hydra of my vices. She has not armed my
body with the menace of a sword which might pacify them, nor bound my
plumed corselet with a mesh of steel, crowned my head nobly with a lofty

---

[149] *Arch.* 1. 225–33.   [150] *Arch.* 1. 248–311.   [151] *Arch.* 1. 312–19.
[152] The contrast is with the snakes which cannot injure the austerity-hardened
Psyllus (*Arch.* 1. 308–11).

helmet, nor offered me the protection of a shield. Those whom Nature so favors do not fear the Stymphalian darts of sin, and the arrows of sinfulness that wound by stealth do not dismay them.]

Architrenius accordingly decides that he must go through the world in search of Nature in the hope of regaining her favour.

> Quid faciam novi: profugo Natura per orbem
> Est querenda michi. veniam, quacumque remotos
> Abscondat secreta lares, odiique latentes
> Eliciam causas et rupti forsan amoris
> Restituam nodos.[153]

[I know what to do: I must seek out Nature by roaming the world. I will discover that far-off place, wherever it be, where she dwells in secret, bring to light the hidden causes of her hostility, and perhaps repair the broken bond of love.]

But he seems to be wrong about Nature. In the body of the poem, the provisions of Nature and her demands are frequently invoked as guides to consumption.[154] In sexual matters Nature is said to shun homosexuality.[155] It is clear from this, despite Architrenius' criticism, that Nature does offer moral guidance. When Nature finally appears in the poem, what she says seems to disarm Architrenius' criticism. Having eventually found Nature, the hero delivers his complaint.[156] He asks 'Compaterisne tuam seclerum, Natura, flagellis | Affligi subolem' [And can you, Nature, allow your offspring to be tormented by the scourge of wrong],[157] but Nature denies that she is unmotherly, claiming rather that in her *bonitas*, which she associates with God, she has behaved with great generosity towards humanity.

> Nec matris feritas est illa, nec illa
> Fellificor taxo. semper tibi sedula grates
> Et meritum perdo; gratamque, ingrate, bonorum
> Indulsi saciem, misero felicia fudi
> Non merito, donumque tenes donoque teneris.
> Sollicitis hominem studiis limavit et orbem
> Officiosa dedit, cumulato larga favore

---

[153] *Arch.* 1. 320–4.
[154] *Arch.* 2. 180 f.; 2. 325 f.; 2. 357 f.; 2. 476–80; 6. 257–60; 6. 266–9; 6. 335–8; 7. 169–72.
[155] *Arch.* 7. 70–86.   [156] *Arch.* 9. 156–210.   [157] *Arch.* 9. 178 f.

Nostra Iovi bonitas cognata et cognita. numquam
Plenior exhibuit veram dilectio matrem.
Non egresco datis, dare non fastidio, rerum
Continuans partus, nec rumpit dextera fluxum
Muneris incisi, nec dandi rustica donum
Diminuit torpendo manus; sed dona minoris
Credis, ubi dono est plus quam contenta voluntas.
    Oculit ubertas precium, saciesque sapori
Derogat et tenuat accepti copia grates.[158]

[This cruelty is not your mother's, and no such poison embitters me. Though I am ever zealous on your behalf, I gain neither thanks nor reward. I have graced you, ingrate, with an abundance of delightful gifts, and showered happiness on your undeserving wretchedness. All that you possess is my gift to you, and it is through my gift that you are sustained.

Our goodness, closely akin to Jove's, and sanctioned by him, fashioned man with wearisome labor, and in our abundant largesse we willingly bestowed the universe upon him. Never did a more loving act reveal the true mother. And my power to give has not grown feeble, nor am I grudging in my gifts. Constantly bringing new creatures to birth, my hand never interrupts the pouring forth of its bounty, and no laziness or clumsiness in its bestowal diminishes its value. But you consider that an inferior gift by which your wishes are more than fulfilled. Abundance appears of less worth, what is plentiful loses its savor, and a bounteous gift reduces the gratitude of him who receives it.]

Thus Nature vindicates herself. This does not, however, altogether meet the case, for it does not deny what is the ground of Architrenius' complaint, that he is left naturally the prey of vice. Whatever she may feel about the legitimacy of that complaint, Nature recognizes that she can do something in response to it.

At quia sedulitas homini mea servit eique
Fundit opes et opem, meriti secura, malorum
Radicem fodiam, morbos a sedibus imis
Eiciam. paucis—cupias scivisse—docebo.
. . . Iam debita menti
Canicies aderit et maturabitur intus,
Ne viridis putrescat homo, dabiturque petenti
Dulce, quod ad saciem siciens delibet alumpnus,
Quo puer ex animo sordensque infancia cedat.[159]

[158] *Arch.* 9. 213–28.   [159] *Arch.* 9. 229–32, 237–41.

[But since it is my constant care to be of service to man, to shower him with my wealth and succor with no concern for reward, I will dig out the root of these evils, cast out the disease from your innermost being, and offer a brief lesson; take pains to understand what I say . . . Now your mind will assume the white-haired gravity that befits it, and grow inwardly mature, rather than rotting while still green. To him who seeks it a sweetness will be granted which the eager nursling may taste until satisfied, and which will clear your mind of immaturity and the decayed remains of childishness.]

The means of achieving this is to give Moderancia to Architrenius in marriage:

> longo Moderancia nobis
> Cognita convictu, rerum cautissima, morum
> Ingenio felix, Virtutis filia, natu
> Nobilis et thalamos meditanti nubilis anno,
> Pulchra—pudica tamen—dabitur tibi, sacra ligabo
> Federa, que nulla caveas diffibulet etas.
> Ipsa quidem vicii pravos exosa susurros,
> Haut immunda pati poterit consorcia, semper
> Expavit tetigisse picem. contagia toto
> Pectore declines, alioquin vincula rumpet
> Coniugii, passum maculas non passa maritum.[160]

[Moderation, well known to me from long intimacy, most prudent in all things and blessed with a keen moral sense. As the daughter of Virtue, she is of noble birth and of an age to consider the marriage-bed. Beautiful yet chaste, she will be yours, and I myself will tie the sacred knot which, you may be sure, no length of time will undo. For she so detests the lewd whisperings of vice that she will never consent to any impure relations; she has ever shuddered at the thought of touching pitch. Steer clear of taint with your whole heart, lest otherwise she should break the bonds of marriage, not suffering a husband who suffers from defilements.]

These two passages suggest that in the attempt to follow Nature lies the route to virtue and that to follow Nature is essentially to behave with moderation, the fruits of which, right action, will no doubt be brought forth in Architrenius' marriage.[161] The explicit association of Nature and Moderancia has been foreshadowed in earlier remarks

---

[160] *Arch.* 9. 291–301.
[161] This is very much in line with Stoic thinking. See above, n. 98.

on consumption, in which natural requirements are invoked as a moral guide,[162] and this structuring of man's nature indicates that Nature has in fact, despite Architrenius' complaint, made certain provisions for man's moral well-being. We might perhaps say that Architrenius' initial complaint is uttered out of a consciousness of his fallen condition, now lacking original righteousness; righteousness is not thrust upon fallen humanity, not automatic for it, and salvation now has to be worked for, but the behaviour that leads to it is something to which their nature, fallen though it is, inclines human beings. Hence on the one hand the need to search strenuously for Nature and on the other the provision by Nature of the solution to the viciousness of the human condition.

In the recommendation of the marriage between Architrenius and Moderancia moral and procreative concerns on Nature's part mingle. Nature says that Architrenius has an obligation to procreate:

> Sancio nostra virum sterili marcescere ramo
> Et fructum sepelire vetat, prolemque negantes
> Obstruxisse vias. commissi viribus uti
> Seminis et longam generis producere pompam
> Religio nativa iubet, ne degener alnum
> Induat aut platanum, semper virguncula laurus,
> Aut salicem numquam parienti fronde puellam,
> Aut si qua est vacuo folio vel flore pudica.[163]

[Our decree forbids man to wither on the barren bough, bury his talent in the ground, or prevent conception by blocking its channels. Natural religion bids a man exercise the seminal power entrusted to him and give rise to a long procession of offspring, lest he remain ever virgin like the laurel, be reduced to the state of the barren alder, the plane-tree, the maiden willow whose boughs never bear, or any other plant so chaste as to be devoid of leaf or blossom.]

Nature also speaks against sex with prostitutes and adultery, thus hedging about her injunction to procreate with traditional moral directives.[164] Nature, we may take it, stands opposed to illegitimate sexual behaviour in general, not just to the perversion of homosexuality. In this she is true to what is implied in her sponsorship of

---

[162] See n. 154 above.   [163] *Arch.* 9. 242–9.   [164] See *Arch.* 9. 250–67.

marriage between Architrenius and Moderancia: she is unequivocally on the side of virtue and reason.[165]

The twelfth-century texts which we have considered in this
chapter offer images of Nature which in some respects differ. The
Architrenius' Nature perhaps has the widest competence and the
greatest moral efficacy, there being no emphasis on her incapacity
in respect of a higher power, and natural and right behaviour on
man's part apparently being within her gift.[166] She and the Nature of
the *De planctu Naturae* appear to be responsible for the endowment
of humanity with its whole nature, whereas the Natures of the
Cosmographia and the *Anticlaudianus* are unable to create the human
soul. Whatever the differences and whatever the limitations some of
the figures display, the Natures in all these works are trying to work
for the good: as agents of creation and procreation, they have their
appointed place in the divine plan; furthermore, the three later
figures explicitly desire virtuous behaviour in the human being.
But this ambition for the good does not deny a problematic aspect
to the natural. The treatment of Nature in the *Architrenius* seems
intended to show that the problems perceived in the natural dispensation are only apparently there,[167] but it is very possible to come
away from the two works of Alan of Lille which we have considered
feeling that they in some way license the reservations we might
entertain about Nature. These reservations do not simply come
down to the fact of Nature's lack of salvific reach in comparison
with the direct activity of the divine through Grace; as well as

[165] There is one point in the text where Nature may be set authoritatively in close
association with what tends towards vice. The philosopher Xenocrates says: 'Est satis ad
vires in nostra pericula dandas | Coniuga Nature mundo concessa libido, | Quantum
prolis amor et sacra iugalia poscunt' (7. 87–9). This Wetherbee translates as follows:
'Suffice it to say of these powers bestowed to our peril, that lust has been granted to the
world as Nature's partner, to perform what the love of offspring and the rites of marriage
require.' I suspect, however, that the true meaning is 'The sexual desire, partner of
Nature, permitted [*or:* the concession of sexual desire, partner of Nature] to the chaste
man to the extent that the love of offspring and the rites of marriage require, is sufficient
for giving us strength against what is dangerous to us.' Our tendency to sexual excess can
be combated effectively by means of the legitimate fulfilment of sexual desire in marital
and procreative sex, a process which is in accord with Nature.

[166] Wetherbee (*Architrenius*, p. xxv f.) thinks the poem essentially ethical and non-
theological in its omission of a sense of the limitation of Nature.

[167] See, however, n. 145 above. The very registering of possible problems in the
Architrenius testifies at least to a sense that concern about Nature's moral status has some
degree of plausible justification.

registering what Nature cannot do, we experience discomfort about the arrangements Nature actually does make. Her associations with the body and sex are already obscuring her moral glory, and the damaging effects of those associations will be allowed greater play as the Nature tradition develops.

CHAPTER FOUR

The *Roman de la Rose*

The Nature figures considered in the previous chapter, whatever their shortcomings, want to endorse and promote that which the texts they inhabit conceive as the highest good. Whether this is the case with the *Roman de la Rose*, however, is far from clear[1]—but then, not a great deal about the moral position of the *Roman* is clear; the famous fifteenth-century debate over the poem is early testimony to the difficulty of arriving at a consensus of judgement about the work, and the difficulty remains.[2] Is the poem a paean to plenitude[3] and are Nature's urgings to procreation therefore to be unreservedly approved, or do these urgings proceed from a Nature vitiated by the Fall who misguidedly seeks to remedy the effects of that catastrophe by a physical rather than a spiritual combat with death; in which case we, properly informed by Christian orthodoxy,

---

[1] Guillaume de Lorris's part of the *Roman* was written *c*.1230, that of Jean de Meun *c*.1270 (though see n. 6 below). The edition of the *Roman* used here is that of Félix Lecoy, 3 vols. (Paris, 1965–70), the translation that of Frances Horgan (Oxford, 1994) with occasional alterations.

Most of the discussion of Nature is found in Jean de Meun's part of the *Roman*. Guillaume, however, does say that Nature established the fountain of Narcissus (1425–38). The fountain is very likely an emblem of the folly of love: see Robertson, *Preface*, 91–5, John V. Fleming, *The Roman de la Rose* (Princeton, 1969), 92–6, 231 f., and Charles Dahlberg's comments in his translation of the *Roman* (Princeton, 1971), 579, 581. (Contrast, however, Erich Köhler, 'Narcisse, la fontaine d'amour et Guillaume de Lorris', *Journal des savants* (1963), 86–103). The question of the relation between Nature and amatory desire becomes a major issue in Jean de Meun's section of the poem.

[2] For the Querelle see *Le Débat sur le Roman de la Rose*, ed. Eric Hicks (Paris, 1977). Some of the texts from the Querelle are considered in the next chapter. Sylvia Huot's *The Romance of the Rose and its Medieval Readers* (Cambridge, 1993) has made it clear that right from the outset the *Roman* generated different responses in its readers. On the reception of the *Roman* in France in the Middle Ages see also Pierre-Yves Badel, *Le Roman de la Rose au XIVe siècle: étude de la réception de l'œuvre* (Geneva, 1980). For an account of critical opinion see Heather M. Arden, *The Romance of the Rose* (Boston, 1987) and her *The Roman de la Rose: An Annotated Bibliography* (New York, 1993).

[3] See Alan F. Gunn, *The Mirror of Love: A Reinterpretation of 'The Romance of the Rose'* (Lubbock, Tex., 1952).

should distance ourselves from the counsels of Nature and her priest Genius?[4] Which of the many voices of the text has authority and in what degree?[5] Or is it improper to seek a hierarchy of authority working to the production of a single, self-consistent message in a text which is at play?[6] Fortunately it is possible to be clear about certain aspects of the Nature figure in the *Roman*, even without resolving some fundamental questions as to how to approach and interpret the work as a whole.[7] This means that, though we are faced with the most perplexing difficulties in relation to the intentions of the original authors of the *Roman* and its 'meaning', it is less difficult to see how the *Roman* would have provided a licence and a stimulus for later writers to reflect on the natural in a particular light and to develop the Nature figure in a particular direction. For the *Roman* makes Nature something radically different from what she is in Alan of Lille.[8]

---

[4] See Fleming, *Roman,* and the same author's *Reason and the Lover* (Princeton, 1984); also Pelen, *Latin Poetic Irony*, 142 f.

[5] Fleming has argued that Reson is the voice of authority. However, Michael D. Cherniss, 'Irony and Authority: The Ending of the *Roman de la Rose*', *MLQ* 36 (1975), 227–38, supposes that because all the figures who claim to know about love in the *Roman* are limited by the secularity of the poem's world, none of them is authoritative (230). In *The Romance of the Rose* (London, 1995), 47, Sarah Kay writes: '[The] poly-phonic character of [Jean de Meun's] *Rose* is one of the principal sources of irony within it: it is hard for the reader to know if any of these conflicting voices possesses the authority to be right, and to put its competitors in the wrong . . . I . . . regard [Jean de Meun's] text as a compilation, or montage, of different subject positions all held in play.'

[6] We should, of course, remember that the text is (probably; but see Roger Drag-onetti, *Le Mirage des sources* (Paris, 1987), 200–25, where it is suggested that the *Roman* is a pseudonymous work by a single author) the work of two authors, though it may be that Jean de Meun has so thoroughly appropriated the work of Guillaume de Lorris that this duality does not imply divided vision in the poem as finally presented by Jean.

[7] Kay, it should be said, sees Nature as the most mobile and elusive figure of Jean's text (*Romance*, 112 f.). I think the desire to proclaim contradiction and disruption within the text leads Kay to exaggerate the instability and elusiveness of Jean de Meun's Nature figure. It seems to me that some of what she offers to demonstrate the self-contra-dictoriness of the figure does not do so, resolution of the supposed contradictions being possible. Further, her claims regarding what the text proposes as 'natural' reach beyond what the text's own nature terminology suggests. However, the different inheritances which shape Jean's Nature figure do impose a certain strain on the coherence and consistency of that figure. We shall find ourselves asking, for instance, whether the high moral stance of Alan of Lille's Nature, to some extent at least transferred to Jean's figure, is really consistent with the latter's major concerns.

[8] On the relationship between the two figures see, e.g., Economou, *Goddess*, Baker, 'Priesthood', and Winthrop Wetherbee, 'The Literal and the Allegorical: Jean de Meun and the *De planctu Naturae*', *Medieval Studies*, 33 (1971), 264–91. The difference between

It is towards the end of the poem that Jean de Meun brings on stage his versions of the Alanian figures Nature and Genius, but before their arrival there has been reference to and discussion of Nature. Reson, reintroduced into the poem at the beginning of Jeun de Meun's section, speaks of a Nature who presides over procreative activity. Having encouraged the Lover to practise a general social love,[9] Reson goes on to contrast to this another kind of love common to beast and man:

> Autre amor naturel i a,
> que Nature es bestes cria,
> par quoi de leur feons chevissent
> et les aletent et norrissent.
> De l'amor don je tiegn ci conte,
> se tu veuz que je t'en raconte
> quels est li defenissemenz,
> c'est naturiex enclinemenz
> de volair garder son semblable
> par entencion convenable,
> soit par voie d'engendreüre,
> ou par cure de norreture.
> A ceste amor sunt presz et prestes
> ausinc li home com les bestes.
> Ceste amor, conbien qu'el profite,
> n'a los ne blame ne merite,
> n'en font n'a blamer n'a loer.
> Nature les i fet voer,
> force leur fet, c'est chose voire,
> n'el n'a seur nul vice victoire;
> mes sanz faille, s'il nel fesoient,
> blasme recevoir en devroient.[10]

Alan's and Jean's Natures was noted in the Querelle by Jean Gerson (see next chapter). It is Alan who is crucial in Jean de Meun's Nature inheritance. For Jean de Meun and Bernardus Silvestris see Wetherbee, *Cosmographia*, 59 f. Wetherbee, *Architrenius*, p. xxviii, suggests that Jean de Meun may not have known the *Architrenius*.

[9] This love involves doing as one would be done by (5421–4), a precept familiar to us as the prime directive of the natural law in some understandings, but not here explicitly linked to Nature or the natural.

[10] *RR* 5733–54. G. Paré, *Les Idées et les lettres au XIIIe siècle* (Montreal, 1947), 92 f. relates the kind of love of which Reson here speaks to the *appetitus naturalis* or *amor naturalis* of the scholastics. One of his supporting quotations (Aquinas, *ST* I. 2 q. 94 a. 2) refers to the Ulpianic definition of the law of nature; for the relation of Jean's Nature to that behind the Ulpianic definition of natural law, see below. One wonders whether

[There is another, natural, kind of love, which Nature created in the animals and that enables them to produce their young, and to suckle and rear them. If you wish me to define for you the love of which I speak, it is a natural and properly motivated inclination to wish to preserve one's likeness, either by engendering or by seeing to rearing. Men and beasts are equally well fitted for this love, which, however profitable it may be, carries with it no praise or blame or merit, and those who love thus deserve neither blame nor praise. In truth, Nature pledges them to it by force, and it does not involve any victory over vice, but if they did not practise it, they would most certainly deserve blame.]

Reson claims that the Lover is not concerned with this kind of love. The Lover's love she regards as a problematic 'maladie de pensee':

> Amors, se bien sui apensee,
> c'est maladie de pensee
> antre .II. persones annexe,
> franches entr'els, de divers sexe,
> venanz a genz par ardeur nee
> de vision desordenee,
> pour acoler et pour besier
> pour els charnelment aesier.
> Amant autre chose n'entant,
> ainz s'art et delite en tant.
> De fruit avoir ne fet il force,
> au deliter sanz plus s'esforce.[11]

[Love, if my judgement is correct, is a mental illness afflicting two persons of opposite sex in close proximity who are both free agents. It comes upon people through a burning desire, born of disordered perception, to embrace and to kiss and to seek carnal gratification. A lover is concerned with nothing else but is filled with this ardent delight. He attaches no importance to procreation, but strives only for pleasure.]

Reson considers this disregard of procreation criminal:

> Sachiez que nus a droit n'i va
> ne n'a pas entencion droite
> qui, sanz plus, delit i couvoite;

Reson here, and Genius later when he enjoins universal procreative endeavour, are guilty of confusing individual and communal obligation. Aquinas argues that procreation is not obligatory for each human individual but for humanity in the aggregate. See *ST* 2. 2 q. 152 a. 2 ad 1and n. 92 below.

[11] *RR* 4347–58.

> car cil qui va delit querant,
> sez tu qu'i se fet? Il se rant
> conme sers et chetis et nices
> au prince de trestouz les vices,
> car c'est de touz maus la racine.[12]

[You should know that no one can love as he ought or with the right intentions if he desires only delight. Do you know what he does, the man who seeks delight? He surrenders, a wretched and foolish slave, to the prince of all the vices, for such behaviour is the root of all evils.]

According to Reson the proper function of sex is, orthodoxly enough, procreative, and it is to ensure procreation that sex has been made pleasurable:

> quar puis que pere et mere faillent,
> Nature veust que li filz saillent
> pour recontinuer ceste euvre,
> si que par l'un l'autre requeuvre.
> Pour ce i mist Nature delit,
> pour ce veust que l'en si delit,
> que cist ovrier ne s'en foïssent
> et que ceste euvre ne haïssent,
> quar maint n'i treroient ja tret,
> se n'iert deliz qui les atret.
> Ainsinc Nature i sotiva.[13]

[For since fathers and mothers pass away, Nature wants their children to spring up to continue this work, so that one is replaced by another.

---

[12] *RR* 4392–9. Reson cites Cicero, *De senectute* (12), in support of this opinion. It was certainly orthodox to suppose that to have sex for pleasure was wrong, even within marriage (See, e.g., Noonan, *Contraception*, 196 ff.), but is the quest for sexual pleasure 'de touz maus la racine'? Are we meant to recall an alternative Pauline opinion (1 Timothy 6: 10) that the love of money is the root of all evils? Perhaps Reson's views are unbalancedly puritanical; certainly she herself will speak (see next quotation) in such a way as to suggest that in making sex pleasurable Nature provides an inducement necessary for securing the good of procreation, and this seems to render the moral issue over sexual pleasure anything but clear-cut. Aquinas attributes the pleasure of sex to 'divina providentia'; see next note. On the moral status of sexual pleasure see, e.g., Noonan, *Contraception*, 193 ff., 292 ff., and Payer, *Bridling*, 30–4.

[13] *RR* 4381–91. Aquinas writes: 'ad excitandum ad actum quo defectui speciei subvenitur, divina providentia delectationem apposuit in actu illo, quae etiam bruta movet, in quibus non est infectio originalis peccati' (*Sent.* 4 d. 31 q. 1 a. 1 ad 1, cited by Noonan, *Contraception*, 293 f.) [in order to stimulate to the act by which provision is made against the species' loss, the divine providence set pleasure in that act, pleasure which also moves the brute animals, in whom there is not present the infection of original sin].

Therefore Nature made the work pleasurable, desiring that it should be so delightful that the workmen should not take to their heels or hate it, for there are many who would never perform this task unless they were attracted by pleasure.

Thus Nature used her ingenuity.]

Reson seems happy enough with this arrangement, but there is a problem over the relation of pleasure to procreation, which the activity of the personifications of the poem exposes, as we shall see later.

We should also note that Reson's discussion of the love which Nature stimulates makes no mention of marriage. Paré goes so far as to comment:

selon Raison la procréation est la seule loi qui régisse l'union charnelle. Il n'est pas question du mariage dans son exposé; elle laisse même entendre que l'union libre n'est qu'une louable obéissance aux lois de nature.[14]

Whether we are exactly given to understand this about free love by Reson is open to question, but her conception of Nature is clearly alignable with that involved in the Ulpianic definition of natural law; the love which Nature stimulates, as the passage at 5733 ff. shows, is something taught to all the animals.[15] If the Ulpianic conception does back Reson's idea of Nature, it would be entirely appropriate and entirely in tune with orthodox scholastic thinking for her not to introduce considerations of marriage, plural sexual relations being standardly acknowledged to be in accordance with this kind of natural law.[16]

The naturalness of plural sexual relations is the burden of what La Vieille, one of the personages who (unlike Reson) tries to further

---

[14] Paré, *Les Idées*, 317 [according to Reson procreation is the only law that should regulate carnal union. There is no question of marriage in her exposition; she even gives it to be understood that free union is simply a praiseworthy obedience to the laws of nature]. However, Huot, *Romance*, 98 thinks we must assume that Reson means sex to occur within marriage. This is the explicit position of the K text's Raison; see Huot, *Romance*, 170.

[15] The statement that the exercise of this kind of love is not subject to praise or blame may remind us of a similar statement in respect of Ulpianic natural law made by William of Auxerre. See above, Ch. 1 at n. 84.

[16] See above, Ch. 1.

the Lover's attempt on the Rose, has to say about Nature.[17] She tells us, for instance, that Nature was not 'si sote' as to make one man for one woman and vice versa: rather she intended everyone to be for everyone else. Law, however, has intervened to disallow the original freedoms:

> D'autre part el sunt franches nees;
> loi les a condicionees,
> qui les oste de leur franchises
> ou Nature les avoit mises;
> car Nature n'est pas si sote
> qu'ele face nestre Marote
> tant seulement por Robichon,
> se l'antandement i fichon,
> ne Robichon por Mariete,
> ne por Agnés ne por Perrete,
> ainz nous a fez, biau filz, n'en doutes,
> toutes por touz et touz por toutes,
> chascune por chascun conmune
> et chascun conmun a chascune.[18]

[Moreover, women are born free; the law has bound them by taking away from them the freedoms Nature had given them. For Nature, if we apply our minds to the question, is not so stupid as to create Marote simply for Robichon, nor Robichon for Mariete or for Agnes or for Perrete; on the contrary, fair son, you may be sure that she has made all women for all men and all men for all women, every woman common to every man and every man to every woman.]

Marriage is evidently, for La Vieille, a restriction imposed by law on natural freedom. But she also says that one of the reasons for marriage is to secure proper care of offspring, a care neglected prior to the institution of marriage.[19] This may give us pause. What Nature teaches all animals includes 'educatio' according to Ulpian (and Isidore), and theologians can argue that monogamy is natural to human beings precisely because it is what is accommodated to the purpose of bringing up children.[20] It may be that we are being

---

[17] The sequence in which La Vieille lays out her position begins at 12351. For the figure of La Vieille Jean de Meun draws on an extensive antifeminist tradition, in which the Ovidian *Vetula* and the writings of Jovinian as recorded by St Augustine are among the seminal texts.

[18] *RR* 13845–58.   [19] *RR* 13859–64; 13883–6.   [20] See above, Ch. 1.

prompted to retort to La Vieille that in sponsoring marriage Law only formally prescribes what is in fact natural for human beings. On the other hand, there is nothing explicit to this effect in the *Roman* and, as we have seen in Chapter 1, the theological writings openly concede that there is a sense of natural law according to which sex outside marriage is in accord with the natural order.

La Vieille's utterances involve a parodying of Boethian discourse about Nature. Various moves are made which have the effect of lowering the dignity natural processes enjoy in the *De consolatione*, as if Jean de Meun is interested in querying the Boethian celebration of the natural. So, for instance, La Vieille seeks to prove a natural inclination in women towards the liberty which marriage in her view removes by adducing the illustration of the caged bird found in the *De consolatione*. This, though well treated in captivity, always desires its freedom.[21] So far, this is sufficiently Boethian, but then La Vieille draws a parallel with women:

> Ausinc sachiez que toutes fames,
> saient damoiseles ou dames,
> de quelconques procession,
> ont naturele entencion[22]
> qu'el cercheroient volentiers
> par quex chemins, par quex sentiers
> a franchise venir porroient,
> car torjorz avoir la vorroient.[23]

[In the same way, I assure you, all women, whether maidens or ladies and whatever their origin, are naturally disposed to search willingly for ways and paths by which they might achieve freedom, for they would always like to have it.]

La Vieille further thinks that those in religious orders feel the pressure of Nature towards 'franchise' and she cites Horace on the recrudescence of Nature to prove her case.[24] She reflects that

---

[21] *CP* 3. m. 2.

[22] Boethius' *naturalis intentio* (see above, Ch. 3) is here parodied.

[23] *RR* 13929–36.

[24] *RR* 13989–96. The reference is to Horace, *Epistles* 1. 10. 24 (ed. O. A. W. Dilke (Letchworth, 1954). Fleming, *Roman*, 180, thinks we are to find La Vieille's citation not valid as support of her views, but one suspects a more equivocal state of affairs. Certainly the citation is used straight and with similar (un-Horatian) reference to sexual instinct by Guillaume Saignet in his treatise against compulsory clerical celibacy, *Lamentacio*

the desire of all creatures to return to their nature, another Boethian topos,[25] constitutes a justification for sexual licence:

> Toute creature
> veust retourner a sa nature,
> ja nou lera por violance
> de force ne de couvenance.
> Ce doit mout Venus escuser
> qu'el vouloit de franchise user,[26]
> et toutes dames qui se geuent,
> conbien que mariage veuent,
> car ce leur fet Nature fere,
> qui les veust a franchise trere.
> Trop est fort chose que Nature,
> el passe neïs nourreture.[27]

[Every creature wants to return to its nature, and will not fail to do so, however violent the pressure of force or convention. This should excuse Venus for wishing to make use of her freedom, and all those ladies who take their pleasure although they are bound in marriage, for it is Nature, drawing them towards their freedom, who makes them do this. Nature is very strong, stronger even than nurture.]

In a lowering transformation of Boethius' 'tame' lion,[28] La Vieille asserts the existence of an ineradicable natural impulse in cats to chase rats and mice. There is a similarly ineradicable impulse in male horses to pursue mares, an impulse which admits no discrimination as to colours.[29] Analogous lack of discrimination operates in human sexual desire, which does not tend to monogamy:

> Et ce que je di de morele
> et de fauvel at de fauvele
> et de liart et de morel,
> di je de vache et de torel
> et des berbiz et du mouton,
> car de ceus mie ne douton

humanae Nature adversus Nicenam constitutionem interdicentem conjugatis sacerdotium (written 1417–18). For this work and details on de Saignet see Nicole Grévy-Pons, *Célibat et Nature* (Paris, 1975). The citation of the Horatian sententia by Saignet's Natura occurs at 143, l. 285.

[25] *CP* 3. m. 2.
[26] Venus was married to Vulcan, but committed adultery with Mars, as La Vieille has just told us (see 13805 ff.).
[27] *RR* 13997–4008.   [28] *RR* 14009 ff. See *CP* 3. m. 2.   [29] *RR* 14031 ff.

qu'il ne veillent leur fames toutes;
ne ja de ce, biau filz, ne doutes
que toutes ausinc touz ne veillent,
toutes volentiers les acueillent.
Ausinc est il, biau filz, par m'ame,
de tout houme et de toute fame
quant a naturel appetit,
don lai les retret un petit.
Un petit? Mes trop, ce me samble;
car quant lai les a mis ensamble,
el veust, soit vallez ou pucele,
que cil ne puisse avoir que cele,
au mains tant con ele soit vive,
ne cele autre, tant con cil vive.
Mes toutevois sunt il tanté
d'user de franche volanté,
car bien sai que tel chose monte;
si s'an gardent aucun por honte,
li autre pot poor de peine,
mes Nature ausinc les demeine
con les bestes que ci deïsmes.[30]

[My remarks about the black mare, the sorrel horse and mare, and the grey and black horse are also true of the cow and the bull and the ewes and the rams. We have no doubt that every male desires every female, nor should you doubt, fair son, that in the same way, every female desires every male and receives him gladly. And where natural appetites are concerned, fair son, upon my soul it is just the same for every man and every woman, though law does restrain them a little. A little? Too much, in my view, for when law has joined a young man and maiden together, it will not allow that young man to have any other maiden, at least during her lifetime, nor will it allow the maiden to have any other young man. Nevertheless, they are all tempted to use their free will, for I know how important this is. Some are restrained by shame, others by fear of punishment, but Nature drives them all, just as she does the beasts that we have been talking about.]

Now La Vieille, of course, is by no means of exemplary moral character and her invocations of the natural are not inspired by the highest moral ideals, but it is not obvious that her understanding of Nature is illegitimate or her appeals to the idea invalid, for all that

---

[30] *RR* 14047–73.

she does not present Nature as a figure of high moral dignity.[31]
Certainly scholastic orthodoxy would want to supplement La
Vieille's account: in the first place, the end of procreation, about
which La Vieille fails to speak, would be mentioned; secondly, a
demonstration that the monogamous sexual behaviour sanctioned
by orthodox morality was required by the total nature of the human
being would be given. But in the light of what the theologians write
in respect of the natural law understood in Ulpianic terms as 'quod
omnia animalia docuit', we might feel that La Vieille is justified in
claiming that there is a natural impulse towards unrestricted sexual
liaison between men and women.[32]

However Nature appears in the remarks of Reson and La Vieille
and whatever academic conceptions ground those remarks, when
she eventually arrives in the poem *in propria persona*, it is apparent
that there is a close relation between her and the Nature of Alan of
Lille's *De planctu Naturae*. So, for instance, Nature tells us that she is
God's deputy, guarding the golden chain which binds the elements
and having under her jurisdiction all that that chain encloses:

> tant m'honora, tant me tint chiere
> qu'il m'an establi chamberiere;
> servir m'i lesse et lessera
> tant con sa volantez sera . . .
> Por chamberiere? certes vaire
> por connetable et por vicaire . . .
>   Si gart, tant m'a Dex honoree,
> la bele chaene doree
> qui les .IIII. elemanz enlace
> tretouz anclins devant ma face;
> et me bailla toutes les choses
> qui sunt en la chaene ancloses,
> et conmanda que ges gardasse

---

[31] This is not to say, to be sure, that La Vieille's argument for unrestricted sexual
behaviour is meant to be taken with complete seriousness, let alone as authorially
sanctioned, but the less obviously unsound her arguments in support of her central
position on free love, the more difficult her position will be for the reader to counter
intellectually. Jean de Meun may well wish to lend plausibility to La Vieille's position, so
as to disrupt orthodox clarities and incite questioning which does not issue easily in
answers; so much the radically differing understandings of the poem proposed from the
beginning of its reception would seem to suggest.

[32] See above, Ch. 1, for opinion on how certain animals do not naturally, according
to the Ulpianic definition, know 'sua'.

> et leur fourmes continuasse,
> et voust que toutes m'obeïssent
> et que mes regles apreïssent
> si que ja mes nes obliassent,
> ainz les tenissent et gardassent
> a tourjorz pardurablement.[33]

[[God] showed me such honour and love that he made me chamberlain of all; he allows and will allow me to serve him there as long as it is his will....As chamberlain? Truly, as constable indeed, and vicar...

God has done me the honour of placing in my keeping the fair golden chain that links the four elements, all of which bow before my face. He also entrusted to me all the things enclosed within the chain, and ordered me to guard them and maintain their forms. He wanted all things to obey me and learn my rules so well that they would never forget them, but would observe and keep them throughout all eternity.]

Genius, as in the *De planctu Naturae* Nature's priest,[34] also affirms Nature's status as God's deputy:

> Nature,
> qui de tout le monde a la cure
> conme vicaire et connestable
> a l'ampereeur pardurable
> qui siet en la tour souveraine
> de la noble cité mondaine
> don il fist Nature ministre,
> qui touz les biens i amenistre
> par l'influance des esteles,
> car tout est ordené par eles
> selonc les droiz anperiaus
> don Nature est officiaus,
> qui toutes choses a fet nestre
> puis que cist mondes vint an estre,
> et leur dona terme ansemant
> de grandeur et d'acroissemant,
> n'onques ne fist riens por noiant
> souz le ciel...[35]

---

[33] *RR* 16741–4, 16751–2, 16755–67.
[34] *RR* 16242 etc. In the *Roman* Genius is specifically Nature's confessor. On the significance of this see below.
[35] *RR* 19475–92. That 'God and Nature do nothing in vain' is an Aristotelian commonplace. Bernardus Silvestris identifies 'elementans Natura' with the influence

[Nature, custodian of the whole world, vicar and constable of the eternal emperor who sits in the sovereign tower of this noble city, the world, and who made Nature its minister, to administer all its riches through the influence of the stars (for everything is ordered by the stars, according to the imperial right exercised by Nature); by her authority who has brought all things to birth since this world began, and likewise given them their allotted time for growth and increase, and who has never made anything that had no purpose beneath the heaven...]

As in the *De planctu Naturae*, Nature is charged with ensuring the continuity of the species; she produces new individuals to replace those who die and thus keeps Death at bay:

> Nature, qui pansoit des choses
> qui sunt desouz le ciel ancloses,
> dedanz sa forge antree etoit,
> ou toute s'antante metoit
> an forgier singulieres pieces
> por continuer les espieces;
> car les pieces les font tant vivre
> que Mort ne les puet aconsivre,
> ja tant ne savra corre aprés.[36]

[Nature, whose thoughts were on the things enclosed beneath the sky, had entered her forge, where she was concentrating all her efforts upon the forging of individual creatures to continue the species. For individuals give such life to species that, however much Death pursues them, she can never catch up with them.]

Now all this is sufficiently Alanian, and in the moral sphere also Nature is capable of voicing sentiments which align her with the Nature of the *De planctu*. So she criticizes rational creatures who fail to follow the guidance of their reason:

---

of the stars. See above, Ch. 3 at n. 45. Lucie Polak, 'Plato, Nature and Jean de Meun', *Reading Medieval Studies*, 3 (1977), 80–103 (88) suggests that the control Nature apparently has over the stars may bring her into conflict with what is good and right, since the tendencies instilled in individuals by the stars sometimes have to be resisted if the good is to be done (*RR* 17029–70). But the provision of that tendency to evil in human beings does not necessarily mean Nature is opposed to the right; we might recall how Nature in the *De planctu Naturae* says she has created man with his reason and sensuality at odds, precisely in order that reason shall overcome the bad tendencies of the sensuality (see above, pp. 87–8).

[36] *RR* 15863–71.

> resonable creature,
> soit mortex hom, soit divins anges,
> qui tuit doivent a Dieu loanges,
> s'el se mesconnoit comme nice,
> cist defauz li vient de son vice,
> qui le sans li trouble et anivre,
> car il pot bien reson ansivre
> et pot de franc voloir user,
> n'est riens qui l'an puisse escuser.[37]

[as for rational creatures, whether mortal men or divine angels, all of whom ought to praise God, if such a creature is so foolish as not to know himself, this failing is the result of his wickedness, which dulls and fuddles his senses, for he is perfectly capable of being guided by reason and of using his own free will, and nothing can excuse him from doing so.]

She later issues a general moral condemnation of humankind:

> Orgueilleus est, murtriers et lierres,
> fel, couvoiteus, avers, trichierres,
> desesperez, gloz, mesdisanz,
> et haïneus et despisanz,
> mescreanz, anvieus, mantierres,
> parjurs, fausaires, fos, vantierres,
> et inconstanz et foloiables,
> ydolatres, desagraables,
> traïstres et faus ypocrites,
> et pareceus et sodomites:
> briefmant tant est chetis et nices
> qu'il est sers a tretouz les vices
> et tretouz an soi les herberge.[38]

---

[37] *RR* 17832–40. See also Nature's insistence, in the context of a discussion of astrological determinism (*RR* 17029 ff.), that reason, if its power is believed in, can stop men and women from following the evil course to which their particular natures (*propre nature*) press them (17057–61).

[38] *RR* 19195–207. Nature refers to humanity's estrangement from her in the lines immediately preceding these. It is possible that this estrangement is expressed in these vices. Towards the end of his Sermon Genius (see *RR* 20607–17) instructs his audience to honour Nature and toil hard (*laborer*) in her service. 'Laborer' may well have exclusive sexual reference, but some moral injunctions not obviously sexual follow (to return what belongs to others, not to kill, to keep hands and mouth clean, to be loyal and merciful), and these may also be meant to be taken as ways of honouring Nature. The matter is complicated further by the fact that similar injunctions occur in the *Ars amatoria* of Ovid where it is suggested that such behaviour will keep on one's side the Jupiter who laughs at the perjuries of lovers (*Ars am.* 1. 633 ff. (ed. J. H. Mozley, Loeb Classical

[Man is a proud, murderous thief, a cruel, covetous, miserly traitor, a desperate, scandalmongering rascal, full of hatred and contempt, suspicion and envy. He is a deceitful, perjured liar, a foolish boaster, an unpredictable madman, an ungrateful idolater, a false and treacherous hypocrite, an idle sodomite. In short, he is such a wretched fool that he is the slave of every vice, and harbours them all within himself.]

But if these Alanian motifs tend towards establishing Nature as a figure of dignity, power, and moral authority, other elements in this sequence of the poem by no means co-operate.[39] In the first place Nature *confesses*; and though what she says in confession consists largely of the kind of complaint against humankind which her counterpart in the *De planctu* makes, we are invited to think in terms of a Nature having done something wrong.[40] And in the process of this confession, Nature's dignity is undercut. Nature cannot help being implicated in the criticism of women made by Genius in the antifeminist tirade which precedes her confession, despite Genius' claim that what he has said does not apply to her.[41] Nature herself includes her own confession under a general comment on the irritating character of the way women speak.[42] Given this interest in presenting Nature as very much a fallible woman,[43] it is not surprising that close inspection of what she does shows limitation in her capacity and her concern.

Library (London, 1929))). Huot (*Romance*, 171 f.) suggests that a Genius who is 'on the verge of turning into the old *lascivi praeceptor Amoris* [instructor in lascivious love] himself, with Nature, his presiding deity, assuming the role of the god who smiles on the perjuries of lovers', is here using virtuous behaviour as a code for heterosexual activity.

[39] On this see Polak, 'Plato', 82.

[40] The perceived fault would seem to be making man, an action Nature eventually explicitly says she regrets at 19180. Arguably this regret is in itself faulty, since it questions God himself, he being ultimately responsible for the creation of human beings. (Kay, *Romance*, 96, 99, however, thinks the fault in question is not Nature's, for all that she confesses, but man's in failing to pursue procreation.)

[41] *RR* 16671–6.

[42] *RR* 18265 ff. and see also Nature's comment (19188 ff.) on how, being a woman, she cannot keep silent (about man's vices). Wetherbee (*Platonism*, 261–3) finds in the disorderliness of Nature's discourse evidence of 'the very denaturing forces which have aroused [Nature's] anger' (261). He also sees Nature's relations with Genius as reflecting the 'confusion and duplicity of the world of human experience' (264). See also Susan Stakel, *False Roses* (Saratoga, Calif., 1991); Stakel registers how Nature is not always reasonable or orderly and comments also on the problematic character of Nature's interest in (distorting) mirrors (81).

[43] On which see Rosemond Tuve, *Allegorical Imagery* (Princeton, 1966), 267 ff.

For all the affirmation of the reach into the heavens of Nature's authority, her attentions in the poem are very much directed towards things 'dessous le ciel' [beneath the heavens].[44] On her first appearance as an actor in the poem, in a passage quoted above, she is thinking about these things and has entered into her forge to repair the depredations of Death. That the first thing we should learn about the figure is that she is involved in a struggle against the effects of Death emphasizes her implication in the sub-heavenly realm of mutability.[45] It is consonant with this emphasis, though here she differs from her counterpart in the *De planctu Naturae*,[46] that her endowment of human beings should not include the *antandement*, which is a capacity of the human being's immortal soul:

> n'i n'a pas, se je ne li done,
> quant a la corporel persone,
> ne de par cors ne de par mambre,
> qui li vaille une pome d'ambre,
> ne quant a l'ame vraiement,
> fors une chose seulement:
> il tient de moi, qui sui sa dame,
> .III. forces, que de cors que d'ame,
> car bien puis dire, san mentir,
> jou faz estre, vivre sentir; . . .
> il a son estre avec les pierres,
> et vit avec les herbes drues,
> et sent avec les bestes mues;
> oncor peut il trop plus an tant
> qu'il avec les anges antant . . .[47]
>
>   San faille, de l'antandemant
> connois je bien que vraiemant
> celui ne li donai je mie.

[44] Even in respect of the heavens Nature's presidence seems to be presidence over the material, elemental creation: the heavens are enclosed within the chain of the elements. The limitation to the material, as we have seen, features in some writings of the Chartrian tradition, though the *De planctu Naturae* does not so limit Nature.

[45] See Stakel, *False Roses*, 79, on the way the priority of this image to that of Nature as presiding over the golden chain undercuts Nature's dignity. What lay beneath the moon was traditionally regarded, in accordance with Aristotelian cosmology, as a realm subject to change and decay (see J. D. North, *Chaucer's Universe* (Oxford, 1988), 16), and with this realm Nature came to be associated (see e.g. Chaucer's *Physician's Tale, CT* 6. 22 f.).

[46] Nature does of course confess to other kinds of limitation in the *De planctu*.

[47] The understanding of human nature here is grounded in Aristotle.

> La ne s'estant pas ma baillie,
> ne fui pas sage ne poissant
> de fere riens si connoissant.
> Onques ne fis riens pardurable;
> quan que je faz est corrumpable.[48]

[except for what I give him, [man] has nothing in his body, trunk, or limbs that would buy him so much as a pomander, nor indeed in his soul, except for one thing; only man, who has received three physical and spiritual forces from me, his mistress (for I can truthfully say that it is I who give him existence, life, and feeling) . . . [he has] existence in common with the stones, life with the thick grass, and feeling with the dumb beasts, and he is capable of still more in that he has understanding in common with the angels; . . .

Undoubtedly, as I know very well, it was not I, in truth, who gave him his understanding. That is outside my province, and I had neither the wisdom nor the power to make anything so intelligent. I have never made anything eternal, and whatever I make is corruptible.]

Whilst in the *De planctu Naturae* Alan was prepared to speak of Nature giving human beings both reason and sensuality, here Nature's provision is limited to physical matter and the vegetative and sensitive souls: the rational soul, possession of which distinguishes human beings from the other animals, is understood to be provided directly by God.[49] This conception is in line with Guillaume de Lorris's statement that Nature did not create Reson.[50] Nature's denial that she is the provider of the *antandement* in fact aligns her with understanding of Nature behind the Ulpianic definition of natural law: she is to be associated with the sub-rational capacities which man shares with the animals rather than with his rational side.[51]

---

[48] *RR* 18999–9008; 19016–20; 19025–32.

[49] William of Conches reserved to God the creation of the souls of Adam and Eve: otherwise creation occurred through secondary causes and in particular the stars. See above, Ch. 3 at n. 35. Gower makes the soul the direct creation of God in contrast with Nature's provisions for the body at *CA* 7. 490–3.

[50] *RR* 2969 ff. Though in medieval literature it is not always appropriate to take Reason as the human faculty of reason (see Alford, 'Idea'), that Guillaume says Reson is made in the image and likeness of God suggests that we are to think of the rational soul.

[51] Polak, 'Plato', sees Nature as claiming 'a part in the fashioning of the whole man including his reason' (90), on the strength of Nature's having decreed that man shall turn his face heavenward and her saying that she makes man in God's image (18993–6). But if there is any such claim, it is, as Polak recognizes, immediately cancelled by the passage just quoted in the main text.

This association with the animal, the sub-rational, seems to shape, and from an orthodox point of view distort, Nature's moral perspective. Despite her wide-ranging condemnation of human sinfulness quoted above, she says she will leave most of the sins to God to deal with; she is herself immediately concerned to do something only about behaviour which fails to lead to procreation, seeing procreative activity as the *treu* humankind owes her. We recall how she appears first in the poem as one seeking to counter the depredations of death, and perhaps wonder whether her moral commitments are not secondary to her concern that species shall continue.[52] At any rate, Nature's list of sins at lines 19195 ff. does not include fornication and adultery. Nature makes no stipulation that sexual activity is to be conducted within the framework of marriage: what she is interested in is getting things reproduced, and fornication and adultery stand a chance of furthering this aim, just as sexual abstinence thwarts it. In this failure to condemn what are orthodoxly considered to be illegitimate forms of sexual activity, Nature brings to mind the scholastic meditations on whether fornication and the like are against nature, and their conclusions that, if nature is understood in a certain way, they are not.[53] It may, indeed, be this understanding that contributes most to the formation of the Nature who appears as actor in the *Roman*, as, indeed, it seems to underpin Reson's and La Vieille's accounts of Nature. Nature in the *Roman* may be at bottom the Nature who teaches all animals.[54] The investment of such a figure with Alanian trappings which show forth Nature's power in the universe perhaps constitutes Jean de

[52] See *RR* 19293 ff. Polak, 'Plato', 92, thinks Nature's complaining of humanity's vices at 19192 ff. 'rather [an] inappropriate bow to the *De Planctu*', and finds that her concentration on sins against her as procreatrix comes about because 'unlike Alain's Natura, the only evil she knows is primaeval chaos'. Stakel, *False Roses*, 80, speaks of Nature's 'obsession' with propagation, which causes her to limit the scope of her moral concern.

[53] The theologians we examined in Ch. 1 do not seek to validate unorthodox sexual behaviour. However, Bishop Tempier's condemnations of 1277 suggest that the legitimacy of sexual behaviour outside the orthodox limits was being canvassed in the 13th century in a way troubling to orthodoxy. See Polak, 'Plato', 96. For Tempiers's condemnations, see *Chartularium Universitatis Parisiensis*, ed. H. Denifle and A. Chatelain (Paris, 1889–97), vol. i.

[54] Polak, 'Plato', 95, finds that Nature and Genius in the *Roman* have been 'reduced to the force of instinct'. In contrast to any affirmation that Nature in the *Roman* is an essentially coherent figure, it might be argued that Jean keeps different conceptions of Nature in play without resolving them, so that Nature becomes a site of contradiction.

Meun's challenge to Neoplatonic conceptions, demanding that we recognize the possibility that what organizes the universe, under God, should not be conceived as a principle concerned to mediate God's rationality and goodness to the created order but is in fact a much less elevated, less spiritual, more material force which expresses itself in the animate creatures of its domain through a blind instinctualism, unconditioned by rational considerations.[55]

How satisfactory such a principle is as a shaper of human actions is, for all that Nature is a divine appointee, very much open to question. The question is perhaps put most sharply by what Genius, Nature's close associate, has to say about the way to salvation. Genius, speaking at Nature's behest, condemns not only perverted sexuality in the fashion of Alan of Lille's *De planctu*, but also the failure to be sexually active.[56] So Genius holds admission to the paradisal park, a clear figure of the Christian heaven, presided over as it is by a white Lamb, the Virgin's Son, to be conditional not only on avoiding the vices mentioned by Nature, but also on actively working for procreation.[57] Where, one wonders, would this leave the virgin saints, or, indeed, the Lamb himself and his Mother?

Even if this view is taken, however, Jean's parodying of the *De planctu* throws the emphasis onto those aspects of his Nature figure which mark the difference between her and Alan's *Natura* (see Polak, 'Plato', 92–5). Jean's intertextual procedures demand that we attend to what is new in his figure, to what marks out his Nature as different. The challenge to Neoplatonism to which I refer in the text is still operative even with a non-unitary Nature. It would also remain true that Jean's Nature would tend to urge thinking and writing about the natural in the particular direction suggested by what is new in her. But in any case, it may be that the general moral concern Nature shows in the *Roman*, something which might seem at odds with her sponsoring of animal instinct, is not in fact out of line with an Ulpianic conception of her, since animal behaviour is appealed to to support a wide range of orthodox moral positions in medieval writing. See Chs. 2 and 6. And however that may be, the fictive mode Jean employs may well tolerate the expression of moral opinions by a Nature understood to figure the sub-rational impulses; after all, even the Ulpianic natural law moves to what is good, and is in the service of God. A personified Nature drawn on Ulpianic lines might reasonably be allowed to perceive and object to behaviour which goes against God's laws, even if these are not the laws she is herself charged by God to promote.

[55] See Polak, 'Plato', 94 ff., and Wetherbee, *Platonism*, 255–66, on Jean de Meun's subversion of 12th-century Neoplatonic ideas.
[56] See *RR* 19513 ff. for the condemnation of abstinence and 19599 ff. for the condemnation of perversion.
[57] There is even the possibility that his advocacy of apparently non-sexual virtues is in fact geared to the pursuit of love. See Huot, *Romance*, on the Ovidian nature of Genius' closing remarks (above, n. 38).

The extremity of Genius' advocacy of procreation, which leads him to such a bizarre position (although an intelligible one for him, if he figures the reproductive urge, or (male) sexuality, or the genitalia),[58] requires us to wonder about his and Nature's moral balance.[59] The enterprise of preserving the species through procreation is a reasonable one,[60] but that does not mean that everyone is required to procreate,[61] or that those who do procreate should make sex the urgent and exhausting priority Genius would have it be.[62] Further, an unreserved commitment to procreation may lead down some morally questionable paths and into some unwholesome alliances. When Nature sends Genius to excommunicate those who oppose her and absolve those who observe her rules by seeking to

---

[58] For such figuration see Kay, *Romance*, 92 f., and Sarah Kay, 'Sexual Knowledge: The Once and Future Texts of the *Romance of the Rose*', in Judith Still and Michael Worton (eds.), *Textuality and Sexuality* (Manchester, 1993), 69–86. Genius seems likely to be a complex figure, so these meanings need not exclude one another or other ones. See next note.

[59] Recent critics seem on the whole to be less ready than used to be the case to suppose that Genius is articulating the author's own position, though Piehler, *Visionary Landscape*, 108, thinks 'Genius's exhortation to fecundity can be regarded as an appropriate synecdoche of a general exhortation that lovers should follow virtue'. Others tend to agree in finding Genius wrong, but there is an issue as to how wrong. Polak, 'Plato', 97, thinks him a bogus theologian and a fraudulent spiritual teacher; Fleming, *Roman*, 193 f., sees him as *naturalis concupiscentia* and, inasmuch as he exceeds the proper limits of that capacity, as 'both a fraud and a buffoon' (209 f.), but Wetherbee, 'Literal', is more charitable, supposing him to symbolize the best in ungraced human nature (284). Thomas D. Hill, 'Narcissus, Pygmalion, and the Castration of Saturn: Two Mythographical Themes in the *Roman de la Rose*', *SP* 71 (1974), 404–26, sees Genius as both absurd, and pathetic in that he harks back to a time lost, but not quite forgotten, when 'there was no conflict between moral imperatives and man's natural desire to perpetuate himself' (423). Kathryn L. Lynch, *The High Medieval Dream Vision* (Stanford, Calif., 1988) thinks that Genius comes to represent imaginative failure (135): though he has not lost all access to that archetypal memory which had given Alan's Genius his authority, he fails 'to submit the spark of his imaginative perception to the disciplines of reason' (136).

[60] As we have seen, Reson approves it. For some scholastic opinions that generation for the increase of the species would have occurred even in Paradise see G. Paré, *Le Roman de la Rose et la scolastique courtoise* (Paris, 1941), 152 f.

[61] See n. 10 above.

[62] See *RR* 19671 ff. Polak, who argues that Jean de Meun holds up to ridicule a tendency in 12th-century thought to make the sex-urge the ground of a moral scheme, writes of Genius' Sermon ('Plato', 96): 'Though there is, of course, a profound and obvious connection between the Creator, Providence and the "opus naturae" which gives the speech of Genius some undeniable validity, it is the equation of the christianized *anima mundi* . . . with, not only the principle of fertility, but its instrument, sexual instinct, which constitutes the *reductio ad absurdum* of these neo-platonic speculations about nature which the message of Genius is.'

procreate, her cavalier promise of pardon to the latter rather mitigates the force of her insistence that the vices she has earlier condemned should be avoided—for it is just these vices which will be
pardoned:

> car ges doi touz amis clamer,
> por leur ames metre en delices,
> mes qu'il se gardent bien des vices
> que j'ai ci devant racontez,
> qu'il effacent toutes bontez.
> Pardon qui bien doit soffisanz
> leur donez, non pas de .x. anz,
> nou priseroient un denier,
> mes a tourjorz pardon plenier
> de tretout quan que fet avront,
> quant bien confessier s'en savront.[63]

[I call all such my friends and I will fill their souls with delight, provided
they avoid those vices of which I have spoken and which wipe out every
merit. Give them a pardon that will be amply sufficient: not just for ten
years, for that would not be worth twopence to them, but a perpetual,
plenary pardon for everything they have done, when they make a good
confession.]

One is led to wonder, not for the first time, how much she really
cares about the vices she condemns.

Particularly suggestive is the fact that, though it is Nature who
instructs Genius to excommunicate those who fail to obey her,
Genius delivers his sermon under the aegis of Venus and the God
of Love. At the end of Nature's confession he takes off his chasuble,
alb, and surplice and, tellingly, puts on less cumbersome secular dress,
'si con s'il alast queroler' [as if he were going to a dance], before he
goes off to carry out Nature's injunctions.[64] But when he reaches the
forces of Love, the God of Love and Venus fit him out again:

---

[63]   *RR* 19358–68. We might also feel uncomfortable about the way Genius appears to
relegate the obligation to confess, with its commitment to doing good and renouncing
evil, and to call on God beneath the duty to have sex: 'Et quant assez avrez joué | si con
je vos ai ci loué, | pansez de vos bien confessier, | por bien fere et por mal lessier, | et
reclamez le dieu celestre | que Nature reclaime a mestre' (*RR* 19861–6). [And when you
have played enough in the way I have recommended, remember to make a good
confession so as to do good and renounce evil, and call upon the heavenly God,
whom Nature acknowledges as her master.]

[64]   *RR* 19398–448.

Tantost li diex d'Amours affuble
a Genius une chasuble;
anel li baille et croce et mitre
plus clere que cristal ne vitre.
N'i quierent autre paremant,
tant ont grant antalentemant
d'oïr cele sentance lire.
Venus, qui ne cessoit de rire
ne ne se poait tenir quaie,
tant par estoit jolive et gaie,
por plus anforcier la natheme
quant il avra feni son theme,
li met ou poign un ardant cierge,
qui n'estoit pas de cire vierge.[65]

[Then the God of Love arrayed Genius in a chasuble and handed him a ring, crosier, and mitre, clearer than glass or crystal. They sought no other ornament, for they greatly longed to hear him read the sentence. Venus laughed continually and could not keep quiet in her joy and gaiety; in order to lend added force to his anathema, when he had finished his speech, she put into his hands a lighted candle, which was not made of virgin wax.]

So now whose priest, or rather bishop, is Genius?[66] And what purpose exactly will his anathema serve? Clearly Venus and the God of Love think it will be theirs; but then what of Genius' and Nature's concern for procreation? We know, after all, on the strength of what Reson has told us about the Lover that Venus and the God of Love, the powers directly presiding over erotic love, are interested not in procreation but in pleasure.

Here is the problem we pointed to earlier when considering what Reson said about Nature. The trouble is that to pursue her legitimate end of procreation Nature uses a dangerous mechanism, since people may start ignoring the end and have sex simply for the pleasure—after all 'maint n'i treroient ja tret, | se n'iert deliz qui les atret'.[67] On the other hand these lines also suggest that the end of

---

[65] *RR* 19447–60.

[66] One wonders what precisely the significance of the change from priest to bishop is. In the investment of Genius with this higher, episcopal authority by the deities of love Jean is perhaps pointing to the critical importance of the notion of procreation in any justification of sexual behaviour.

[67] *RR* 4389 f. See above, at n. 13.

the preservation of the species might not be achieved were it not for sexual pleasure.[68] What is clear is that, even if sex is indulged in for pleasure, it may still achieve its orthodoxly proper end of procreation. There is at least the suggestion that this is what actually happens at the end of the poem:[69]

> A la parfin, tant vos an di,
> un po de greine i espandi,
> quant j'oi le bouton elloichié.
> Ce fu quant dedanz l'oi toichié
> por les fueilletes reverchier,
> car je vouloie tout cerchier
> jusques au fonz du boutonet,
> si con moi samble que bon et.
> Si fis lors si meller les greines
> qu'el se desmellassent a peines,
> si que tout le boutonet tandre
> an fis ellargir et estandre.[70]

[I can tell you that at last, when I had shaken the bud, I scattered a little seed there. This was when I had touched the inside of the rose-bud and explored all its little leaves, for I longed, and it seemed good to me, to probe its very depths. I thus mingled the seeds in such a way that it would have been hard to disentangle them, with the result that all the rose-bud swelled and expanded.]

That procreation can occur where there is no procreative intent may well be why Nature sends her priest Genius to urge the barons of Love to assault the Rose Castle. It has been suggested that Nature fails to see that Venus and her cohorts are not interested in procreation,[71] but it seems at least as likely that Nature sees very clearly and accurately that the more heterosexual behaviour there is—she dis-

[68] This is a point taken up in *Renart le Contrefait*. See Ch. 5.

[69] This has been doubted, in spite of the following passage. See, e.g., Pelen, *Latin Poetic Irony*, 146 and n. 65, and Douglas Kelly, *Internal Difference and Meanings in the Roman de la Rose* (Madison, 1995), 148, for whom the passage need only indicate the sexual arousal of the Rose. The language of mixing 'greines' however, at least puts one in mind of conception. It is possible that an ambiguity here neatly and teasingly encapsulates the critical difficulty about sex—that one cannot disentangle procreation and pleasure—and dramatizes the futility of trying to do so. Kelly, *Difference*, 113, speaks of any sexual activity which does not serve Nature's purpose of continuing the species as being unnatural, but this may be naively clear-cut.

[70] *RR* 21689–700.

[71] So Economou, *Goddess*, 121–3; see also Robertson, *Preface*, 201 f.

approves, as we might expect, of homosexual activity[72]—the more chance there is that procreation will occur; in this the end of the poem very possibly vindicates her.[73]

The co-operation between Venus and Nature expresses a sense of the inseparability of the orthodoxly acceptable end of procreation from the orthodoxly dubious principle of sexual pleasure. Sex is to be regarded as natural even though it does not consciously aim at procreation. It is Nature after all, who arranged for pleasure to be experienced in sex (a fact on which Reson agrees with La Vieille,[74] who remarks that Nature regulates us by inciting our hearts to pleasure—an agreement we might feel to be fraught with rather alarming implications for the moral status of Nature). The association of Nature and Venus in the *Roman* in a scenario very possibly designed to contrast with the rebellion of Venus from Nature in the *De planctu* seems to be commenting on Alan's treatment of the two figures.[75] The Nature of the *De planctu* seeks to detach herself from Venus and thereby from responsibility for the seamier side of sexual behaviour. Jean suggests that this is an evasion: in the first place in the *De planctu* Nature is responsible for the position in the procreative system of those sexual urges represented by Venus, the prosecution of which can nevertheless so easily be de-coupled from the pursuit of procreation; in the second place, a corrupt Venus now contaminates the procreative processes of Alan's Nature, and Jean's arrangement of the action of his poem dramatizes how the natural drive towards procreation may indeed go forward through channels

[72] See *RR* 19204, where sodomy occurs in the list of sins condemned by Nature. Sodomy may refer rather generally to non-inseminative sexual activity. At 19599 ff. Genius condemns homosexual sex. Scholastic opinion sometimes sees homosexual activity as against Nature in a specifically Ulpianic sense (see n. 82 below).

[73] As it may give an appropriateness to Genius' preaching against the Garden of Deduit (in comparison with the Park of the Lamb) in that very Garden (see Piehler, *Visionary Landscape*, 109); this homiletic situation might suggest the co-opting of the drive to procreation for the interests of pleasure, but the possibility that the action of the poem ends in procreation means that it might equally suggest the reverse. Perhaps Jean is pointing to the inextricability of the drive for pleasure and that for procreation (see n. 69 above).

[74] *RR* 14127 f. Wetherbee, 'Literal', 278 cites a passage from *Chaucer and the French Tradition* (Berkeley, 1957), 75, in which Charles Muscatine speaks of the proximity of La Vieille and Reson. In his *Sentences* commentary Aquinas sees sexual pleasure as a God-ordained stimulus to the activity which will ensure the species survives (see n. 13 above).

[75] Nature calls Venus 'm'amie' at *RR* 19313, something she would hardly be able to do in the *De planctu* or the *Anticlaudianus*.

less than pure.[76] Thus it would be impossible to deny that Nature is in some sense operative in at least all heterosexual sexual behaviour, even if one might wish to say that in such an action as the conquest of the Rose there is something in accordance with nature and something against nature.[77]

I have suggested that the Nature of the *Roman* may appropriately be understood with reference to the idea of Nature backing the Ulpianic conception of natural law. But can sex without procreative intent, to which I am arguing the *Roman*'s Nature in effect turns (despite her official protestations) a blind eye, be reckoned natural according to the Ulpianic paradigm? The 'coniunctio maris et feminae' which is specified as one of the things Nature teaches all animals according to the Ulpianic definition of the law of nature tends to be understood by later writers as 'ad multiplicationem speciei' [for the multiplication of the species] or 'ad generandum' [for generation], and the Ulpianic definition itself mentions *procreatio* after *coniunctio* in its list of what is taught by Nature. But *ad* in such comments presumably marks a purpose in *Nature* that sex should bring about generation and multiply the species, a purpose which, as the end of the *Roman* appears to show, can be fulfilled without specific human intent[78]—and do animals, after all, intend to *procreate*? Where the sexual behaviour leaves room for Nature's procreative purposes to be fulfilled, it would seem that sex without specific procreative intent need not be conceived as against Nature and may be understood as being prompted by Nature in the Ulpianic sense.[79] This would seem to be confirmed by theological commentary. For instance, the Alexandran *Summa* is prepared to regard fornication as natural in the Ulpianic sense,[80] and one presumes the writer does not suppose that fornication necessarily includes pro-

---

[76] We have seen how the candle which Venus hands to Genius and which is used, it seems, to figure the universality of sexual desire in women (at least) (see *RR* 20640–8) is described at *RR* 19460 as not being made of virgin wax.

[77] See the remark by the Wycliffite writer cited in Ch. 2, at n. 59.

[78] See P. M. Kean's succint comments on the *Roman* in her review of Economou, *Goddess*, RES NS 25 (1974), 190–2 (191).

[79] We may feel that Kelly, *Difference* (113–15), too easily brackets the Lover's taking of the Rose (in which we may presume there is no procreative intent) with sexual activity which cannot serve Nature's purpose to continue the species and which is therefore unnatural.

[80] *ST* 3. 366 ad 1 (see above, Ch. 1 at n. 79).

creative intent.[81] On the other hand the *Summa* regards the *peccatum sodomiticum*, where procreation is an impossibility, as against nature in the Ulpianic sense.[82] Likewise, sex without procreative intent also apparently qualifies as natural in Augustine's discussion of sexual behaviour in the *Opus imperfectum contra Julianum*.[83] Augustine there defines the 'usus naturalis' as that in which the male uses the female organ 'quo natura ejusdem generis animantium propagatur'. Adultery and fornication, though illicit, are taken to be natural in this sense and less reprehensible, therefore, than the 'usus contra naturam'. Augustinian and Ulpianic natural sex clearly have much in common. Nature in the *Roman* behaves in ways readily intelligible in terms of such perspectives on what is natural in sex. She advocates procreation—her purpose in arranging the *coniunctio* of male and female and that pleasure that incites to it—and only stands against those sexual practices which *cannot* achieve that end.

If we return to the relationship between Alan of Lille and Jean de Meun, we may reflect that Jean's Nature, considered whole, stands less close to his Reson than does Alan's Natura to his Ratio.[84] In the *Roman* Reson disapproves of the Lover's behaviour and this kind of behaviour Nature, through her alliance with Venus, encourages.[85] Reson is not against procreative sex, but she is not prepared to have the Lover go forward in his immoral non-procreative purposes and in the madness of his Amor-inspired infatuation. Nature, on the

---

[81] At *Summa contra Gentiles* 3. 122 n. 5, n. 9 (in *Opera omnia*, ed. R. Busa, 7 vols. (Rome, 1980), vol. ii) Aquinas argues against fornication on grounds including the wrongness of the emission of semen in such a way that procreation cannot occur, suggesting that he supposed fornicators not to be, as a rule, interested in having children.

[82] Alexander of Hales, *ST* 3. 366 ad 1. At *ST* 1.2 q. 94 a. 3 ad 2 Aquinas speaks of the *concubitus masculorum* as 'specialiter' against nature, nature being understood in the Ulpianic sense (all sins are against nature inasmuch as they are against reason, possession of which distinguishes human from animal nature).

[83] See above, Ch. 1, p. 45.

[84] This in spite of Reson's not explicitly stipulating marriage as the proper form of sexual behaviour (but see n. 14) and her failure to commend celibacy at all.

[85] Venus' hostility to Reson is explicit in a speech to Honte, Reson's daughter: 'Certes, Honte, ja n'ameré | ne vos ne Reson, vostre mere, | qui tant est aus amanz amere. | Qui vostre mere et vos creroit, | ja mes par amors n'ameroit' (20748–52) [It is certain, Shame, that I shall never love you or your mother, Reason, who is so harsh to lovers. No one who listened to you or your mother would ever be a true lover].

other hand, *is* prepared to sanction both these things, since they may bring about what she desires.[86] As is in large measure the case with Natura in the *De planctu Naturae* Reson's priorities are derived from a concern with what is in accord with reason: the *Roman*'s Nature, on the other hand, does not provide human reason, and her priorities in respect of what happens in the poem (whatever she may say about her cosmic status and wide moral concern) are those of an Ulpianic Nature. Whereas Alan's Natura, presiding over the whole of human nature, is on the side of reason and condemns behaviour in which the *sensualitas* is indulged as bestial wantoning,[87] Jean's Nature, not providing the *antandement* but only that part of human beings which they share with the beasts,[88] approves the self-expression of that part since that self-expression is geared towards the maintenance of the species.[89]

Jean's offering of a Nature committed to the animal dimension of human beings licenses his reader to suppose that to follow Nature risks failure to fulfil the higher demands of the nature of the human creature as a rational and moral being. In fact the literary tradition now features a Nature figure who can be taken as happily urging people to what, seen in a wider perspective than this Nature wishes to entertain, is not right.[90] The unrighteousness would involve a submission to the animal side of human nature, but the *Roman*, by configuring Nature as it does, pushes the reader to understand this side of human nature as *the* natural side (in line with a clear tradition in theological discourse). This suggests that, in a conflict between parts of themselves, their being most truly themselves, i.e. most natural, has a tendency to lead humans into sin; this further

---

[86] In view of this, Kelly, *Difference*, 119, seems to me wrong to claim that in the *Rose* unnatural sex 'includes any human sexuality not governed by reason'. See below, pp. 157–9, on *Les Echecs amoureux*.

[87] See above, Ch. 3.

[88] Whatever counter-indicators one might find (see n. 51 above), this is the situation in the most explicit formulation.

[89] At *SCG* 3. 122 n. 9 Aquinas speaks of the good of nature which is the conservation of the species and at *Sent.* 4 d. 26 q. 1 a. 3, co of an inclination of nature 'to the procreation of offspring through which the nature of the species is conserved'.

[90] The Natura of the *De planctu* may as we have seen be understood as implicated in the moral unsatisfactoriness of the sexual system she initiated, but she is certainly not happy about the way things now work in that system and her perspective is not limited in the same way and to the same degree as Nature's in the *Roman* is (or at least as Nature is in the dominant conception of her in the poem).

implies that by their very design as creatures they are, as it were, programmed towards failure as moral beings. There is another point: when the *Roman* allows Nature to be understood as the sponsor of the animal side of human beings and yet the vicar of God, the minister of divine purposes, the inevitable suggestion is that that side, although it has a deep-seated tendency to deflect human beings from the path of right morality, is nevertheless in itself good and has its own proper aims. Ought we not then to accommodate its God-ordained drives? The problems then may not lie simply in the difficulty of suppressing what is most truly natural in us, but in a positive obligation to ensure the ends of our natural, animal side; for in fulfilling this obligation in the sphere of sex we are, given the inextricability of the legitimate pursuit of procreation from the illegitimate pursuit of pleasure (not to mention the experience of pleasure[91]), inevitably involving ourselves in sin.[92]

It may be possible to submerge anxiety about this in a claim that, notwithstanding the movement of the natural within human beings towards sin, that movement produces a compensatory good. This would be one way of taking the engendering of the child at the end of the *Roman*. So Wetherbee comments eloquently:

The world [the *Roman*] presents is as far from the ideal harmony of the Platonic cosmos of Alain and Bernardus as it is from the park of the Good Shepherd. But when the Lover ... blindly assumes responsibility for the future of mankind, he is responding to a creative impulse which seeks to realize both of these lost ideals. And in understanding this we recognize the almost miraculous fertility of that human nature which, hidden beneath

---

[91] The hard-line view was that the *experience* of sexual pleasure was always itself sinful (see Noonan, *Contraception*, 197 f.).

[92] At *SCG* 3. 136 Aquinas refutes the notion that perpetual continence is not a good by distinguishing between what is required of each individual and what is required of humanity as a whole. But though this shows that not all need procreate, it allows that some ought to and so leaves a moral uncertainty about the submission of individuals to what Aquinas (*SCG* 3. 136 n. 3) calls the *vis concupiscibilis incitans*, if this *vis* is indeed God-ordained (*ex divina ordinatione*) and yet the pursuit of pleasure in sex wrong, as in the dominant Augustinian view. Noonan, *Contraception*, 294, noting Aquinas's claim in his *Commentary on the Sentences* (see n. 13 above) that 'divina providentia' made sex pleasurable to ensure procreation, points out the contradiction between this position in which the pursuit of pleasure in sex is effectively a response to a directive from God and the dominant view, which would have held that one must not succumb to the instinct to pleasure.

the proliferation of conflicting desires and false visions, is the rock and loam from which all such impulses must necessarily and perpetually spring.[93]

It might be supposed that the Lover's dubious intentions have a certain tendency to bring about something good, because they are grounded in the natural order, which in itself remains good, for all that human beings cannot with complete success accommodate both its demands and those laid on them by the higher, immediately divine authority of God.[94] But such optimism is not obligatory: one can instead focus on the tendency of the natural in human beings to draw them away from goodness and concentrate on the way in which they are, alarmingly, more or less determined by the most fundamental part of their being into behaviour which is in an eschatological perspective against their own best interests. It seems to me that in Gower, in the end, and rather often in Chaucer, Nature is seen in this pessimistic way. One might even suggest that this way of seeing Nature, perhaps opened up for these English writers by a reading of the *Roman de la Rose*, led to a certain general pessimism about the position in the world of human beings.

[93]   Wetherbee, *Platonism*, 265 f.
[94]   In *Piers Plowman* Langland finds a way of accommodating an acknowledgement of natural tendencies to sin within a vision of the natural that sees the good that arises from it as much more significant. What needs to be avoided at all costs is *unkyndenesse*, unnaturalness; see White, *Nature and Salvation*, 89–111.

CHAPTER FIVE

Further French Natures

Where the twelfth-century writers considered in Chapter 3 and, indeed, the academic theorists of natural law reviewed in Chapter 1 seek to keep the morally problematic associations of nature with sex under firm control, the *Roman de la Rose* lets them run loose. In this chapter I want to consider some writings in French on which the impact of the *Roman* is apparent and examine how they respond to the idea of a Nature who condones and encourages behaviour orthodoxly regarded as sinful.

At the beginning of the fifteenth century Jean Gerson wrote against the *Roman de la Rose* in the famous Querelle which also involved Christine de Pisan on the anti-*Rose* side and Jean de Montreuil and the brothers Gontier and Pierre Col as defenders of the poem.[1] Gerson wants to put the de Meunian genie back in the Alanian bottle:

je parleroie comment en la persone, maintenant de Nature, maintenant de Genius . . . il enhorte et commande sans differance user de toute charnalité, et maudit toux ceulx et celles qui n'en useront; et ja de mariaige ne sera faicte mencion—qui toutes fois par nature est ordonné . . . Vray est que

---

[1] The texts in the Querelle have been edited by Eric Hicks under the title *Le Débat sur le Roman de la Rose* (Paris, 1977) and translated by Joseph L. Baird and John R. Kane in *La Querelle de la Rose: Letters and Documents* (Chapel Hill, NC, 1978). This edition and this translation are used here.

Gerson also involved himself in controversy with Guillaume Saignet, a counsellor and diplomat for the house of Anjou in the first part of the 15th century. For Saignet's text see Ch. 4 n. 24 above. Saignet wrote against priestly celibacy on the grounds that it obstructed the divinely ordained reproductive purposes of Nature and involved an unrealistic attempt to control what are legitimate urges of the flesh. Saignet does not associate Nature with completely unrestrained sexual behaviour; his Nature is against fornication and adultery and in favour of marriage (Grévy-Pons, *Célibat*, 144). But the position Saignet constructs for Nature sets her in vigorous opposition to that state orthodoxly regarded as of the highest virtue. One might compare Gower at *CA* 8. 2333 ff. on the need for the holy man to 'withdrawe | His kindly lust' against Nature's law.

ceste ficcion poetique fut corrumpuement estraitte du grant Alain, en son livre qu'il fait *De la plainte Nature*; . . . Et qui ces euvres et oultraiges veult excuser par Nature qui parle, je respons pour vous, dame Nature, que onques vous ne concillastes pechié, onques ne voulsistes que persone fist contre aucuns des dis commandemens (lesquelx nous appellons vos commandemens) les conmandemans de Nature; dire le contraire seroit erreur en la foy (c'est assavoir dire que selonc droit de nature euvre naturelle d'omme et de fame ne fust pechié hors mariaige).[2]

[I could say how sometimes in the person of Nature, sometimes of Genius . . . he exhorts and encourages to all forms of carnality indiscriminately; and he curses all men and women who do not indulge in it. Nor does she make mention of marriage, which nevertheless is ordained by Nature . . . It is true that this poetic fiction was abstracted from Alanus' great book, *The Complaint of Nature*—but corruptly . . . Therefore, whoever desires to excuse this man's intolerable works by saying that it is Nature who speaks, I answer for you, Lady Nature, that you never did counsel sin, nor did you wish anyone to act against the ten commandments, which we call in fact your commandments, the commandments of Nature. He who would say otherwise and contrary—that, according to the Law of Nature, the natural act between man and woman outside marriage is not a sin—would be erring in the Faith.]

Elsewhere Gerson objects to those who 'ne tenoient compte de quelconque chastete, mais looyent Luxure et disoient qu'elle estoit selon nature', attributing this opinion to the *Roman de la Rose*.[3] Yet his own language points to a difficulty: if the 'euvre *naturelle* d'omme et de fame' can occur outside marriage, is it not legitimate to create a personification called Nature which exhorts to sex regardless of marriage?[4]

---

[2] *Traitié contre Le Roman de la Rose*, ed. Hicks, *Débat*, 80 f.

[3] *Poenitemini* 5, ed. Hicks, *Débat*, 184.

[4] Even Christine de Pisan, hostile to the *Roman* though she is, does not register an objection to Jean's conception of Nature as prepared to sponsor extra-marital sexual activity, activity which can be designated 'lechery'; she seems to accept that lechery is ascribable to Nature. Discussing Genius' sermon, Christine writes (*Epistre au Prevost de Lisle*) that the author of the poem correctly says that the virtuous will go to paradise. She continues (Hicks, *Débat*, 53): 'et puis conclut que tous entendement— hommes et femmes sans esparnier—a parfunir et exerciter les euvres de Nature; ne en ce ne fait excepcion de loy, comme se il voulzist dire—mais dit plainement!—qu'ilz seront sauvez. Et par ce semble que maintenir vueille le pechié de luxure estre nul, ains vertu—qui est erreur et contre la loy de Dieu' [but he concludes that everyone, men and women alike, should know how to perform and exercise the functions of Nature; nor in this does he make any exception of law, as if he wished to say, and

Other writers certainly do think it legitimate to take up and rework the *Roman*'s notion of a Nature urging to sexual behaviour unrestricted by the orthodox moral considerations. The *Lamentations* of Matheolus was written (in Latin) towards the end of the 13th century apparently by a cleric who had married a widow. Because of this marriage he found himself technically a bigamist and consequently at a disadvantage in obtaining preferment.[5] His response to his unfortunate situation is a work complaining against marriage and women. The *Lamentations* were translated into French in the 1370s by Jean Le Fèvre, and this version proved extremely popular. There is some evidence that the Latin text was influenced by the *Roman de la Rose*, but that influence is more clearly evident in the the French version, and it is the idea of nature found in that version which I consider here.[6]

Nature is implicated in certain kinds of female misbehaviour standardly itemized in medieval anti-feminist writings.[7] For instance, women resent being kept at home by their husbands, but

> se partout va franchement
> Esbatre et sans empeschement,
> La nature tousjours l'atire
> A luxure par avoutire.[8]

indeed says plainly, that they will all be saved. And by this it appears that he wishes to maintain that the sin of lechery is nothing, rather a virtue, which is error and against the law of God]. The phrase *euvre naturelle*, which brings Gerson close to self-contradiction, is used again here. The phrase would seem to be a set euphemism for copulation and therefore, perhaps, the connection with the idea of Nature may not necessarily be strongly felt (this may be why Gerson writes as he does). But given that Christine is discussing Genius' sermon in which sexual activity is explicitly related to the power Nature, it seems unlikely that she would not be thinking of the *euvre de Nature* as something sponsored by the power Nature. For a clear instance of Nature the personification associated with 'her' *fait*, see *Les Echecs amoureux*, fo. 29b (quoted below, p. 157).

[5] See *Les Lamentations de Matheolus et le Livre de leesce de Jehan Le Fèvre, de Resson*, ed. A. G. van Hamel, 2 vols., Bibliothèque de l'École des Hautes Études, Sciences Philologiques et Historiques, 95, 96 (Paris, 1882, 1905), vol. ii, pp. cx–cxvii. References to the *Lamentations* and the French version by Jean Le Fèvre are to this edition.

[6] See Badel, *Roman*, 178–200.

[7] For an introduction to such writing see Alcuin Blamires (ed.), *Woman Defamed and Woman Defended* (Oxford, 1992).

[8] *Lam.* 2. 4045–8.

[if she goes everywhere freely and without hindrance to frolic, nature always draws her to lechery through adultery.]

It is impossible to keep effective watch on a wife—nature will out:

> Qui femme garde, il pert sa paine.
> Autant vaut arer la riviere.
> Haye, mur, porte n'estriviere,
> Buye ne cep, fer ne closture,
> Ne peut contrester a nature;
> Car tel chatel se laisse embler,
> Quant a autre puet assembler,
> Pour accomplir son appetit.[9]

[Whoever tries to keep a woman under control is wasting his time. You might as well plough a river. Hedge, wall, gate, or stirrup-leather, chain or prison, iron or enclosure cannot resist nature. For a possession of this kind is off whenever she has the chance to consort with somebody else to accomplish her desire.]

However, rather than standing as part of a condemnation of promiscuity, these remarks lead into a recommendation of it—at least for men:

> Et se tu en veuls prendre aucune,
> Je lo, soit blanche, bise ou brune,
> Que d'une seule ne te payes,
> Mais que pour une cent en ayes.
> S'omme a seule femme s'alie,
> De mille chayennes se lie.
> Qui des femmes a un millier,
> Lors ne le puet on essillier;
> Franchement vit, tousjours est siens
> Par la franchise de ses biens.[10]

[And if you want to take one of them [i.e. women], I advise that you should not be satisfied with one, be she fair, dark or brunette, but that you should have a hundred of them instead of just one. If a man allies himself to one woman alone, he binds himself with a thousand chains. The man who has a thousand women cannot then be hounded out. He lives in freedom and is always his own man because of the freedom with which he gives his goods.]

---

[9] *Lam.* 2. 4058–65.   [10] *Lam.* 2. 4071–80.

The justification of this attitude lies in the fact that Nature has not instituted monogamy (we hear the tones of La Vieille in the *Roman de La Rose*):[11]

> Nature ne te crea mie
> Pour faire seule compaignie
> A une femme seulement.
> Mais tu fus creés telement
> Com je diray, se tu m'escoutes:
> Toutes por tous, et tous pour toutes.[12]

[Nature did not create you to be the sole company of one woman alone, but you were created such as I shall say, if you listen to me—all women for all men and all men for all women.]

This idea is recurrent:

> E ne m'a pas creé nature
> Pour une seule creature.
> Nennil, elle est a tous commune,
> Elle fait chascun pour chascune.[13]

[And Nature has not created me for one single creature—not at all; she is indiscriminate, she makes every man for every woman.]

and again:

> En n'est pas nature si vile
> Que seulement creast Sebile
> Pour Werry, ne Werry pour elle,
> Ne moy aussi pour Perrenelle.
> Quant les gens ensemble apparie,
> Chascun pour chascune approprie.
> Mais mariage est au contraire:
> Le seul veult a la seule traire;
> Dont nature est forment contrainte
> Et souvent troublée et estainte;
> Retourner veult a sa franchise.[14]

[Nature is not so low as only to have created Sebile for Werry and Werry for her, nor me for Perenelle either. When she brings people together she provides every man for every woman. But marriage is the reverse of this, wanting to attach one to one. Nature is rigidly constrained by

---

[11] See *RR* 13845 ff.   [12] *Lam.* 2. 4081–6.
[13] *Lam.* 3. 1081–4.   [14] *Lam.* 3. 1241–51.

this and frequently troubled and enervated. She wants to return to her freedom.]

As well as these passages, the text features an Old Woman, derived from La Vieille in the *Roman de la Rose*, who encourages sexual behaviour against the prohibitions of the clergy, which are, according to her, hypocritical:

> Se le clergié en fait deffense,
> C'est mal dit, qui a droit y pense.
> Pourquoy dient il le contraire
> De la chose qu'il convient faire?
> Il n'en y a nul, tant soit sage,
> Qui n'aint la coustume et l'usage
> De gesir avecques mouiller...
> Leur commandement ne doit nuire.
> Aux fais, non pas aux dis pren garde.
> Se je te ment, je vueil qu'en m'arde.
> Ceste euvre n'est point reprouvée;
> Ou seroit ceste loy trouvée?
> On doit obeïr par droiture
> Aux commandemens de nature.
> Je te le di en verité,
> Qu'il est pure necessité
> D'exercer euvre naturelle
> A jouvencel et a pucelle.[15]
> Dieux a fait la porte du ventre
> Et veult que Priapus y entre.
> S'il voulsist, on la tenist close.
> Cy ne convient pas longue glose;
> Ceste sentence est toute voire.
> Et d'autre part, c'est fort a croire
> Que Dieux, qui est pere de vie,
> Comdampnast l'amant pour l'amie.
> Ce seroit chose trop inique.
> Le cuer qui a amer s'applique
> Aime Dieux et tient en chierté.
> Mais il het orgueil et fierté.

---

[15] This is, of course, to ignore the power of the free will to combat natural pressures (contrast the comment of Gace de la Buigne quoted below, at n. 29, and consider the implication of the passage from Jean de Condé's *Messe des oiseaux* quoted below, at n. 25). It is worth noting that there is no mention of the natural in the Latin at this point.

Dieux aime le cuer amourable.[16]
Ceste chose est moult favourable.
Pour ce ne la voist nul blasmant!
Quant Dieux voit parjurer l'amant,
Il rit et est plain de leesce.
Amour est droit fait de noblesce
Et veult le cuer loial et ferme;
Le dit du poëte l'afferme,
Fols est qui contre amor estrive.[17]

[If the clergy forbid it, they're wrong, if you think about it rightly. Why do they say the opposite of what it suits them to do? There's not one of them, however wise he may be, who doesn't habitually sleep with women... Their commandment ought not to be heeded. Pay attention to what they do, not what they say. If I'm lying to you may I be burnt. This deed is not forbidden—where can you find that law? One ought by rights to obey the commands of nature. I tell you truly that to do the work of nature is a matter of pure necessity for a young man and a maid. God has made the door of the belly and he wants Priapus to enter it. If He'd wanted, it would have been kept closed. This doesn't need a lengthy gloss—what I say is completely true. And besides, it's hard to believe that God, who is the father of life, would condemn the lover for having his girl: that would be too unfair. God loves the heart which applies itself to loving and holds it dear, but He hates arrogance and pride. God loves the amorous heart. This is a very good thing; He doesn't see anything wrong in it. When God sees the lover perjure himself he laughs and is full of joy. Love is the proper deed of nobility and desires a heart loyal and firm. As the poet says: he is a fool who strives against love.]

Now clearly this kind of thing needs to be taken with a full pinch of salt; something must surely be awry in an outlook which proposes that God is amused at perjury.[18] But our awareness that La Vieille's perspective is skewed here and that the sufferings of Matheolus himself are likely to distort his vision also does not force us to suppose that what Matheolus and La Vieille say about Nature is entirely incorrect. There may be no absolute necessity forcing young people to make love, and it may not always be right to

---

[16] Compare the claim that 'God loveth, and to love wol nought werne' at *TC* 3. 12.

[17] *Lam.* 2. 1883–9, 1892–923.

[18] We are presumably intended to recognize how the passage perverts Christian teaching on charity with the erotic doctrines of Ovid. For God laughing at the perjury of lovers see *Ars am* 1. 633, 'Iuppiter ex alto periuria ridet amantum' and see Ch. 4 above, n. 38.

obey the commands of nature, but it may equally still be legitimate
to think of Nature as urging towards sexual activity with no regard
to moral considerations.

   A similar situation, in which a dubious statement on sex includes
what may be a legitimate conception of a Nature very un-Gersonian
in the unrestricted sexual pressure she exerts, obtains in Jean Le
Fèvre's *Livre de leesce*, a kind of rebuttal of the *Lamentations*.[19] Le
Fèvre mounts arguments to the effect that God, desiring generation,
has established sexual pleasure. At one point such an argument is
followed by a proviso that sexual activity should be performed
'licitement, sans abuser',[20] and this seems sufficiently in tune with
orthodox morality. But there is also this passage in which the
pressure of love and nature towards divinely instituted sexual pleasure produces the unconstrained sexual activity of Solomon:

> Dieux, qui voult generacion,
> L'omme fourma et puis la femme
> Et en leur corps inspira l'ame.
> Amour y mist et compaignie
> Pour faire et pourcreer lignie.
> Et ne fait pas a oublier
> Qu'il commanda multiplier
> Et croistre pour remplir la terre.
> Ce ne fu pas signe de guerre;
> Il voult que propagacion
> Venist par delectacion.
> Homme et femme sont raisonnables
> Et plus discrès et plus notables
> Que ne soit autre creature.[21]
> Amour puissant avec nature

---

[19] 'Dans le *Livre de L[e]esse* Le Fèvre réfute point par point les assertions de Matheolus' (Badel, *Roman*, 196) [In the *Livre de leesce* Le Fèvre refutes the assertions of Matheolus
point by point]. Jean opens the work by asking pardon of ladies for having translated
Matheolus and tells them that the current work will show how women ought not to be
blamed but rather praised and honoured (*LL* 1–40).

[20] *LL* 3012.

[21] There appears to be a suggestion here that the influence of human rationality,
understood as militating against sexual activity, needs to be broken down. For this
sentiment see also *Renart le Contrefait*, and perhaps *Les Echecs amoureux*, where the God of
Love, who may be conceived as non-reasonable, claims that he is needed to draw human
beings to the sexual act necessary for Nature's reproductive project. These texts are
treated below.

Les fait mouvoir a deliter
Et a charnelment habiter
Pour continuer nostre espece,
Que la mort corrompt et despece;
Car qui s'en tenroit pour tencier,
Tout seroit a recommencier.
Salemon fu riche homme et sage;
De nature savoit l'usage;
Il fu roy et non pas hermite,
Si ne voult estre sodomite;
Sodomite est plus lais pechiés
Dont l'homme puist estre entechiés.
Pour ce prist il des concubines
Et des femmes et des roïnes
Et jouvenceles a plenté
En usant de sa voulenté.
Il compila par grant science
Ecclesiastes, Sapience
Et proverbes et paraboles,
Dont on lit en maintes escoles;...
Se par amour, qui le lya,
Aux femmes tant s'umilia
Que leur plaisir voult du tout faire,
Maistre Mahieu s'en doit bien taire.[22]

[God who desires generation formed man and then woman and gave life to the soul in their bodies. He placed love and companionship there to make and procreate lineage. It should not be forgotten that he gave the command to multiply and increase to fill the earth. This was no sign of war: he wanted propagation to come about through pleasure. Man and woman are endowed with reason and are wiser and more remarkable than any other creature. Powerful love with nature makes them move to take pleasure and live together carnally to continue our species, which death corrupts and decimates. For if one abstained from this act out of some objection to it, everything would have to be started again. Solomon was a mighty and wise man; he knew the way Nature operates. He was a king and not a hermit and he didn't want to be a sodomite. Sodomy is the worst sin of which man can be guilty. So he took concubines and wives and queens and plenty of young girls, giving his desire its head. He put together, through his great learning, Ecclesiastes, Wisdom and proverbs and parables which are studied in many schools.... If on account of love which bound him he

[22] *LL* 826–60, 863–6.

humbled himself so greatly before women that he wanted to do their pleasure in everything, Master Matthew had better shut up.]

Now there may be irony here, for though calling Solomon 'sage' and citing his Wisdom writings appears to lend weight to the contention that his uninhibited sexual behaviour is a laudable submission to a divinely instituted directive, Solomon's attachment to his concubines was regularly understood as an egregious foolishness which led him into sin.[23] The comment here on how he humbled himself to women in pursuing their pleasure, though on the surface apparently intended to win our approval, seems quite as likely, given the orthodoxy about the proper power relations between men and women, to excite our condemnation. Perhaps we should distance ourselves from this celebration of Solomon's sexuality. Nevertheless, such distancing would not inevitably entail a scepticism about the conception of Nature as stimulating in unconstrained fashion heterosexual sexual activity, whilst standing opposed to homosexuality, for such a Nature is recognizably Ulpianic, animal, generic, and as such assimilable to orthodox theological understandings.

The moral position of Nature appears more clearly, free of the blurring effect of the possibility of irony, in other works. In Jean de Condé's *La Messe des oiseaux*, the author offers an apparently subversive demonstration that nuns have as much right in Nature to take lovers as do canonesses; this notion is then allegorized in such a way as to disarm its subversiveness.[24] This allegorizing move, however, does not involve a denial that Nature's pressure is towards love, which in the case of the nuns and the canonesses is a pressure towards evil. In a conclusion which affirms the reasonableness of married love and the appropriateness of celibacy to religious Jean writes:

> Chanonesses et vous nonains,
> De coi la tenche fu orains,
> En folie vous deliteis
> Et en vous cuers maint vaniteis.

---

[23] See 1 Kings 11 for Solomon's being drawn into idolatry by his foreign wives.

[24] Jean de Condé, on whom see Jacques Ribard, *Un ménestrel du XIV siècle* (Geneva, 1969), was born *c.*1275–80 and died in 1345. For edition see *La Messe des oiseaux et le Dit des Jacobins et des Fremeneurs*, ed. Jacques Ribard, Textes Littéraires Français (Geneva, 1970). The translation is that in *Chaucer's Dream Visions: Sources and Analogues*, trans. B. A. Windeatt (Cambridge, 1982) with occasional adjustments.

> Trop vous a Venus decheües,
> Quant en ses las iestes cheües,
> Car Amours, dont Venus est dame,
> Ele est du tout contraire a l'ame
> Et dampnation li enorte,
> Ja soit che Nature l'aporte.[25]

[You canonesses and nuns who quarrelled just now, you take delight in folly and fill your heart with many vain things. Too much has Venus deceived you when you fell into her snares, for Love—of which Venus is the mistress—is utterly contrary to your souls and damnation goads it on, even though Nature contributes it.]

It is probably the special circumstances of religious women, committed as they are supposed to be to celibacy, which gives rise to the strong language of damnation, but still, Nature is evidently conceived as having a tendency to prompt women in general towards sexual behaviour without regard to its moral acceptability. These authorial words confirm firstly the close co-operation of Nature and Venus of which Venus herself has spoken earlier:

> Je ai, aprés Dieu et Nature,
> Pooir sour toute creature
> Qui naist de marle et de femiele,
> Qui alaitie est de mamielle
> U par autre guise nourie.
> Sour chascune ai ma seignourie
> Selonc ce que le me consent
> Nature, qui a moi s'assent,
> Cui je tieng a ma souveraine,
> Qu'ele oevre en terre premeraine
> Aprés Dieu, ki commenchemens
> Est deseur tous et finemens;
> Nature establi et crea
> Et sa poissance li grea,
> Et de Nature sui creee
> Ki ma maistrie m'a greee.
> Quant son pooir au mien assamble,
> Et il s'acordent bien ensamble,
> Sans le souverain Creatour
> Ne porroit nus hons querre tour

---

[25] *Messe des oiseaux* (*Messe*), 1527–36.

> Dont vers nous tenser se peüst
> Pour forche ne sens qu'il eüst.[26]

[I have—after God and Nature—dominion over every creature that is born, male or female, suckled at the breast or nourished in any other way. I have my dominion over everybody, in accordance with what is granted to me by Nature, who is at one with me. For she is the primary active principle on earth after God, who is above everything, the beginning and end of all. It is He who established and created Nature, and accorded to her her power, and I was created by Nature, who has established my authority. When her power unites with mine and they accord well together, then without the aid of the Sovereign Creator no man can find means to protect himself against us by whatever strength or wit that he has.]

and again:

> Envers cui que eles mesfachent
> Quant eles aiment, en che point,
> Voir, envers moi ne meffont point.
> Pour coi dont les renfuseroie?
> Encontre Nature seroie,
> Quant Nature a amer semont
> Toutes creatures del mont.[27]

[Whoever they [the nuns] do wrong to in as much as they love, truly in this respect they do no wrong at all to me. Why should I reject them for that? I would be against Nature, when Nature urges all creatures of the world to love.]

But the words the author puts *in proprium os* at the end of the text also confirm what these remarks of Venus imply—the morally anarchic potential in Nature as she co-operates with Venus.

The *Roman des deduis* of Gace de la Buigne is a treatise on hunting in the form of a debate between Love of Dogs and Love of Birds.[28] The main body of the work is preceded by a lengthy section in which Gace discusses what vices the hunter must avoid and what virtues he must practise, for hunting is not merely a technique, but also has moral requirements to make of its practitioners. In the course of this preliminary exposition Gace finds cause to counter excuses for wrong behaviour which argue that nature inclines to evil—his concern at this point is with *gloutonnie* and *luxure*:

[26] *Messe* 957–78.   [27] *Messe* 1092–8.
[28] Gace, a Chaplain of the Kings of France, wrote the *Roman des deduis* between 1359 and 1377. The edition used here is that of Åke Blomqvist (Karlshamn, 1951).

> mais [se] descort
> As a moy et tu veulles dire
> Que nature a pechié t'encline,
> Si as tu franche volenté,
> Combien que y soies encliné.[29]

[But if you disgree with me and want to say that nature inclines you to sin, you still have free will, however much you may be inclined to it.]

Gace does not deny the claim about nature and sin, apparently conceding that there may be a natural inclination to certain kinds of evil. That Gace supposes Nature to incline to the sins of the flesh is clearly evident when he offers a psychomachia in which the seven deadly sins confront the virtues and Nature fights, along with Venus, Amours, Delit, and Oiseuse, among others, in the company of Luxure and Gloutonnie, who command the force most powerfully threatening to virtue. Deduit des Oiseaux complains to Reson about Nature in the following terms:

> Mais Nature par son pouoir,
> Qui a fait Luxure esmouvoir
> Telement en mon prejudice
> Que je n'en puis avoir justice,
> Par tout elle tient son escolle
> Et mes gens de tous poins affolle, . . .
> Par tout veult lire ces leçons.
> Trop lonc seroit a reciter
> Ou Nature la fait ouvrer
> Et Oiseuse sa chamberiere.
> L'une li treuve la matiere,
> Et l'autre la semont au fait,
> Si que tout mon fait en deffait.[30]

[But Nature, who by her power has stirred up Lechery to my prejudice in such a way that I cannot have justice, everywhere keeps her school and makes my people go utterly mad. . . . Everywhere she wants to read these lessons. It would take too long to recount where Nature puts her to work, and Idleness her chamberlain. One of them finds her the material and the other summons her to the deed in such a way that she undoes everything I accomplish.]

---

[29] RD 1736–40.   [30] RD 3255–60, 3264–70.

Nature is the standard bearer for Luxure in the fight against Continence, Chastee, Abstinence, and their forces; Luxure is in fact her daughter:

> Nature porte sa baniere,
> Qui contre Chastee est fiere,
> Si a juré Sainte Marie
> Qu'elle li fera villenie,
> Car la poindra de tel pointure
> Que sa fille dame Luxure
> De lui fera tout son plaisir.[31]

[Nature carries her banner, Nature who is disdainful towards Chastity. She has sworn by Holy Mary that she will do her harm, for she will pierce her with such a point that her daughter Dame Lechery will do all her pleasure with her.]

But the virtues, of course, win in the end: Luxure flees to Paris, where she has friends, pursued by Chastee;[32] Nature protests that she will fight to the death but is eventually seized by the throat by Vieillesse and yields to her;[33] on seeing Nature thus caught Venus flees.[34]

Gace, then, connects Nature with a sexuality seen as opposed to the good and with the morally ill-disposed flesh in general (for Nature is allied with Gloutonnie as well as Luxure, and Oiseuse can also be considered a sin of the flesh[35]) and has her prompting evil. And it is clear that, as Gace presents it, the effective remedy against Nature's influence lies not in the exercise of virtue, but in growing old: there is here an implicit acknowledgement of the immense power of Nature, which human free will seems unable to control.[36]

Though Gace sets a limit to Nature's power in having her overcome by Vieillesse, such a limit is not obligatory. Henri d'Andeli has

---

[31] *RD* 4925–31. The inappropriate oath by the Virgin Mary is perhaps a pointer to Nature's eventual defeat.

[32] *RD* 5108–14.

[33] *RD* 5115–28.

[34] *RD* 5131 f.

[35] For Sloth as sin of the flesh see Morton Bloomfield, *The Seven Deadly Sins* (East Lansing, Mich., 1952), 147, 213.

[36] Contrast the affirmation of Nature in the *Roman de la Rose* that free will equips the human being to combat the pull of evil successfully (*RR* 17029 ff.).

Nature triumphant over age in his *Lai d'Aristote*.[37] In this work
Aristotle, old man that he is,[38] acknowledges Nature's power in
causing him to fall under the spell of the young woman he loves:

> Oïl, fait il, ma douce dame.
> Por vos metrai et cors et ame,
> Honeur et vie en aventure!
> Tant m'a fet Amors et Nature
> Que de vos partir ne me puis.[39]

[Yes, he said, my sweet lady. For you I will put my body and soul, my
honour and my life in jeopardy. So much have Love and Nature done to
me that I cannot part from you.]

But the power of Nature is dangerous: his enslavement is not something Aristotle enjoys or approves. He warns Alexander of the risk
he faces from love and nature, especially since he is young:

> Quant ge, qui sui plains de viellece,
> Ne poi contre Amor rendre estal
> Q'ele ne m'ait torné a mal
> Si grant com vos avez vëu.
> Quant que g'ai apris et lëu
> M'a desfait Nature en une eure,
> Qui tote science deveure
> Puis qu'ele s'en velt entremetre....
>   bien savoie la doutance
> Et l'anui et la mesestance
> Qui de Nature vient et muet.
> Puis que par force m'en estuet
> Faire folie si aperte,
> Voz n'en poiez aler sanz perte
> Ne sanz blasme de vostre gent![40]

---

[37] It should be said that this work (?*c*.1225) antedates Jean de Meun's portion of the
Roman de la Rose. For details of the work and its author see the edition by Maurice
Delbouille (Paris, 1951), from which the quotations here are taken.

[38] The issue of the relation between old age and Nature in sexual matters is important
with regard to Gower's *Confessio Amantis*, as we shall see in the next chapter. It has been
argued (I think wrongly) that Gower holds love in old age to be unnatural. That does,
however, seem to be the view expressed in Matheolus' *Lamentations*. There Nature takes
exception to Aristotle's elderly sexual infatuation (1. 1079–128) and condemns him for
pushing himself beyond his physical capacities (1. 1125–7).

[39] *Lai d'Aristote* 406–10.

[40] *LA* 485–92, 496–502.

[when I, who am full of age, am unable to fight against love and prevent her from turning me to evil as great as you have seen. Whatever I have learnt and read, Nature defeated me in a single hour, Nature who consumes all knowledge, when she wishes to interfere... I was well acquainted with the fear, the pain and the misery which comes from Nature and originates in it. Since I am made by force to do such open folly, you cannot get away from it unscathed and without the censure of your people.]

But the moral of the story is that 'amors vaint tout et tout vaincra | Tant com cis siecles durera'⁴¹ [Love conquers all and will conquer all while this world lasts] and the authorial voice finds exoneration for Aristotle in this power of Nature:

> s'il l'ot par force entrepris,
> En doit il estre en mal repris?
> Nenil! Car amors l'esforça
> Et volentez, qui la force a
> Sor toz et sor totes ensanble.
> Dont n'a li maistres, ce me sanble,
> Nule coupe en sa mespresure,
> Quant ne mesprist par apresure,
> Mais par nature droite et fine.⁴²

[if it was under duress that he undertook it [love] ought he to be blamed for it? Not at all! For Love constrained him, and Desire, which has power over every man and and every woman alike. So the master [Aristotle], it seems to me, incurs no blame in his wrongdoing, since he did not do wrong as a matter of habit, but by nature fair and square.]

The exoneration of Aristotle, however, does not constitute an exoneration of Nature.

We can see in this French writing, then, widely divergent views on the moral status of Nature. At the one extreme, Gerson refuses to allow Jean de Meun's association of Nature with dubious sexual behaviour, and at the other Gace de la Buigne makes a straightforward connection between Nature and Lechery, a connection more straightforward, in fact, than that made in the *Roman de la Rose* itself.

If different works manifest very different views about Nature, single texts also can present opposing attitudes, as they respond both to Nature's claims to general moral authority and to a sense that her

---

⁴¹ *LA* 578–9.   ⁴² *LA* 534–42.

influence in certain spheres—particularly the sexual—is not entirely benign. *Les Echecs amoureux* is very explicit about the close association of Nature and Reason.[43] Nature informs the poet that God has given humankind a sensual side which it has in common with the animals and also reason which distinguishes it from them and she counsels him to follow the path of reason and not to be seduced by the sensual:

> Car Raison a virtu saccorde
> Et li sentimens corporeulx
> Nentent qua delit sauoureux
> Et a mondaines vanites. . . .
> Pren dont le chemin de Raison
> Et de vertu toute saison
> Et fuy ce que Raison desprise.[44]

[For Reason accords with virtue, and bodily sense only inclines to delight of the senses and worldly vanities . . . so take the path of Reason and of virtue at all times and flee what Reason despises.]

This is strongly reminiscent of the *De planctu Naturae*,[45] and the Alanian tendencies of *Les Echecs* are in evidence again when Pallas, a figure associated with reason and wisdom, takes the poet to task for his attachment to Venus and Amours, her son. Venus and Amours are interested in the first place in pleasure rather than the profit of procreation,[46] and Pallas is severe on this commitment to delight:

> Car delis donne occasion
> De faire fornicacion
> Et adulteres deffrenes
> Horriblez et desordonnes
> Descorde fraude traisons
> Et tout dautres grans mesproisons
> Questre ne pourroient comprises.[47]

---

[43] This work was written between 1370 and 1380. There exists a commentary in French on the first part of the poem dating from about 1400 and John Lydgate's *Reson and Sensuallyte* (before 1412) is a translation of part of it. Quotations from the poem are taken from E. Sieper, *Les Echecs amoureux*, Litterarhistorische Forschungen 9 (Weimar, 1898).

[44] *EA* fo. 4b/5a (Sieper, *Echecs*, 13).

[45] See above, Ch. 3.

[46] See Sieper, *Echecs*, 57 on *EA* fo. 30b.

[47] *EA* fo. 48a (Sieper, *Echecs*, 80).

[For delight gives occasion to commit fornication and unbridled adulteries, horrible and uncontrolled, discord, fraud, treason, and all the other great misdeeds which you would not believe existed.]

Pallas recurs to the distinction between reason and the part humanity shares with the animals and argues that the life of Venus reduces human beings to the level of animals when they should be pursuing reason and the virtues:

> Pour ce quil a entendement
> Et Raisonnable Jugement
> Qui le fait des Dieux approuchier
> Si com luy doit bien Reprouchier
> Quant Il veult les bestes ensuiure
> Car Il doit plus noblement viure. . . .
> Homs doit laissier deliz aux bestes
> Et entendre a chosez honnestes
> Ou Raisons et vertus enclinent.[48]

[Since he has understanding and rational judgement which makes him come close to the Gods, he ought to be reproached when he wants to follow the beasts, because he ought to live more nobly. . . . Man ought to leave pleasure to the beasts and attend to honourable things where Reason and virtue lead.]

It is natural for the animals to pursue sensual satisfaction, but human beings, because they possess reason as well as a sensual side, would actually be going against Nature were they to abandon reason in favour of sensuality.[49] So Pallas tells the poet that there is no doubt

> Que tu fais contre la droiture
> Et de Raison et de nature
> Qui veulx ainsy viure en loyseuse
> De la vie delicieuse
> Ou venus fait les folz cuers traire
> Qui tant est a tout bien contraire.[50]

[that you are acting against the rule of both Reason and Nature in wanting to live in the idleness of the life of delight, to which Venus, who is so contrary to all good, draws foolish hearts.]

---

[48] *EA* fo. 52a (Sieper, *Echecs*, 87).
[49] See *EA* fos. 46a and 52a (Sieper, *Echecs*, 79, 87).
[50] *EA* fo. 51a (Sieper, *Echecs*, 85).

However, this Alanian paradigm coexists with one much more sympathetic to the vision of the *Roman de la Rose*. Amours tells the poet, after the fashion of the *Roman*'s Reson, that Nature has put delight in the sexual act,[51] but he goes further than this in a passage which reflects extremely interestingly on the stance of Reson in the *Roman*. It is, according to Amours, not only sexual pleasure that Nature uses:

> Secondement nature y vault
> Mettre aussy lamour que moult vault
> Pour la chose parfaire adroit
> Qui aultrement petit vauldroit
> Car deliz ne laccorde
> Ne pourroit attraire a sa corde
> Lumain cuer ce nest mie doubte
> Mais quant amour au cuer se boute
> Lors fait elle sans nul discort
> Le cuer et le delit daccort
> Si quez le cuer art et desire
> A venir ou deliz le tire. . . .
> Ainsy attrait les cuers humains
> Nature a son fait soirs et mains
> Et les fait a sa forge courre
> Pour lespiece humaine secourre.[52]

[Secondly Nature wants to send love in as well, which is of great merit, to have the thing done properly, which otherwise would be worth little: for neither pleasure nor harmony, without any doubt, could attract the human heart to her bond; but when love enters the heart, then she acts irresistibly in such a way that the heart burns and desires to come where pleasure draws it. . . . Thus Nature attracts human hearts to her deed day and night and makes them run to her forge to help the human species.]

This seems to question the distinction made in the *Roman de la Rose* by Reson between a kind of love that Nature sanctions, which pursues the end of procreation, and the love presided over by the God of Love which is not interested in procreation. In *Les Echecs* the God of Love claims that what he stands for is an essential part of Nature's procreative scheme, bidding for a respectability refused his counterpart in the *Roman de la Rose* by the Reson of that poem. However, despite this claim and though Amours apparently

---

[51] *EA* fo. 29a (Sieper, *Echecs*, 54 f.).   [52] *EA* fo. 29a, b (Sieper, *Echecs*, 55).

personifies something operating at a higher pyschological level than the basic animal impulsion towards sex—presumably the attraction between two particular persons, the love into which one can fall—Amours still would seem, given his relationship to Venus and the pursuit of pleasure condemned as anti-Reason by Pallas (and given also the relationship between this poem and the *Roman de la Rose*), to stand opposed to Reason.[53] So though we are perhaps offered some kind of rehabilitation of Amours in this poem founded on the countering of the contention of the *Roman*'s Reson that the love presided over by the God of Love is something to be distinguished from natural procreative drives, the alignment of Amours and Nature, the fact that Nature uses Amours, nevertheless tends to drive Nature and Reason apart.

It is just possible, perhaps, that we are being invited to remember and approve what Reson says about the God of Love in the *Roman de la Rose* and reject what Amours has to say about himself in *Les Echecs* as special and invalid pleading, though one can see easily enough that a reading of the end of the *Roman de la Rose* might well have prompted the idea, entertained quite unironically, that the co-operation of Nature, Venus, and Amours is necessary for the successful achievement of Nature's procreative ends. But even if we should not accept what Amours says here about himself without reservation, it is more difficult to feel that we ought to dismiss the link he proposes between procreation and pleasure; Pallas may be right that Venus is interested only in pleasure, but the pursuit of sexual pleasure is in Amours's account part of Nature's procreative system. That account derives here from Reson in the *Roman de la Rose*, and has the authority of that figure behind it. However, if the pursuit of sexual pleasure is indeed ordered to natural procreative ends, if, in fact, Nature can legitimately be understood to have created sexual pleasure, then the terms in which Pallas speaks of Venus and Nature do not do justice to the relationship which exists between them, implying rather simplistically sheer opposition where there is evidently much co-operation. We are, after all, told of how Venus gets ready the tools used in Nature's forge.[54] For all

---

[53] For another kind of claim that unReason is necessary for the survival of the species see *Renart le Contrefait*, 24367 ff., quoted below.

[54] *EA* fo. 30a (Sieper, *Echecs*, 56). In this picture of Venus forwarding the work of Nature's forge, the author may be acknowledging explicitly what the *De planctu Naturae*

that Pallas thinks the pursuit of delight bestial and anti-rational, and supposes 'la vie delicieuse' to be contrary to Nature, Nature uses delight to fulfil her purposes.[55] Are we then to suppose that the irony is directed at Pallas? The difficulty here is that Nature herself speaks of how one should follow reason and flee what reason despises rather than pursuing bodily pleasure in terms very similar to those of Pallas.[56] It does seem as though Alanian and de Meunian paradigms collide in this poem in a fashion which may well prohibit resolution.

Renart le Contrefait is another poem in which the treatment of Nature shows signs of a desire to accommodate two irreconcilable conceptions of that figure.[57] The difficulty, as with *Les Echecs*, lies in the issue of Nature's relationship on the one hand to reason and on the other to sex. But whereas *Les Echecs* never explicitly offers Nature for condemnation, the problems attaching to her being implicit in her relationship with Venus, *Renart le Contrefait*'s Nature is very evidently problematic, though for much of its course the poem does not seem to want to acknowledge this.

Renart le Contrefait invests a great deal of energy in suggesting that Nature, correctly understood, is always at one with reason and the right. Renart informs us that his arts do not come from Nature:

> Mes ars ne vient pas de Nature,
> Et pour ce n'ay je de lui cure:
> Naistre nous fait, vivre et sentir,

seems not to wish clearly to confess, that a morally dubious Venus is inevitably part of the reproductive scheme over which Nature now presides.

[55] One might seek to distinguish between 'la vie delicieuse' and the occasional—and natural—pursuit of delight, but this seems to go against the grain of Pallas' moral philosophy in which any pursuit of delight for its own sake seems contrary to the rational nature of the human being. Pallas might allow the enjoyment of sexual pleasure arising from an act performed with the intention of procreation, but this would show a stricter concern for purity of intention than does Nature, who is happy to use the intention to achieve sexual pleasure as a means to her procreative ends.

[56] See the lines from *EA* fos. 4b/5a, quoted above, at n. 44.

[57] *Renart le Contrefait* is an extremely lengthy work which exists in two versions written by the same author (a bigamous clerk of Troyes). The first version was composed between 1319 and 1322, the second was started in 1328 and left incomplete around 1342. See the introduction to the edition by G. Raynaud and H. Lemâitre, 2 vols. (Paris, 1914). This edition, from which the quotations below are given, prints the second version of the work as the main text, with significantly variant material from the first version given in the annotation.

Mais mal ne fait pas consentir,
Car mal ne vient pas de Nature;
Pour ce mon art n'a de lui cure.
Mais bien vient naturelement
Dès le premier commencement
Que Dieu la Nature ordonna,
Et telz dons de lui luy donna
Que par Raison s'ordonneroit,
Ne ja aultre maistre n'aroit.
Adez vault Raison le sieusist
Et de tous ses fais le duisist,
Ne nulle foiz sans lui n'alast,
Feïst, deïst, ouvrast, parlast,
Et s'il estoit que la venist
Que elle autre chemin tenist
Que Raison ne feïst sa cure,
Elle perdroit [*ed.* par droit] nom de Nature,
Tant comme sans lui ouvreroit,
Mauvais nom en recouvreroit.
Pour quoy Nature sans Raison
Ne doit aler nulle saison.
Ainsi l'ordonna qui le fist,
Qui oncques maulx en lui ne mist.
Nature et Raison mist ensamble,
Et se Nature s'en dessamble,
Elle n'est Nature appellée,
Mais tressote et desordonnée.
Tout cil en grant foulour se tient
Qui dist mal par Nature vient
Ne que Nature y mecte cure.[58]

[My arts do not come from Nature and so I have no time for her. She gives us birth, makes us live and feel, but she does not make us consent to evil, for evil does not come from Nature. Therefore my art does not bother about her. But good comes naturally, since the first beginning when God set up Nature and gave her such gifts from him that she should govern herself by Reason and never have another master. And he requires that Reason should take her and guide her in all her doings and that she should never go without Reason, or do or say or work or talk without it. And if it were to happen that she should come to take a road other than that which

---

[58] *RC* 6107–39. At 6257 ff. the unnaturalness of Avarice is affirmed, whilst *pacïence* and *souffisance* are said to come from 'bonne Nature'.

Reason was in charge of, she would lose the name of Nature; as long as she operated without Reason, she would get a bad name because of it. So Nature should not at any time go without Reason. He ordained it thus who created her, who never put any bad in her. He put Nature and Reason together, and if Nature detaches herself she is no longer called Nature, but is utterly foolish and out of order. Any person who says that evil occurs through Nature and that Nature doesn't bother about it is a complete fool.]

All vice is contrary to Nature and human beings are born to do good and please God, ordered to this end by the nature God has given them.[59] Unfortunately, custom can alter the directions of Nature, and it is custom which teaches human beings vice:

> Tous telz vices tient et aprent,
> Mais Nature ne scet neant,
> Dont ne doit on mie retraire
> Que Nature lui face faire,
> Fors coustume tant seulement.[60]

[All such vices he [man] holds and learns, but Nature knows nothing of them: so one should never object to what Nature makes man do, but only what custom makes him.]

A reworking of the Boethian exemplum of the tree constrained artificially to grow in a certain way follows, with less optimism than Boethius shows for the tree's capacity to return to its original and proper natural course of development,[61] and this is used to illustrate how

---

[59] See *RC* 6310–13.

[60] *RC* 6321–5. Custom is able to corrupt Nature at 6219 ff. In the *Roman de Silence* (second half of the 13th century) Nature and Norreture each claim that the other is responsible for Adam's Fall, but Nature wins the argument. In this romance the heroine's return to her natural womanhood, after being reared as a male, is spoken of as a recovery of Nature's rights (*droiture*) and it does seem (with the death of the evil queen, Silence's marriage to the king, and the recovery of women's right to inherit which are all part of the denouement) to be the most satisfactory resolution of the action one can conceive. Nevertheless, the work certainly raises questions as to whether Norreture cannot improve on Nature. There are remarks, for instance, which suggest that, just as Nature is responsible for producing the admirable Silence, so she endows people with evil natures also (see 2295 ff.). She is explicitly presented as capable of ill humour and carelessness (see 1835 f.). For the *Roman de Silence* see the edition and translation by Sarah Roche-Mahdi (East Lansing, Mich., 1992); pp. xvii–xix of the introduction to this edition consider the topos of Nature/Norreture opposition.

[61] See *RC* 6326 ff. and Boethius *CP* 3. m. 2. (See also *RC* 6291 ff. for animals along the lines of Boethius.)

> acoustumance
> Fait toute mauvaise ordonnance,
> Et qui naturelment se maine,
> Raison le met en son demaine.
> Raison et Nature est un point,
> Nul ne va pas sans l'autre point.[62]

[Custom creates all bad behaviour, and Reason takes under her wing the person who directs himself according to Nature. Reason and Nature are a single item—you never find them apart.]

For all this strong linkage between Reason, the good, and Nature, however, the first of these passages does envisage the possibility of Nature's operating without Reason and going wrong, and though it claims that Nature so operating is no longer Nature, in making that claim it still refers to that which supposedly disqualifies itself from being Nature as Nature. Such a paradoxical way of speaking concedes the difficulty of separating off this unacceptable motive force of human behaviour from Nature, reasonable and good. The difficulty would seem to lie in the perception that the errant force is constituted out of, or, if one prefers it, gives conceptual shape to, exactly those things in the human being which constitute or are designated by the acceptable Nature. A similarly paradoxical use of language occurs in the following passage, which comes after we have been told, in terms Alanian enough, that God established Nature on earth and that everything is under her jurisdiction:[63]

> Elle doit regner par Raison,
> Par Raison lui fut baillié voye;
> Or si se gard qui la fourvoye!...
> Tant que Nature tient sa voye,
> Par Raison point ne se fourvoye;
> Et quant elle passe le point,
> Que Raison ne le conduit point
> Et qu'en ses fais ne le convoye,
> Certainement elle fourvoye
> Et va contre l'ordonnement
> Que Dieu lui fist premierement.
> Tant com lez Raison va et vient,

---

[62] *RC* 6361–6.
[63] *RC* 6525 ff. See also 6059 ff. and 6398 ff., this latter affirming that God puts Nature in charge of the defectible material creation.

Elle son propre nom maintient,
Icellui que Dieu lui donna
Qui a ceste fin l'ordonna,
Ne aultrement ne le doit faire,
Et quant elle fait le contraire,
Lors n'est plus Nature appellée,
Mais est gloutte et desmesurée. . . .
Ne doit pas Nature estre dicte
Si tost que sans Raison habite;
Aultrement n'est ja fourvoyé,
Se de Raison n'est eslongié.[64]

[She ought to rule in accordance with Reason. A certain path was appointed for her in accordance with Reason. Now watch out if you lead her astray. . . . Whilst Nature holds her course, through Reason she does not go astray, and when she goes beyond a certain point and Reason ceases to lead her and does not accompany her in what she does, then to be sure she goes astray and goes against the mode of procedure that God first appointed for her. Whilst she comes and goes in the company of Reason she maintains her proper name, which God gave her, who appointed her to this end: she should not do otherwise. And when she does the opposite, then she is no longer called Nature, but she is bloated and excessive. . . . She should not be called Nature whilst she lives without Reason. Otherwise she is never led astray when she is not separated from Reason.]

This way of talking about Nature testifies to an unhappiness with the notion that she causes evil, but also to an implicit recognition that what most strongly characterizes Nature is not accordance with Reason, but kinds of operation evident in evil behaviour as well as good. So what we might call the Alanian impetus to build reasonableness into the definition of Nature, an impetus which gives us the explicit claims of these passages, is thwarted by the projection, through the way in which those claims are expressed, of a Nature in fact unreasonable. That defining Nature in terms of Reason is, to say the least, problematic becomes very evident later on,[65] when Nature herself—whose identity as Nature can hardly be questioned—tells us that she does not always obey her mistress

---

[64] *RC* 6534–6, 6547–62, 6565–8.

[65] 'Later on' in the sequence of the text, and also, it would seem, considerably later on in time of composition. We may be dealing with a change over time in the conception of Nature on the author's part, though if this is so the new conception, clearly separating Reason and Nature, would seem to have been latent already in the earlier one which associated Reason and Nature only at the cost of some logical awkwardness, as we have seen.

Reason. Though Nature's speech begins in a celebration of moderation and reason such as one might expect from a loyal servant of Reason, it is not long before she is speaking in such a way as to suggest that there is no necessary accommodation of natural activities to what is right:

> Se tu voeulx vivre longuement,
> Boy et menguë par raison.
> En tout temps, en toute saison
> Raison voeult en trestous lieux estre;
> Elle est ma dame et est mon maistre. . . .
> Ne je ne doy nulle rien faire
> Qu'a son voloir et a son plaire.
> Parfois seroie dissolue,
> Se par el n'estoie tenue;
> Avec lui devons tous aller.
> Combien que soit de ravaller,
> Maintz me suivroient volentiers,
> Se Raison n'estoit es sentiers.[66]

[If you want to live long, drink and eat in accordance with reason. At all times, on all occasions, Reason wishes to be present in all places; she is my mistress and my master. . . . I must do nothing but at her will and her pleasure. I would sometimes be dissolute if I were not held in check by her. We must all follow her lead. However much they might be lowering themselves, many would follow me willingly if Reason were not in accompaniment.]

A certain tension between moral imperatives and the impulses of Nature is in evidence here. That tension is also apparent when Nature goes on to explain[67] how Honte (Shame), the daughter of Reason, causes Nature's works to be held cheap and the opportunity of pleasure given over and how God ordained that Nature should work and rule in accordance with Reason because:

> quant je regne sans Raison,
> Ne puis estre en bonne saison
> N'a grant honneur n'a sceureté,
> Combien que soit ma volenté.[68]

[when I rule without Reason, I cannot be appropriate or greatly honoured or in a position of security, however much I might wish it.]

[66] *RC* 24324–8, 24333–40.   [67] *RC* 24341 ff.   [68] *RC* 24363–6.

That the notion of Nature working without Reason is no mere hypothesis is evident from Nature's confession that she is not, in fact, completely obedient to Reason—the need for procreation, according to her, demands otherwise:

> Mais, combien qu'elle soit ma dame,
> Tout son voloir ne fay, par m'ame.
> Maint homme peu s'en loëroient,
> Et les dames m'en blasmeroient,
> Ces beaulx varlès et ces pucelles
> Et ces dames cointes et belles
> Qui s'entr'ayment et par moy oeuvrent,
> Quant ilz en privé s'entretroeuvent,
> Ne loëroient pas ma joye,
> Se par Raison ouvrer volloye.
> De Raison ung dé ne douroient,
> Ne en ce riens ne le croiroient,
> Qui plus est meilleur et souvent
> Quant l'un l'autre entre sez bras tient
> Et s'esbatent en lieu privé.
> Par moy sont tel mil engenré,
> Et tel mil en naissent sur terre,
> Se vouloient Raison enquerre,
> Qui ja engenrés ne seroient,
> Ne ja sur terre ne naistroient.
> Ainsi le monde feniroit,
> Trop petitte durée aroit.
> De cent ung il ne seroit pas,
> Se Raison estoit mes compas
> Que ne peüsse que par lui,
> Mais n'en prendray conseil a lui,
> Mais ouvreray de mes bateaulx.[69]

[But however much she [Reason] is my lady, I do not, on my soul, do all her will. Many men would not be very pleased [?] and the women would find fault with me, these handsome young men and these maidens and these charming and beautiful ladies who love one another and act through me when they come together in private—they would not praise the joy I give if I wished to work in accordance with Reason. They wouldn't give a fig for Reason or give her any credit as to that activity which is much better

---

[69] RC 24367–93. Nature goes on to talk about how she and Reason govern the animals; we have again the motif of natural animal sexuality, in contrast with human sexuality, being unproblematic for the right ordering of the world.

and comes about when one holds the other in his arms and they frolic in a private place. By me are so many thousands engendered, so many thousands brought to birth on earth who would never be engendered or born on earth if reason were followed. And so the world would come to an end, it would not last long enough. There would not be one person in a hundred if Reason were my guide so that I could not do anything without her; however, I shall not take counsel of her, but I shall do things off my own bat.]

What Nature says here about unreasonable behaviour serving the end of procreation reminds one of how Nature in the *Roman de la Rose* in colluding with Venus endorses sexual behaviour which goes against Reson. Perhaps Nature's commitment to sexual pleasure in *Renart* is more enthusiastic than that of her counterpart in the *Roman*, where sexual pleasure is emphatically a means to Nature's prime end, rather than something she celebrates in its own right, but this only serves to point up and reinforce the *Roman*'s understanding that sexual pleasure and procreative impulse are inextricably bound together and both of them natural. Nature in *Renart* may understand Reason as restrictive of sexual activity in various ways; one restriction, on which Reson in the *Roman de la Rose* is clear, might be that there should be procreative intent in sexual behaviour. It may be that this *Renart* passage is raising the issue of whether, if a legitimizing procreative intent were indeed to be waited upon, the reproductive purposes of Nature would be fulfilled. In any case, Nature is suggesting that the world needs unReason of one kind or another to survive[70] and in the distance Nature sets between herself and Reason is evidence that behaviour unconditioned by Reason in this sexual sphere can nevertheless be understood as natural—this despite the earlier protestations that Nature properly so called is always in accord with Reason.

The desire for procreation is only one aspect of Nature's concern for life, a concern which in fact tends against Reason otherwise than as it promotes sex:

> Mais je sçay de vray que Nature
> Nul temps a mort penser n'a cure.
> Nature est a la char amie

---

[70] Compare the claims in *Les Echecs amoureux* of the God of Love, presumably not a force in harmony with Reason, to be essential for the prosecution of the work of Nature's forge (see above, at n. 52).

Et lui dist: 'Tu ne morras mie,
Esperance ayes d'autre part!',
Qu'il en rebaille bien sa part.
Se la mort qui trestout engoulle,
Tenoit ung homme par la goulle
Et tous les menbres fussent mors
Et tout le remanant du corps,
Esperance adez lui diroit
Que il tresbien eschaperoit,
Et le conforteroit Nature
Qui nul tempz de morir n'a cure.
S'en ung lieu cent mil home estoient,
Qui tous ochis estre devroient,
Qu'on leur deüst les chiefz copper,
N'en deüst q'ung seul eschapper,
Ung chascun Esperance aroit
Que ly eschappé il seroit.
Esperance en toute saison
Et Nature guerroient Raison.[71]

[But I know truly that Nature never troubles to think about death. Nature
is the friend of the flesh and says to it 'You will never die, have hope
instead!', so that it rebels utterly against its lot. If death, which consumes all,
were to hold a man by the throat and all his limbs were dead and all the rest
of his body, Hope would still say to him that he would certainly escape, and
Nature, who never has any concern about dying, would comfort him. If
there were a hundred thousand men in one place who were all going to
have their heads chopped off and only one of them was going to escape,
Hope would say to each one that he was going to be the one to escape. At
all times Hope and Nature war against Reason.]

Nature thinks looking after oneself properly a means of preventing
death, which is something that happens to other people:

'. . . Laisse morir ces gens meschans
Que la mort ne poeuent tarder,
Et qui ne se scevent garder.
Qui toudis bien se garderoit,
Jamais nul jour il ne moroit.
Nul ne se mouert, a brief parler,
Que cil qui ne se scet garder.'
Ainsi fait Nature sçavoir.[72]

[71] RC 39133–54.   [72] RC 39166–73.

['Let those unfortunate people die who cannot put death off and who do not know how to look after themselves. The person who can look after himself well will never ever die. No one will die, in short, except the person who does not know how to look after himself.' This is the kind of knowledge Nature gives.]

Nature's refusal here to countenance the possibility of death[73] is perhaps derived from the idea that there is an inalienable and unalterable natural impulse in all living things to resist death.[74] But whereas in Boethius the existence of such a sub-rational impulse could be used as evidence for the goodness of Nature (though Boethius noted the possibility that it might be necessary to go against the natural impulse for self-preservation[75]), here the absoluteness of the drive for survival is rendered as opposition to Reason; it is a perverse refusal to acknowledge the inevitable which encourages the morally dubious 'char' and endangers the soul. For

> par iceulx empeschemens,
> Par telz manieres d'argumens
> Sont maintes personnes dampnées.[76]

[through these hindrances and this kind of argument many people are damned.]

The association of Nature with the flesh is readily intelligible, since Nature here clearly does not include Reason, and the flesh covers those motions in the human being which are functions of corporeality and not to do with the rational soul to which Reason speaks. But there are strongly negative moral connotations to 'the flesh', so that linking Nature to it does her few favours. In fact, the Nature/Reason duality takes on something of the moral colouring of the traditional body/soul opposition; Nature's final intention—promotion of life—may be respectable enough, but her operations in human beings to secure this end, expressed as they are in the sub-

---

[73] This attitude seems odd when set against the notion that the very purpose of Nature is to combat death. See, for example, *Roman de la Rose* 15861 ff. with its picture of a Nature taking the reality of death very seriously, working in her forge to counter Death's depredations so that the species may continue.

[74] See Boethius *CP* 3. p. 11 42 ff. We might recall also (Ch. 1 at n. 103) Alan of Lille's definition of *natura* as 'naturalis calor', the vital heat which keeps bodies alive. See below for similar meanings of *kynde* in *The Book of the Duchess* and *Confessio Amantis*.

[75] See *CP* 3. p. 11 91–3.

[76] *RC* 39185–7.

rational, animal side, can cut across the pursuit of good to which the rational soul urges. So Nature's sponsoring of the non-rational side of human beings can be read in morally disapprobatory terms as connivance with those dubious entities the body and the flesh, standardly taken to be engaged in a permanent warfare with the soul.[77]

However, despite the opposition between Nature and Reason here over the question of death, a desire to see Nature as good breaks through into the text again—and does so in such a way as to cast some doubt on what I have been arguing. In the lines following the passage just quoted we find an exoneration of Nature, properly understood:

> Nature n'y a coulpe,
> Car ice de Raison je tien
> Que Dieu fist Nature en tout bien,
> Et quancques Dieu fist, est bien fait;
> Donc n'a point Nature meffait;
> Se homs va en desordonnance,
> Ce n'est fors par acoustumance.
> Et male acoustumance ont prise
> Qu'ilz ont en leur nature mise,
> Tant l'ont en eulx souvent murée
> Qu'ilz l'ont en eulx ennaturée.
> Pour ce, vont en desordonnance
> Par leur malvaise acoustumance
> Et puis vont disant le contraire
> Que Nature leur fait ce faire,
> Et que Nature ainsi le voeult,
> Et qu'autrement faire ne poeult.
> De ceste responce n'ay cure,
> Que ja en maint mal nul n'a cure;
> Celle que Dieu a en lui mise,
> Ne il ne l'a par lui acquise,
> Mais on poeut bien telle acquerir
> Qui la maine jusqu'a perir.
> Mais ce n'est pas celle nature
> A qui Dieu a bailliet la cure
> D'homme faire vivre et sentir.

---

[77] Compare the position implied by the dubious company Nature keeps in the *Roman des deduis* (see above, pp. 151–2).

S'a celle se voeult consentir,
Ne poeut aller que bonne voye.
Mais ung aultre a qui il s'avoye,
A en sa complexion mise
Et par acoustumance acquize,
Car par celle au monde s'avoye
Et laisse sa premiere voye.[78]

[Nature is not to blame in this matter, for from Reason I hold this view, that God made Nature completely good, and whatever God made is well made. So Nature has not done amiss; if man goes astray, it is only through habit. And they have taken bad habits and put them in their nature; they have so frequently enclosed them in themselves that they have become a part of their nature. So men go astray through their bad habits and then go about saying the contrary—that Nature makes them do this, and that Nature so wills it and cannot do otherwise. I have no time for this reply, since Nature never had to do with evil in man. The nature God put in man he has not acquired by himself, but it is possible to acquire such a nature which leads the original one to destruction. But this is not that nature to which God committed the job of making man live and feel. If man wishes to consent to this nature, he can only tread a virtuous path. But he has set in his constitution another to which he commits himself and acquired it through habit, for through this nature he entrusts himself to the world and leaves his original path.]

As with earlier passages we can see here a desire to avoid calling something which prompts to evil 'Nature' coexisting with a sense that this is a legitimate usage.[79] Here, however, there is less of a feeling of uneasy contradiction within the passage itself than is the case earlier in the poem where evil is attributed to habit rather than Nature: here habit and Nature gone astray are more or less identified so that two understandings of Nature are clearly discriminated and hierarchized and we are invited to suppose that the 'natural' refusal to countenance death of which we have just been informed is the operation only of ingrained habit, of 'nature' only in a secondary and less proper sense. However, whether this satisfactorily resolves matters for the whole poem is very much open to question. The Nature whom we met earlier explaining how she disobeys Reason in sexual matters goes on to say that she encourages a manner of living which ignores death:

[78] *RC* 39190–222.   [79] For the earlier passages see above, pp. 159–63.

Et deça mer, et dela mer
Fay je l'un et l'autre entr'amer,
Mener bonne vie et joieuze,
Et esbatant et amoureuze,
Sans avoir paour de perir
Et sans point penser a morir.[80]

[and on this side of the sea and beyond it I make people love one another, lead a good and happy life, frolicsome and amorous, without having fear of perishing and without thinking of death.]

Yet Reason, no doubt thinking precisely of how men are brought to 'live and feel', is quite content to acknowledge this Nature as her 'chanbriere'[81]—and this is surely an unlikely designation for an entity understood as ingrained habit. It also seems unlikely that Reason would be allowed to dignify Nature by calling her noble[82] were Nature already conceived as that second unsatisfactory Nature as which she is later reinterpreted. And in any case, as I have already suggested, it would seem to impose an intolerable strain on the literary mode employed in *Renart le Contrefait* deliberately to give what amounts to the wrong name to a personification.

The treatment of Nature in *Renart le Contrefait* indicates an awareness in the literary realm of the problematic quality of the idea of the natural, an awareness very likely stimulated by the detachment of Nature from Reason and the moral countenanced by the *Roman de la Rose*. *Renart le Contrefait* seems to be striving to accommodate Jean de Meun's Nature, with her morally dubious commitment to procreation, to an abiding conviction that what is truly natural to human beings is morally acceptable, indeed, that Nature is by definition—God's definition—good. The trouble that is taken over this issue indicates a strong desire, such as we have seen in scholastic discourse also, to rescue the idea of the natural for the side of right and reason. That desire is not at all surprising: very uncomfortable implications, moral and metaphysical, lie in the notion that sin is natural to human beings. But the inevitable

---

[80] *RC* 24425–30.   [81] *RC* 24531.

[82] *RC* 24532. Not that Reason regards Nature at this point as entirely satisfactory. Note that the poem's earlier contrasting of nature and custom (see above, pp. 161–2) does not represent custom as creating a second nature, though it does suggest that nature can be corrupted by custom.

tendency of the treatment of Nature in the *Roman de la Rose* is to promote a less than sanguine attitude to claims that what is natural is good and given the potential moral and spiritual repercussions of such an attitude it is no surprise that Gerson was alarmed and indignant at what Jean had done to Alan's Nature.[83]

The subversive force of the Nature of the *Roman de la Rose* lies in her representing, at least primarily, the animal in the human being and in thus insisting on the naturalness to the human being of an urge to reproduce which generates a tendency to behave in ways unacceptable to orthodox morality. Jean's alliance between Nature and Venus may be a way of symbolizing the impossibility of drawing lines of distinction between the natural procreative urge and sexual desire—at least heterosexual sexual desire; it may be that Jean conceives all such sexual desire as precisely the expression of the natural procreative urge—this is how we might understand Reson's comment about Nature putting delight in the sexual act to ensure procreation.[84] If this is not exactly the case, Jean nevertheless certainly implies that whether or not a sexual act—perhaps we should say an inseminative sexual act—is consciously directed at procreation, it is natural—a view even Gerson seems implicitly, though perhaps unwittingly, to endorse when he uses the phrase 'euvre de nature' of illegitimate sexual activity in which procreative intent seems unlikely. But—paradoxically, in view of Nature's insistence in the *Roman* on her procreative role—this sense of the inevitable mutual implication of sexual desire and procreation may result in a turning of the emphasis in the literary tradition away from Nature as sponsor of procreation to Nature as sponsor of sexual desire; it is true, at any rate, that the insistence on Nature as *procreatrix* on which was founded Alan of Lille's separation of Nature and Venus is not very marked in several important treatments of Nature after the *Roman de la Rose*. Thus in the *Roman des deduis* Nature's concern for procreation is no longer apparent, and when Gower and Chaucer speak of Nature it is not as the perpetuator of species at work in her

---

[83] Though, as we have seen, what Jean did could find support in the intellectual tradition—and perhaps, we might say, in the language itself, seeing that even Gerson fails to avoid entirely the kind of contradiction with respect to what exactly is natural into which *Renart le Contrefait* appears rather more consciously to enter. See above, p. 140.

[84] *RR* 4381–91.

forge that they present her: their emphasis falls on Nature as stimu-
lator of sexual behaviour. Given that its procreative function was the
surest legitimization of which sexuality, morally problematic as it
was, could avail itself, this development does nothing at all to
reinforce Nature's moral authority.

CHAPTER SIX

Gower

If the great English writers of the Later Middle Ages could be summoned to a disputation over which of them attributed the greatest importance in their work to the idea of nature, Gower would undoubtedly mount an impressive case.[1] The significance of nature for him is apparent simply in the frequency with which he uses nature terms and is perhaps more tellingly evidenced in the fact that he often uses them when his sources do not.[2] The word-counts suggest, I think, rightly that there is something talismanic about the natural for Gower, and I shall later propose reasons why this should be so.

The main text of this chapter will be largely concerned with *Confessio Amantis*, Gower's great English work.[3] Most of this work consists of speech by characters and this raises the question of whether what is said about Nature is wholly reliable, or whether it should be subjected to a scrutiny informed by an apprehension of shortcomings in the speaker. In particular, may we trust Genius, who has most to say about Nature? Some critics seek to expose a lack of authority, even an absurdity, in Genius, who they find fails, for

---

[1] Besides Gower and Chaucer, who are treated in this book, Langland and Julian of Norwich invest very heavily in the idea of nature.

[2] The *Concordance to John Gower's Confessio Amantis*, ed. J. D. Pickles and J. L. Dawson, Publications of the John Gower Society 1 (Cambridge, 1987) lists 365 uses of *kinde* and *nature* terms. It has been suggested by R. F. Yeager, 'Trilingual', that Gower makes a distinction of usage between *kinde* and its related terms on the one hand and *nature* and *nature*-related terms on the other. I think a thoroughgoing distinction unlikely. One telling piece of evidence is at *CA* 2. 3251, where Gower uses a feminine possessive adjective with *kinde*. This indicates clearly enough that Gower conceives of Kinde here in terms of Romance literature's Goddess Nature (contrast Langland's male personification Kinde), demonstrating how the native and romance terms can be equivalent for Gower at least in one very important area.

[3] Reference to his other works will occur mainly in the footnotes. It should be said that there is not complete consonance between *Confessio Amantis* and Gower's other works in their dealings with Nature.

some of the poem at least, to deliver teaching in line with orthodox Christian moral doctrine.[4] James Simpson, for example, argues with great subtlety that Genius, along with Amans, develops in the course of the poem towards a perspective more informed by reason than the one he exhibits at the beginning of the poem.[5] Genius' initially flawed perspective, according to Simpson, affects the way he speaks about Nature. To begin with, Genius over-exaggerates Nature's power, only later acquiring and promulgating a proper sense of the capacity and responsibility of human reason for controlling the natural drives.[6] Genius' authority is certainly not beyond question[7], but neither, in my view, is the morally optimistic view of the poem that sees it as affirming the power of human free will to bring the

[4] See Anthony E. Farnham, 'The Art of High Poetic Seriousness: John Gower as Didactic Raconteur', in Larry D. Benson (ed.), *The Learned and the Lewed*, Harvard English Studies 5 (Cambridge, Mass., 1974), 161–73, David W. Hiscoe, 'The Ovidian Comic Strategy of Gower's *Confessio Amantis*', *PQ* 64 (1985), 367–85, Thomas J. Hatton, 'John Gower's Use of Ovid in Book III of the *Confessio Amantis*', *Mediaevalia*, 13 (1987), 257–74, Georgiana Donavin, *Incest Narratives and the Structure of Gower's Confessio Amantis*, ELS Monograph Series 56 (Victoria, 1993), 29 ff.

[5] James Simpson, *Sciences and the Self in Mediaeval Poetry* (Cambridge, 1995). See also Donavin, *Incest*, 29–32.

[6] See Simpson, *Sciences*, e.g. 194, 216. It should, however, be noted that in *VC* at 5. 193–6 Gower is prepared to have the narrative voice offer sentiments similar to those of Genius (at, e.g., *CA* 3. 148–60) on the ineluctability of love: 'O, quia per nullas amor est medicabilis herbas, | Nec vis nec sensus effugit eius onus; | Nullus ab innato valet hoc evadere morbo, | Sit nisi quod sola gracia curet eum.' [O that love cannot be healed by any herbs and no power or sense escapes its burden. No one is able to escape this innate disease, unless it be that grace alone should cure him.] (Translations of *VC* are taken from (or on occasion adapted from) E. W. Stockton (trans.), *The Major Latin Works of John Gower* (Seattle, 1962). For edition see *Works*, ed. G. C. Macaulay, 4 vols. (Oxford, 1899–1902).) Kurt Olsson, *John Gower and the Structures of Conversion*, Publications of the John Gower Society 4 (Cambridge, 1992), 105, thinks Genius 'gradually shift[s] the basis of his argument from sentient to rational nature' and moves from making reference to an Ulpianic law of nature to championing a law of nature 'grounded in reason and the tenets of Christian faith'.

[7] Consider, for instance, Genius' opinion that 'Love is an occupacion, | Which for to kepe hise lustes save | Scholde every gentil herte have' (*CA* 4. 1452–4); the marginal note, which very likely derives from the author, reads *Non quia sic se habet veritas, set opinio Amantum* [not that this is the truth, but the opinion of lovers]. Genius himself shows embarrassment at his role as the priest of Venus (see *CA* 5. 1382 f.) and at the end of the poem (see *CA* 8. 2060–148) comes out against love in a way that implicitly asks questions of much that he has said before, in fact of the whole project of a confession of love. The radically ironic perspective we are encouraged to adopt to the bulk of the work by Genius' rejection of love is founded, I would say, precisely on Gower's sense of the ineluctability of love—a view of love which Simpson, however, thinks Gower corrects in Genius in the course of the poem.

natural erotic impulses into a proper subordination to reason. As we shall see, there is much towards the end of the poem not issuing from the mouth of Genius about the essential disorderedness of love and the impossibility, or near-impossibility, of ordering that passion or protecting oneself from its influence. Moral safety in respect of love, because love always threatens to generate internal anarchy, is perhaps only given to those who commit themselves to a life of professional holiness and seek to escape from love, and this escape is something indeed *given* in grace.[8] The poem, to be sure, does encourage a countenancing of the possibility that reason and the impulse to love might be harmonizable, but the fact that it ends with its narrator figure, Amans/John Gower, not effecting that harmony but leaving love behind both as a personal experience and as a subject for writing would seem to indicate that it is less committed than Simpson suggests to the promotion of this harmony as the goal of human endeavour. The shape of the frame narrative, in fact, does not suggest that the poem is an unequivocal celebration of the possibility of integrating into a unity directed to the moral good the divisions of the self. [9]

Whatever we suppose about Genius' authority, and even if detachment from some of his remarks is appropriate, it is not clear that everything he says about Nature is distorted. Many of his comments in fact seem quite unexceptionable, and so do not prompt a driving of a wedge between view of character and real opinion of author. Thus, for instance, when Genius condemns something as *unkynde*, unnatural, as he rather often does, it seems to be a perfectly authorial view. This designation *unkynde* speaks of the way in which certain behaviour goes against the natural order. Albinus, for instance, has his wife Rosemund drink unwittingly out of a cup made from her father's skull and then gloats over this to her:

> Tho was ther mochel Pride alofte,
> Thei speken alle, and she was softe,
> Thenkende on thilke unkynde Pride,

---

[8] See *CA* 8. 2775–9; also *CA* 5. 6395*–411* and the *VC* quotation in n. 6 above. Holiness is achieved only by the few; see *CA* 8. 2330–7.

[9] See further below. David Aers' contention that the poem is to be seen as a paratactic structure, collocating without harmonizing different positions, is germane here. See David Aers, 'Reflections on Gower as "*Sapiens* in Ethics and Politics"', in R. F. Yeager (ed.), *Re-Visioning Gower* (Asheville, NC, 1998), 185–201.

> Of that hire lord so nyh hire side
> Avanteth him that he hath slain
> And piked out hire fader brain,
> And of the Skulle had mad a Cuppe.[10]

The *unkynde* here, I think, points to the way in which Albinus' shocking behaviour is at odds with an order of action and feeling conceived as normal and appropriate to the relationship between man and wife—indeed as automatically, spontaneously present in it. The standing that naturalness of this sort has for Gower is apparent in a recurrent pattern of usage of the idea of *unkynde*ness. In more than one passage Gower offers us the appalling, and yet satisfying, picture of *unkinde* crime matched by *unkinde* requital. The pattern emphasizes the high dignity of the natural order, for our satisfaction indicates to us that the violation of the natural order is so monstrous that retribution can only be satisfactory if of a similarly monstrous kind. So, following the murder of Agamemnon, Orestes speaks to Clytemnestra these words:

> O cruel beste unkinde,
> Hou mihtest thou thin herte finde,
> For eny lust of loves drawhte,
> That thou acordest to the slawhte
> Of him which was thin oghne lord?
> Thi treson stant of such record,
> Thou miht thi werkes noght forsake;
> So mot I for mi fader sake
> Vengance upon thi bodi do,
> As I comanded am therto.
> Unkindely for thou hast wroght,
> Unkindeliche it schal be boght,
> The Sone schal the Moder sle,
> For that thou whilom seidest yee
> To that thou scholdest nay have seid.[11]

and, in revenge for the rape and mutilation of her sister Philomena by Tereus, Progne cooks her son by Tereus and serves him as a *sewe* for his father to eat:

[10] *CA* 1. 2563–9.
[11] *CA* 3. 2055–69. Simpson, *Sciences*, thinks that a limitation in the law of *kinde*, which 'cannot decide the issue' (191) between two parties guilty of *unkynde* behaviour, is here displayed; reference to a higher kind of law is shown to be necessary. Simpson

> With which the fader at his mete
> Was served, til he hadde him ete;
> That he ne wiste hou that it stod,
> Bot thus his oughne fleissh and blod
> Himself devoureth ayein kinde,
> As he that was tofore unkinde.[12]

The incestuous Amon suffers *unkindely* in similar fashion:

> Of this sotie also I finde,
> Amon his Soster ayein kinde,[13]
> Which hihte Thamar, he forlay;
> Bot he that lust an other day
> Aboghte, whan that Absolon
> His oghne brother therupon,
> Of that he hadde his Soster schent,
> Tok of that Senne vengement
> And slowh him with his oghne hond:
> And thus thunkinde unkinde fond.[14]

These passages, then, affirm the high status of the natural order. They also show us something of the content of that order—that it embraces certain very basic arrangements for human families. Those arrangements would seem to include certain spontaneous emotions which we could call instinctive: the love of son for mother or of brother for brother, for instance. This sense of the natural as something below the level of rational operation is characteristic of Gower's understanding of the idea of nature.

If to do things in contravention of the natural order results in perverse and heinous crime, there is also a peculiar perversity in the kind of bad behaviour towards which there is no prompting in the natural order. So Ire is

---

thinks this marks an important stage in the development of Amans and Genius towards a greater adhesion to reason. I am not convinced that Gower wishes to point up an inability to decide the issue. The point is rather that terrible things are set in train by a violation of the law of *kinde* and this tends to enhance its status in our eyes. That later passages present *unkinde* crimes met by *unkinde* retributions raises questions about the attribution to the Orestes passage of the critical importance Simpson gives it.

[12] *CA* 5. 5901–6.

[13] In the Alexandran *Summa* (see 3. 254 and 3. 367) we find a distinction made between fraternal incest and incest across generations. Only the latter is deemed fundamentally and unequivocally against the law and order of Nature.

[14] *CA* 8. 213–22.

A vice forein fro the lawe,
Wherof that many a good felawe
Hath be distraght be sodein chance;
And yit to kinde no plesance
It doth, bot wher he most achieveth
His pourpos, most to kinde he grieveth,
As he which out of conscience
Is enemy to pacience:[15]

Genius makes similar remarks about Avarice:

Mi Sone, I have of thee no wonder,
Thogh thou to serve be put under
With love, which to kinde acordeth:
Bot, so as every bok recordeth,
It is to kinde no plesance
That man above his sustienance
Unto the gold schal serve and bowe,[16]
For that mai no reson avowe.[17]

The same idea is used to condemn Envy:

[15] *CA* 3. 5–12. Ire seems to go against a natural impulse for inner peace. At *MO* 4297–308, Tençon, the second daughter of Ire, is 'de nature l'anemie' [the enemy of nature] (4300) at least partly because she works against the peace of the person under her influence. Translations of *MO* are taken (sometimes adapted) from William Burton Wilson (trans.; rev. Nancy Wilson Van Baak], *John Gower: Mirour de l'omme* (East Lansing, Mich., 1992). Nature is said to complain of Ire at *MO* 5101–12, where a comparison with Greek fire, which burns more fiercely in contact with water, is presumably meant to enforce the idea of Ire's unnaturalness.

[16] According to the headnote to *CA* book 5 'obstat avaricia . . . nature legibus' [avarice stands against the laws of nature]. At *MO* 7597–608 Avarice is compared to *idropesie*, one of the symptoms of which is a 'soif desnatural' [unnatural thirst], which requires more quenching the more liquid it is given. Nature and Moderation are traditionally associated, and in this *CA* 5. 117–24 passage one's natural desires guide one towards moderation. At *MO* 16537–72 Nature encourages moderate consumption of food. At *VC* 1. 2045 Natura is said to rejoice in moderation.

[17] *CA* 5. 117–24. The passage claims, I think, that no natural impulse validates the pursuit of wealth beyond the point at which this suffices for survival. Were we to take the last line as explaining why avarice offers no 'plesance to kinde', we might find the suggestion that no natural impulsive prompting to that which reason did not approve exists, or alternatively that the talk of nature here does not have to do with impulses, but with a natural, reasonable order of things. In either case, a close connection between the natural and reason would be asserted. However, in *CA* the natural is not usually defined in terms of reason, and Amans' love, here said to accord with *kinde*, is certainly considered by Genius to clash with reason; it seems either that the connection made by 'for' is not a very logically rigorous one or that the last line asserts the impossibility of reason supposing that avarice might offer 'plesance to kinde'.

> For thus the wise clerkes telle,
> That no spirit bot of malice
> Be weie of kinde upon a vice
> Is tempted, and be such a weie
> Envie hath kinde put aweie
> And of malice hath his steringe,
> Wherof he makth his bakbitinge,
> And is himself therof desesed
> So mai ther be no kinde plesed;
> For ay the mor that he envieth,
> The more ayein himself he plieth.[18]

This sense of the self-damaging quality of Envy is present too in an earlier passage from this book:

> it acordeth noght to kinde
> Min oghne harm to seche and finde
> Of that I schal my brother grieve;
> It myhte never wel achieve.[19]

Here, I think, the *kinde* covers a certain basic instinctual order, the order in which one automatically seeks one's welfare in such things as physical sustenance and mental contentment. Ire and Avarice and Envy cannot find legitimization in this natural impulsive order.[20] Naturalness is the marker of a certain degree of moral status here; things are less excusable where there is no justification for them at the level of basic natural impulse.

---

[18] *CA* 2. 3136–46. A little earlier the unnaturalness of Envy is exhibited through physiological considerations: 'And ek he brenneth so withinne, | That kinde mai no profit winne, | Wherof he scholde his love plese: | For thilke blod which scholde have ese | To regne among the moiste veines, | Is drye of thilke unkendeli peines | Thurgh whiche Envie is fyred ay' (*CA* 2. 3119–25). (Compare *MO* 3817–28 where, however, the heat seems also to have a metaphorical extension into the spiritual realm.) In this passage *kinde* would appear to specify a force within the organism by which it is kept alive and in health, a sense of *kinde* which goes back ultimately to an understanding of φύσις in Greek thought. See also *CA* 4. 3303–5 and 6. 657–64. At *CA* 1. 2046–7 we are told of two old men how 'Ther was of kinde bot a lite, | That thei ne semen fulli dede' and at 2.1747–8 death is described as 'The maladie of which nature | Is queint in every creature'. Envy may also be unnatural in going against a natural inclination to *felaschipe* (see *CA* 2. 3100–4 and compare *CA* 5. 4697–703).

[19] *CA* 2. 369–72.

[20] The unnaturalness of Jealousy at *CA* 5. 670–1 may involve a similar opposition to the spontaneous impulses which define the true and proper directions of the self: 'Bot thilke unkynde Jelousie, | Which everemor the herte opposeth.'

These two kinds of appeal to the natural are very different in implication; the first insists upon the absolute unacceptability of what is unnatural whilst the second intimates the relative excusability of what is natural. But both appeals are to a basic impulsive order, and this understanding of what the natural is, this sense that it is connected with intuitive, instinctive motions, is, as I have said, strong in Gower.[21] We can see from other uses of the idea of nature in moral contexts that Gower understands nature as a moral authority of a particular kind and that its distinctness from other authorities lies in its association with the order of impulse. The distinctness appears in the following passage on War, one of the effects of Wraththe:

> So forto speke in this matiere
> After the lawe of charite,
> Ther schal no dedly werre be:
> And ek nature it hath defended
> And in hir lawe pes comended,
> Which is the chief of mannes welthe,
> Of mannes lif, of mannes helthe.[22]

Here Nature and her law are placed against the law of charity, the two distinguishable authorities both enjoining peace. The law of charity can, as we have seen, be understood as identical to the natural law, but Gower does not seem to be so regarding it here. The law of charity here is perhaps to be understood as something promulgated in the Christian revelation. That seems to be what is in question with 'Cristes lore' in the following passage, where *kinde* is this time involved in a tripartite distinction.

> For who that pite wol biholde,—
> It is a poynt of Cristes lore.
> And for to loken overmore,

---

[21] In 'Natural law and John Gower's *Confessio Amantis*', *Medievalia et humanistica*, NS 11 (1982), 229–61 (repr. in Peter Nicholson (ed.), *Gower's 'Confessio Amantis'*, Publications of the John Gower Society 3 (Cambridge, 1991), 181–213), Kurt Olsson discerns five different meanings of the law of nature at work in *CA* . However this may be, I would want to insist on the primacy in the moral discourse of *CA* of the understanding of nature as it bears on humankind as something intuitive, instinctive, pre-rational.

[22] *CA* 3. 2260–6.

It is bihovely, as we fynde,
To resoun and to lawe of kynde.[23]

That *resoun* should here be distinguished from the law of *kinde*
suggests that, besides being distinct from the revealed Christian
moral law, the law of *kinde* is regarded as something other than the
law of natural reason.[24] If Gower is thinking here in terms of the
traditional understandings of the law of nature, then it would seem
to be the Ulpianic conception, according to which the law of nature
is 'quod natura omnia animalia docuit' [what nature has taught all
animals], which he has in mind. This conception would certainly be
appropriate to the nature terms in the following passage:

For who that wolde ensample take,
The lawe which is naturel
Be weie of kinde scheweth wel
That homicide in no degree,
Which werreth ayein charite,
Among the men ne scholde duelle.[25]
For after that the bokes telle,
To seche in al this worldesriche,
Men schal noght finde upon his liche
A beste forto take his preie:
And sithen kinde hath such a weie,
Thanne is it wonder of a man,
Which kynde hath and resoun can,

[23] *CA* 7. 3156*–3160*. At *MO* 4885–7 Moedre 'occit encontre sa nature | Sans avoir
mercy ne pité' [kills against its nature without having mercy or pity], where there may
well be reference to a natural impulse towards mercy and pity.
[24] *Kinde* and reason are made distinct in the comments on *Delicacie* at *CA* 6.1147 ff.,
where we are told that the folly of *Delicacie* 'whilom was schewed eke, | If thou these
olde bokes seke, | Als wel be reson as be kinde, | Of olde ensample as men mai finde'.
The opposition of *Delicacie* to *kinde* may lie in its going beyond a simple preparedness to
take the best available by way of food and drink—a functioning of appetite which may
be regarded as natural—into an over-concern with the pleasures of the stomach that can
impair health (that is, in fact, do damage to *kinde* in the sense reviewed in n. 18).
[25] At *MO* 4921–9 Nature is in harmony with God in condemning Homicide, though
here Nature makes the condemnation apparently because Homicide destroys what nature
makes live (compare *Piers Plowman* B 17. 274–6). This may be what is in mind at *MO* 4979
where murders are said 'nature contrelie[r]' [to go against nature]. At *MO* 5041–50
however, an appeal is made, in the manner of the *CA* passage, to the behaviour of the
animals in order to show how Homicide preys on his neighbour and friend 'desnature-
lement' [unnaturally]. At *MO* 24133–44 the shedding of human blood is *comme desnaturé*
[unnatural, as it were], where the employment of the nature term is probably bound up

That he wol owther more or lasse
His kinde and resoun overpasse,
And sle that is to him semblable.[26]
So is the man noght resonable
Ne kinde, and that is noght honeste,
Whan he is worse than a beste.[27]

The law of nature is here defined by the behaviour of the animals.[28] It is also apparent that *kinde* can be used to specify, in distinction from reason, that part of the human being which is had in common with the animals.[29] The behaviour of the animals is again invoked to prove that the *unkindenesse* which is ingratitude is unnatural:

with the claim that the apostrophized murder sheds 'ton sanc' [your own blood]: the unnaturalness may lie in the violation of natural impulses in respect of one's kin (in this case understood to include all humankind), or perhaps (depending on how one reads 'ton sanc') of the perverse self-thwarting to which, as we have seen, several *CA* passages make reference. At *MO* 15001–7 the sinner of whatever sort is said to be the murderer of the soul; he 'ad fait tuer [L'Alme] de vile ordure | Encontre resoun et nature' [has killed the soul with vile filth contrary to reason and nature]. Here the grounds of the unnaturalness are perhaps the self-harm involved. At *CA* 7. 3356 Lichaon's killing of his guests is said to be 'ayein the lawe of kinde', possibly not because all homicide is unnatural, but rather because Gower supposes there to be an instinctive revulsion from harming guests.

[26] See *MO* 24133–44.

[27] *CA* 3. 2580–98. There is a somewhat similar passage in *VC* (7. 1173–62) in which, nevertheless, the relation of reason to nature is very different: 'Est homo nunc animal dicam, set non racionis, | Dum viuit bruti condicione pari. | Nescia scripture brutum natura gubernat, | Iudicis arbitrium nec racionis habet: | Est igitur brutis homo peior, quando voluntas | Preter naturam sola gubernat eum. | Corporis, heu! virtus per singula membra revoluens | Naturam viciis seruit ad acta foris; | Ac anime racio carnis viciata vigore | De virtute nichil interiore sapit.' [Now, I should say that man is an animal, but not a rational animal, as long as he lives in a condition like a brute beast's. A nature ignorant of learning governs a brute beast, and it has no power of judgement or reason. Man is therefore worse than a beast, when his will alone governs him contrary to nature. Alas! The body's strength coursing through all parts of the body serves the vices in doing things beyond [the limits of] nature. And the soul's power of reason, corrupted by the vitality of the flesh, knows nothing of inner virtue.]

[28] This understanding of the 'lawe which is naturel' as animal behaviour coheres with the idea of Nature's unproblematic control of the animal world in the literary tradition, where the animals' obedience to her directives can be contrasted with human disobedience. See, for example, *DPN* 2. 232–8, cited above, p. 89. In *MO* Nature's control over the animal world is evident at 4786–8, whilst 16567–72 set animal behaviour under Nature and, associating it with *Mesure*, use it to point a moral lesson for human beings. See also *MO* 6841–52. Medieval moralists commonly make the behaviour of animals a pattern for human actions.

[29] In her Fordham dissertation, 'The Concept of Kynde in John Gower's Confessio Amantis' (1972), Henriette A. Klauser remarks, 'Man should follow kinde and the animals, but in a very different way than the animals—he must use his intelligence'

> The bokes speken of this vice,
> And telle hou god of his justice,
> Be weie of kinde and ek nature[30]
> And every lifissh creature,
> The lawe also, who that it kan,
> Thei dampnen an unkinde man.
>   It is al on to say unkinde[31]
> As thing which don is ayein kinde,
> For it with kinde nevere stod
> A man to yelden evel for good.
> For who that wolden taken hede,
> A beste is glad of a good dede,
> And loveth thilke creature
> After the lawe of his nature
> Which doth him ese.[32]

This distinction between reason and nature where the natural is the animal is evident in *Cinkante Balades* also. Gower writes:

> Sibien les choses qe sont natural,
> Com celles qe sont d'omme resonal,
> Amour par tout sa jurediccioun
> Claime a tenir, et par especial
> Amour s'acorde a nature et resoun.[33]

(72). This perhaps exaggerates the difference between human and animal following of *kinde*. Humans share impulses with the animals, impulses which press upon them as upon the animals prior to any application of intelligent choice, and which often prompt to right action. Human action also has reason to guide it, but that guidance is something super-added to the directives of *kinde*, the impulsive, animal side.

[30] The word-order of this line is probably distorted, 'and ek' being out of place; the thought is probably 'and Nature also [condemns the *unkinde* man, expressing herself in this respect] *be weie of kinde*'. On such distortion see H. Iwasaki, 'A Peculiar Feature of the Word-Order of Gower's *Confessio Amantis*', *SE Lit*. 45 (1969), 205–20.

[31] *Unkinde* here is the equivalent of *ingratus*, the term used in the Latin headnote to the section; *ingratitudo* appears in a marginal note at the beginning of the section. Since 'unkynde' in this passage is to be understood as ungrateful, ll. 5. 4923–4 at the beginning of the second paragraph here are less tautologous on first reading than might appear, though Gower can make the point about *unkindenesse* being against nature the more forcefully by claiming tautology.

[32] *CA* 5. 4917–31. See *CA* 3. 2631–2: 'For every lawe and every kinde | The mannes wit to merci binde', where *kinde* may refer to impulse of an instinctive nature. See also *MO* 4885–7.

[33] *CB* 50. 12–16. *CB* 35. 19 also separates nature and reason: 'Plus poet nature qe ne poet resoun' [Nature can do more than Reason]. The poet is contrasting his fortune in love (as a human being possessed of reason) with that of the birds.

[Love claims jurisdiction everywhere; over natural things as well as those having reason. And in particular, love makes its accord with nature and reason.]

The understanding of the natural as natural instinct, of a kind with that possessed by animals, seems to be the dominant, though perhaps not exclusive, conception in *Confessio Amantis*. It is a conception in line with that in the *Roman de la Rose*. There, as we have seen, Nature does not give human beings reason. This is because the immortal human soul is understood to be created directly by God, and with this immortal soul comes the rational capacity. The same distinction between the creative spheres of God and Nature is visible in *Confessio Amantis* where it is congruent with the distinction between reason and *kinde* within the human being which we have just been examining. A lengthy passage at the beginning of book 7 describes the human complexions and the disposition of the bodily organs within the human body.[34] For these things Nature is responsible, but she is not given responsibility for the soul:

> And thus nature his pourveance
> Hath mad for man to liven hiere;
> Bot god, which hath the Soule diere,
> Hath formed it in other wise.[35]

The direct creation of the soul by God is here affirmed and Nature is limited to the material. That limitation seems to be operative in the following passage also:

> O thou divine pourveance,
> Which every man in the balance
> Of kinde hast formed to be liche,
> The povere is bore as is the riche
> And deieth in the same wise,
> Upon the fol, upon the wise
> Siknesse and hele entrecomune;
> Mai non eschuie that fortune
> Which kinde hath in hire lawe set;
> Hire strengthe and beaute ben beset
> To every man aliche fre,
> That sche preferreth no degre
> As in the disposicioun

---

[34] *CA* 7. 393 ff.   [35] *CA* 7. 490–3.

Of bodili complexioun:[36]
And ek of Soule resonable
The povere child is bore als able
To vertu as the kinges Sone.[37]

'And ek' in line 3257 probably marks a movement away from the
sphere of *kinde*.

In these last two passages, but also implicitly where he distinguishes *kinde* from reason, Gower is aligning Nature with the
body.[38] Body and soul, of course, are traditionally at loggerheads,
a state of affairs on which Gower reflects pessimistically just after the
first of these passages:

Bot ofte hir [the Soul's] wittes be mad blinde
Al onliche of this ilke point,
That hir abydinge is conjoint
Forth with the bodi forto duelle:
That on desireth toward helle,
That other upward to the hevene;
So schul thei nevere stonde in evene,
Bot if the fleissh be overcome
And that the Soule have holi nome
The governance, and that is selde,
Whil that the fleissh him mai bewelde.[39]

---

[36] Nature's egalitarian dispensation receives comment at *MO* 17341 ff. and 23101 ff.

[37] *CA* 2. 3243–59.

[38] At *CA* 4. 2230 ff. the physical matters of birth and death are in the realm of *kinde*
and have nothing to do with true *gentillesse*, which is dependent on the condition of
the soul. At *VC* 2. 297 ff. Nature provides the body ('Corpora natura dedit' (300)),
whilst the grace of God provides the *virtutes animae* [powers of the soul]. At *VC* 5. 263–4
the lover's extravagance is said to be such that 'Quod sibi natura, sibi vel deus attulit
omne, | Corpus, res, animam, tot dabit inde bona' [He will give up so many good
things for it [a woman's love]—his body, his soul, his property, everything that Nature
or God has imparted to him]. Here again Nature is probably to be taken as giving
the body and God the soul (the *res* may be the gift of God, or perhaps of the unmen-
tioned Fortune—a distinction between the gifts of Nature, Fortune, and Grace is
traditional). Elsewhere, however, Gower writes as if certain non-bodily virtues are in
Nature's gift. So Amans says of his Lady that 'Nature sette in hire at ones | Beaute with
bounte', 5. 2594–5. See also *CB* 13. 8 ff. and 38. 15–18. In the latter passage the
separation between Nature's and God's endowment of the lady seems not to run
along the body/soul divide. In passages such as these Gower's erotic discourse deploys
a well-established topos in which Nature gives the beloved charms beyond the physical.
See Ch. 7 n. 1.

[39] *CA* 7. 500–10.

Such an attitude might seem to imply that the influence of nature on human beings will not be benign, Nature being associated with the body, but, as we have seen, this is by no means always the case in *Confessio Amantis*. In fact, it may be that the idea of Nature is for Gower the focus for a vision of the healing of the fundamental division between soul and body and hence a talismanic concept. The critical nature of this division is emphatically set before us when Gower makes it responsible for the Fall.[40]

> The bodi and the Soule also
> Among hem ben divided so,
> That what thing that the body hateth
> The soule loveth and debateth;
> Bot natheles fulofte is sene
> Of werre which is hem betwene
> The fieble hath wonne the victoire.
> And who so drawth into memoire
> What hath befalle of old and newe,
> He may that werre sore rewe,
> Which ferst began in Paradis:
> For ther was proeved what it is,
> And what desese there it wroghte;
> For thilke werre tho forth broghte
> The vice of alle dedly Sinne.[41]

This is stark, to be sure, but the idea of nature offers a way of viewing the bodily, instinctual impulses in human beings in a more favourable light. This is because what is natural can readily be understood as divinely ordained—it is God who institutes the law of nature, even when that is understood as the law of animal impulse. So to present the impulsive as natural is a way of encouraging a view of it as in essence morally respectable. The affirmation of moral acceptability implicit in the language of nature may be critical in encouraging Gower to explore the possibility that, after all, there may be no irreconcilable division between the impulsive and the rational as these bear on moral behaviour, but that they may rather lend one another support as they prompt towards what is right. The general

---

[40] For Gower's sensitivity to the dividedness of things and his response to it see Hugh White, 'Division and Failure in Gower's *Confessio Amantis*', *Neophilologus*, 72 (1988), 600–16.

[41] *CA* prol. 995–1009.

strategy of *Confessio Amantis* seems to be designed with a view to entertaining claims about the unifiability of aspects of the human being which at first sight might seem irreconcilable. If the prologue affirms division, the fact, nevertheless, that sin against love can be analysed in terms applicable to sins against the Christian moral code, and presented as a subset of the larger category of sin-in-general, implies that the erotic side of human nature, in which bodily impulse expresses itself, can be regulated in such a way as to produce morally approvable actions; the expressions of the bodily in the sexual sphere do not, the implication seems to be, have to be contrary to the directions the immortal rational soul sets for human beings. The figure Genius holds together the two poles of this distinction between soul and body, sacred and erotic, being at once a priest and a priest of Venus and having therefore obligations both to morality and to the sexual dimension of human life.[42] Genius is very explicit about his dual responsibility, his double nature,[43] and this is one of the signs that Gower undertakes the enterprise of *Confessio Amantis* in an acute awareness of division and perhaps as an attempt to lay to rest some of the anxieties that that awareness generates. In the end it seems to me that Genius confesses his inability to sustain obligations both to the impulsive and to the moral and that this constitutes a movement away from the original presentation of Genius, a movement which is testimony, I think, to Gower's understanding that, attractive though the prospect might be, and though the idea of nature gives the attempt some plausibility, it is impossible to sustain a sense of the human predicament in which the sting has been drawn from division.[44] But to this we shall return.

The moral benignity of a nature distinct from reason is made apparent, then, on several occasions in *Confessio Amantis*, as Gower suggests that at the instinctual level human beings are in tune with the right, that the natural, *kynde*, instinctual human being is a moral one.[45] However, his idea of the goodness of natural human instinct coexists with darker suggestions about nature-as-impulse. We have

---

[42]   On the double aspect of Genius see Baker, 'Priesthood'.
[43]   See *CA* 1. 233–88 and 8. 2075–83. See also below.
[44]   See White, 'Division'.
[45]   The link between the *kinde* and the animal helps sustain this suggestion, because animals were often used in moral discourse as indicators of how humans should behave.

seen something of this already: in the passages quoted above which speak of Ire and Envy in relation to the doing of *plesance* to *kinde*, there is a hint that if these sins actually proceeded from *kinde* impulses, they would be in some degree excusable. At 5. 117–19, being 'put under | With love' to serve occasions no surprise because it is natural, and the lack of surprisingness seems to indicate a preparedness to accept and perhaps even to excuse. Had Avarice been similarly natural, it might have been in some degree excusable. Similarly Ire is a vice *forein* from the law and yet it does no *plesance* to *kinde*, as if it conceivably might have done that *plesance* and in doing it found some measure of excuse. There seems to be a willingness here to entertain the possibility that what is sinful might be naturally impelled, though the very language of nature provides a means of doing something to rehabilitate, make acceptable up to a point, the behaviour that in all moral strictness is sinful. If the natural is not right, at least it is understandable, excusable: the rhetoric of nature can here be seen to provide a fall-back position of some attractiveness, one might feel, to anyone wanting to think well of the impulsive and attempting to find the fundamental division between soul and body something less than tragic.

So much may be said out of reflection on passages already discussed. It is, however, not with Ire and Envy, but with sex that Nature's capacity to stimulate vice, to go against reason and to invite pardon for it, becomes clearly apparent. Nevertheless an invocation of Nature or the natural in the sexual sphere does not always bring moral condemnation with it. That Nature should be responsible for sexual activity is, of course, deeply inscribed in the tradition we are considering and Gower quotes an authority who makes her responsible for the first human sexual act:[46]

---

[46] That sexual behaviour is one of Nature's laws is made clear at the outset of the book 1 of *CA* where the Latin verses inform us that 'Naturatus amor nature legibus orbem | Subdit' [Created love to Nature's laws subdues | This orb]. The verses continue, 'et vnanimes concitat esse feras' [and causes beasts to share one mind], which links natural sexual activity with the animal world in line with Gower's favoured conception of the natural in *CA*. The translations here are taken from Siân Echard and Claire Fanger, *The Latin Verses in the Confessio Amantis: An Annotated Translation* (East Lansing, Mich., 1991). In glossing these verses Echard and Fanger, 14, draw attention to a passage at *VC* 4. 571 f., 'Crescere nature sunt iura que multiplicare, | Que deus in primo scripsit ab ore suo' [Nature's laws are to increase and multiply; from God's own mouth this was written in the beginning].

> Metodre seith . . .
> Hou that Adam and Eve also
> Virgines comen bothe tuo
> Into the world and were aschamed,
> Til that nature hem hath reclamed
> To love, and tauht hem thilke lore,
> That ferst thei keste, and overmore
> Thei don that is to kinde due,
> Wherof thei hadden fair issue.[47]

It is difficult to be sure what the moral resonance of this is as regards Nature; perhaps the conquest of shame together with the very fact that sex as we know it ('*thilke* lore') is a post-lapsarian phenomenon points to the problematic aspects of this natural process; on the other hand, that nature should be involved perhaps vindicates this process, which can lead to '*fair* issue'. What is clear is that a view is presented in *Confessio Amantis* according to which the natural impulse to sex can be satisfied within morally acceptable limits:

> For bot a mannes wit be swerved,
> Whan kinde is dueliche served,
> It oghte of reson to suffise.[48]

Indeed, here one might say that natural sexual appetite provides moral guidance, its satisfaction, and no more, indicating what is legitimate.[49] Other lines tell us that there is no necessity in nature for polygamous sexuality; the natural sexual drive can be accommodated within a monogamous relationship:

> The Madle is mad for the femele,
> Bot where as on desireth fele,
> That nedeth noght be weie of kinde.[50]

---

[47] *CA* 8. 48, 51–8. Metodre is Methodius. This view that there was no sex in Paradise is orthodox. Augustine's view in *De Genesi ad litteram* that there would have been sex even had the Fall not occurred eventually came to hold sway in the Middle Ages. See Cohen, *Be Fertile*, 223–65 and Payer, *Bridling*, 19–28.

[48] *CA* 7. 4569–71.

[49] On nature and moderation see n. 16 above. There remains, however, the possibility that the natural urge for sex presses beyond its 'due' satisfaction'; see below. At *MO* 9198–202 Foldelit is accused of working up sexual desire beyond the appetite which nature provides (and at *MO* 9505–6 Nature is said to complain about Foldelit).

[50] *CA* 7. 4215–17. *CB* 34 seems to suggest that Nature teaches the birds monogamy: there is perhaps the implication that Nature is providing a moral lesson for human beings, who should follow the example of the birds as the poet represents himself doing.

In the following passage, which comments on the Tale of Apollonius, incest is against 'kinde', the natural here clearly being on the side of the right; it may even be that here love against kinde is implicitly identified with love against reson:

> Lo thus, mi Sone, myht thou liere
> What is to love in good manere,
> And what to love in other wise:
> The mede arist of the servise;
> Fortune, thogh sche be noght stable,
> Yit at some time is favorable
> To hem that ben of love trewe.
> Bot certes it is forto rewe
> To se love ayein kinde falle,
> For that makth sore a man to falle,
> As thou myht of tofore rede.
> Forthi, my Sone, I wolde rede
> To lete al other love aweie,
> Bot if it be thurgh such a weie
> As love and reson wolde acorde.
> For elles, if that thou descorde,
> And take lust as doth a beste,
> Thi love mai noght ben honeste;
> For be no skile that I finde
> Such lust is noght of loves kinde.[51]

It is possible that the passage justifies its remark about love and reason by the observation about love and kinde, with the *forthi* of line 2020 making the connection. In this case we would have here a conception of *kinde* as reason, rather than what human beings share with the animals; that would be powerful testimony to the goodness of the *kinde* even in the sphere of sex.[52] I suspect, however, that *forthi* does not have precise and exclusive reference to the previous sentence; certainly the general tendency of the writing on love and nature in *Confessio Amantis* is to raise questions about the attunedness of the natural to reason.

As we have seen in Ch. 1 scholastic theologians could establish the naturalness of monogamy through reference to the behaviour of at least certain kinds of bird—and find an implication for what is natural to humans in this.

[51] *CA* 8. 2009–28.

[52] Henry Ansgar Kelly, *Love and Marriage in the Age of Chaucer* (Ithaca, NY, 1975), 147, reads this passage as indicating that 'for man unreasonable love is unnatural'.

Despite these passages which might reasonably incline one to think well of Nature's moral standing in the sexual sphere, when we consider the poem's treatment of types of sexual activity not orthodoxly acceptable, its position turns out not to be simple. In the case of homosexuality, the story of Iphis and Iante suggests that Nature on the one hand condemns homosexuality and yet stimulates to it on the other. Iphis, in fact a girl, has been brought up as a boy and has fallen in love with Iante (uncomplicatedly a girl):

> and ofte abedde
> These children leien, sche and sche,
> Which of on age bothe be.
> So that withinne time of yeeres,
> Togedre as thei ben pleifieres,
> Liggende abedde upon a nyht,
> Nature, which doth every wiht
> Upon hire lawe forto muse,
> Constreigneth hem, so that thei use
> Thing which to hem was al unknowe;
> Wherof Cupide thilke throwe
> Tok pite for the grete love,
> And let do sette kinde above,
> So that hir lawe mai ben used,
> And thei upon here lust excused.
> For love hateth nothing more
> Than thing which stant ayein the lore
> Of that nature in kinde hath sett:
> Forthi Cupide hath so besett
> His grace upon this aventure,
> That he acordant to nature,
> Whan that he syh the time best,
> That ech of hem hath other kest,
> Transformeth Iphe into a man,
> Wherof the kinde love he wan
> Of lusti yonge Iante his wif;
> And tho thei ladde a merie lif,
> Which was to kinde non offence.[53]

[53] *CA* 4. 478–505. At *MO* 9509–14 Sodomy is repellent to God and Nature. In scholastic writing the expenditure of seed where conception cannot result is against nature. For scholastic opinion as to the unnaturalness of sodomy/homosexual sex in an Ulpianic sense see above, pp. 45, 135 n. 82.

It looks here as if Nature prompts to immorality, though the peculiarity of Iphis' upbringing makes it difficult to know how much of an indictment of Nature this represents. What we can say is that Gower has chosen to implicate Nature in sin by ascribing to her responsibility for the sexual feelings of Iphis and Iante. It would have been easy enough to make no reference to Nature, or indeed to speak of the unnaturalness of the sexual attraction, presenting Nature's benign regulative influence as overridden by the force of peculiar circumstances. Instead, Gower allows one to feel that Nature may be so intent on sexual activity that she is even prepared to operate against her own arrangements for its channelling. The presentation hints that at the bottom of the human psyche lies a naked, unconditioned, undifferentiating sexual impulse—and that suggests something morally anarchic at the bottom of the totality one calls Nature.[54] Bizarre circumstance has exposed how one cannot rely on the impulses to secure virtuous action. Yet that is to draw out implications in a way the passage quite remarkably fails to do. No attempt is made to resolve the paradox of unnatural action prompted by Nature: indeed the passage refuses even to countenance this paradox. Perhaps Gower's attachment to the idea of a Nature on the side of morality inclines him to turn a blind eye to the difficulties that emerge here out of his conception of the natural for human beings as the impulsive: any such willed blindness would only be encouraged by the real difficulty of discerning responsibilities in moral waters muddied by the perversity of the parental contribution to what goes on.[55]

For all that—and whether Gower likes it or not—Nature is in this passage presented as both reassuringly moral in her orientations

[54] In commenting on the stories of Iphis and Iante and of Canace and Machaire, Kelly, *Love and Marriage*, 140, writes, 'The law of nature in question here, then, is the "unmodified" instinct that man shares with beasts, an instinct that takes no notice of person, number, or gender.' In *MO* improper sexual activity can be associated with nature: see *MO* 8629–40 and 17185–91.

[55] One might contrast the Iphis and Iante story with the story of Achilles and Deidamia, where nature asserts itself over against nurture: though Achilles has been brought up as a girl, his natural instincts as a male reassert themselves so that he and his bedfellow Deidamia make love. Gower writes of the power of nature to reassert itself in terms which may remind us of Boethius: 'Wher kinde wole himselve rihte, | After the Philosophres sein, | Ther may no wiht be therayein: | And that was thilke time seene. | The longe nyhtes hem betuene | Nature, which mai noght forbere, | Hath mad hem bothe forto stere: | Thei kessen ferst, and overmore | The hihe weie of loves lore | Thei gon, and al was done in dede, | Wherof lost is the maydenhede' (*CA* 5. 3058–68).

and at the same time worryingly unreliable from a moral point of view. A similar double perspective can be detected across the range of Gower's references to incest. Again, this may have to do with Gower's desire to think of the natural as supportive of right morality and yet to conceive it as something impulsive and non-rational. We have seen already that Antiochus' incest is held to be *ayein kinde*[56] and that so is Amon's.[57] However, incest can also be regarded as stimulated by nature. Before Abraham sexual relations between brother and sister were readily countenanced:

> as nature hem hath excited,
> Thei token thanne litel hiede,
> The brother of the Sosterhiede
> To wedde wyves, til it cam
> Into the time of Habraham.[58]

This pre-Abrahamitical incest was not sinful; after the Flood, so few people remain on earth that conditions are more or less the same as they were at the beginning of the world, of which period we hear that

> that time it was no Sinne
> The Soster forto take hire brother,
> Whan that ther was of chois non other.[59]

Nevertheless, the picture pre-Abraham seems to show a basic natural sexual instinct which *might* have been modified, though in fact it was not, with regard to kinship relations. This suggests that the difference post-Abraham lies not in any change to the configuration of basic instinct, such that it becomes against this instinct to desire close kin sexually, but in the fact that now it is customary and appropriate to 'take hiede of the Sosterhiede', though nature might perhaps excite one in the direction of one's sister. This is to say that when, as nowadays, incest is sinful, nature can still properly be said to incite to it. This perspective—that nature urges to incest—is certainly operative in Genius' account[60] of what happened to Canace and Machaire:

---

[56] See the passage at *CA* 8. 2009–28, quoted above; also *CA* 8. 2005, where Antiochus is said to have set his love *unkindely* on his daughter.

[57] See *CA* 8. 213–22, quoted above.   [58] *CA* 8. 94–8.   [59] *CA* 8. 68–70.

[60] The question of the reliability of Genius arises here. See above pp. 174–6. Donavin, *Incest*, 35–6, thinks Genius wrong to suggest that Canace and Machaire's

Be daie bothe and ek be nyhte,
Whil thei be yonge, of comun wone
In chambre thei togedre wone,
And as thei scholden pleide hem ofte,
Til thei be growen up alofte
Into the youthe of lusti age,
Whan kinde assaileth the corage
With love and doth him forto bowe,
That he no reson can allowe,
Bot halt the lawes of nature:
For whom that love hath under cure,
As he is blind himself, riht so
He makth his client blind also.
In such manere as I you telle
As thei al day togedre duelle,
This brother mihte it noght asterte
That he with al his hole herte
His love upon his Soster caste:
And so it felle hem ate laste,
That this Machaire with Canace
Whan thei were in a prive place,
Cupide bad hem ferst to kesse,
And after sche which is Maistresse
In kinde and techeth every lif
Withoute lawe positif,
Of which sche takth nomaner charge,
Bot kepth hire lawes al at large,
Nature, tok hem into lore
And tawht hem so, that overmore
Sche hath hem in such wise daunted,
That thei were, as who seith, enchaunted.
And as the blinde an other ledeth
And til thei falle nothing dredeth,
Riht so thei hadde non insihte.[61]

Here the arrangements that precipitate the incest are, unlike those pertaining in the case of Iphis and Iante, quite normal ('as thei scholden pleide hem ofte'). There is no exoneration available for

incest is prompted by natural law, but she leaves out of account the Ulpianic conception of that law.

[61] *CA* 3. 148–81.

Nature in the perverseness of human influence on the situation. It seems clear enough that in this case Nature is regarded as presiding over an unconditioned sexual instinct which is capable of expressing itself in behaviour contrary to reason and also to the positive human law which demands moral action and which yet cannot adequately constrain the natural impulses which may impel people away from moral behaviour. Here the distinctness of nature from reason becomes opposition between the two, as the law of reason is suspended in favour of the laws of nature.

With Canace and Machaire Nature's influence produces an action that ought not to be condoned. Yet we seem to be given permission—or even to be encouraged—to adopt an attitude to Nature not altogether negative. Nature is said to be 'Maistresse in kinde' and this may well remind us of other treatments of the Nature figure in which she has been placed over the realm of nature by God; she can, in fact, be seen as having a kind of authority, so that is possible to react to her imperious unconcern for human law as an appropriate response to an attempt at *lèse-majesté* (and a puny one at that). Furthermore, though Nature cannot strictly excuse herself through reference to perverse human influence, there is perverse human behaviour in the story, behaviour that may, indeed, be thought to be unnatural, and this behaviour means that it is not, as might have been the case, Nature who is the villain of the piece. The story is an illustration of *Malencolie*, this being instanced in the fearful revenge on his child, Canace, and his grandchild taken by Eolus. In the face of the ties of blood which should restrain him, Eolus demands that Canace kill herself and has the baby exposed. It is on these appalling effects of *Malencolie* that the last indignant lines of the story dwell:

> Ha, who herde evere singe or rede
> Of such a thing as that was do?
> Bot he which ladde his wraththe so
> Hath knowe of love bot a lite;
> Bot for al that he was to wyte,
> Thurgh his sodein Malencolie
> To do so gret a felonie.[62]

[62] *CA* 3. 330–6.

The moral perspective that Gower adopts for the Canace and Machaire story tends to protect Nature from censure by turning our attention to the father's culpability, as he overreacts to something presented as a natural necessity. This is how Genius puts matters:

> Forthi, my Sone, how so it stonde,
> Be this cas thou miht understonde
> That if thou evere in cause of love
> Schalt deme, and thou be so above
> That thou miht lede it at thi wille,
> Let nevere thurgh thi Wraththe spille
> Which every kinde scholde save.
> For it sit every man to have
> Reward to love and to his miht,
> Ayein whos strengthe mai no wiht:
> And siththe an herte is so constreigned,
> The reddour oghte be restreigned
> To him that mai no bet aweie,
> Whan he mot to nature obeie.
> For it is seid thus overal,
> That nedes mot that nede schal
> Of that a lif doth after kinde,
> Wherof he mai no bote finde.
> What nature hath set in hir lawe
> Ther mai no mannes miht withdrawe,
> And who that worcheth therayein,
> Fulofte time it hath be sein,
> Ther hath befalle gret vengance.[63]

Not only is it suggested that the incest of Canace and Machaire is excusable, being a necessity caused by the ineluctable operation of natural law, but the final lines speak of the liability to *vengance* of those who stand in the way of its operation; they thereby imply that such opposition involves opposing the desires of the powers which run the universe, in whose hands the exercise of *vengance* lies. It follows that the operations of Nature are divinely sanctioned and that actions which proceed from them are at least in some degree vindicable, in some measure due and appropriate. This position is validated through the story of Tiresias and the snakes. Whilst Tiresias is out walking he sees

[63] *CA* 3. 337–59.

Tuo Serpentz in his weie nyh,
And thei, so as nature hem tawhte,
Assembled were, and he tho cawhte
A yerde which he bar on honde,
And thoghte that he wolde fonde
To letten hem, and smot hem bothe:
Wherof the goddes weren wrothe;
And for he hath destourbed kinde
And was so to nature unkinde,
Unkindeliche he was transformed,
That he which erst a man was formed
Into a womman was forschape.[64]

This incident is offered in commentary on the story of Canace and
Machaire, and the parallel between the stories suggest that the incest
of brother and sister is, just like the normal copulation of animals,
undepraved. What Nature teaches the snakes is clearly unexceptionable, and there is accordingly a strong implication that what Nature
teaches Canace and Machaire is likewise unexceptionable. Genius
withdraws a little from what the parallel implies in his final comment:

Lo thus, my Sone, Ovide hath write,
Wherof thou miht be reson wite,
More is a man than such a beste:
So mihte it nevere ben honeste
A man to wraththen him to sore
Of that an other doth the lore
Of kinde, in which is no malice,
Bot only that it is a vice:[65]
And thogh a man be resonable,
Yit after kinde he is menable
To love, wher he wole or non.
Thenk thou, my Sone, therupon
And do Malencolie aweie;
For love hath evere his lust to pleie,
As he which wolde no lif grieve.[66]

---

[64] *CA* 3. 366–77. As elsewhere, the heinousness of the action against nature is marked
in the appropriate unnaturalness of the punishment.

[65] Kelly, *Love and Marriage*, thinks this passage expresses a difference between the way
in which animals and human beings are subject to love and comments, 'That is, no vice
can exist without malice, and malice requires reason' (which only humans have), 139. I
think, rather, that Gower is making a distinction between malice and unmalicious vice.

[66] *CA* 3. 381–95.

Here it is acknowledged that the teaching of Nature can incite to vice, but it is a kind of vice in which there is no malice (this in the case of Envy was shown to be against *kinde*),[67] and to succumb to the pressure of sexual instinct, which, amiably enough, desires no one's harm, is in some degree excusable, deserving less harsh reaction and punishment than might otherwise be appropriate.

So different and contradictory attitudes towards Nature are discernible in this sequence of *Confessio Amantis*. On the one hand—and most clearly in the Tiresias exemplum—Nature is closely connected with the divine order: though Nature may be conceived along Ulpianic lines, what it teaches the animals and, implicitly, human beings is regarded as appropriate. On the other hand, there is the presentation of Nature as an irresistible force working against reason, inciting moral blindness, and promoting vice (albeit not malicious vice). The movement of the sequence suggests a desire to vindicate natural behaviour, a desire so strong that we are offered the next thing to an explicit justification of incest. The uneasy coexistence of conflicting conceptions of the natural and the approach of the text to moral solecism—or maybe its arrival at it—might perhaps be explicable in terms of an overcommitment to love on Genius' part; but it is also possible that they take their rise from a determination in Gower to think well of Nature in spite of a countervailing awareness that natural human sexuality is a threat to the moral order.[68]

What seems unarguable, and not to be ironized away, given the association of nature with untrammelled sexual instinct both in the juridico-theological and the literary traditions, is that this sequence proclaims Nature's potential moral anarchy. She can work against the positive law with which human beings seek to bind their own behaviour;[69] the sequence is also explicit on how Nature and reason

---

[67] See above, at n. 18.

[68] Perhaps Gower conceals behind Genius' confusion an uncertainty over how to reconcile different ideas about Nature.

[69] Compare the comment in the *Knight's Tale* that 'positif lawe and swich decree | Is broken al day for love in ech degree' (*CT* 1. 1167–8), where positive law is in implicit contrast with a law of nature which promotes sexual behaviour. Kelly, *Love and Marriage*, 144, thinks *lawe positif* at *CA* 3. 172 'refers to the law of reason that God has given only to men' and not to the animals; earlier he writes, 'the positive law must be taken as the equivalent of the moral law itself, of nature informed by reason' (141). Kelly risks obscuring how Gower is pointing to the difficulty of controlling natural instinct.

can come into collision: in several other places supportive of reason, as we have seen, here Nature causes human beings not to allow the laws of reason. Other passages in *Confessio Amantis* also bear witness to a tension between nature and reason in the sphere of sexual love. The following clearly identifies the natural as the animal and the impulsive within the human being and hints that unrestrained naturalness would lead to lechery, a lechery regardable as bestial; for though human beings share *kinde* or *nature* with the animals, their having reason demands of them a different kind of behaviour from that of the animals, demands that they shall hold (animal) *nature* in check so that what would be for them wrong behaviour shall not be perpetrated:

> For god the lawes hath assissed
> Als wel to reson as to kinde,
> Bot he the bestes wolde binde
> Only to lawes of nature,
> Bot to the mannes creature
> God yaf him reson forth withal,
> Wherof that he nature schal
> Upon the causes modefie,
> That he schal do no lecherie,
> And yit he schal his lustes have.[70]

The modification of natural urges is also required in the following:

>   and over this
> The fifte point, so as it is
> Set of the reule of Policie,
> Wherof a king schal modefie
> The fleisschly lustes of nature,
> Nou thenk I telle of such mesure,
> That bothe kinde schal be served
> And ek the lawe of god observed.[71]

Other lines in book 7 deploy the language of restraint and measure:

>   And thus therfore
> The Philosophre upon this thing

---

[70] *CA* 7. 5372–81. On this see Götz Schmitz, *The Middel Weie*, Studien zur Englischen Literatur 11 (Bonn, 1974), 78 f.

[71] *CA* 7. 4207–14.

Writ and conseileth to a king,
That he the surfet of luxure
Schal tempre and reule of such mesure,
Which be to kinde sufficant
And ek to reson acordant,
So that the lustes ignorance
Be cause of no misgovernance,
Thurgh which that he be overthrowe,
As he that wol no reson knowe.
For bot a mannes wit be swerved,
Whan kinde is dueliche served,
It oghte of reson to suffise.[72]

Here the object of tempering is not designated 'nature' but 'luxure', and this passage earlier provided an illustration of the moral force of nature even in the field of sex. But the passage is double-edged—the moral potential of the *kinde* here lies in the way the satisfaction of natural appetite provides a measure for consumption, but this does not rule out the possibility that natural appetite may press beyond the 'due' measure of its satisfaction. One can sense an apprehensiveness about the natural in the last sentence.

Indeed, all these passages cut two ways; they suggest that an accommodation of the natural sexual urge can be made, but they point to the necessity of restraint of the natural. Nature may be a domesticable threat to morality, but it is a threat nevertheless. The story of Toby and Sara (from the conclusion of which the passage at 7. 5372–81 just quoted comes) registers a double effect of a similar kind. It certainly demonstrates that the requisite restraint of sexual desire can be achieved. Each of Sara's first seven husbands has been destroyed by the fiend Asmod for failing to accommodate his sexual desires to the demands of law. This unfortunate iteration eventually comes to an end:

Whan sche was wedded to Thobie,
And Raphael in compainie
Hath tawt him hou to ben honeste,
Asmod wan noght at thilke feste,
And yit Thobie his wille hadde;
For he his lust so goodly ladde,
That bothe lawe and kinde is served,

[72] *CA* 7. 4558–71.

> Wherof he hath himself preserved,
> That he fell noght in the sentence.[73]

This is very well, to be sure, but *kinde* stands in tension with law here and the story points up how strong a challenge is offered by *kinde* to right moral performance. The marginal comment at the beginning of book 8 puts neatly the condition of Sara's first husbands, all of whom fail to achieve the necessary balance between the demands of nature and the impositions of law:

nonnulli primordia nature ad libitum voluptuose consequentes, nullo humane racionis arbitrio seu ecclesie legum imposicione a suis excessibus debite refrenantur.

[Some people in the pursuit of pleasure follow the basic impulses of nature at will and are not restrained as they should be from excess by any judgement of human reason or through the imposition of the laws of the Church.]

This allows the passage into excess to be regarded as a natural one—it does not propose a certain point ('whanne kinde is dueliche served') beyond which we are indulging in a *luxure* understandable as unnatural,[74] and it fails to suggest that Nature provides or implies the necessary boundaries. This anarchically abandoned natural appetite is surely operative in the Toby and Sara story, for which, however, the bland *nonnulli* of the marginal comment seems over-optimistic. *Plurimi* would be more accurate for a story in which getting things right requires eight attempts and an archangel. This puts in perspective the story's celebration of achieved balance—a little reflection allows us to see not only that nature has a tendency to pull against reason, but that in the normal course of events it pulls this way rather successfully.

So a current of moral pessimism about nature in the sexual sphere is discernible even in this superficially optimistic story. But *Confessio Amantis* contains stronger pessimism; it is, for instance, evident—for all the exculpations—in the stress on the ineluctability of natural pressures to vice in the Canace and Machaire story. It seems to me that such pessimism characterizes the moral vision which lies deep-

---

[73] *CA* 7. 5357–65. On the Toby and Sara story and the question of the legitimacy of seeking sexual pleasure in marriage, see Kelly, *Love and Marriage*, 274–85.

[74] Compare *DPN* 10 in which the failure to restrain Cupido is regardable as unnatural because it is against Nature's desires (see above, p. 91).

est in the text. As we shall see, reflections about the impossibility of securing oneself with certainty against the influence of love or of ordering that condition from within its grip[75] are offered by a variety of different voices and in a variety of different places in the poem. That variety seems to me to call into question interpretations which seek to devolve the resignation about the impossibility of coping with love onto Genius or Amans or the erotic mode of the main body of the work.[76] I find it hard to believe that a poem which is concerned to affirm with full conviction the cheering possibility that we can harmonize an accommodation of our sexual drives with a fidelity to the moral imperatives to which we are subject would end with the poet disengaging from love and proclaiming its essence—and that of the law of *kinde*—to be irrationality.[77] The Tale of Apollonius may be felt to pick up on suggestions as to the possibility of harmony within the human being made in book 7 and demonstrate that harmony triumphantly, but the subsequent unfolding of the story of Amans/John Gower and the explicit comments about love and nature mean that the triumphal is not the final tonality of the poem. Gower seems to me more impressed with the tendency of things to fall out of always precarious harmonies and balances than with their capacity to achieve these. Love does sometimes go right, but it is not human judgement that makes it do so. The story of Toby and Sara shows the erotic ordered by a supernatural intervention— and in so doing suggests the rarity of such ordering;[78] elsewhere the secular language of *aventure* makes the same point about the incapacity of human free choice in this area and the unusualness of *mesure*.[79] At the beginning of book 1 Gower tells us that he will leave the matter of the prologue and speak of love:

[75] Gower often seems not to make a clear distinction between these two things.

[76] As does Simpson. Besides *Sciences and the Self* see also James Simpson, 'Ironic Incongruence in the Prologue and Book 1 of Gower's *Confessio Amantis*', *Neophilologus*, 72 (1988), 617–32.

[77] See *CA* 8. 3138–51.

[78] See the passages cited in n. 8 for the necessity of grace for producing the desired condition in respect of love, which is in these cases immunity from or healing of love. In these passages reference to grace indicates the rarity of the achievement of the desired condition.

[79] It may be relevant that the achievement of harmony between love and morality occurs in stories which are two degrees more fictional than the realm in which John Gower (no longer the fiction Amans, who hears fictions) is sent away from love and back to his books of moral virtue. The implication may be that achieved harmony is a fairy tale.

In which ther can noman him reule,
That of tomuche or of tolite
Welnyh is every man to wyte,
And natheles ther is noman
In al this world so wys, that can
Of love tempre the mesure,
Bot as it falth in aventure:
For wit ne strengthe may noght helpe,
And he which elles wolde him yelpe
Is rathest throwen under fote,
Ther can no wiht therof do bote.
For yet was nevere such covine,
That couthe ordeine a medicine
To thing which god in lawe of kinde
Hath set, for ther may noman finde
The rihte salve of such a Sor.
It hath and schal ben everemor
That love is maister wher he wile,
Ther can no lif make other skile;
For wher as evere him lest to sette,
Ther is no myht which him may lette.[80]

Here it is a matter of 'aventure' whether that proportion and 'mesure' which ought to characterize human living in all its aspects is achieved over love. But the chances of it being achieved are much less than evens, for a tendency to disproportion is of the very nature of love. This entitles love to be regarded as a disease, albeit a disease endemic in the natural God-given order, the *lawe of kinde*.[81] It is, of course, no surprise that the diseased condition of the inner self should find expression in wrong behaviour, as with Amans in this passage which follows his confession of the dominance within him of the conflict between reason and love-sponsoring will:

Thou dost, my Sone, ayein the riht;
Bot love is of so gret a miht,

---

[80] *CA* 1.17–38. Very similar language is used at the end of the poem (8. 3138 ff.) by the narrator, who by this stage is released from love and about to celebrate the love of God, and so cannot be said to be providing a perspective skewed by commitment to the erotic. This seems to me to put pressure on Simpson's notion that the poem moves away from such views on the irresistibility of love as are expressed at the opening of book 1— though it should be said that in the concluding passage there is no absolutely explicit affirmation that 'love is maister wher he wile'.

[81] *VC* 5. 193–6 treats amor as an *innatum morbum* [innate disease]; see n. 6.

> His lawe mai noman refuse,
> So miht thou thee the betre excuse.
> And natheles thou schalt be lerned
> That will scholde evere be governed
> Of reson more than of kinde.[82]

The last lines here state an ideal in which reason dominates *kinde*, an ideal in line with the comments in book 7. However, the sense of antagonism between reason and *kinde*, as they compete for domination of the will, is sharper than in book 7, and that seems appropriate when the projected ideal is presented as unrealizable—the first lines of the passage indicate that whatever *should* be the case, *kinde* and love are not in fact amenable to reason.

That sharp sense of the antagonism between love on the one hand and reason and morality on the other and a consciousness of the unmanageability of the natural sexual impulses are what dominate the ending of *Confessio Amantis*. Because love and reason are incompatible, because they cannot safely and securely be balanced in mutual accommodation, Genius requires Amans to give up love:

> For love, which that blind was evere,
> Makth alle his servantz blinde also.
> My Sone, and if thou have be so,
> Yit is it time to withdrawe,
> And set thin herte under that lawe,
> The which of reson is governed
> And noght of will.[83]

Unsurprisingly, this does not persuade Amans. His release from love is not freely willed and rationally decided upon, but occurs by the decision of the capricious deity Venus and through the immediate

---

[82] *CA* 3. 1193–9. At *VC* 5. 199–200 wrongdoing in the erotic sphere is laid at the door of a human nature which cannot be escaped; here, however, though it seems sexual sin is naturally inevitable, there is no excuse in the fact that one is naturally constrained to it: 'O natura viri, poterit quam tollere nemo, | Nec tamen excusat quod facit ipsa malum' [O the nature of man which no one will be able to remove—and it nevertheless does not excuse the evil which it commits itself]. The legitimacy of offering the naturalness of the sexual drive as an excuse is called into question at *MO* 20713–24, but here it is only priests who are explicitly denied the excuse, vowed as they are to chastity. It is recognized that priests may be subject to an 'inclinacion' which leads them to a 'naturele ardure' [natural ardour].

[83] *CA* 8. 2130–6.

agency of the blind god Cupid.[84] This again seems likely to figure
the operation of chance, of factors unpredictable to and uncontrol-
lable by reason, in matters of love; we should note how Venus
releases this old man from love but not those others who as the
company of Elde remain in her court, a fact which suggests that we
are not in the realm of regular and governable process.[85]

One might perhaps attempt to accord reason some kind of control even over the desperately love-sick Amans by arguing that
Amans' healing is precipitated by his coming to understand that
his position in love is hopeless. Venus tells Amans that he should
'Remembre wel hou thou art old'[86] and these lines follow:

> Whan Venus hath hir tale told,
> And I bethoght was al aboute,
> Tho wiste I wel withoute doute,
> That ther was no recoverir;
> And as a man the blase of fyr
> With water quencheth, so ferd I;
> A cold me cawhte sodeinly,
> For sorwe that myn herte made
> Mi dedly face pale and fade
> Becam, and swoune I fell to grounde.[87]

What is then experienced in the swoon, and in particular the
removal of the 'fyri Lancegay' of love by Cupid,[88] might figure a
subconscious detachment of the self from love. However, it is by no
means clear that we must read things this way, that the despair is to
be seen as in any way rational or as a trigger of change. It does not
seem inevitable that Amans will be healed following his despairing
of his predicament—as far as we can see he might have gone on
loving without hope. The attempt to grant reason any sort of power
over love at this point in the poem goes against the implications of
the way Gower presents matters. His swoon means that the end of

---

[84] *CA* 8. 2362–76, 8. 2745–802. See *CA* 8. 2377–86 for Venus' capriciousness and 1. 39 ff. for that of 'love', a blind, male power presumably identical with Cupid.

[85] There is not even, I think, an ungovernable regularity constituted by a person's impotence and its consequences for his status as a lover; considerations about sexual potency are raised by Venus in relation to Amans' exclusion from her court, but there are doubts over Solomon's sexual capacity and he remains a member of the court.

[86] *CA* 8. 2439.

[87] *CA* 8. 2440–9.

[88] *CA* 8. 2792 ff.

love comes while Amans's rational faculties are in suspense, and within the swoon the crucial things happen to Amans rather than being achieved by him.[89] It is true that he contemplates his old age in a mirror given him by Venus, but the contemplation occurs *after* the removal of the *lancegay*: if the contemplation is a fulfilment of Venus' command to remember his old age, its occurring where it does suggests that rational reflection can happen only after the passion of love has ended and does not bring about that end.[90] Reason's incapacity in the psyche of the lover and the irreconcilability of love and reason are indicated by the lines describing how Amans, the dart of love now removed, awakens from his swoon:

> And thus thenkende thoghtes fele,
> I was out of mi swoune affraied,
> Wherof I sih my wittes straied,
> And gan to clepe hem hom ayein.
> And whan Resoun it herde sein
> That loves rage was aweie,
> He cam to me the rihte weie,
> And hath remued the sotie
> Of thilke unwise fantasie,
> Wherof that I was wont to pleigne,
> So that of thilke fyri peine
> I was mad sobre and hol ynowh.[91]

Reason does something towards completing the healing of Amans here—perhaps cause Amans to rebuke and register properly his own absurdity—but, critically, Reason's operation cannot begin, he cannot come to Amans, until 'loves rage' is 'aweie'. The blindness of the lover, as Genius has told us, removes the capacity for rational self-rule.

In his petition to Venus and Nature Amans reflects on how rational self-rule is beyond him, as Nature constrains him to love and yet refuses to satisfy his longing:

---

[89] Amans' passivity and the capriciousness of the forces working upon him are means by which Gower acknowledges the mysterious, involuntary causality which leads to a falling out of love.

[90] The positioning of the mirror sequence also suggests that the despair which leads to the swoon is not caused by the reflection Venus recommends, and this encourages one to see that despair as a product of passion rather than reason.

[91] *CA* 8. 2858–69.

Ferst to Nature if that I me compleigne,
Ther finde I hou that every creature
Som time ayer hath love in his demeine,
So that the litel wrenne in his mesure
Hath yit of kinde a love under his cure;
And I bot on desire, of which I misse:
And thus, bot I, hath every kinde his blisse.[92]

The resoun of my wit it overpasseth,
Of that Nature techeth me the weie
To love, and yit no certein sche compasseth
Hou I schal spede, and thus betwen the tweie
I stonde, and not if I schal live or deie.
For thogh reson ayein my will debate,
I mai noght fle, that I ne love algate.[93]

This is a version of the topos of the distinction between the harmony of the animals' relation to Nature and the disharmony of the human race's,[94] only here the emphasis falls not on human depravity, but on the way in which human beings are the victims of their natural impulses. For if Nature impels humans to love and yet provides no certain satisfaction of that urge, Nature appears as a tyrant operating according to no appropriate and rationally intelligible order, but rather generating a cruel teleological suspension where an end clearly proposed in her arrangements cannot be brought into actuality.[95] Now, we are, to be sure, dealing here with a self-pitying Amans, but what he says about Nature's frustrating dispensation for human sexuality is not obviously discredited by that self-pity.

---

[92] The contrast between the birds, who are successful in love, and an unsuccessful human protagonist is found also in *CB* 35. The *Parlement of Foules* (which we might note dramatizes the conception of a bird Parliament on Valentine's day found in Gower's balade) may well allegorize a similar picture, and through it make uncomfortable suggestions about the role Nature plays in human experience. See Ch. 7.

[93] *CA* 8. 2224–37.

[94] As in *DPN* (2.230 ff.), where Nature's *tunica* is torn only at the point at which humanity is depicted.

[95] The sense of victimhood would be enhanced were we to understand that humans were *compelled* to love; this sense may be carried in the idea of Nature teaching to love, and at ll. 2239 f. we are told that 'whilom Pan, which is the god of kinde' was overcome by love, perhaps indicating that all natural creatures, humans included, lack the power to resist love.

A sense of Nature's power, not necessarily benign, draws forth from Venus the concession that though she may have released Amans from love, there remain for him negotiations with Nature:[96]

> For I thi bille have understonde,
> In which to Cupide and to me
> Somdiel thou hast compleigned thee,
> And somdiel to Nature also.
> Bot that schal stonde among you tuo,
> For therof have I noght to done;
> For Nature is under the Mone
> Maistresse of every lives kinde,
> But if so be that sche mai finde
> Som holy man that wol withdrawe
> His kindly lust ayein hir lawe;
> Bot sielde whanne it falleth so,
> For fewe men ther ben of tho.[97]

This apparently suggests that Amans/John Gower, for all his recovery of reason and psychic calm, remains at risk of succumbing again to the turbulence of overmastering sexual feelings—unless, that is, he becomes one of the few holy men, a condition towards which he is, in fact, arguably moving at the end of the poem, with his *Por reposer* beads and his intercession for the peace of the realm and his pointing to the love of God in the last lines of the work. But clearly, whatever is the case with Amans/Gower, most people remain at risk from their natural sexual feelings, feelings which are inimical to holiness, which perhaps we may understand as virtue of the highest kind.

But if Nature threatens rational calm and is at odds with holiness in her promotion of sexual instinct, her moral status here at the unillusioned end of the poem is not wholly negative. Venus' lines on Nature just quoted continue into this:

[96] The distinction between the two powers may relate to a distinction between a particular attachment in love and the basic sexual impulse. At certain other points in the poem where the language distinguishes between Cupid and Nature, or love and nature (see e.g. 3. 148 ff., 3. 403), Gower may possibly be separating amatory attachment from sexual impulse, but it is unclear how much the language represents a real conceptual distinction. Such a distinction does not seem to be carried by the different terms at *CA* 1. 29–36 and 8. 51–8.

[97] *CA* 8. 2324–36.

> Bot of these othre ynowe be,
> Whiche of here oghne nycete
> Ayein Nature and hire office
> Deliten hem in sondri vice,
> Wherof that sche fulofte hath pleigned,
> And ek my Court it hath desdeigned
> And evere schal; for it receiveth
> Non such that kinde so deceiveth.
> For al onliche of gentil love
> Mi court stant alle courtz above
> And takth noght into retenue
> Bot thing which is to kinde due,[98]
> For elles it schal be refused.[99]

Perhaps Gower's attachment to the idea of nature as a force for good calls forth these lines as some sort of counterbalance to the lines on the antagonism between Nature as sponsor of *kindly lust* and the holiness which repudiates Nature's sexual law.[100] But however that may be, it is clear that the strand in the poem which takes a positive view of the moral dimensions of the impulsive order is confronted in the closing lines with an emphasis on the moral unsatisfactoriness of love and the natural.

We can say then that the image of Nature's morality in *Confessio Amantis* is a divided one. On the one hand the idea of Nature seems to be used to suggest how the impulsive realm in which human beings find themselves implicated offers support to human efforts to behave well. Even for the sexual realm we find suggestions that natural behaviour is good behaviour and there are some passages which give us to understand that the natural sexual urges are at least

---

[98] J. A. W. Bennett interprets this as if it were a remark about the debt of sexual activity payable to nature, but the sense of 'due' seems rather to be 'appropriate to' or 'consonant with'. See Bennett, 'Gower's "Honeste Love"', in J. Lawlor (ed.), *Patterns of Love and Courtesy: Essays in Memory of C. S. Lewis* (Evanston, Ill., 1966), 120. Exactly what Gower is thinking of here is not entirely clear; the remark may have to do with the standard conception of unnatural sexual behaviour as non-inseminative. How far Venus would meet her own strictures is also questionable, given the account of her activities in book 5. But the continuation of the passage shows Amans, a long-standing member of Venus' court, vindicated as natural: 'Wherof I holde thee excused, | For it is manye daies gon, | That thou amonges hem were on | Which of my court hast ben withholde; | So that the more I am beholde | Of thi desese to commune' (2350–5).

[99] *CA* 8. 2337–49.

[100] We have noted before in the tradition and in *CA* itself how the natural sometimes has intermediate moral status.

accommodatable to good morality. But these variously positive accounts of the impact of the impulsive on human beings as moral creatures coexist with a strand of witness which recognizes that the sexual urge has a tendency to send human behaviour off the moral rails. Affirmations of the moral dubiousness of the natural, though, tend to add riders that offer various kinds of rehabilitations of problematic natural behaviour. There may, for instance, be reflections on the difficulty of escaping the power of the natural and on how succumbing to that power is excusable, or natural wrong behaviour may be shown to be preferable to wrong behaviour which cannot be called natural. This rather wavering view of the moral position of the natural is, I think, part of a larger hesitancy in *Confessio Amantis* in deciding between a view of the world which sees it as harmonious in its basic component elements and one which affirms its radical dividedness. Ultimately, in my view, division triumphs: Gower tends to imagine the world in terms of profound antagonisms between opposites in which harmonious balancing of claims is not achievable, but in which peace and stability could only be attained by the elimination of the influence of one of the opposites, an elimination not in fact likely to occur.[101] Nevertheless, he wants, I think, at least to entertain the view that harmony between opposites is available. This, as I understand it, is what he is doing in constructing a work which uses a moral framework for dealing with love. Gower wants to entertain the idea that sexual love is regulable according to orthodox moral categories—and is therefore, at the minimum, morally acceptable—against a view which affirms the essential moral problematicness of sex and the body. This is why he presents Genius in the way he does. Genius is both a servant of Venus and a priest, and this is so, I would suggest, because Genius is a major piece of equipment in Gower's experiment in holding love and morality together. The importance of his dual function is indicated by the insistence with which its duality is detailed by Genius:

> Thi schrifte to oppose and hiere,
> My Sone, I am assigned hiere,

---

[101] See, e.g., the passage on the soul and the body at *CA* 7. 490 ff., where soul and body can 'nevere stonde in evene | Bot if the fleissh be overcome | And that the Soule have holi nome | The governance, and that is selde, | Whil that the fleissh him mai bewelde' (506–10), and see White, 'Division', 601–3.

Be Venus the godesse above,
Whos Prest I am touchende of love.
Bot natheles for certein skile
I mot algate and nedes wile
Noght only make my spekynges
Of love, bot of othre thinges,
That touchen to the cause of vice.
For that belongeth to thoffice
Of Prest, whos ordre that I bere,
So that I wol nothing forbere,
That I the vices on and on
Ne schal thee schewen everychon;
Wherof thou myht take evidence
To reule with thi conscience.
Bot of conclusion final
Conclude I wol in special
For love, whos servant I am,
And why the cause is that I cam . . .
     it is noght my comun us
To speke of vices and vertus,
Bot al of love and of his lore,
For Venus bokes of nomore
Me techen nowther text ne glose.
Bot for als moche as I suppose
It sit a prest to be wel thewed,
And schame it is if he be lewed,
Of my Presthode after the forme
I wol thi schrifte so enforme,
That ate leste thou schalt hiere
The vices, and to thi matiere
Of love I schal hem so remene,
That thou schalt knowe what thei mene.[102]

However, this double service, harmonizing two kinds of obligation, two kinds of priesthood, is one which finally cannot be maintained.[103] By the end of the poem Genius is effectively denying his mistress Venus[104] and demanding, as we have already seen, that

---

[102] *CA* 1. 233–52, 267–80.
[103] See Baker, 'Priesthood', on the double service and White, 'Division', on its collapse. Genius expresses embarrassment at Venus' sexual activities at *CA* 5. 1382 f.
[104] See Cherniss, *Boethian Apocalypse*, 114 f.

love be refused in favour of reason and morality. His sense that his obligations to Venus have receded behind the claims of a morality hostile to sexual love appears in lines at the beginning of the speech which culminates in the declaration of how love leads to misrule of the self and moral blindness:[105]

> I behihte thee that yifte
> Ferst whanne thou come under my schrifte,
> That thogh I toward Venus were,
> Yit spak I suche wordes there,
> That for the Presthod which I have,
> Min ordre and min astat to save,
> I seide I wolde of myn office
> To vertu more than to vice
> Encline, and teche thee mi lore.
> Forthi to speken overmore
> Of love, which thee mai availe,
> Tak love where it mai noght faile:
> For as of this which thou art inne,
> Be that thou seist it is a Sinne.[106]

If at the beginning of the poem Genius is insistent on his status as servant of Venus and rather tentative about his capacities as moral educator, here near the end both that insistence and that tentativeness have vanished as sexual love is dismissed in favour of morality. Genius' revised sense of his capacities and obligations is perhaps a sign of how the poem's initial generosity towards love has given way to an ascetic vision which focuses on the unsatisfactoriness of human sexual love, its irreconcilability with the claims of morality, and which sees clearly the need to turn to a love beyond this world.[107]

It should be acknowledged that despite the advice he gives him Genius eventually agrees to present Amans' petition for aid

---

[105] See above, at n. 83 It is important to be aware that Genius is not simply condemning Amans' love in this speech, but that for Genius, Love makes *all* his servants blind (*CA* 8. 2130 f.). See further below.

[106] *CA* 8. 2075–88.

[107] This perspective is clearly dominant in the words of the narrator at the end of the poem (*CA* 8. 3138–72). The sentiments of the narrator here are very similar to those of Genius in the speech from which I have just quoted and confirm that taking love where it may not fail means turning to the love of God. Genius is not advising Amans to turn to some other kind of human love.

in his love-cause to Venus, and because of this can be regarded as furthering love and retaining a degree of loyalty to his mistress.[108] This preparedness in Genius to turn away from a well-understood moral truth may come about because Gower knows that the advice to give up love, though it recommends the right course, recommends it in the face of the ineluctability of the erotic impulse—and perhaps its necessity if the world is to continue (we recall Genius' role in the tradition as a power of reproduction). But Genius, to the extent that he is loyal to love and to Venus at the end of the poem, is so against his own moral convictions, and in this his dividedness, not merely his duality now, is apparent.

Whatever Genius' delivery of Amans' petition may signify, he certainly champions the ascetic point of view, a point of view which dominates the end of the poem. In this attachment to the ascetic ethos Genius becomes a significantly different figure from the Genius Gower originally presented, and, indeed, one estranged from the Geniuses of the earlier tradition. The configuration of the poem's new Genius acknowledges, I think, the failure, perhaps a planned failure, of its original Genius to be the means of a harmonization of the claims of love and of morality. The triumph of the ascetic produces also a disintegration of the other major figure through which *Confessio Amantis* investigated the possibility of a bringing together of love and morality. Amans ceases to be a lover; he loses his name and the identity it specifies. He gains the name John Gower, and this suggests—because it is the poet's true name—that in the ending of love a true identity has been recovered.[109] The identity recovered is both personal and artistic. Gower is sent off to

---

[108] *CA* 8. 2200–9; 2301–9.
[109] The marginal note at 1. 61 speaks of the author 'fingens se esse Amantem'[pretending that he is a lover]. We might think of the identity recovered at the end of the poem as being that of the non-feigning poet John Gower who *in propria persona* gives us the moralistic Prologue and the unillusioned lines on love prior to 1. 61. To write about love *in extenso* may require the poet to hold in abeyance his normal attitudes and to adopt the more sympathetic stance of an actual lover. In the return to the territory and attitudes of the beginning of the poem and particularly in the use of the poet's real name, as the I of the poem is detached from love and entertains again the kind of sentiment found before the adoption of the role of Amans, a declaration of the provisional, experimental quality of the bulk of *Confessio Amantis* is made, the author setting a distance between the attitudes he presents as those of his 'true' self and the major part of his poem.

> go ther vertu moral duelleth,
> Wher ben thi bokes, as men telleth,
> Whiche of long time thou hast write[110]

This would seem to suggest that *Confessio Amantis* itself, a different kind of book, has been something of a false direction, a failure.

The idea of nature is implicated in this failure, genuine or contrived. This is perhaps not surprising in view of the traditional associations between Nature and Genius: if Genius does not 'work', then how can Nature? If the poem is exploring the relationship between soul and body, between love and morality, between this world and the next, entertaining in some way the hope that it will be possible to reconcile the demands of these divided poles, one can see that Gower might very well be interested in the idea of Nature. For all that he associates Nature with the body and with the sexual impulse, the ideas of the law of nature and of Nature as God's deputy give much countenance to the notion that the instinctual is legitimate and in tune with the demands of the divine on humanity. Like Genius (though perhaps less as a result of poetic artifice and more because of a conceptual structure deeply inscribed in medieval culture and which Gower can hardly avoid), Nature straddles the moral and the erotic and gives promise of being a concept through which the two can be reconciled, the erotic moralized, the moral made to accept the erotic. But the pull of division requires a perception of Nature in this one crucial area of sexuality as ultimately unattuned to the production of right moral order. In the end it is made to appear that the natural sexual drive is not morally trustworthy and that the Nature who deals out sexual impulses to human beings does not, in so doing, enhance their chances of behaving well or even being happy. In the last analysis, because of Nature's lack of concern for morality in a sphere which nevertheless needs moral controls, Nature and Reason have to be seen as antagonistic.

Some critics, however, think that *Confessio Amantis* proclaims a subtle attunedness of the natural to the demands of good morality: it affirms that the natural process of ageing brings a diminished sexuality and so tends to a promotion of holiness. Even the laws of nature, it is

[110] *CA* 8. 2925–7.

argued, connive to bring a person to salvation;[111] what is required of Amans is not a transcending of but a conforming to the laws of nature.[112] There certainly is a sense in the poem that age is sexually incapacitating,[113] but it is not clear that Nature inevitably tends to release a person from sexuality with age in a way that would make the retention of sexual interest counter-natural. Venus comments on how her court does not take 'into retenue | Bot thing which is to kinde due'[114] and yet Elde's company of aged lovers are of that court. Venus' remarks at *CA* 8. 2322 ff. that, whatever she herself does, Amans will need to treat with Nature in the matter of love, imply that Nature may stimulate sexual feeling even in the elderly. Gower's use of nature terms, in fact, does not suggest that Amans' aged love is unnatural. The nearest Gower gets to affirming the contrary is when some of the lovers who assemble round the swooning Amans

> weren wo that I [Amans] so ferde,
> And seiden that for no riote
> An old man scholde noght assote;
> For as thei tolden redely,
> Ther is in him no cause why,
> But if he wolde himself benyce;
> So were he wel the more nyce.[115]

Others argue, though, that

> the wylde loves rage
> In mannes lif forberth non Age;
> Whil ther is oyle forto fyre,
> The lampe is lyhtly set afyre,
> And is fulhard er it be queynt.[116]

The issue here is never explicitly resolved, but Amans' case suggests the latter opinion is correct.[117] He has been struck by Cupid's dart

---

[111] So Donald Schueler in 'Gower's Characterization of Genius in the *Confessio Amantis*', *MLQ* 33 (1972), 240–56 (246).

[112] See John Burrow, 'The Portrayal of Amans in "Confessio Amantis"', in A. J. Minnis (ed.), *Gower's Confessio Amantis*, (Cambridge, 1983), 5–24 (17 f.)

[113] See *CA* 8. 2398–439.

[114] *CA* 8. 2347 f.

[115] *CA* 8. 2764–70.

[116] *CA* 8. 2773–7.

[117] Kelly, *Love and Marriage*, 156, points out that this opinion is accorded a *Nota* in the marginal commentary.

and seems dependent on Cupid for its removal. No doubt in the natural course of things there will be fewer elderly lovers than young ones—the company of aged lovers is smaller than that of young lovers, though it is still a 'gret compaignie'[118]—but that does not imply any perverse unnaturalness on the part of aged lovers. Rather, in them there is realized that susceptibility to love which is a general law of nature, a nature which it is almost impossible—perhaps impossible without the assistance of grace—to transcend but which, in this erotic sphere, powerfully jeopardizes good moral behaviour.[119]

That Nature and Reason are fundamentally antagonistic, then, is the view of the end of the poem. This should be sufficiently apparent from passages already quoted, but the seal is set on this perspective as Gower takes his 'final leve':

> But now uppon my laste tide
> That y this book have maad and write,
> My muse doth me forto wite,
> And seith it schal be for my beste
> Fro this day forth to take reste,
> That y nomore of love make,
> Which many an herte hath overtake,
> And ovyrturnyd as the blynde
> Fro reson in to lawe of kynde;
> Wher as the wisdom goth aweie
> And can nought se the ryhte weie
> How to governe his oghne estat,
> Bot everydai stant in debat
> Withinne him self, and can noght leve.[120]

This view of love, nature, and reason is a world away from that celebrating their harmony in *Cinkante Balades* 50: 'Amour s'acorde a

---

[118] *CA* 8. 2667–80. At 7. 1044 ff. it is 'the youthe of every creature' which 'love of his pointure stingeth | After the lawes of nature', and see the comments on Canace and Machaire at *CA* 3. 152–7.

[119] See *CA* 8. 3138 ff. The question of the naturalness of love in old age is discussed in Hugh White, 'The Naturalness of Amans' Love in *Confessio Amantis*', *Medium Aevum*, 66 (1987), 316–22.

[120] *CA* 8. 3138–51. It should be noted that this passage revises heavily the equivalent lines in the earlier version (3070*–3087*). It seems, however, to render more emphatic a negative assessment of erotic love already present at the end of the original version. See Kelly, *Love and Marriage*, 157–60.

nature et resoun.' Here in *Confessio Amantis* love and nature stand opposed to reason. In the final vision of the poem nature is not seen as one pole of a harmony of opposites but rather as a disintegrative pressure on human beings, something on the side of that division which is for Gower at the root of the world's ills. The best that can ultimately be said of nature is that the sins it prompts are excusable— but that is rather a muted claim to make. As such, though, it accords excellently with the tonality of the conclusion of *Confessio Amantis*, where the enterprise of love ends in a reasonably dignified failure, and where the poem invites us to look a little askance at what it has done, terminating in something less than a blaze of self-congratulation.

Finding an excuse for behaviour in its being something to which human beings are compelled need not mean that the agent of compulsion is also protected from blame. However, with Gower's treatment of the morally dubious pressures of Nature it does seem that various attempts are made to prevent the possibility of unequivocal condemnation of Nature as a force which viciously victimizes a helpless humankind. Human beings may be more or less helpless in the face of Nature, but, after all, Nature and her law carry many associations with right order and this perhaps makes difficult a thoroughgoing and unequivocal repudiation even of those of her operations which push humanity towards vice. So, as the beginning of book 1 has it, the world has to go on through love, and though love may be a *Sor*, it is something which God has set 'in lawe of kinde'. There are intimations here of a divine purpose being worked out through the sometimes anti-rational influences of nature. The way in which Gower frequently presents instinct as a force for moral good may indicate that he would like to believe in a mysterious but ultimately benign purpose in the ineluctable and apparently sometimes baneful influence of the sexual impulse on human beings. Likewise, his readiness to designate the dubious instinctive animal side of humankind 'kinde', a term which has so many positive connotations, seems to point to a determination to see that side as acceptable, despite some evidence pointing in the other direction. But Gower does not evade that evidence: he confronts squarely the fact of nature's inclinations to vice. By doing this, he allows play to anxiety about the human predicament. Human beings find themselves borne down upon by natural forces impossible, or all but impossible, to control and which militate against their efforts at reasonable and holy living. In this predicament can the thought that vice is only natural offer legitimate consolation, or would it be more appropriate to take the depressing view that humanity is alarmingly open to the influences of a truly evil power? The world may have to stand by love, but the world is not only God's creation, but also one member of a triad of evil influences, the other two being the flesh and the devil, which work to bring human beings to damnation. And when love is designated 'huius princeps mundi' in the headnote to book 1, we should recall that this is a title of the devil.[121] The final directions of the poem suggest that one might do well not to put too much trust in the fact that love and nature are permitted their power over humankind by God. The same is true of the devil himself, but to succumb to his power means damnation. In the background here seem to be alarmed questions about the purposes of God which would have to be met by sheer faith in God's mercy. For what cannot be demonstrated in reassurance, even through the promising term nature, is that the constitution and existential situation of human beings are designed to move them towards salvation. Rather, it has to be confessed that nature lines up with the forces of unreason, its influence in the critical area of human sexual love tending to operate against reason and goodness, and that therefore one ought ideally to seek to liberate oneself, near impossible though this seems to be—an acutely worrying fact—from natural sexual impulse. This fatally compromises any attempt to celebrate the things of this world as if they were not at root irreconcilable with the things of heaven and this is why *Confessio Amantis* ends in renunciation and a proclamation of its own failure.

---

[121] See St John's Gospel 12: 31, 14: 30, 16: 11.

CHAPTER SEVEN

Chaucer

In the last chapter it was suggested that Gower struggles to believe that Nature is on the side of Good and in the end finds such belief impossible to sustain. This predicament has much to do with the conception of the natural as the instinctive being strongly dominant in *Confessio Amantis*. Chaucer's understanding of the natural seems less centralized than Gower's, his writings more expressive of the range of possible meanings for nature and the natural available in the Middle Ages; one could not plausibly argue for Chaucer, as one can for Gower, that all his references to the natural imply an Ulpianic Nature, such that what is understood as natural to human beings is what they share with the animals.[1] Yet it seems to me that Chaucer, when he engages most deeply with ideas of the natural, is more deliberately, even programmatically, sceptical than is Gower about the benignity of Nature. Several of Chaucer's poems make extensive use of the figure Nature or the idea of the natural and of the notion that the natural is good and right, but these works seem deliberately to invite us to go through a process of disillusion with Nature which ends in scepticism. In them, we are initially encouraged to understand the natural as benign or morally normative in various ways, but then made to reflect on how problematic this is.

---

[1] So in the *Parson's Tale* Chaucer uses the traditional division of the goods of Nature, Fortune, and Grace, within which the goods of nature are divided into those of body and of (the rational, non-animal) soul ('Goodes of nature of the soule been good wit, sharp understondynge, subtil engyn, vertu natureel, good memorie' (*CT* 10. 453)). Chaucer also sometimes works within an erotic discourse which sees the virtues of character of the beloved, as well as her beauty, as gifts of Nature. So at *BD* 1195–8, Nature is seen as responsible for lady White's *bounte*; in the *Squire's Tale*, Nature is held to have set 'verray wommanly benignytee' in Canacee's 'principles' (*CT* 5. 484–7); at *PF* 372–6 the formel is seen as a work of Nature and said to be superlatively *benygne, gentil,* and *goodly*—indeed 'in her was everi virtue at his reste' (376). (See also *Complaynt d'Amours*, 50–8.) In *The Complaint of Venus*, on the other hand, it may be that Nature's endowment is confined to physical 'forming' (9–15).

This scepticism about the natural is, I think, Chaucer's deepest response to various strands of optimistic naturalism in his cultural inheritance. It is not, however, always in evidence. Sometimes the natural is taken as good and no reservations are indicated. It is not surprising, given the frequent recourse moralists of the period make to the idea of nature as moral norm, that instances should occur in the moralizing prose of the *Tale of Melibee* and the *Parson's Tale*. The following passage from *Melibee* displays a morally authoritative Nature of wide competence, a conception deriving via Cicero from Stoicism:

For the lawe seith that 'ther maketh no man himselven riche, if he do harm to another wight.' | This is to seyn, that nature deffendeth and forbedeth by right that no man make hymself riche unto the harm of another persone. | And Tullius seith that 'no sorwe, ne no drede of deeth, ne no thyng that may falle unto a man, | is so muchel agayns nature as a man to encressen his owene profit to the harm of another man.'[2]

The *Parson's Tale* makes reference to a natural order which has straightforward moral implications, as when condemning a variety of Envy:

The speces of Envye been thise. Ther is first, sorwe of oother mannes goodnesse and of his prosperitee; and prosperitee is kyndely matere of joye; thanne is Envye a synne agayns kynde.[3]

In these instances, the order of nature is not defined with reference to animal instinct and that the understanding of Nature in the *Parson's Tale* is basically non-Ulpianic is evident in some remarks on fornication and marriage:[4]

Of Leccherie, as I seyde, sourden diverse speces, as fornicacioun, that is bitwixe man and womman that been nat maried, and this is deedly synne

---

[2] *CT* 7. 1583–6. As we shall see, *The Book of the Duchess* suggests human sorrow is in a sense all too natural.

[3] *CT* 10. 491. Note how here what makes envy unnatural is a feature of an abstract natural order; in Gower, Envy is unnatural because it works against the instinct for one's own welfare (see above, pp. 179–80). It is possible that, as with some of Gower's uses, the Parson's condemnation of this kind of Envy as 'agayns kynde' marks it as particularly heinous.

[4] The Parson does, however, refer to 'unkyndely synne, by which man or womman shedeth hire nature in manere or in place ther as a child may nat be conceived' (*CT* 10, 577), using a traditional designation for non-inseminative sexual practices which seems to be predicated on an understanding of the natural which ties it to animal behaviour.

and agayns nature. Al that is enemy and destruccioun to nature is agayns nature.[5]

It seems possible that this passage is confuting Ulpianic conceptions, such as we met in Chapter 1, to the effect that fornication is something to which their animal instincts urge human beings. The apparent tautology in the last sentence can be seen as involving the proof that fornication is against nature; all that is 'enemy and destruccioun' to nature is (obviously) against nature, and fornication is such 'enemy and destruccioun'—presumably because it is understood that sex in accordance with nature always occurs within marriage.[6] Marriage in the following passage is certainly understood as part of the natural law, part indeed of the prelapsarian, ur-natural law: 'This is verray mariage, that was establissed by God, er that synne bigan, whan natureel lawe was in his right poynt in paradys.'[7]

Within *Melibee* and the *Parson's Tale*, whatever arises out of their existence within the Canterbury collection as a whole, Chaucer does not seem interested in applying sceptical pressure to their visions of things. However, even in the *Parson's Tale*, there is the occasional indication that the natural is not absolutely satisfactory as a moral guide. So natural impulses will not necessarily take us the whole way down the path of virtue:

For Crist seith: 'Loveth youre enemys, . . . ' | For soothly, nature dryveth us to loven oure freendes, . . . | And in as muche as thilke love [of enemies] is the moore grevous to parfourne, so muche is the moore gret the merite.[8]

More worrying are the connections with that dubious entity, the flesh, whose evil promptings Nature may be said to encourage:

---

[5] *CT* 10. 865–6.

[6] It is perhaps just possible that non-inseminative behaviour is what is 'enemy and destruccioun to nature'; and, indeed, 'nature' might mean 'semen' (and its equivalent in women) in accordance with the sense of 'nature' employed by the Parson in the passage quoted in n. 4 above. On fornication and non-insemination in theological writing see Ch. 1.

[7] *CT* 10. 921. For some consideration of medieval writers distinguishing pre- and post-lapsarian natural law see e.g. Carlyle, and Carlyle, *History*, v. 14 ff. According to the Parson, in a passage indebted to St Augustine (see *De civitate Dei* 19. 15), *thraldom* is not an aspect of the 'natureel condicion' of things, and *thraldom* is a punishment for sin, not something deserved by 'nature' (*CT* 10. 755–7). There seems to be a certain tendency in the *Parson's Tale* to associate the natural with the prelapsarian.

[8] *CT* 10. 526 f., 529.

Now as for to speken of goodes of nature, God woot that somtyme we han hem in nature as muche to oure damage as to oure profit. | As for to speken of heele of body, certes it passeth ful lightly, and eek it is ful ofte enchesoun of the siknesse of oure soule. For, God woot, the flessh is a ful greet enemy to the soule, and therfore, the moore that the body is hool, the moore be we in peril to falle. | Eke for to pride hym in his strengthe of body, it is an heigh folye. For certes, the flessh coveiteth agayn the spirit, and ay the moore strong that the flessh is, the sorier may the soule be. | And over al this, strengthe of body and worldly hardynesse causeth ful ofte many a man to peril and meschaunce.[9]

Here Nature's provision of physical health is viewed as something of a disadvantage in the pursuit of virtue, Nature being seen as a sort of arms-dealer supplying the wrong side in a war between body and soul. Nature cannot here be seen as unequivocally an agent of the good. Though it is possible to view Nature's provision of the morally dubious body in a positive light as an aspect of her beneficence,[10] that is not the case in this passage, where the war between body and soul is seen in purely negative terms, as a threat, rather than as an incitement, to virtue, and where it seems to be suggested that human beings would be better off without the physical 'goods' of Nature.

Even the *Parson's Tale* then, though it is happy to invoke the natural unquestioningly as a moral norm, contains within it some not wholly positive reflections on aspects of the natural order. Configured in this way in respect of the natural, the *Parson's Tale* is representative of the kind of moralistic writings considered in Chapter 2. These understand the natural in a fundamentally positive way but offer some purchase to scepticism about the goodness and beneficence of the natural as regards human beings. If we were to seek to trace a literary genealogy for Chaucer's scepticism, we would not look to this kind of writing first; we shall see later, however, that the *Physician's Tale* stimulates doubts about the true goodness of Nature's goods which the Parson might indeed endorse. Chaucer's scepticism might have been nourished, at least, by some of what is written about the natural in works such as those which the *Parson's Tale* adapts or which are of a kind with it.

---

[9] *CT* 10. 457–60.
[10] In the *De planctu Naturae*, as we have seen, Nature presents her provision of the dubious *sensualitas* as offering an opportunity for human beings to triumph in virtue and earn a due reward.

However, it is not within this kind of discourse that Chaucer engages most creatively—and sceptically—with ideas of nature; unless, that is, one can count the *Consolation of Philosophy* as of this kind. For Chaucer certainly deals both creatively and sceptically with Boethius' conception of the natural. We can see this very clearly in two passages from different Canterbury Tales which share the same ultimate origin in Boethius' *Consolation of Philosophy* 3 *metrum* 2.[11] The procedures behind these two passages can be aligned quite closely with what occurs in other texts in which Chaucer gets to grips with Nature. In these other texts, as we shall see, Chaucer invites from the reader, in response to an optimistic conception of Nature presented within the poem, the kind of sceptical re-evaluation of such a conception made by himself outside and prior to the poem in these Boethius-derived passages. Furthermore, both these two passages and the other texts are engaged with the erotic; for, as with Gower, Chaucer's scepticism about Nature seems to be triggered by concerns as to her operation in the sphere of human love.

In *Boece* Chaucer renders book 3 *metrum* 2 as follows:

It liketh me to schewe by subtil soong, with slakke and delytable sown of strenges, how that Nature, myghty, enclyneth and flytteth the governementz of thynges, and by whiche lawes sche, purveiable, kepith the grete world; and how sche, byndynge, restreyneth alle thynges by a boond that may nat be unbownde. Al be it so that the lyouns of the contre of Pene beren the fayre chaynes, and taken metes of the handes of folk that yeven it hem, and dreden hir stourdy [maistre] of whiche thei ben wont to suffre betynges; yif that hir horrible mouthes ben bybled (that is to seyn, of beestes devoured), hir corage of tyme passed, that hath ben idel and rested, repeireth ayen, and thei roren grevously, and remembren on hir nature, and slaken hir nekkes from hir cheynes unbownde; and hir mayster fyrst, totorn with blody tooth, assaieth the wode wratthes of hem (this to seyn, thei freten hir maister). And the janglynge brid that syngeth on the heghe braunches (that is to seyn, in the wode), and after is enclosed in a streyte

---

[11] The treatment of the Boethius passage in the *Roman de la Rose* needs also to be taken into account in considering these two Chaucerian passages. Benson (*The Riverside Chaucer*, ed. Larry D. Benson (3rd edn., Boston, 1987), 953) suggests that Chaucer is probably using *RR* 13911–28 and *RR* 14009–22 in the *Manciple's Tale*, but it seems more than likely, especially if we accept that the *Manciple's Tale* is a late work, that Chaucer, even if working directly from *RR,* would have been aware of the relation with Boethius.

cage, althoughe that the pleyinge bysynes of men yeveth [hym] honyed drynkes and large metes with swete studye, yit natheles yif thike bryd skippynge out of hir streyte cage seith the agreables schadwes of the wodes, sche defouleth with hir feet hir metes ischad, and seketh mornynge oonly the wode, and twytereth desyrynge the wode with hir swete voys.[12]

In the next *prosa* Boethius draws the parallel between these animals returning to their natural forms of behaviour and human beings, whose 'naturel entencioun', though sometimes suppressed, leads them towards the 'verray good'.[13] So the context, as I have already suggested in Chapter 3,[14] as well as the celebration of Nature with which the passage opens (cf. 2 *metrum* 8), shows that the creatures' return to nature is to be understood as something good. A later exchange between Philosophy and the Prisoner encapsulates succinctly Philosophy's positive view of the natural, asserting its attunedness to the will of God: ' "Thanne is ther nothyng," quod sche, "that kepith his nature, that enforceth hym to gon ayen God." "No," quod I.'[15]

Chaucer's versions of material in *Consolation of Philosophy* 3 m. 2 completely subvert the original drift; they convert evidences which Boethius offers for an optimistic view of the natural into pointers to what one might call its perversity. This is what the Manciple says:

> But God it woot, ther may no man embrace
> As to destreyne a thyng which that nature
> Hath natureelly set in a creature.
>   Taak any bryd, and put it in a cage,
> And do al thyn entente and thy corage
> To fostre it tendrely with mete and drynke
> Of alle deyntees that thou kanst bithynke,
> And keep it al so clenly as thou may,
> Although his cage of gold be never so gay,
> Yet hath this brid, by twenty thousand foold,
> Levere in a forest that is rude and coold
> Goon ete wormes and swich wrecchednesse.
> For evere this brid wol doon his bisynesse
> To escape out of his cage, yif he may.
> His libertee this brid desireth ay.
>   Lat take a cat, and fostre hym wel with milk

---

[12] *Boece* 3. m. 2 1–31.   [13] *Boece* 3. p. 3 6–7.
[14] See above, p. 72.   [15] *Boece* 3. p. 12 102–5.

> And tendre flessh, and make his couche of silk,
> And lat hym seen a mous go by the wal,
> Anon he weyveth milk and flessh and al,
> And every deyntee that is in that hous,
> Swich appetit hath he to ete a mous.
> Lo, heere hath lust his dominacioun,
> And appetit fleemeth discrecioun.[16]

The Manciple adds a further example from the animal world before making the connection with the world of human beings:

> A she-wolf hath also a vileyns kynde.
> The lewedeste wolf that she may fynde,
> Or leest of reputacioun, wol she take,
> In tyme whan hir lust to han a make.
>   Alle thise ensamples speke I by thise men
> That been untrewe, and nothyng by wommen.
> For men han evere a likerous appetit
> On lower thyng to parfourne hire delit
> Than on hire wyves, be they never so faire,
> Ne never so trewe, ne so debonaire.
> Flessh is so newefangel, with meschaunce,
> That we ne konne in nothyng han plesaunce
> That sowneth into vertu any while.[17]

This unattractive she-wolf, not present in the *Consolation of Philosophy*, and her unpleasing behaviour confirm emphatically what is already evident earlier, that an un-Boethian perspective is here operative. The changes undergone by the examples which do occur in the *Consolation* in themselves demonstrate how Boethius' drift has been transformed and his favourable assessment of the natural inverted. Boethius offers us a lion nobly shaking off the chains of captivity on tasting blood; this magnificent beast becomes in Jean de Meun and Chaucer a domestic pet indulging a dubious appetite for vermin. As for Chaucer's bird, the attractions of the captive life are more stressed than in the *Consolation*, as is the negative side of freedom (the forest is 'rude and cold'; in Chaucer the pleasing detail

---

[16] *CT* 9. 160–82.
[17] *CT* 9. 183–95. The she-wolf occurs at *RR* (7761–66) at some distance from the other *RR* material used in this *Manciple's Tale* passage. The exemplum of the she-wolf is in fact widespread (see T. B. W. Reid, 'The She-Wolf's Mate', *Medium Aevum*, 24 (1955), 16–19).

of how the freed bird 'siluas dulci uoce susurrat' is omitted, whilst on the other hand the loaded 'Goon ete wormes and swich wrecched-nesse' (not in Jean de Meun), is added. Thus the bird's return to its wild condition is not seen as something to be celebrated, but as the satisfaction of an inappropriate and uncontrolled desire. What bird and cat do comes from an unreasonable *lust*, a word the use of which encourages us to associate their behaviour, for all its evident natur-alness, with the debased activity of men to which the animals' actions are made parallel.[18] Equally, as the Maniciple makes his application to the human realm, we are encouraged to see what 'nature | Hath natureely set' in mankind as something which levels him with the animals, an instinctive, unreasonable, and indeed perverse appetite, located—a mark both of its physicality and its moral dubiety—in the 'flessh'. The Maniciple sees the operation within men of what Boethius calls the *naturalis intentio* as something which pulls them down rather than raising them towards the hea-vens. His claim that there is a natural inclination in the human male[19] to adulterous promiscuity means that here to follow one's nature is precisely 'to gon ayen God'. Nature here is anything but morally normative, and her provision for humankind, in a moral frame of reference, anything but benign.

Knowledge of the ultimate source of these reflections on Nature, Boethius, might permit us to condemn what the Maniciple says as a travesty of the truth produced out of a distasteful and unacceptable cynicism evident in the Tale as a whole. But to take this line may be to behave rather as does Phebus in that Tale: Phebus spurns the Crow only for telling a truth he would rather not hear, and which, indeed, he tries to claim as a falsehood. Unfortunately, much occurs in the human sphere to justify the Maniciple's unflattering view of human nature. Furthermore, as we saw in Chapter 1, the notions first that it is natural for human beings to be non-monogamous and second that the instinctive level of human motivation is the most truly natural aspect of it are articulated in the academic literature of the Middle Ages. These notions do not have to be worked into a

[18] Though 'lust', of course, does not always possess its modern meaning in Middle English texts.
[19] The insistence that it is men and not women to whom the animal examples relate is presumably ironic, given the immediately preceding reference to the *she*-wolf and the immediately subsequent reference to Phebus' wife's adultery.

view of Nature such as the Maniciple's but they do lend such a view considerable support. Perhaps, in fact, we should not read the confrontation with Boethius as evidence of the Manciple's error, but allow that his idea of the natural, however little we relish the fact, is one we ought to take seriously, one, indeed, which asks some legitimate and difficult questions of the optimistic Boethian view.

It is not once but twice that Chaucer offers what might be called an anti-nature version of *Consolation* 3 *metrum* 2; he seems at least intrigued by the possibility of turning Boethius' moral naturalism on its head. In the *Squire's Tale* Canacee's hawk speaks as follows of the bird which has jilted her:

> I trowe he hadde thilke text in mynde,
> That 'alle thyng, repeirynge to his kynde,
> Gladeth hymself;' thus seyn men, as I gesse.
> Men loven of propre kynde newefangelnesse,
> As briddes doon that men in cages fede.
> For though thou nyght and day take of hem hede,
> And strawe hir cage faire and softe as silk,
> And yeve hem sugre, hony, breed and milk,
> Yet right anon as that his dore is uppe
> He with his feet wol spurne adoun his cuppe,
> And to the wode he wole and wormes ete;
> So newefangel been they of hire mete,
> And loven novelries of propre kynde,
> No gentillesse of blood ne may hem bynde.[20]

As in the *Manciple's Tale* the emphasis is on the perversity of the bird's action, and 'kynde' drags down rather than elevates. 'Gentil' blood is unable to refine raw nature, which is accordingly shown to be very much the lowest common denominator in the constitution of individuals. As with the *Manciple's Tale* what is natural for animals and what for human beings are set together—here, in fact, they are explicitly the same 'newefangelnesse'—in such a way as to suggest that, as they operate in accordance with their natures, human beings are expressing an instinctive side of their being which they share with the animal creation.[21] We may wonder how a knowledge of Boethius, which here the reference to 'thilke text' invites us to bring

---

[20]   *CT* 5. 607–20.
[21]   This is the effect, I think, despite the anthropomorphization of the avian in parts at least of this *Squire's Tale* passage.

to bear, should affect our reading of this passage. Should we allow it to refute Canacee's hawk's negative opinions on how Nature operates in birds and men? She is, after all, likely in her situation to take a jaundiced and therefore questionable view; and we might feel that this dubiousness of what she is saying is reflected in the somewhat awkward use she makes of the behaviour of Boethius' bird's return to its original way of life to exemplify 'newefangelnesse'. We might, however, suppose the hawk to be voicing, albeit perhaps in rather an overwrought manner, a perfectly legitimate opinion, and explain the awkwardness with reference not to the character but to the author's fascination with this passage of Boethius and how it can be turned so as to reverse its original direction.

What both these passages do is modify an originally favourable presentation of Nature in such a way as to permit sceptical thoughts about that presentation. In these cases the original presentation lies outside the Chaucerian text (though the *Squire's Tale* explicitly draws our attention to the existence of this antecedent text). Elsewhere, and repeatedly, Chaucer writes into his own texts a favourable presentation of the natural which he then encourages his readers to reassess sceptically. One such text is *The Book of the Duchess*. At the beginning of this poem the narrator's sorrowful sleeplessness is said to be contrary to nature:

> And wel ye woot, agaynes kynde,
> Hyt were to lyven in thys wyse,
> For nature wolde nat suffyse
> To noon erthly creature
> Nat longe tyme to endure
> Withoute slep and be in sorwe.
> And I ne may, ne nyght ne morwe,
> Slepe; and thus melancolye
> And drede I have for to dye.[22]

'Nature' in the third line here should probably be understood as something like 'natural vigour' or 'natural vitality':[23] this natural

---

[22] *BD* 16–24.

[23] See *MED*, s. v. 'nature' 2. (b) and *OED*, s. v. 'nature' II. 6. a, though this is not a meaning recognized by N. Davis (ed.), *A Chaucer Glossary* (Oxford, 1978). For this meaning in Gower and its derivation see above, Ch. 6 n. 18 (and also pp. 39–41). See also *BD* 715–16. The description of the dying Arcite's condition at *CT* I. 2757–61 involves references to nature which seem to have a similar meaning. On this see

vigour may be exhausted or, perhaps rather, overcome[24] by certain kinds of behaviour. In this case, the narrator's sorrowful sleeplessness threatens to exhaust or overcome 'nature' within him, and since the order of nature requires the functioning of 'nature' within the organism, it would be 'agaynes kynde' for the narrator to survive, to 'lyve', to continue alive, in the condition in which he currently finds himself.[25] 'Agaynes kynde', however, is not value-free; it carries normative suggestions. In running against the dispositions naturally in place for the functioning of living organisms the narrator's protracted depressive sleeplessness cuts across a right and proper order, and it may be that, in allowing himself to continue in this state, the narrator is to be understood as culpable.[26]

Later in the poem the description of the Black Knight suggests his extreme grief also is 'agaynes kynde' in a way similar to that in which the condition of the narrator is:

Bennett, *Parlement*, 205, who cites Albertus Magnus on Nature's healing activity; see also Noguchi, 'Chaucer's Concept of Nature', 29–31.

[24] 'nat suffyse' might mean either 'be insufficient', in which case we should think of an amount of energy being exhausted, or 'not have the power', in which case we should think of an inferior force overcome.

[25] See also the opening of *A Complaint to his Lady*: 'The longe nightes, whan every creature | Shulde have hir rest in somwhat as by kynde, | Or elles ne may hir lif nat longe endure' (1–3). I am not sure that 'ageyns kynde' in the *BD* passage ought to be understood to have immediate reference to the moral law of nature as Bennett, *Parlement*, 208 n.3, seems to suggests, though contrariety to the natural physical order has, as I argue in the text, a moral dimension.

[26] In the *Tale of Melibee* Chaucer shows himself aware of Ciceronian censure of sorrow as unnatural, 'And Tullius seith that "no sorwe, ne no drede of deeth, ne no thyng that may falle unto a man, | is so muchel agayns nature as a man to encressen his owene profit to the harm of another man"' (*CT* 7. 1585–6). Interestingly, this citation from *De officiis* (3. 5. 21) couples sorrow and dread of death which, given that *melancolye* is linked to fear of dying in *BD*, suggests that it might be this particular understanding of certain things as unnatural which underpins the discourse of unnaturalness in *BD*. On the other hand, what *BD* sees as problematical is *extreme* sorrow, and it may be the association of Nature with *mesure* (also, of course, found in the Stoic-influenced Cicero) which calls forth the designation 'unnatural' for the extreme sorrows of *BD* (in *BD* Nature has made White's eyes open and close 'by mesure' (870–3)). Erzgräber, 'Kynde', 119 f., draws attention to the Aquinan notion that there is a natural inclination in all substances, human beings included, to look to self-preservation, an inclination which is to be regarded as part of the law of nature. See Aquinas, *ST* 1. 2 q. 94 a. 2. I doubt, however, that reading the nature terms of *BD* with Erzgräber's close reference to Aquinas really explains the physiological aspects of the nature terminology. In general, his imposition of Aquinan meanings on Chaucer's texts seems not wholly satisfactory.

> Hit was gret wonder that Nature
> Myght suffre any creature
> To have such sorwe and be not ded.[27]

The wonder is felt, I think, because such grief is so contrary to the natural vitality of the human organism that one would have expected death to supervene in that natural course of events superintended by Nature. However, besides these physiological considerations, we might find in the language of this passage suggestions that Nature has suspended an appropriate punishment, suggestions, in fact, that the Knight is culpable—as the narrator may be also—in his unnatural grief. Certainly the conversation between Dreamer and Knight invites us to see the Knight's grief as blameworthy; the Knight, according to the dreamer, should pull himself together and not give in in the face of adverse Fortune.[28] From this perspective, when the Dreamer urges the Knight to 'Have some pitee on your nature | That formed yow to creature',[29] we can find the Knight guilty of failure to respect the natural ordering of the human organism, something Nature, the force ultimately in charge of that natural ordering, might well see as a criminal disrespect for her own authority. A further suggestion that the Knight is guilty of disrespect for the natural order is to be found in the anger of Pan, 'that men clepeth god of kynde', at the Knight's sorrows:

> So, throgh hys sorwe and hevy thoght,
> Made hym that he herde me noght;
> For he had wel nygh lost hys mynde,
> Thogh Pan, that men clepeth god of kynde,
> Were for hys sorwes never so wroth.[30]

---

[27] *BD* 467–9; see also *BD* 715–16.

[28] See *BD* 714–19.

[29] *BD* 715–16.

[30] *BD* 509–13. For Pan as 'totius Naturae deus' [the God of all nature] see Isidore, *Etymologiae* 8. 11. Though one might see here a condemnation of the Knight for unnatural sorrow, it is also possible that Pan is sympathetic to the Knight (see E. T. Donaldson (ed.), *Chaucer's Poetry* (New York, 1958), 952 f.) and 'wroth' on his behalf, rather than with him. Pan may be indignant that human grief has the potency it does in the realm he superintends. The remark may, in fact, indicate the irremovable presence of human grief in the natural realm. Perhaps, again, Pan's responsibilities are particularly to those physiological forces which support life (often specified in *BD* by 'nature' or 'kynde') and which are compromised by the Knight's grief, natural though in a wider perspective it may be seen to be. See further Hugh White, 'Chaucer Compromising Nature', *RES* NS 40 (1989), 157–78 (161 f.).

The concept of *kynde* also appears in the introduction to the story of
Seys and Alcyone, and may bear on this question of extreme sorrow:

> And in this bok were written fables
> That clerkes had in olde tyme,
> And other poetes, put in rime
> To rede and for to ben in minde,
> While men loved the lawe of kinde.[31]

These lines may indicate that the story of Seys and Alcyone was
written to promote or to confirm love of the law of nature. One
way of understanding this, a way encouraged by the parallels between
Alcyone's story and that of the narrator and the Black Knight with
their nature terms, would be to suppose that in giving way to extreme
sorrow at the death of Seys, a sorrow which she refuses to abandon
despite the admonition which she receives from Morpheus inhabit-
ing the corpse of Seys to 'let be your sorwful lyf',[32] and which
accordingly leads to her death, Alcyone is acting culpably 'agaynes
kynde'. In submitting to her grief she is running counter to the natural
physical dispositions for the health of the organism, and this, it may be
argued, is blameworthy;[33] further, in her unassuageable grief she is
failing to accept the natural order which includes the death of those
we love and the transitoriness of all earthly happiness ('I am but
ded . . . To lytel while our blysse lasteth', says Morpheus/Seys).[34]

---

[31] *BD* 52–6.   [32] *BD* 202.

[33] Erzgräber, 'Kynde', 119–21, citing Aquinas, sees Alcyone as failing to look to a
natural law duty of self-preservation. He thinks the reference to the law of *kinde* to be a
reference to the law of natural reason (118). Natural reason would prompt Alcyone
towards self-preservation, because reason recognizes that the natural urge in substances
for self-preservation is part of the proper order of things.

[34] *BD* 204, 211. Another way of taking the reference to the *lawe of kinde* is to see it as
pointing to how the exemplary marital devotion of Seys and Alcyone is the ideal
fulfilment of a law of nature. See Phillips (ed.), *The Book of the Duchess*, 143 and John
M. Fyler, *Chaucer and Ovid* (New Haven, 1979), 71. I suggest below that it may be
possible to regard Alcyone's death from the extreme grief which her devotion to Seys
precipitates as in a sense a working out of the law of nature. It is also possible that the law
of *kinde* reference marks the story of Seys and Alcyone as pagan; the covert point then
might be that though the absence in a pagan dispensation of the Christian doctrine of
resurrection means Alcyone's suicidal grief is natural and legitimate, the situation of the
Knight, in some sense a figure for the Christian John of Gaunt, is critically altered by the
hope which the resurrection makes available. However, the absence of explicit reference in *BD* to the hope of resurrection would then seem rather strange—though, of
course, a judgement of what might or might not be deemed appropriate by Chaucer in a
poem which touches so closely the person of John of Gaunt is very difficult to make.

Against the unremitting griefs of the humans in the poem are set the rhythms of the earth. The anthropomorphic language of the following passage requires us to compare the non-human response to suffering and sorrow with that of human beings. The earth

> had forgete the povertee
> That wynter, thorgh hys colde morwes,
> Had mad hyt suffre, and his sorwes;
> All was forgeten, and that was sene,
> For al the woode was waxen grene;
> Swetnesse of dew had mad hyt waxe.[35]

The suffering and sorrow of winter turns for the earth to the joy of Spring and can be forgotten and put aside. We are invited, I think, to feel that this forgetfulness would be appropriate, in due season, for the human griefs of the poem also. The non-human world, perfectly expressive, no doubt, of Nature's will,[36] is offered as a norm by which we may judge the human mourners; we are invited to find their sorrow excessive and in that excess unnatural.[37]

Such a judgement, nevertheless, may on reflection come to seem inappropriate, ill attuned to the reality of intense sorrow. It is by no means clear that it is supported by the way the poem unfolds. At lines 1312–13 a pun on 'hert-huntyng' links the Dreamer's attempts to 'ese' the Knight's heart[38] with the pursuit of the *herte*, and if, as appears to be the case, the *herte* escapes, we may have an indication that the parallel heart, the Knight's, escapes the Dreamer's attempts to regulate it, an escape which might point us to how consolatory pieties and moral exhortation are inefficacious to assuage extreme grief. Certainly, the Dreamer finds it impossible to continue his consolatory endeavour in the face of an unadorned statement of the Knight's position:

> 'Bethenke how I seyde here-beforn,
> "Thow wost ful lytel what thow menest;

---

[35] *BD* 410–15.

[36] Cf. *DPN* 8. 10 ff. and see Ch. 1 n. 109.

[37] For *BD* seen as recommending a 'natural' equanimity in the face of grief see L. V. Sadler, 'Chaucer's *The Book of the Duchess* and the "Lawe of Kynde"', *An. M.* 11 (1970), 51–64, and Duncan Harris and Nancy L. Steffen, 'The Other Side of the Garden: An Interpretive Comparison of Chaucer's *Book of the Duchess* and Spenser's *Daphnaida*', *JMRS* 8 (1978), 17–36.

[38] See *BD* 556.

> I have lost more than thow wenest."
> God wot, allas! Ryght that was she!'
>   'Allas, sir, how? What may that be?'
>   'She ys ded!' 'Nay!' 'Yis, be my trouthe!'
>   'Is that youre los? Be God, hyt ys routhe!'
> And with that word ryght anoon
> They gan to strake forth; al was doon,
> For that tyme, the hert-huntyng.[39]

The Dreamer's bafflement may constitute the poem's acknowledgement of the propriety of the Knight's inconsolable grief.[40]

As we reflect on the problems of consolation in the poem, we see that the parallelism the poem proposes between human and non-human worlds is also problematic. The alienation of the sorrowing Knight from his joyful springtime surroundings may not figure a temporary and remediable state of affairs but rather express a profound difference between two kinds of experience. For the fact is that whilst an annual cycle transforms the earth, for human beings there is no cyclic regeneration, and this must make their experience of mutability, transience, and death very different from what goes on in the regenerable non-human world.[41]

The impossibility of aligning human experience with what goes on in the vegetable world casts the poem's talk of Nature in a new light. For as nature terms are applied to human beings in the poem they seem to have primary reference to the physical aspect of human existence, with what a medieval writer might think of as the vegetative capacities of the soul; from the natural state of affairs on this physical level, certain moral implications then appear to arise. But

---

[39] *BD* 1304–13.

[40] Many critics, however, think that the Knight is in some degree healed or consoled. See, e.g., J. Norton-Smith, *Geoffrey Chaucer* (London, 1974), 13 ff., and P. M. Kean, *Chaucer and the Making of English Poetry*, shortened edn. (London, 1982), 30. Jörg O. Fichte, *Chaucer's 'Art Poetical': A Study in Chaucerian Poetics* (Tübingen, 1980), 43, robustly, and I think rightly, affirms that this is not the case. See also Dieter Mehl, *Geoffrey Chaucer* (Cambridge, 1986), 35–6. For *BD* as a consolatory poem see also A. J. Minnis, *The Shorter Poems: Oxford Guides to Chaucer* (Oxford, 1995) 135–60.

[41] Fyler, *Chaucer and Ovid*, 74, considers that Chaucer contrasts 'the blithe unconsciousness of spring' with the inability of human beings 'to forget that winter will come again'. I would endorse this understanding that human consciousness constitutes a highly important differentiating factor between the human and the non-human world, but would also want to register how in *BD* human mortality as opposed to non-human regenerability is a crucial consideration.

though human beings do indeed in some measure share this physical, vegetative aspect of their existence with parts of the non-human living world,[42] they also clearly exist on higher levels, having sensitive and rational dimensions to their souls. We are entitled to ask to what extent human beings lie under the jurisdiction of moral laws derived from the physical side of their nature and how binding on them such 'natural' imperatives are. May it not be that human nature considered whole has on its higher levels an entirely natural susceptibility to emotional stress which can come into conflict with its lower-level drives towards physical well-being? In fact, if we look again at the account of the Knight's grief at lines 467–9, we find that, surprising as it is, Nature does permit the extreme sorrow he undergoes. It is possible to find here a suggestion that, though it may be debilitating of the physical organism, extreme human sorrow is not just because of this contrary to the order of Nature. It becomes possible to conceive of the order of Nature as including both the energies that seek to keep organisms alive and also emotions that run counter to those energies; the contradiction may be a 'wonder' but it is a fact of nature. This wider understanding of the idea of nature in the poem may lead us to suppose that the implication of the reference to the law of *kinde* in the introduction to the story of Seys and Alcyone is not that Alycone stands condemned but that her death from grief is part of the total economy of Nature as that embraces human beings in their wholeness.[43] And whether the Dreamer is to live on in sorrow, as does, for the moment, the Knight, or is to suffer the death he fears, it is possible to see both fates as sanctioned by Nature.

The conclusions reached in the last paragraph depend on one's drawing certain implications from the statement that 'Hit was gret wonder that Nature | Myght suffre any creature | To have such sorwe and be not ded'. It may, however, be felt that I have pressed this remark too insistently in deriving from it the notion of a Nature

[42] 'In some measure', for they are not, as we have seen, subject to a cyclical physical regeneration as is vegetation. This difference may be in the end what validates extreme sorrow, for which there would be no occasion were human beings fully engaged in the natural regenerative cycle.

[43] W. W. Skeat, *The Works of Geoffrey Chaucer*, 7 vols. (Oxford, 1894–7), thought that the reference to the law of *kinde* when the story of Seys and Alcyone is introduced was a reference to 'the natural promptings of passion' (i. 463 on l. 56).

not bound to the physical functionings of the organism and sanctioning a suffering which tells against physical vitality. But however this may be, difficulties arise for the idea of regulating human behaviour 'according to nature'. If Nature in the poem is limited to the physical, then, as I have suggested, its scope seems insufficient to justify a straightforward, unarguable derivation from it of moral laws. If, on the other hand, another kind of Nature is discernible, questions may be asked of the beneficence of its dispensation for humankind. Why does Nature permit the kind of suffering the Knight, the Dreamer, and Alcyone undergo; why is human relationship fraught with such perils; why, indeed, are human beings subject to death, when much of the world which Nature superintends is subject only to a cycle of change?[44]

Chaucer, then, offers us a Nature apparently invested with benign, morally regulative authority, only to incite us to question whether Nature is rightly so understood. This is entirely consonant with the way in which the *Manciple's Tale* and the *Squire's Tale* rework the positive Boethian presentation of Nature in the passages we have examined. It is also consonant with what happens in the *Parlement of Foules* where Nature's claims to be at the centre of a satisfying moral system and to preside over a beneficent world order are treated with more than a touch of scepticism.

In the *Parlement*, Chaucer is, I take it, as Lumiansky suggested,[45] interested in reconciling the pursuit of sexual love with the demands of a morality which insists on other-worldly perspectives ('Know thyself first immortal' (73)) and unselfish commitment to the common good (46 ff., 74 f.). This morality is presented in the rehearsal of what Africanus says in the *Somnium Scipionis*; here the only mention of sexual love occurs when we are told of the punishment of 'likerous folk'.[46] This Africanan dismissiveness of sexual love seems to be confirmed as the appropriate stance towards that force by the Cupid

---

[44] There would, of course, be theological answers to these questions; but *The Book of the Duchess* makes no explicit investment in Christian discourse.

[45] R. M. Lumiansky, 'Chaucer's *Parlement of Foules*: A Philosophical Interpretation', *RES* 24 (1948), 81–9.

[46] *PF* 79. Minnis, *Shorter Poems*, 269 notes that whereas in Cicero the pleasure seekers *are* the law-breakers, Chaucer puts 'likerous folk', lechers, on a par with law-breakers, 'thereby affording their sin a specific category and status which highlights both its importance and its nature'.

and Venus scene in the dream.[47] This pictures a sexual love with so many undesirable elements as to make any revaluation of it against the implied criticism of the Africanan perspective seem unviable. However, with the introduction of the Goddess Nature the dream proposes a way of reconciling sexual love with the demands of Africanan morality. The scene over which Nature presides suggests that the harmony between individuals which sexual love promotes is to be understood as an aspect of cosmic order expressive of the divine will. So the fulfilling of individual sexual drives may be felt to serve a wider purpose also, may, in fact, be regarded as serving that 'commune profit' the claims of which Africanus promotes. Further, though this is not emphasized in the *Parlement*,[48] a procreative concern is a prominent characteristic of Nature both in Alan of Lille's *De planctu Naturae*, to which Chaucer specifically draws our attention, and in the Nature tradition at large. We may be meant to understand that such a procreative concern on the part of the *Parlement*'s Nature contributes to the 'commune profit' in achieving the preservation of the various species. From this Nature-centred perspective an accommodation of this world and the 'nede' (384) of individuals within it can respectably be made because sexual love is seen not merely as serving the here and now and the physical but also as capable of fulfilling the kind of moral demands Africanus makes and attunable to an essentially spiritual vision of things.[49]

Chaucer takes care to associate Nature with the divine and with an ordered harmony of creation expressive of the divine purposes:

> Nature, the vicaire of the almyghty Lord,
> That hot, cold, hevy, lyght, moyst, and dreye
> Hath knyt by evene noumbres of acord.[50]

[47] See, however, David Aers, 'The *Parlement of Foules*: Authority, the Knower and the Known', *Chaucer Review* (1981), 1–17 (8). Minnis, *Shorter Poems*, 284 f., warns against importing the moralizing perspective of the gloss on the Boccaccian source into a reading of Chaucer's presentation of the Temple of Venus, but the amount of suffering in the Temple seems to solicit a negative judgement on the place. And it is certainly very easy to suppose that we are meant to find something morally wrong about a Priapus bent on rape and a Venus taking her pleasure with her Porter Richesse.

[48] See Minnis, *Shorter Poems*, 275.

[49] Among critics who see something of this sort as the 'message' of the *Parlement* are Bennett, *Parlement*, and Economou, *Goddess*, 125–50.

[50] *PF* 379–81. Earlier personifications of Nature suggest that we should take 'That' here to refer not to 'Lord' but to 'Nature' (see e.g. *CP* 2. m. 8 and *DPN* 7. 1 ff.) and this is, in any case, the easier way of taking the Chaucerian sentence.

This harmonious binding of the elements is recalled in the description of Nature's pairing off of the birds towards the end of the poem: 'To every foul Nature yaf his make | By evene acord.'[51] In this way sexual love is associated with elemental harmony. Nature's ordering and harmonizing power is further evident in her bringing together birds of very different types among which peaceful relations are by no means universal into (relatively) ordered assembly, as also in her directing the course of their parliament by her 'ryghtful ordenaunce' (390) and restoring order when chaos threatens (519 ff., 617 ff.). This magnificent and beneficent harmonizing force presents a strong contrast to the dissolute Venus[52] in whose Temple we have encountered only disharmony of various kinds in the sphere of sexual love. We may even feel that we have discovered a resolution of the paradox presented by the inscriptions above the gate giving entrance to the dream garden[53]—under Venus human beings are doomed to find trouble in love, under Nature they can find joy.

Chaucer claims his Nature is 'right as Aleyn, in the Pleynt of Kynde, | Devyseth [her] of aray and face'.[54] But one very significant difference between the *Parlement*'s Nature and that of the *De planctu Naturae* lies in the relation of the two figures to Reason. In the *De planctu Naturae* there is, as we have seen, no distance between Nature and Reason: to follow Nature is to follow Reason.[55] In the *Parlement*, however, Nature, addressing the formel, makes this very revealing remark:

> But as for counseyl for to chese a make,
> If I were Resoun, thanne wolde I
> Conseyle yow the royal tercel take,
> As seyde the tercelet ful skylfully,
> As for the gentilleste and most worthi,
> Which I have wrought so wel to my plesaunce
> That to yow hit oughte to been a suffisaunce.[56]

[51] *PF* 667–8.
[52] We may find ourselves reminded of the relationship between Nature and Venus in the *De planctu Naturae* (see, e.g., *DPN* 10. 131 ff.).
[53] See *PF* 127–40.
[54] *PF* 316–17.
[55] See above, Ch. 3.
[56] *PF* 631–7.

Why is Nature here made to separate herself so deliberately from Reason and the line Reason would take?[57] Nature's remark comes just after she has insisted that the formel should be free to make up her own mind about which of her suitors shall marry her and just before she grants the formel her 'firste bone' (643), which turns out to be not to mate at all 'as yit' (652–3). Nature's unwillingness to ally herself straightforwardly with Reason may perhaps be accounted for by her awareness of the obligations she is under towards the irrational desires of individuals.[58] It is the function of the reason to argue the will, if necessary, into the right course of action, but Nature, at any rate in the sphere of love, respects the will's unreasonableness.[59] Earlier in the poem Nature showed her respect for the wishes of the females of all the species of birds:

> But natheles, in this condicioun
> Mot be the choys of everich that is heere,
> That she agre to his eleccioun,
> Whoso he be that shulde be hire feere.
> This is oure usage alwey, fro yer to yeere.[60]

In the case of the noble birds this respect for the will of the individual apparently leads to the frustration of Nature's intentions.

Nature's insistence on the formel's liberty to choose puts her own plan for the mating of the birds at risk and thus threatens her harmonizing purpose, and, if these are indeed a concern of the *Parlement*, her procreative purposes too. It also poses a double threat to what Reason would recommend: the formel might make an unreasonable choice of partner or, as proves to be the case, might

---

[57] Certain manuscripts read 'If it were Resoun' in l. 632, but 'If I were Resoun' is very much the editorial preference. The reading with 'it' would give us a Nature lacking in confidence in her right or ability to give moral advice. (Its presence in the manuscript tradition might possibly indicate a sense on the part of a scribe of an oddness about the proposed identification of Nature and Reason.)

[58] Erzgräber, 'Kynde', 131, however, sees in Nature's reference to Reason here a Nature pressing for behaviour in accordance with Reason. 'Natura handelt weiterhin entsprechend den Geboten der Ratio, als sie die letzte Entscheidung dem Adlerweibchen selbst überlässt, dabei aber mit einem vernünftigen Rat nicht zurückhält' [Nature behaves in accordance with the commands of Reason when she leaves the final decision to the female eagle, but does not hold back with a reasonable piece of advice].

[59] R. W. Frank, 'Structure and Meaning in the *Parlement of Foules*', *PMLA* 71 (1956), 530–9, remarks 'She is Nature, not Reason. Reason has very little to do with love. Love is irrational' (538). Perhaps this covers the unreasonableness of the formel's *not* loving.

[60] *PF* 407–11.

refuse to make a choice at all. We may of course imagine that
next year all will go according to Nature's plan as far as a pairing
off goes, and even that the formel will then choose the royal tercel,
thus putting herself in accord with Reason; but we have no right,
I suspect, to suppose that either of these things will certainly occur.[61]
What is certain is that the poem has shown us how the desires of
an individual can produce action which goes against Reason, and
in some sense, Nature, and yet that such 'unnatural' unreasonableness has to be sanctioned by a Nature insistent on freedom of
erotic choice.[62] The unreasonableness of human behaviour is
not, it seems, unnatural, being an integral part of the domain of
Nature, and so, as with *The Book of the Duchess*, the category of the
natural turns out not to provide human beings with secure moral
guidelines.

   The *Parlement* invites us to contrast Nature and Venus and to find
ourselves repelled by the sterility, debauchery, and pain over which
Venus presides and delighted by the fertility and joyful harmony,
ultimately in the service of the divine, which Nature's rule brings
forth. The behaviour of the noble birds, however, calls this neat
distinction into question.[63] They are clearly part of the domain of
Nature—indeed Nature's treatment of the formel suggests the noble
birds are at the pinnacle of Nature's order[64]—but the formel, with a
regard to her own wishes rather than that 'commune profit' for
which Nature, it is suggested, is concerned, fails to fulfil the purposes Nature has apparently established for her, and thus, it may be

[61] Henry M. Leicester, 'The Harmony of Chaucer's *Parlement*: A Dissonant Voice',
Chaucer Review, 9 (1974), 15–34, likewise suggests that the formel might continue her
resistance to Nature's plan beyond the term of a year (32). See also David Lawton,
Chaucer's Narrators (Cambridge, 1985), 42; Elaine Tuttle Hansen, *Chaucer and the Fictions
of Gender* (London, 1990), 127. Minnis, *Shorter Poems*, 302, rejects Hansen's view,
supposing that the formel 'utterly accepts that she will marry' (257); this, however,
seems to go beyond what is clear from the text.
[62] Leicester, 'Harmony', 25, 27, thinks that the focus of the poem is on the disruptive
force of individual personality, which Nature seeks to channel into institutional forms. It
seems difficult, however, since Nature very explicitly gives permisson for the exercise of
free choice, to exonerate Nature completely from blame for the disruption caused by
the formel.
[63] Fyler, *Chaucer and Ovid*, 89, finds that 'the more one looks at this antithesis of
Venus and Nature, the less sharply defined it seems'. He suggests that through the tercels
Venus invades Nature's realm (93).
[64] See *BD* 372 ff., where Nature is described holding the formel on her hand,
admiring her and kissing her.

felt, sets herself against fertility and harmony.[65] The tercels seem doomed to the 'sykes hoote' (246) 'engendered with desyr' (248) which fill the Temple of Venus: for at least two of them this state will, it would seem, exceed the year's term, and the influence of 'the bittere goddesse Jelosye' (252), felt in the Temple, will surely be felt by the tercels too. The formel's action and its consequences indicate how for human beings frustration in love is a not unnatural state of affairs; yet such frustration is at the centre of the experience of love under Venus, as is emblematized by the statue of Priapus 'In swich aray as whan the asse hym shente | With cri by nighte' (255–6) which stands 'in sovereyn place' (254) in the Temple.[66] The formel herself blurs the distinction between love under Nature and love under Venus when she deflects Nature's invitation to choose a suitor, saying:

> I wol nat serve Venus ne Cupide,
> Forsothe as yit, by no manere weye.[67]

Chaucer has, at the beginning of the poem, affirmed with some emphasis Love's capacity to throw into confusion the person who contemplates it:

> The lyf so short, the craft so long to lerne,
> Th'assay so hard, so sharp the conquerynge,
> The dredful joye alwey that slit so yerne:
> Al this mene I by Love, that my felynge

---

[65] In *Chaucer's Language and the Philosophers' Tradition* (Cambridge, 1979), 129 J. D. Burnley states that the formel's 'sensitivity...joins the sensuality of the Temple of Venus as elements destructive of natural, rational and ultimately divine order'. As I understand it, however, human free will, with its destructive potentialities, is in a strong sense part of the natural realm.

[66] See Emerson Brown, Jr., '*Hortus Inconclusus*: The Significance of Priapus and Pyramus and Thisbe in the *Merchant's Tale*', *Chaucer Review*, 4 (1970), 31–40. In a later article, 'Priapus and the *Parlement of Foulys*', *SP* 72 (1975), 258–74, Brown finds a link between Priapus' frustration and the eagle suitors (268).

[67] *PF* 652–3. B. F. Huppé and D. W. Robertson, Jr., *Fruyt and Chaf* (Princeton, 1963), 141–2, think that the formel realizes that Nature's suggestion as to whom she should choose is a recommendation, unbeknown to Nature, of an unnatural and unreasonable love (i.e. of the kind sponsored by Venus and Cupid): in good conscience the formel cannot do as Nature suggests. However, the formel's 'as yit' casts doubt on this suggestion. Economou, *Goddess*, 147 regards the formel as deluded in supposing that she will have to serve Venus and Cupid—her love could be natural. Reviewing Economou's book (*RES* NS 25 (1974), 190–2) P. M. Kean pertinently asks why, if this is the case, Nature does not disabuse the formel.

> Astonyeth with his wonderful werkynge
> So sore, iwis, that whan I on hym thynke
> Nat wot I wel wher that I flete or synke.[68]

The poet's invalidation of the distinction he offers us for making sense of love is consonant with this initial stress on the difficulty of the subject.[69] Love turns out to be irresolvably ambivalent; both inscriptions on the gate into the dream garden are always relevant, the one indissociable from the other.[70] In retrospect we can see that the presence of Venus and Nature in the same garden should have alerted us to the impossibility of holding them apart.[71] In the *De planctu Naturae* Venus' rebellion distances her from Nature's purposes, but Venus retains the power Nature has delegated to her, and so her rebellion defines the way in which (for all Nature's laments) the influence of Nature works upon human beings.[72] In the *Parlement* the love of the Temple of Venus is perhaps to be seen as a force of Nature.[73] There are certainly good reasons to view with scepticism any notion that Nature exerts an unqualifiedly benign influence upon human beings and always directs their behaviour down approvable channels.

Like *The Book of the Duchess* the *Parlement* may deal in two ideas of nature, one relating to the non-human world, the other to humanity. The formel is apparently the only bird whose will runs counter to Nature's, and in this the formel (with the other noble birds) may be standing for humanity, with its natural capacity for free choice, as against the lower birds,[74] representative of animal sexual desire, a

---

[68] *PF* 1–7.

[69] Fyler, *Chaucer and Ovid*, pointing out how the oppositions which the poem presents blur as it proceeds, considers that *PF* shows us how 'as fallen, conscious man faces instinctive Nature, the systems that the mind discovers in the world, or imposes on it, verge on collapse' (82).

[70] An indissociability noted by several critics, including W. H. Clemen, *Chaucer's Early Poetry* (London, 1963), 139 f., and Kean, *Chaucer*, 53. See also Minnis, *Shorter Poems*, 289.

[71] See D. S. Brewer (ed.), *The Parlement of Foulys* (London, 1960; repr. 1972), 31.

[72] See above, pp. 94–5.

[73] On the closeness of Nature and Love in *PF* see Bennett, *Parlement*, 115 f., and Kean, *Chaucer*, 49–53. Fyler, *Chaucer and Ovid*, 89 f., insists that Venus is part of Nature's realm.

[74] See, among others, Victoria Rothschild, '*The Parliament of Fowls*: Chaucer's Mirror up to Nature?', *RES* NS 35 (1984), 164–84 (174 f.). Erzgräber ('Kynde', 130 f.) supposes that the noble birds, as opposed to the lower birds, represent a truly human kind of loving which is in tune with the law of nature understood as the law of reason.

desire which seems to move instinctively and without difficulty to its proposed end. The joyful harmony at the end of the poem may be founded upon an absence of free will. The roundel sung by the birds near the poem's close celebrates a natural cycle:

> Now welcome, somer, with thy sonne softe,
> That hast thes wintres wedres overshake,
> And driven away the longe nyghtes blake![75]

A feature of this cycle is the 'recovering' by each bird of his *make* (68). But the 'human' birds stand outside the charmed circle of non-human nature, their experience not delimited by the yearly cycle, the difficulties of that experience unresolved.[76]

There would seem to be no satisfying resolution for the narrator of the *Parlement* either.[77] He is left still not, apparently, having the thing he desires (91) and committed to further reading (695 ff.). This suggests that the poem he has produced remains open-ended, failing in the end to provide the satisfaction that it had promised when proffering its resolutions. In these respects the poem as a whole differs from the roundel it includes. The roundel settles the issue between *winter* and *somer* unproblematically and returns to its beginning to achieve harmonious closure, but it does not emblematize what has happened in the poem as a whole, or provide closure for it. The end of the whole poem dissatisfyingly suggests misdirected effort and the need painfully to proceed further outside the limits of the poem. Perhaps in the sphere of artistic as of sexual performance failure and lack of fulfilment are part of the natural human condition.[78] But in any case, symbolically speaking, winter and the

He does not, however, register the problems arising from the possibility of human beings choosing freely not to follow reason.

[75] *PF* 680–2.

[76] In *CA* Amans laments the difference between himself and the animal creation in that the latter are guaranteed to find satisfaction in love (*CA* 8. 2224–35). Fyler, *Chaucer and Ovid*, finds the behaviour of the noble birds a symbol of the problems of human consciousness as against the unproblematic instinctiveness of the natural realm (see, e.g., 93 f.). B. Bartholomew, *Fortuna and Natura: A Reading of Three Chaucer Narratives* (The Hague, 1966), 44, speaks of 'the near impossibility of a completely "natural" love for complicated humanity'.

[77] See, however, Lawton, *Narrators*, 44.

[78] Lawton, *Narrators*, 43 f., on the other hand, sees roundel and poem as equally showing forth an achieved delight on the part of the small birds and the Dreamer, who are not implicated in the pain of being servants of Love. Art, in Lawton's reading of the

black nights, despite the rejoicing the poem records and which it enshrines in the roundel, have not been dispelled for the (human) poet or, it would seem, for the birds who may figure humanity, and this may remind us of how the Black Knight in *The Book of the Duchess* sits unconsoled amidst the signs of spring.

If the natural human situation is not marked by order and harmony, doubts about the presence of these qualities even in the non-human world are stimulated by certain features of the *Parlement*. The catalogue of birds at 330 ff. characterizes them in terms which suggest that their kingdom is riddled with strife and which display various unpleasantnesses in many of the species.[79] One might well ask what kind of a benign dispensation this is. Perhaps we might go as far as to ask why the universe has been constituted at the elemental level a *concors discordia*: why this basic component of strife in the relation of things?[80] The course of the parliament itself sets clearly before us the tendency of disparate entities not to get along easily together. Though Nature eventually secures some kind of harmonious close, this should not cancel our awareness that uncomfortable antagonisms seem fundamental to the structure of things. We might begin to suspect that the unsatisfactoriness of the way things are in the human realm is only an unsurprising reflex of a disharmony endemic to the universe as a whole.

A Nature in the tradition of the Alanian *vicaria Dei* appears again in the *Physician's Tale*. The beautiful Virginia is the handiwork of this Nature and is an advertisement, as it were, for her supreme creative ability:

> For Nature hath with sovereyn diligence
> Yformed hire in so greet excellence,

poem, is superior to Love (which is a metaphor for all human experience) in being able to provide for us a world we wish to inhabit.

[79] Frank, 'Structure and Meaning', 536, notes that 'a disturbing number [of the birds] are described in terms suggesting nature red in tooth and claw'. See also Fyler, *Chaucer and Ovid*, 90 f., who in addition finds disagreeable attributes in the catalogue of trees at ll. 176–82. We might note that when the cuckoo claims to be speaking 'for comune spede' (507), this ironically displays a tendency in the realm of Nature for Africanus' 'commune profit' to be ignored in favour of self-centred individual drives.

[80] Kean, *Chaucer*, 45 remarks on how Nature in *PF* 'is shown presiding over a world of matter which contains a fundamental core of conflict'. Gardiner Stillwell, 'Unity and Comedy in Chaucer's *Parlement of Foules*', *JEGP* 49 (1950), 470–95, claims that Nature's universe 'is not so well-ordered as it might be' (480).

As though she wolde seyn, 'Lo! I, Nature,
Thus kan I forme and peynte a creature,
Whan that me list; who kan me countrefete?
Pigmalion noght, thogh he ay forge and bete,
Or grave, or peynte; for I dar wel seyn
Apelles, Zanzis, sholde werche in veyn
Outher to grave, or peynte, or forge, or bete,
If they presumed me to countrefete.
For He that is the formere principal
Hath maked me his vicaire general,
To forme and peynten erthely creaturis
Right as me list, and ech thyng in my cure is
Under the moone, that may wane and waxe,
And for my werk right no thyng wol I axe;
My lord and I been ful of oon accord.
I made hire to the worshipe of my lord;
So do I alle myne othere creatures,
What colour that they han or what figures.'[81]

There is a certain complacency in this imagined self-presentation, as well as a not altogether attractive self-aggrandizement; and yet the course of the story might incline us to wonder how justified Nature's self-satisfaction is. Despite Nature's 'cure' the sublunary world is plainly not penetrated by the harmony Nature might be supposed to sponsor as she works to further the divine plan. Nature in fact seems to be responsible for some of the unsatisfactoriness of the world. She produces the superlative beauty of a Virginia only, apparently, when she feels like it ('Whan that me list'). This remark and the reference to 'alle myne othere creatures' reminds us that physical humanity is by no means universally attractive. It seems legitimate to wonder exactly how Nature's unattractive productions promote God's 'worshipe'. This consideration may be relevant in the moral sphere also: if Nature is to be understood to produce Virginia's moral excellence, she would then seem also to be responsible for the depravity of other creatures such as Apius.[82] Futhermore, the actual effect of Nature creating Virginia so beautiful is disastrous. Harry Bailey's comments on the tale draws attention to this:

[81] *CT* 6. 9–28.
[82] Virginia's moral character is not explicitly said to be given her by Nature (see n. 1 above).

Allas, to deere boughte she beautee!
Wherfore I seye al day that men may see
That yiftes of Fortune and of Nature
Been cause of deeth to many a creature.
Hire beautee was hire deth, I dar wel sayn.[83]

Whatever we may feel about the adequacy of this, it is certainly the case that Virginia's beauty stimulates evil and sets in train a series of appalling events which invite us to review the complacent self-eulogy imagined for Nature with some scepticism. If we go further than Harry Bailey into the causes of the tragedy and discover male sexual predatoriness at their centre, this too raises questions about Nature; for it is through sex that the procreative purposes of Nature are effected, a means, indeed, which Nature in the tradition is understood to have established. Scepticism will be further stimulated if we register the futility in Nature's production of her masterpiece: Virginia goes to waste in an untimely death, and does so as a virgin who has contributed nothing to the creative performance on which Nature so prides herself. And we might detect an ironic self-defeatingness in what is going on here; Nature creates her masterpiece of beauty which in the natural course of things, because of the natural sexual attraction established, one may suppose, by Nature with a view to her end of procreation, attracts the ultimately fatal attention of Apius which defeats the natural end of procreation. Furthermore, the fragility of Nature's great creation, Virginia, suggests that the conventional topos of the superiority of her creativity to that of human artists requires close examination. Rather as in other works we have examined, in the *Physician's Tale* Chaucer presents an apparently benign Nature, powerful and creative, only to compromise that presentation by implicating Nature in debility, disorder, depravity, and destruction.[84]

In *Troilus and Criseyde* also Chaucer begins by presenting Nature positively and then incites us to ask sceptical questions. The notion of *kynde* is first introduced into the poem as part of a sequence in which the narrator comments on Troilus' falling in love. The

---

[83] *CT* 6. 293–7.

[84] As is appropriate for a superintendent of the sublunary realm. When Chaucer presents a personified or quasi-personified nature, he never clearly, it seems to me, accords this figure jurisdiction over the stable realm above the moon (but see Economou, *Goddess*, 149, who supposes otherwise in the case of the *Parlement*).

dismissive attitude towards love which Troilus possesses before he sees Criseyde is represented by the narrator as both foolish and morally reprehensible:

> O blynde world, O blynde entencioun!
> How often falleth al the effect contraire
> Of surquidrie and foul presumpcioun;
> For kaught is proud, and kaught is debonaire.
> This Troilus is clomben on the staire,
> And litel weneth that he moot descenden;
> But alday faileth thing that fooles wenden.[85]

The ensuing comparison with 'proude Bayard', the horse, enforces further the absurdity and immorality of Troilus' presumptuous defiance of the God of Love.[86] Bayard attempts to cast off the law of his own nature before he considers: 'Yet am I but an hors, and horses lawe | I moot endure.'[87] The invocation of the idea of law reinforces the feeling that it would be improper to go against the (natural) course of one's being. All this prepares us to understand the immutable law of *kynde* by which love has irresistible power over human beings as something which constrains them *appropriately*— Troilus' scorn, like Bayard's revolt, besides being futile, flies in the face of the proper natural order:

> Forthy ensample taketh of this man,
> Ye wise, proude, and worthi folkes alle,
> To scornen Love, which that so soone kan
> The fredom of youre hertes to hym thralle;
> For evere it was, and evere it shal byfalle,
> That Love is he that alle thing may bynde,
> For may no man fordon the lawe of kynde.[88]

Here the benign moral connotations of the natural law are being used to suggest the propriety of the natural instinctive process of sexual engagement.[89] Troilus' submission to the natural and inevitable is further suggested to be good in the following stanzas. The

---

[85] *TC* I. 211–17.

[86] See *TC* I. 183–210.

[87] *TC* I. 223–4. These lines, like the Bayard passage before, and the reflections which follow in the next four stanzas, have no equivalent in *Il Filostrato*.

[88] *TC* I. 232–8.

[89] The pre-rational instinctive order itself has a degree of normativity, but moral authority is also here being borrowed from the idea of the law of nature as a rational

wisest, strongest, worthiest, and 'grettest of degree' have all been overcome by love (1. 241–4):

> And trewelich it sit wel to be so,
> For alderwisest han therwith ben plesed;
> And they that han ben aldermost in wo,
> With love han ben comforted moost and esed;
> And ofte it hath the cruel herte apesed,
> And worthi folk maad worthier of name,
> And causeth moost to dreden vice and shame.
>
> Now sith it may nat goodly ben withstonde,
> And is a thing so vertuous in kynde,
> Refuseth nat to Love for to ben bonde,
> Syn, as hymselven liste, he may yow bynde;
> The yerde is bet that bowen wole and wynde
> Than that that brest, and therfore I yow rede
> To folowen hym that so wel kan yow lede.[90]

The recognition of the coerciveness of love, which enslaves, removes freedom, and has to be bowed before, and the affirmation of the goodness of love, which 'may nat goodly ben withstonde', is 'so vertuous in kynde'[91] and 'so wel kan yow lede', might be thought to coexist rather uneasily. This unease will, I think, make itself felt strongly in a rereading of the passage in the light of the whole work—indeed, our knowledge of Criseyde's eventual betrayal of Troilus may give rise to some disquiet on a first reading—but the conviction of the narrator encourages us to suppress these doubts and to enthuse about Troilus' submission to so good an overlord, and take the law of *kynde* as something which orders human life according to a proper pattern.

---

moral law. It seems clear that the *lawe of kynde*, which is here introduced in reference to an irresistible erotic impulse, cannot be taken as the law of rational human nature, as Dunleavy ('Ethical Absolute', 201–2) would wish.

[90] *TC* 1. 246–59.

[91] *Kynde* here may have reference to love's own nature—it is so taken by Nevill Coghill in his rendering of *Troilus and Criseyde* (Harmondsworth, 1971)—but it is also possible that it refers to general Nature and so suggests a division in respect of virtue between what is *kynde* and what is not. Pandarus later divides love 'of kynde' from love 'celestial' (see below), and such a division may be hinted at in the phrase 'vertuous in kynde'. Meanings of 'sensibly' for 'goodly' and 'powerful' for 'vertuous' are available, but strong moral senses are pressed on us by what is said in the previous stanza. In the light of the completed narrative, however, we might care to revise our understanding of 'vertuous'.

In the raptures of his love for Criseyde Troilus would certainly subscribe to this view. He desires for everyone the binding of love, which he associates with the divinely authored natural order:

> So wolde God, that auctour is of kynde,
> That with his bond Love of his vertu liste
> To cerclen hertes alle and faste bynde,
> That from his bond no wight the wey oute wiste;
> And hertes colde, hem wolde I that he twiste
> To make hem love.[92]

Troilus' praises of love here are, of course, inspired by Boethius,[93] in whose vision love is the great force for harmony throughout the cosmos, a chain linking together the different parts of creation; here, then, Troilus' imagery of binding carries a positive sense of secure fixedness within an ordered structure (the passages from book 1 discussed above offer such resonances also). The designation of God as 'auctour . . . of kynde' points to the way in which the natural order and its influences such as love are to be seen as in the service of the divine, for Troilus is offering us a vision of natural sexual love as an aspect of divine love—we recall his previous revealing juxtaposition 'O Love, O Charite!' (3. 1254) and how he speaks in that speech of 'Benigne Love, thow holy bond of thynges' (3. 1261). Pandarus, however, does not share this vision:

> For this have I herd seyd of wyse lered,
> Was nevere man or womman yet bigete
> That was unapt to suffren loves hete,
> Celestial, or elles love of kynde;
> Forthy som grace I hope in hire to fynde.
>
> And for to speke of hire in specyal,
> Hire beaute to bithynken and hire youthe,
> It sit hire naught to ben celestial
> As yet, though that hire liste bothe and kowthe;
> But trewely, it sate hire wel right nowthe
> A worthi knyght to loven and cherice,
> And but she do, I holde it for a vice.[94]

---

[92] *TC* 3. 1765–70.

[93] *CP* 2. m. 8.

[94] *TC* 1. 976–87. These stanzas expand a passage in Boccaccio which does not include the distinction between 'love celestial' and 'love of kynde'.

Unlike Troilus, Pandarus specifically opposes to natural sexual love
the service of heaven in celestial love, and thus raises difficult
questions about the relation of the natural order which includes
sexuality to the divine and therefore to the good. Pandarus' views
point to some sort of answer; sexual love is appropriate (at any rate if
one is beautiful) to a certain stage of life, after which one can commit
oneself to the divine. This, however, would seem too easy, the
problem being that it denies the absoluteness of the demands of
heaven at all stages of one's life. Those demands are acknowledged
in their full exigency in the poem's final exhortation to 'yonge,
fresshe folkes, he or she' to 'repeyre[n] hom fro worldly vanyte'—
which would seem to mean giving up love of *kynde* as Pandarus
understands it in favour of the celestial lover, Christ.[95]

Pandarus seems to think in terms of women having a choice as to
whether they will serve the law of *kynde*, whereas the narrator's
earlier comments on the power of love over Troilus presented love
as something overwhelming against which resistance is futile. It may
be that Chaucer supposes love to affect men differently from the
way in which it does women.[96] Nevertheless, Pandarus still apparently envisages Kynde as a force which exerts a pressure towards
love on Criseyde:

> Peraunter thynkestow: though it be so,
> That Kynde wolde don hire to bygynne
> To have a manere routhe upon my woo,
> Seyth Daunger, 'Nay, thow shalt me nevere wynne!'[97]

With Troilus, the capacity of love entirely to override free will
shows that the law of *kynde* which love's operation manifests is,
whatever benign moral connotations attach themselves to it because
of the existence of other understandings of the law of nature, a law
of pre-rational impulse. The opposition between Kynde and Daun-
ger in Pandarus' imagined Criseydean psychomachia suggests that

[95] See *TC* 5. 1835 ff. In *CA*, where a turn to love celestial in old age is described, the
terms of Genius' insistence that love should be abandoned seem, nevertheless, entirely
non-age-specific (see *CA* 8. 2063–148).

[96] And not just Chaucer; medieval texts often figure female desire as less spontaneous, more chosen, as it were, than male. We might note how the formel in *PF* also has a
choice in respect of love.

[97] *TC* 2. 1373–6. The reference to Kynde is not derived from Boccaccio, to whom
Chaucer is not close towards the end of book 1.

here too the talk of Kynde makes reference, not to the whole of human nature, but to an impulsive side of human beings within which sexual drives are a motivating force; for Pandarus Kynde's priorities are sexual and may run counter to sentiments we might think of as more refined, and which seem to be more conscious.[98] This understanding of Kynde lies behind Pandarus' question to the disconsolate, abandoned Troilus, 'Hath Kynde the wrought al only hire to plese?' (4. 1096). The Kynde imagined here is unconcerned about Troilus' abiding loyal attachment to Criseyde, for such loyalty is unnecessary to fulfil the purposes of Kynde, and indeed may stand in the way of that fulfilment, which lies within the sexual dimension connoted by the idea of Troilus 'plesing' women. Though Pandarus may well be using the normative connotations of Kynde as a means to a kind of moral blackmail of Troilus, for he is implying that what his sexually concerned Kynde urges is the course of action Troilus *ought* to pursue, the natural sexual drive as Pandarus speaks of it begins to look to us disturbingly anarchic. Pandarus' Kynde appears to be something which seeks expression regardless of what the person in whom it operates may consciously desire, and which, indeed, can be seen as *using* human beings as means to its ends, ends which may not be well attuned to the demands of a full humanity.

These Pandaran perspectives on Kynde give us a way of focusing the doubts about the validity of the positive claims made for love and *kynde* in the narrator's remarks when Troilus falls in love, doubts perhaps raised even as the remarks are first offered and certainly stimulated by the way Troilus' story eventually unfolds. We have been offered the view that love is part of a proper natural order and that it tends to promote virtue, but with Pandarus' distinction between love 'celestial' and love 'of kynde' in mind, we can see the claim that love is 'vertuous in *kynde*' as a limiting one: though Troilus is said to grow in virtue,[99] that growth is in the last analysis

[98] Pandarus' remark may well be in contact with the topos in the poetry of *fin amour* that mercy is a quality one expects Nature to give the lady, a mercy on which one can ground a hope of one's love being requited (see *BD* 1195–8; *Complaynt d'Amours*, 50–8); but though Pandarus colours it with courtly language, he seems to be thinking of an impulsive pressure towards erotic engagement, rather than an assent bestowed out of a cool, disengaged virtue.

[99] See *TC* 1. 1079 ff.; 3. 1800 ff.

compromised by an attachment to the things of this world. He and his virtues as a lover, despite what he claims in book 3, appear in the poem's final perspectives to lack a proper relation to the things of heaven: so much is shown as he despises from on high 'this wrecched world' (5. 1817) and human commitment to 'the blynde lust' (5. 1824), and in the narrator's concluding comments.

As for the law of *kynde*, we can, reflecting on the way in which Pandarus' comments reveal a tension between *kynde* sexuality and moral and religious imperatives, ask whether the pattern of behaviour engendered by the force of sexual impulse within human beings really is as readily identifiable as the narrator's enthusiasm for sexual love has suggested with the way things naturally and properly are. Pandarus' talk of *kynde* encourages us to view it in an Ulpianic perspective and to think of it as specifying what man shares with the animals; but however perfectly the animals may express their true natures in accordance with the divine plan through following their instinct, *kynde* as animal instinct is only one component of the human being and its operation is insufficient to ensure that human beings follow their natural and proper course in life. It is not surprising that Troilus' submission to the law of *kynde*, if it is indeed in essence submission to his pre-rational animal impulses, should leave him enmeshed in this world, a victim of 'the blynde lust', floundering in despair, when he should rather, guided by his reason, be following his true direction—towards heaven.

It should be said, however, that to see Troilus' love, which to be sure engages his sexual impulses, as simply reducible to animal sexual impulse would be too crude. Pandarus pictures a Kynde who has made Troilus capable of pleasing more than one woman, but Troilus' submission to the law of *kynde* does not bring with it the capacity to transfer sexual engagement from one object to another in the unconstrained way Pandarus supposes to be part of the scheme of Kynde; for his Kynde seems to desire the kind of easy freedom of sexual expression which characterizes the animal world considered as a whole.[100] It is, we might feel, unfortunate for Troilus that the operations of *kynde* upon him create a psychic condition in which he

---

[100]   See Ch. 1; though some animals were held to be monogamous, it was, as we have seen, possible to suppose that certain kinds of free sexual behaviour were licensed by that law of nature understood to give instruction to 'omnia animalia'.

cannot 'unloven' Criseyde a quarter of a day. Perhaps we see here again a contrast between the problematicness for human beings of what is nevertheless perfectly natural for them and the ease with which the non-human world transacts the natural, a theme we have also detected in *The Book of the Duchess* and *The Parlement of Foules*.[101]

In any case, by the end of *Troilus and Criseyde* the law of *kynde* has been made to appear something subjection to which we should not expect a wise man to celebrate (perhaps telling the story of Troilus educates the narrator, who moves from commitment to and celebration of sexual love to a disparagement of it). Troilus' fate suggests that sexual love does not urge human beings benignly along the path their nature should follow, but leads to a painful entrapment within the ultimately unsatisfying. Considered in the light of the narrative as a whole, the imagery of binding associated with the law of *kynde* confesses fully its attachment to the idea of coercion and so we have, I think, to reject the connotations of harmony and proper order attaching to the notion of binding, just as we have to reject Troilus' Boethian vision of natural sexual love as serving the divine. Love 'of kynde' cannot, regrettably perhaps, be seen as a manifestation of love 'celestial': it is a phenomenon of the sublunary world, and infected with the untrustworthiness of that world. The final perspective offered us is that satisfaction can only be found in a denial of 'feynede loves' (5. 1848), in a movement away from this world of *kynde* and its *kyndely* virtues. But how easy is it to follow the narrator's advice to leave behind the 'worldly vanyte' (5. 1837) of love? The poem's early affirmation of the power of the law of *kynde* is not compellingly contradicted, and we are left with a worry that most will not be able to liberate themselves from its power, for all the narrator's final passionate recommendation of love 'celestial'.[102]

---

[101] In *PF* the goose voices the rather Pandaran sentiment 'But she wol love hym, lat hym love another' (567). Neither here, nor in *Troilus*, however, are we supposed to endorse this kind of free sexual behaviour. Their difficulties invest the noble birds of *PF* and Troilus with some dignity—and tragic as this dignity is in Troilus' case, we would not, I think, have him be either Pandarus (who in any case perhaps only half believes what he is saying about the plurality natural to human sexual behaviour) or Diomede, who clearly knows about serial fornication. But even if this kind of behaviour were more natural—where I think Chaucer is only saying it is more animal—it would not encourage us to see the natural as a benign moral guide for human beings.
[102] We might compare the coerciveness of Nature in *CA*, where it seems that only a holy few can hope to escape her power (*CA* 8. 2330–6 and see above, pp. 202–5, 209).

On several occasions, then, we see Chaucer subjecting the concept of Nature as a beneficent, morally authoritative power to a sceptical scrutiny which ends by replacing this concept with a vision of humanity let down, or even victimized, by Nature. The promise of the possibility of harmoniously ordered living, guided by directives derived from the natural order, gives way to a recognition that humanity's natural lot is to exist painfully and problematically outside the schemes of order which the superseded understandings of Nature teasingly project.

There are contexts in Chaucer, however, as we have seen, where the natural appears to be offered unsceptically as a moral norm. One such context is the *Parson's Tale*, where such a presentation of the natural is rather frequent.[103] This is as we might expect, since here Chaucer abandons the probing complexities of many of his fictions for a discourse altogether more confident of its moral and metaphysical underpinnings. That confidence, however, hardly typifies the Chaucerian vision, to which a sense of the difficulty of reaching epistemological clarity and moral certainty is central. Chaucer's undermining of conceptions of Nature which bid to provide such clarity and certainty manifest that sense.

Perhaps, however, it is possible to see beyond Chaucer the relativist in the poet's dealings with Nature. Chaucer's visions of Nature tend to involve also a conception of human beings as subject to natural imperatives which are not wholly subject to the control of reason. Chaucer is, one supposes, concerned to express doubt about the optimistic Boethian conceptions of the natural with which his reading presents him. But doubt of beneficence may not go far enough; Chaucer may incline to a bleak conviction that the power of Nature over human beings delivers them to an irrationalism which militates forcefully against their best interests as rational moral agents.

Perhaps the apogee both of Chaucer's scepticism about Nature's potential for a benign ordering of human affairs and of his fear that Nature's characteristic way of operating on human beings is to commit them to the deepest experiential unsatisfactorinesses comes in the *Knight's Tale*, where Arcite speaks of how

---

[103] See *CT* 10. 491, 577, 865, 921, discussed at the beginning of this chapter.

> positif lawe and swich decree
> Is broken al day for love in ech degree.[104]

Here the phrasing associates love and its anarchy with the law of nature to which medieval legal writing often opposes positive law. If Arcite is right, the implication is that Nature, at least in the sphere of love, stands for chaos; a considered review of what is said explicitly about Nature in the works in which Chaucer most strenuously engages with that idea does little to make it seem that Arcite is wrong.

[104] *CT* I. 1167–8.

Conclusion

It might be suggested that the unsatisfactoriness of the natural for Chaucer and Gower was inevitable because they were much concerned with nature as promoter of sexual love and in late medieval culture sexual love and reason were inevitably at odds.[1] Nevertheless, even if we can in retrospect see that their cultural predicament made a harmonizing of love and reason impossible, the two poets do not seem happily reconciled to this fact. They are greatly interested in the natural precisely as it offers the prospect of concord between love and reason, the body and the spirit, the self-oriented and the altruistic, earth and heaven. Their discourse of nature expresses a deep longing for a reconciliation between these polarities, and we should not sell short the frustration and disappointment with which they recognize the impossibility of concord.

In fact, whether the reconciliation was indeed impossible within the cultural formation of the times is open to question. Dante certainly moved towards it and in England the *Gawain*-poet was in *Cleanness* emphatically affirmative about the goodness of the natural in sex.[2] Whether this affirmativeness would have survived the closer scrutiny sexual love would have received from him had the *Gawain*-poet been a love-poet is unclear. It seems to me, however, that the benign accommodation of the failures proceeding from the very nature of the human condition (excessive self-love in *Gawain and the Green Knight*, impatient grief in *Pearl*), and the preparedness to see these 'shortcomings' as capable of providing spiritual benefits for the person 'afflicted' by them[3] indicate that the *Gawain*-poet, seeing sex as divinely appointed, might, like Nature in the *De planctu Naturae*, have been prepared to accept the irrationality of Cupid and to receive it with some honour into an order of things firmly centred on the divine.

---

[1] See, e.g., Minnis, *Shorter Poems*, 312 f.

[2] *Cleanness*, in *The Poems of the Pearl Manuscript*, ed. Malcolm Andrew and Ronald Waldron (London, 1978), ll. 697–708.

[3] See further Hugh White, 'Blood in *Pearl*', *RES* NS 38 (1987), 1–13.

The *Gawain*-poet is not a poet of human sexual love, of course, and it may be that it is over-commitment to such love arising from the nature of the discourse within which he is working that sets the medieval love-poet on a collision course with reason and morality. It may also be because he is not over-committed to love that Gower can walk away from that collision relatively unharmed. Gower in the end seems reconciled to not being a poet of sexual love; the division of things is, to be sure, regrettable, but reason and the spirit are the priorities of God and Gower can live with this fact with relative comfort. For Chaucer, though, despite the apparent coolness of his scepticism about claims made for the benignity of the natural, the ultimate impossibility of celebrating its influences on human beings seems much less comfortable. Perhaps this is because Chaucer is a more committed poet of love than is Gower, more anxious that the erotic should be respectably celebratable, accommodatable to the demands of orthodox Christian morality. Perhaps, however, on the other hand, Chaucer's meditations on sex and nature are bound up with wider metaphysical issues, the distress about Nature deriving from and feeding a distress about the dealings in general of God with humanity. Though Chaucer does of course speak of divine mercy,[4] his projections of the divine tend rather to show human beings as victims of God's power, a power not infrequently unreasonable and capricious as far as can be seen.[5] It is noticeable that Chaucer's great contemporaries Langland, the *Gawain*-poet, and Julian of Norwich all affirm strongly the mercy of God and celebrate the natural. With them there seems to be a profound acceptance of the human condition in all its unsatisfactoriness, because it is an arena in and through which a God who is a friend[6] can be found. This acceptance is bound up with a positive affirmation of the natural. Chaucer, it seems, cannot make such an affirmation and so his appreciation of the human comedy is stalked by despair.[7]

[4] As, for instance, at the end of *Troilus and Criseyde*. But the text as a whole can hardly be said to celebrate the mercy of God and its final stanza, very clear on God's power, does not convey an *assurance* of receipt of the mercy of God (contrast, for instance, the ending of *Pearl*).

[5] Consider, for instance, the *Knight's Tale* and the *Clerk's Tale*. The point can also be argued for other of Chaucer's works, such as the *Man of Law's Tale* and the *Prioress' Tale*.

[6] See *Pearl* in Andrew and Waldron, *Pearl Manuscript*, 1204.

[7] On these matters see White, *Nature and Salvation*, esp. 112–16.

References

PRIMARY SOURCES

ABELARD, PETER, *Dialogus* (PL 178, 1609–84).
—— *Expositio in hexameron* (PL 178, 746).
—— *Theologia Christiana* (PL 178, 1113–330).
ALAN OF LILLE, *Anticlaudianus*, ed. R. Bossuat, Textes Philosophiques du Moyen Âge 1 (Paris, 1955).
—— *De planctu Naturae*, ed. N. Häring, *Studi medievali*, 19 (1978), 797–879.
—— *De virtutibus et viciis*, ed. O. Lottin, *Medieval Studies*, 12 (1950).
—— *Liber in distinctionibus dictionum theologicalium (Distinctiones)* (PL 210, 685–1102).
—— *Rhythmus alter* (PL 210, 579–80).
—— *Summa de arte praedicatoria* (PL 210, 109–72).
—— *Theologicae regulae* (PL 210, 621–84).
ALBERTUS MAGNUS, *Super ethica*, ed. Wilhelm Kübel, in vol. xiv of *Omnia opera* (Aschendorff, 1968–72 (books 1–5); 1987 (books 6–10)).
ALEXANDER OF HALES, *Summa theologica*, ed. B. Klumper, 4 vols. (Quaracchi, 1924–48).
AQUINAS, THOMAS, *In quattuor libros sententiarum*, in vol. i of *Opera omnia*, ed. R. Busa, 7 vols. (Rome, 1980).
—— *Summa contra Gentiles*, in vol. ii of *Opera omnia*, ed. R. Busa, 7 vols. (Rome, 1980).
—— *Summa theologiae*, in vol. ii of *Opera omnia*, ed. R. Busa, 7 vols. (Rome, 1980).
ARISTOTELES LATINUS, ed. L. Minio-Paluello (Bruges, 1965).
ARISTOTLE, *De caelo*, ed. W. K. C. Guthrie, Loeb Classical Library (London, 1939).
—— *De generatione animalium*, ed. A. L. Peck, Loeb Classical Library (London, 1943).
—— *De interpretatione*, in *The Organon*, ed. H. P. Cooke, Loeb Classical Library (London, 1949), vol. i.
—— *Metaphysics*, ed. Hugh Tredennick, 2 vols., Loeb Classical Library (London, 1933–5).
—— *Nicomachean Ethics*, ed. H. Rackham, Loeb Classical Library (Cambridge, Mass., 1926).

—— *De partibus animalium*, ed. A. L. Peck, Loeb Classical Library (London, 1937).

—— *Physics*, ed. Philip H. Wicksteed and Francis M. Cornford, 2 vols., Loeb Classical Library (London, 1929, 1934).

The Assembly of the Gods, ed. O. L. Triggs, EETS es 69 (London, 1896).

AUGUSTINE OF HIPPO, *Confessions*, ed. James J. O'Donnell, 3 vols. (Oxford, 1992).

—— *Contra epistolam Manichaei* (*PL* 42, 173–206).

—— *Contra Faustum* (*PL* 42, 207–518).

—— *De bono conjugali* (*PL* 40, 373–96)

—— *De civitate Dei* (*PL* 41).

—— *De libero arbitrio* (*PL* 32, 1221–310).

—— *De natura boni* (*PL* 42, 551–72).

—— *De natura et gratia* (*PL* 44, 247–90).

—— *De spiritu et litera* (*PL* 44, 199–246).

—— *Ennarationes in Psalmos* (*PL* 36, 37).

—— *Opus imperfectum contra Julianum* (*PL* 45, 1049–608).

The Ayenbite of Inwit, ed. R. Morris, EETS os 23 (London, 1866; corr. Pamela Gradon, 1965).

AZO, *Summa institutionum* (Basle, 1563).

BERNARDUS SILVESTRIS, *Cosmographia*, ed. Peter Dronke (Leiden, 1978).

BOETHIUS, *De consolatione Philosophiae* (*The Consolation of Philosophy*), 2nd edn. ed. S. J. Tester, Loeb Classical Library (Cambridge, Mass., 1973).

BONAVENTURE, *Commentaria in IV libros sententiarum*, 4 vols.; vols. i–iv of *Opera theologica selecta* (Quaracchi, 1934–49).

The Book of Vices and Virtues, ed. W. N. Francis, EETS os 217 (London, 1942).

BRACTON, HENRY, *De legibus et consuetudinibus Angliae*, trans. Samuel E. Thorne, 4 vols. (Cambridge, Mass., 1968).

Chartularium Universitatis Parisiensis, ed. H. Denifle and A. Chatelain, 4 vols. (Paris, 1889–97).

CHAUCER, GEOFFREY, *The Riverside Chaucer*, ed. Larry D. Benson (3rd edn., Boston, 1987).

—— *The Works of Geoffrey Chaucer*, ed. W. W. Skeat, 7 vols. (Oxford, 1894–7).

CICERO, *De legibus*, ed. K. Ziegler and W. Görler (Freiburg, 1979).

—— *De natura deorum*, ed. A. S. Pease (Cambridge, Mass., 1955–8).

—— *De re publica*, ed. K. Ziegler (Leipzig, 1969).

—— *Pro Milone*, ed. A. B. Poynton (2nd edn., Oxford, 1902).

Corpus iuris civilis, vol. i (*Digest* and *Institutes*), ed. P. Krueger and T. Mommsen (16th edn., Berlin, 1954).

Cursor Mundi, Southern Version, ed. Sarah M. Horrall et al., 5 vols. (Ottawa, 1978–2000).

DAMASCENE, JOHN, *De fide orthodoxa* (*PG* 94, 781–1228).

DAMIAN, PETER, *De bobo religiosi status* (*PL* 145, 771).

Le Débat sur le Roman de la Rose, ed. Eric Hicks (Paris, 1977).

Dives and Pauper, ed. Priscilla H. Barnum, vol. i, parts 1 and 2, EETS 275, 280 (Oxford, 1976, 1980).

DYMMOK, ROGER, *Rogeri Dymmok liber contra XII errores et hereses lollardorum*, ed. H. S. Cronin (London, 1921).

Les Echecs Amoureux (extracts), in E. Sieper, *Les Echecs amoureux*, Litterarhistorische Forschungen 9 (Weimar, 1898).

English Wycliffite Sermons, ed. Anne Hudson and Pamela Gradon, 5 vols. (Oxford, 1983).

FORTESCUE, Sir JOHN, *De natura legis naturae*, in *The Works of Sir John Fortescue*, ed. Thomas (Fortescue), Lord Clermont (London, 1869).

GACE DE LA BUIGNE, *Roman des deduis*, ed. Åke Blomqvist (Karlshamn, 1951).

GILES OF ROME, *De regimine principum* (Rome, 1556).

GODFREY OF ST VICTOR, *Fons philosophiae*, ed. P. Michaud-Quantin, Analecta Mediaevalia Namurcensia 8 (Namur, 1956).

GOWER, JOHN, *Works*, ed. G. C. Macaulay, 4 vols. (Oxford, 1899–1902).

GRATIAN, *Decretum*, in *Corpus iuris canonici*, vol. i, ed. A. Friedberg (Leipzig, 1879).

GREGORY THE GREAT, *Moralia in Job* (*PL* 75, 513–1162; 76, 9–782).

GUILLAUME DE LORRIS and JEAN DE MEUN, *Le Roman de la Rose*, ed. Félix Lecoy, 3 vols. (Paris, 1965–70).

HERMANN OF CARINTHIA, *De essentiis*, ed. M. Alonso (Comillas, 1946).

Historical Poems of the Fourteenth and Fifteenth Centuries, ed. Rossell Hope Robbins (Columbia, NY, 1959).

HORACE, *Epistles* Book 1, ed. O. A. W. Dilke (Letchworth, 1954).

HUGH OF ST VICTOR, *De Sacramentis* (*PL* 176, 173–618).

—— *De tribus diebus* (*PL* 176, 814b).

—— *Didascalicon*, ed. C. H. Buttimer (Washington, 1939).

ISIDORE OF SEVILLE, *Etymologiae*, ed. W. M. Lindsay (Oxford, 1911).

Jack Upland, Friar Daw's Reply and Upland's Rejoinder, ed. P. L. Heyworth (London, 1968).

JEAN DE CONDÉ, *La Messe des oiseaux et le Dit des Jacobins et des Fremeneurs*, ed. Jacques Ribard, Textes Littéraires Français (Geneva, 1970).

JEAN LE FÈVRE, *Livre de leesce*, in *Les Lamentacions de Matheolus et le Livre de leesce de Jehan Le Fèvre, de Resson*, ed. A. G. van Hamel, 2 vols. Bibliothèque de l'École des Hautes Études, Sciences Philologiques 95, 96 (Paris, 1882, 1905).

JEROME, *Adversus Jovinianum* (*PL* 23, 211–338).

—— *Commentaria in Ezechielem* (*PL* 25, 15–584).

JOHANNES DE ALTAVILLA (Jean de Hautville), *Architrenius*, ed. P. G. Schmidt (Munich, 1974).

JOHN OF SALISBURY, *Entheticus* (*PL* 199, 965–1004).

—— *Metalogicus* (*PL* 199, 835C).

Lai d'Aristote, ed. Maurice Delbouille (Paris, 1951).

LANGLAND, WILLIAM, *The Vision of Piers Plowman: A Complete Edition of the B-Text*, ed. A. V. C. Schmidt (London, 1987).

Liber de Hermetis Mercurii Triplicis de VI rerum principiis, ed. T. Silverstein, AHDLMA 22 (Paris, 1955), 217–312.

LOMBARD, PETER, *Libri IV sententiarum* (*Sententiae*), 2 vols. (2nd edn., Quaracchi, 1916).

Ludus Coventriae, ed. K. Block, EETS ES 120 (London, 1922).

LYDGATE, JOHN, *Reson and Sensuallyte*, ed. E. Sieper, 2 vols. EETS OS 209 (London, 1940).

MATHEOLUS, *The Lamentations*, in *Les Lamentacions de Matheolus et le Livre de leesce de Jehan Le Fèvre, de Resson*, ed. A. G. van Hamel, 2 vols., Bibliothèque de l'École des Hautes Études, Sciences Philologiques 95, 96 (Paris, 1882, 1905).

Middle English Sermons, ed. W. O. Ross, EETS OS 209 (London, 1940).

MYRC, JOHN, *Instructions for Parish Priests*, ed. Edward Peacock, EETS OS 31 (London, 1868).

The Northern Homily Cycle, ed. Saara Nevanlinna, *Mémoires de la Société Néophilologique de Helsinki*, 38, 41 (1972, 1973).

OVID, *Metamorphoses*, ed. Frank Justus Miller, 2 vols., Loeb Classical Library, 2nd edn., vol. ii rev. G. P. Goold (London, 1921, 1984).

—— *Ars amatoria* (*The Art of Love*), ed. John Henry Mozley, Loeb Classical Library (London, 1929).

The Owl and the Nightingale, ed. Eric Stanley (London, 1963).

The Poems of the Pearl Manuscript, ed. Malcolm Andrew and Ronald Waldron (London, 1978).

The Prick of Conscience, ed. R. Morris (Berlin, 1863).

PS-OVID, *De vetula*, ed. Paul Klopsch (Leiden, 1967).

Religious Lyrics of the XIVth Century, ed. Carleton Brown, 2nd edn., rev. G. V. Smithers (Oxford, 1957).

Renart le Contrefait, ed. G. Raynaud and H. Lemaître, 2 vols. (Paris, 1914).

Le Roman de Silence, ed. Sarah Roche-Mahdi (East Lansing, Mich., 1992).

RUFINUS, *Summa decretorum*, ed. H. Singer (Paderborn, 1902).

SAIGNET, GUILLAUME, *Lamentacio humanae Nature adversus Nicenam constitutionem interdicentem conjugatis sacerdotium*, in Nicole Grévy-Pons, *Célibat et Nature* (Paris, 1975).

Selections from English Wycliffite Writings, ed. Anne Hudson (Cambridge, 1978).

The South English Legendary, ed. Charlotte d'Evelyn and Anna J. Mill, 3 vols., EETS 235, 236, 244 (London, 1956–9).

Stoicorum veterum fragmenta, ed. J. ab Arnim, 4 vols. (Leipzig, 1903–24).

THIERRY OF CHARTRES, *De sex dierum operibus*, ed. N. Häring, AHDLMA 22 (Paris, 1955), 184–200.

TREVISA, JOHN, *On the Properties of Things*, 3 vols. ed. M. C. Seymour et al. (Oxford, 1975).

—— *The Governance of Kings and Princes: John Trevisa's Middle English Translation of the 'De regimine principum' of Aegidius Romanus*, David C. Fowler, Charles F. Briggs, and Paul G. Remley, Garland Medieval Texts 19 (New York, 1997).

Two Wycliffite Sermons, ed. Anne Hudson, EETS 301 (Oxford, 1993).

VINCENT OF BEAUVAIS, *Speculum maius* (Venice, 1591).

WILLIAM OF AUXERRE, *Magistri Guillelmi Altissiodorensis summa aurea*, ed. Jean Ribaillier, 4 vols. (Paris, 1981–7).

WILLIAM OF CONCHES, *De philosophia mundi* (*PL* 172 (attributed there to Honorius of Autun), 41–102).

WYCLIF, JOHN (attributed), *Select English Works of John Wyclif*, ed. Thomas Arnold, 3 vols. (Oxford, 1869–71).

—— (attributed), *The English Works of Wyclif Hitherto Unprinted*, ed. F. D. Matthew, EETS OS 74 (London, 1880).

SECONDARY LITERATURE

AERS, DAVID, 'The *Parlement of Foules*: Authority, the Knower and the Known', *Chaucer Review*, 16 (1981), 1–17.

—— 'Reflections on Gower as "Sapiens in Ethics and Politics"', in R. F. Yeager (ed.), *Re-Visioning Gower* (Asheville, NC, 1998), 185–201.

ALFORD, JOHN, 'The Idea of Reason in *Piers Plowman*', in Edward Donald Kennedy, Ronald Waldron, and Joseph S. Wittig (eds.), *Medieval English Studies Presented to George Kane* (Cambridge, 1988), 199–215.

ANDO, SHINSUKE, 'Chaucer's Conception of Nature', in Yoshio Terasawa (ed.), *Key-Word Studies in Chaucer*, i (Tokyo, 1984), 1–14.

ARDEN, HEATHER, *The Roman de la Rose: An Annotated Bibliography* (New York, 1993).

—— *The Romance of the Rose* (Boston, 1987).

BADEL, PIERRE-YVES, *Le Roman de la Rose au XIVe siècle: étude de la réception de l'œuvre* (Geneva, 1980).

BAIRD, JOSEPH L., and KANE, JOHN R. (trans.), *La Querelle de la Rose: Letters and Documents* (Chapel Hill, NC, 1978).

BAKER, DENISE N., 'The Priesthood of Genius: A Study of the Medieval Tradition', *Speculum*, 51 (1976), 277–91.

BARTHOLOMEW, B, *Fortuna and Natura: A Reading of Three Chaucer Narratives* (The Hague, 1966).

BENNETT, J. A. W. *The Parlement of Foules: An Interpretation* (Oxford, 1957).

—— 'Gower's "Honeste Love"', in John Lawlor (ed.), *Patterns of Love and Courtesy: Essays in Memory of C. S. Lewis* (Evanston, Ill., 1966), 107–21.

BLAMIRES, ALCUIN (ed.), *Woman Defamed and Woman Defended* (Oxford, 1992).

BLOOMFIELD, MORTON, *The Seven Deadly Sins* (Michigan, 1952).

BREWER, D. S. (ed.), *The Parlement of Foulys* (London, 1960; repr. 1972).

BROWN, EMERSON, Jr., 'Hortus Inconclusus: The Significance of Priapus and Pyramus and Thisbe in the *Merchant's Tale'*, *Chaucer Review*, 4 (1970), 31–40.

—— 'Priapus and the *Parlement of Foulys'*, *SP* 72 (1975), 258–74.

BROWN, OSCAR, *Natural Rectitude and the Divine Law in Aquinas* (Toronto, 1981).

BRUNDAGE, JAMES A., *Law, Sex, and Christian Society in Medieval Europe* (Chicago, 1987).

BULLOUGH, VERN L., 'The Sin against Nature and Homosexuality', in Vern L. Bullough and James Brundage (eds.), *Sexual Practices and the Medieval Church* (Amherst: N.Y, 1994), 55–71.

BULTMANN, RUDOLF, *Theology of the New Testament*, vol. i (British edn., London, 1952).

BURKE, LINDA BARNEY, 'Genial Gower: Laughter in the *Confessio Amantis'*, in R. F. Yeager (ed.), *John Gower: Recent Readings* (Kalamazoo, Mich., 1989), 39–63.

BURNLEY, J. D., *Chaucer's Language and the Philosophers' Tradition* (Cambridge, 1979).

BURROW, J. A., 'The Portrayal of Amans in "Confessio Amantis"', in A. J. Minnis (ed.), *Gower's Confessio Amantis: Responses and Reassessments* (Cambridge, 1983), 5–24.

CARLYLE, R. W., and CARLYLE, A. J., *A History of Medieval Political Theory in the West*, 6 vols. (Edinburgh, 1903–36).

CHADWICK, HENRY, *Augustine* (Oxford, 1986).

CHADWICK, HENRY, *Boethius: The Consolations of Music, Logic, Theology and Philosophy* (Oxford, 1981).

CHENU, M.-D., *Nature, Man, and Society in the Twelfth Century*, ed. and trans. Jerome Taylor and Lester K. Little (Chicago, 1966).

CHERNISS, MICHAEL D., 'Irony and Authority: The Ending of the *Roman de la Rose*', *MLQ* 36 (1975), 227–38.

—— *Boethian Apocalypse* (Norman, Okla., 1987).

CLAGETT, M., POST, G., and REYNOLDS, R., *Twelfth Century Europe and the Foundations of Modern Society* (Madison, 1961).

CLEMEN, W. H., *Chaucer's Early Poetry* (London, 1963).

COGHILL, NEVILL (trans.), *Troilus and Criseyde* (Harmondsworth, 1971).

COHEN, JEREMY, 'Original Sin as the Evil Inclination: A Polemicist's Appreciation of Human Nature', *Harvard Theological Review*, 73 (1980), 495–520.

—— '*Be Fertile and Increase, Fill the Earth and Master It*' (Ithaca, NY, 1989).

COLISH, M. L., *The Stoic Tradition from Antiquity to the Early Middle Ages*, 2 vols. (Leiden, 1985).

COPLESTON, F. C., *Aquinas* (Harmondsworth, 1955).

CROWE, M. B., 'Synderesis and the Notion of Law in St Thomas', in *L'Homme et son destin d'après les penseurs du Moyen Âge*, Actes du Premier Congrès International de Philosophie Médiévale (Louvain, 1960), 601–9.

—— 'St. Thomas and Ulpian's Natural Law', in *St. Thomas Aquinas 1274–1974: Commemorative Studies* (Toronto, 1974), i. 261–82.

—— *The Changing Profile of the Natural Law* (The Hague, 1977).

DAHLBERG, CHARLES (trans.), *The Romance of the Rose* (Princeton, 1971; repr. Hanover, 1986).

DAVIS, N. (ed.), *A Chaucer Glossary* (Oxford, 1978).

DAWSON, RAYMOND, *Confucius* (Oxford, 1981).

DELHAYE, P., *Permanence du droit naturel*, Analecta Mediaevalia Namurcensia 10 (Louvain, 1960).

D'ENTRÈVES, A. P., *Natural Law* (2nd edn., London, 1970).

DONALDSON, E. T. (select. and ed.), *Chaucer's Poetry: An Anthology* (New York, 1958).

DONAVIN, GEORGIANA, *Incest Narratives and the Structure of Gower's Confessio Amantis*, ELS Monograph Series 56 (Victoria, 1993).

DRAGONETTI, ROGER, *Le Mirage des sources* (Paris, 1987).

DRONKE, PETER, *Fabula: Explorations into the Uses of Myth in Medieval Platonism* (Leiden, 1974).

DUNLEAVY, GARETH W., 'Natural Law as Chaucer's Ethical Absolute', in Willi Erzgräber (ed.), *Geoffrey Chaucer* (Darmstadt, 1983), 196–209.

ECHARD, SIÂN, and FANGER, CLAIRE, *The Latin Verses in the Confessio Amantis: An Annotated Translation* (East Lansing, Mich., 1991).

ECONOMOU, GEORGE D., *The Goddess Natura in Medieval Literature* (Cambridge, Mass., 1972).

—— 'The Two Venuses and Courtly Love', in Joan M. Ferrante and G. D. Economou (eds.), *In Pursuit of Perfection: Courtly Love in Medieval Literature* (Port Washington, 1975).

ERZGRÄBER, WILLI (ed.), *Geoffrey Chaucer* (Darmstadt, 1983).

—— 'Kynde und Nature bei Chaucer', in G. Weber (ed.), *Idee, Gestalt, Geschichte: Festschrift Klaus von See* (Odense, 1988), 116–35.

EVANS, G. R., *Alan of Lille: The Frontiers of Theology in the Later Twelfth Century* (Cambridge, 1983).

FARNHAM, ANTHONY E., 'The Art of High Poetic Seriousness: John Gower as Didactic Raconteur', in Larry D. Benson (ed.), *The Learned and the Lewed*, Harvard English Studies 5 (Cambridge, Mass., 1974), 161–73.

FARRELL, P. M., 'Sources of St. Thomas' Concept of Natural Law', *Thomist*, 20 (1957), 237–94.

FICHTE, JÖRG O., *Chaucer's 'Art Poetical': A Study in Chaucerian Poetics* (Tübingen, 1980).

FLANDRIN, JEAN-LOUIS, *L'Église et le contrôle des naissances* (Paris, 1970).

FLEMING, JOHN V., *The Roman de la Rose: A Study in Allegory and Iconography* (Princeton, 1969).

—— *Reason and the Lover* (Princeton, 1984).

FRANK, ROBERT WORTH, Jr., 'Structure and Meaning in the *Parlement of Foules*', *PMLA* 71 (1956), 530–9.

FYLER, JOHN M., *Chaucer and Ovid* (New Haven, 1979).

GEERTZ, CLIFFORD, *Islam Observed* (New Haven, 1968).

GIBSON, MARGARET (ed.), *Boethius* (Oxford, 1981).

GILSON, E., *The Philosophy of St Thomas Aquinas*, trans. E. Bullough, ed. G. A. Elrington (2nd edn., Cambridge, 1924).

GREGORY, TULLIO, *Anima mundi: la filosofia di Guglielmo di Conches e la scuola di Chartres* (Florence, 1955).

—— *Platonismo medievale* (Rome, 1958).

—— 'L'idea di natura nella filosofia medievale prima dell' ingresso della fisica di Aristotele: ii secolo XII', in *FNM* (Milan, 1966), 27–65.

—— 'La Nouvelle Idée de Nature et de savoir scientifique au XIIe siècle' (with discussion), in J. E. Murdoch and E. D. Sylla (eds.), *The Cultural Context of Medieval Learning*, Boston Studies in the Philosophy of Science 26 (Dordrecht, 1975), 193–218.

—— 'The Platonic Inheritance', in Peter Dronke (ed.), *A History of Twelfth-Century Western Philosophy* (Cambridge, 1988).

GRUBE, G. M. A. *Plato's Thought* (London, 1935; repr. 1980).

GUNN, ALAN M. F., *The Mirror of Love: A Reinterpretation of 'The Romance of the Rose'* (Lubbock Tex., 1952).

HANSEN, ELAINE TUTTLE, *Chaucer and the Fictions of Gender* (London, 1990).

HARRIS, DUNCAN, and STEFFEN, NANCY L., 'The Other Side of the Garden; An Interpretive Comparison of Chaucer's *Book of the Duchess* and Spenser's *Daphnaida*', *JMRS* 8 (1978), 17–36.

HASKINS, C. H., *The Renaissance of the Twelfth Century* (Cambridge, Mass., 1927).

HATTON, THOMAS J., 'John Gower's Use of Ovid in Book III of the *Confessio Amantis*', *Mediaevalia*, 13 (1987), 257–74.

HILL, THOMAS D., 'Narcissus, Pygmalion, and the Castration of Saturn: Two Mythographical Themes in the *Roman de la Rose*', *SP* 71 (1974), 404–26.

HISCOE, DAVID W., 'The Ovidian Comic Strategy of Gower's *Confessio Amantis*', *PQ* 64 (1985), 367–85.

HORGAN, FRANCES (trans.), *The Romance of the Rose* (Oxford, 1994).

HUOT, SYLVIA, *The Romance of the Rose and its Medieval Readers* (Cambridge, 1993).

HUPPÉ, B. F., and ROBERTSON, D. W., Jr., *Fruyt and Chaf* (Princeton, 1963).

IWASAKI, HARUO, 'A Peculiar Feature in the Word-Order of Gower's *Confessio Amantis*', *SE Lit.* 45 (1969), 205–20.

JUNG, MARC-RENÉ, 'Jean de Meun et l'allégorie', *Cahiers de l'Association Internationale des Études Françaises*, 28 (1976), 21–36.

KAY, SARAH, 'Sexual Knowledge: The Once and Future Texts of the *Romance of the Rose*', in Judith Still and Michael Worton (eds.), *Textuality and Sexuality* (Manchester, 1993), 69–86.

—— *The Romance of the Rose* (London, 1995).

KEAN, P. M., review of G. D. Economou, *The Goddess Natura in Medieval Literature*, *RES* NS 25 (1974), 190–2.

—— *Chaucer and the Making of English Poetry*, shortened edn. (London, 1982).

KELLY, DOUGLAS, *Internal Difference and Meanings in the Roman de la Rose* (Madison, 1995).

KELLY, HENRY ANSGAR, *Love and Marriage in the Age of Chaucer* (Ithaca, NY, 1975).

KLAUSER, HENRIETTE A., 'The Concept of Kynde in John Gower's Confessio Amantis' Ph.D. dissertation (Fordham, 1972).

KLIBANSKY, R., 'The School at Chartres', in M. Clagett, G. Post, and R. Reynolds (eds.), *Twelfth Century Europe and the Foundations of Modern Society* (Madison, 1961), 1–23.

KNOWLTON, E. C., 'The Goddess Nature in Early Periods', *JEGP* 19 (1920), 224–53.

—— 'Nature in Middle English', *JEGP* 20 (1921), 186–207.

—— 'Nature in Old French', *MP* 20 (1922), 309–29.

—— 'Genius as an Allegorical Figure', *Modern Language Notes*, 39 (1924), 89–95.

KÖHLER, ERICH, 'Narcisse, la fontaine d'amour et Guillaume de Lorris', *Journal des savants* (1963), 86–103.

KRETZMANN, NORMAN, KENNY, ANTHONY, and PINBORG, JAN (eds.), *The Cambridge History of Later Medieval Philosophy* (Cambridge, 1982).

LACEY, T. A., *Nature, Miracle and Sin* (London, 1916).

LAPIDGE, MICHAEL, 'The Stoic Inheritance', in Peter Dronke (ed.), *A History of Twelfth-Century Western Philosophy* (Cambridge, 1988), 81–112.

LAWLOR, JOHN, 'The Pattern of Consolation in *The Book of the Duchess*', *Speculum*, 31 (1956), 626–48.

LAWTON, DAVID, *Chaucer's Narrators* (Cambridge, 1985).

LEICESTER, HENRY M., Jr., 'The Harmony of Chaucer's *Parlement*: A Dissonant Voice', *Chaucer Review*, 9 (1974), 15–34.

LEWIS, C. S., *Studies in Words* (Cambridge, 1960).

—— *Studies in Medieval and Renaissance Literature* (Cambridge, 1966).

LONG, A. A., *Hellenistic Philosophy* (London, 1974).

LOTTIN, O., *Le Droit naturel chez Saint Thomas d'Aquin et ses prédécesseurs* (2nd edn., Bruges, 1931).

—— *La Doctrine des mouvements premiers de l'appetit sensitif aux 12e et 13e siècles*, AHDLMA 6 (Paris, 1932).

—— *Psychologie et morale aux XIIe et XIIIe siècles*, 6 vols. (Louvain, 1942–60).

LOVEJOY, A. O., and BOAS, G., *A Documentary History of Primitivism and Related Ideas*, i: *Primitivism and Related Ideas in Antiquity* (Baltimore, 1935).

LUMIANSKY, R. M., 'Chaucer's *Parlement of Foules*: A Philosophical Interpretation, RES 24 (1948), 81–9.

LUSCOMBE, D. E., 'Natural Morality and Natural Law', in *CHLMP* (Cambridge, 1982), 705–19.

LYNCH, KATHRYN L., *The High Medieval Dream Vision: Poetry, Philosophy, and Literary Form* (Stanford, Calif., 1988).

MAITLAND, F. W., *Select Passages from Bracton and Azo*, Selden Society 8 (London, 1895).

MEHL, DIETER, *Geoffrey Chaucer* (Cambridge, 1986).

MEHLMANN, J., *Natura filii irae*, Analecta Biblica 6 (Rome, 1957).

MINNIS, A. J., *The Shorter Poems: Oxford Guides to Chaucer* (Oxford, 1995).

MORRIS, C., *Western Political Thought*, i: *Plato to Augustine* (London, 1967).

MOTTO, ANNA L., *Guide to the Thought of Lucius Annaeus Seneca* (Amsterdam, 1970).

MUSCATINE, CHARLES, *Chaucer and the French Tradition: A Study in Style and Meaning* (Berkeley, 1957).

NITZSCHE, JANE CHANCE, *The Genius Figure in Antiquity and the Middle Ages* (New York, 1975).

NOGUCHI, SHUNICHI, 'Chaucer's Concept of Nature', in Toshiyuki Takamiya and Richard Beadle (eds.), *Chaucer to Shakespeare: Essays in Honour of Shinsuke Ando* (Cambridge, 1992), 25–31.

NOONAN, JOHN T., *Contraception: A History of its Treatment by the Catholic Theologians and Canonists* (Cambridge, Mass., 1966).

NORTH, J. D., *Chaucer's Universe* (Oxford, 1988).

NORTON-SMITH, J., *Geoffrey Chaucer* (London, 1974).

OLSSON, KURT, 'Natural Law and John Gower's *Confessio Amantis*', *Medievalia et humanistica*, NS 11 (1982), 229–61 (repr. in Peter Nicholson (ed.), *Gower's 'Confessio Amantis'*, Publications of the John Gower Society 3 (Cambridge, 1991), 181–213).

—— *John Gower and the Structures of Conversion,* Publications of the John Gower Society 4 (Cambridge, 1992).

PARÉ, G., *Le Roman de la Rose et la scolastique courtoise* (Paris, 1941).

—— *Les Idées et les lettres au XIIIe siècle: le Roman de la Rose* (Montreal, 1947).

PAYER, PIERRE J., *The Bridling of Desire* (Toronto, 1993).

PELEN, MARC M., *Latin Poetic Irony in the Roman de la Rose*, Vinaver Studies in French 4 (Liverpool, 1987).

PHILLIPS, HELEN (ed.), *The Book of the Duchess* (Durham, 1984).

PICKLES, J. D., and DAWSON, J. L. (eds.), *A Concordance to John Gower's Confessio Amantis*, Publications of the John Gower Society 1 (Cambridge, 1987).

PIEHLER, PAUL, *The Visionary Landscape: A Study in Medieval Allegory* (London, 1971).

POLAK, LUCIE, 'Plato, Nature and Jean de Meun', *Reading Medieval Studies*, 3 (1977), 80–103.

POTTS, TIMOTHY C., *Conscience in Medieval Philosophy* (Cambridge, 1980).

—— 'Conscience', in *CHLMP* (Cambridge, 1982), 687–704.

RAYNAUD DE LAGE, G., *Alain de Lille: poète du XIIe siècle* (Montreal, 1951).

REID, T. B. W., 'The She-Wolf's Mate', *Medium Aevum*, 24 (1955), 16–19.

RIBARD, JACQUES, *Un ménestrel du XIV siècle* (Geneva, 1969).

ROBERTSON, D. W., Jr., *A Preface to Chaucer* (Princeton, 1962).

ROSS, DAVID, *Aristotle* (5th edn. rev., London, 1949).

ROTHSCHILD, VICTORIA, '*The Parliament of Fowls*: Chaucer's Mirror up to Nature?', *RES* NS 35 (1984), 164–84.

SADLER, L. V., 'Chaucer's *The Book of the Duchess* and the "Lawe of Kinde"', *An. M.* 11 (1970), 51–64.

SCHMITZ, GÖTZ, '*The Middel Weie*': *Stil- und Aufbauformen in John Gowers* '*Confessio Amantis*', Studien zur Englischen Literatur II (Bonn, 1974).

SCHUELER, DONALD G., 'Gower's Characterization of Genius in the *Confessio Amantis*', *MLQ* 33 (1972), 240–56.

SHERIDAN, JAMES J., *Alan of Lille, Anticlaudianus: Translation and Commentary* (Toronto, 1973).

—— *Alan of Lille, The Plaint of Nature: Translation and Commentary* (Toronto, 1980).

SIMPSON, JAMES, 'Ironic Incongruence in the Prologue and Book 1 of Gower's *Confessio Amantis*', *Neophilologus*, 72 (1988), 617–32.

—— *Sciences and the Self in Mediaeval Poetry: Alan of Lille's 'Anticlaudianus' and John Gower's 'Confessio Amantis'* (Cambridge, 1995).

SMALLEY, BERYL, *The Study of the Bible in the Middle Ages* (Oxford, 1952).

SOUTHERN, R. W., *Medieval Humanism and Other Studies* (Oxford, 1970).

STAKEL, SUSAN, *False Roses* (Saratoga, Calif., 1991).

STILLWELL, GARDINER, 'Unity and Comedy in Chaucer's *Parlement of Foules*', *JEGP* 49 (1950), 470–95.

STOCK, BRIAN, *Myth and Science in the Twelfth Century: A Study of Bernard Silvester* (Princeton, 1972).

STOCKTON, E. W. (trans.), *The Major Latin Works of John Gower*, 7 vols. (Seattle, 1962).

TAYLOR, JEROME (trans.), *The Didascalicon of Hugh of St. Victor: A Medieval Guide to the Arts*, with introd. and notes (New York, 1961; repr. 1991).

THORNDIKE, L., *A History of Magic and Experimental Science*, 8 vols. (New York, 1923–58).

TIERNEY, BRIAN, '*Natura, id est Deus*: A Case of Juristic Pantheism?', *JHI* 24 (1963), 307–22.

TUVE, ROSEMOND, *Allegorical Imagery: Some Medieval Books and their Posterity* (Princeton, 1966).

VACANT, A., and MANGENOT, E., *Dictionnaire de théologie catholique* (Paris, 1903–72).

VERBECKE, G., 'L'Influence du Stoicisme sur la pensée Médiévale en Occident', in *Actas del 5o. Congreso Internacional de Filosofía Medieval* (Madrid, 1979), 95–109.

WACK, MARY FRANCES, *Lovesickness in the Middle Ages* (Philadelphia, 1990).

WATSON, G., 'The Natural Law and Stoicism', in A. A. Long (ed.), *Problems in Stoicism* (London, 1971), 216–38.

WEIGAND, RUDOLF, *Die Naturrechtslehre der Legisten und Dekretisten von Irnerius bis Accursius und von Gratian bis Johannes Teutonicus*, Münchener Theologische Studien 26 (Munich, 1967).

WETHERBEE, WINTHROP, 'The Literal and the Allegorical: Jean de Meun and the *De planctu Naturae*', *Medieval Studies*, 33 (1971), 264–91.

—— *Platonism and Poetry in the Twelfth Century* (Princeton, 1972).

—— *The Cosmographia of Bernardus Silvestris: A Translation with Introduction and Notes* (New York, 1973).

—— 'Philosophy, Cosmology, and the Twelfth-Century Renaissance', in Peter Dronke (ed.), *A History of Twelfth-Century Western Philosophy* (Cambridge, 1988), 21–53.

—— *Johannes de Hauvilla: Architrenius*, Cambridge Medieval Classics 3 (Cambridge, 1994).

WHELAN, CHARLES M., 'The "Higher Law" Doctrine in Bracton and St. Thomas', *Catholic Lawyer*, 8 (1962), 218–32, 245.

WHITE, HUGH, 'The Naturalness of Amans' Love in *Confessio Amantis*', *Medium Aevum*, 66 (1987), 316–22.

—— 'Blood in Pearl', *RES* NS 38 (1987), 1–13.

—— *Nature and Salvation in Piers Plowman* (Cambridge, 1988).

—— 'Division and Failure in Gower's *Confessio Amantis*', *Neophilologus*, 72 (1988), 600–16.

—— 'Chaucer Compromising Nature', *RES* NS 40 (1989), 157–78.

WILSON, WILLIAM BURTON (trans.), *John Gower: Mirour de l'omme*, rev. Nancy Wilson Van Baak (East Lansing, Mich., 1992).

WINDEATT, B. A. (trans.), *Chaucer's Dream Visions: Sources and Analogues* (Cambridge, 1982).

WOOLSEY, R. B. 'Bernard Silvester and the Hermetic Asclepius', *Traditio*, 7 (1949), 340–4.

YEAGER, R. F., 'Learning to Speak in Tongues: Writing Poetry for a Trilingual Culture', in R. F. Yeager (ed.), *Chaucer and Gower: Difference, Mutuality, Exchange*, English Literary Studies Monograph Series 51 (Victoria, 1991), 115–29.

Index

Note: Certain terms which occur extensively throughout the book, for example, 'God', 'love', 'nature', 'reason', have not been indexed. References to scholars and critics mentioned in the text are generally provided only where their views are germane to the development of the argument of the book.